WHOIS RUNNING THE INTERNET

WHOIS RUNNING THE INTERNET

Protocol, Policy, and Privacy

GARTH O. BRUEN

Library of Congress Cataloging-in-Publication Data

Bruen, Garth O.
    WHOIS running the Internet : protocol, policy, and privacy / Garth O. Bruen.
        pages   cm
    Includes bibliographical references and index.
    ISBN 978-1-118-67955-5 (hardback)
    1. WHOIS (Computer network protocol)   2. Internet domain names–Government policy.   3. Privacy, Right of.
    I. Title.
    TK5105.5864.B78 2015
    004.67′8–dc23
                                                                                    2015020393

Cover image courtesy of *137867102/Jorg Greuel/Getty 455164793/rozkmina/Getty*

Set in 10/12pt Times by SPi Global, Pondicherry, India

Printed in the United States of America

10 9 8 7 6 5 4 3 2 1

1 2016

This book is dedicated to my father, Robert, who taught me all I know and never stopped teaching.

CONTENTS

INTRODUCTION: WHAT IS WHOIS?

WHOIS is a complex topic, as this book explains, but the simplest explanation is that it is a record system for network resources, mostly, but not exclusively on the Internet. WHOIS is one of the most critical and controversial services on the Internet, yet there has been little or no comprehensive documentation. A WHOIS service can be queried to return a WHOIS record, which details who owns or manages an Internet resource. While this service may seem ordinary, WHOIS is one of the most debated issues in Internet policy. In theory, WHOIS is supposed to simply retrieve contact information; in practice, WHOIS varies widely in composition, access, and use. This text covers the universe of topics and issues including the 40-year evolution of the service, policy changes, comprehensive use instructions, service deployment, and advanced coding for programmers. The text is wide in its breadth and attempts to be somewhat deep in each of the major areas, but there are limitations to coverage in a single text.

Unlike computer programming, networking, or hardware development, WHOIS is a disconnected and esoteric discipline. It has many self-taught adepts as well as almost cultish followers. WHOIS is a deep and wide subject without dedicated texts or classroom instruction, a truly strange and hidden world. Welcome, you are about to become a WHOIS sorcerer.

From RFC1177[1] FYI on Questions and Answers to Commonly asked "New Internet User" Questions (1990)

> *WHOIS: An Internet program which allows users to query a database of people and other Internet entities, such as domains, networks, and hosts, kept at the NIC. The information for people shows a person's company name, address, phone number and email address.*

---

[1] http://tools.ietf.org/pdf/rfc1177.pdf

WHOIS Running the Internet: Protocol, Policy, and Privacy, First Edition. Garth O. Bruen.
© 2016 John Wiley & Sons, Inc. Published 2016 by John Wiley & Sons, Inc.

Same language in the 1991 version[2]

In its modern usage, "WHOIS" has become a bit of a misnomer. A more accurate term would be "WHOOWNS," "WHOCONTROLS," or "WHOISRESPONSIBLE" since the original WHOIS identified personal accounts or machines tied to a specific person or entity. The one-to-one concept of a resource on the Internet simply no longer applies in most cases, and the WHOIS record will in fact reveal multiple parties with their hands on a domain name or Internet Protocol (IP) address.

Performing a domain WHOIS query lookup on "wiley.com" returns this data:

```
John Wiley & Sons, Inc
Domain Administrator
111 River Street
Hoboken, NJ 07030
US
Phone: +1.3175723355
Email: domains@wiley.com
```

The IP address for wiley.com is 208.215.179.146. A WHOIS query lookup on this address returns this data:

```
Name    John Wiley & Sons
Handle        C00546298
Street        432 Elizabeth Avenue
City    Somerset
State/Province      NJ
Postal Code 08875
Country       US
```

These are two very simple examples of a system, which provokes intense concerns about cybercrime, invasion of privacy, and even the survivability of a single global Internet.

The term WHOIS can refer ambiguously to a service program, a database that stores WHOIS records and the WHOIS record itself. The original reason for having these records and making them publicly available is simple: every node on the Internet is capable of passing traffic to another node, which is what makes the Internet work. If one node has functional problems, it threatens the overall operation of the Internet so other administrators must have the ability to contact the owner of a node experiencing a problem somewhere in the chain.

WHOIS as a protocol concept essentially started in 1971 with the creation of Finger, a program that allowed users on a network to retrieve details about other active users on the network. This was most likely the first time it became possible to remotely create a live "online" connection. An updated version in 1977 called Name/Finger actually introduced the term "Whois" as part of the program function. Being able to see who else is on the network and retrieve information about those persons is a fundamental pillar of the Internet, but one also seen as contributing to the decline in personal privacy. There were so few participants on the early network that sharing contact information

[2] http://tools.ietf.org/pdf/rfc1206.pdf

was not considered controversial. As the network steadily grew, some started to see the public availability of this information as a threat. However, it is generally acknowledged that allowing unaccountable parties onto the public network is just as dangerous. A balance must be found between security and privacy. To address this, a sizable portion of the text is dedicated to this debate.

Following the precise path of the growth of the Internet, WHOIS has experienced changes and even mutations. Unknown to most, there is in fact no single WHOIS database or standard for the Internet. There may be as many as 1500 public WHOIS databases, each with its own rules, formatting, and level of service. The number of WHOIS records currently in existence may exceed 200 million. WHOIS is a massive pile of data with names, addresses, phone numbers, and network resources that explains who owns what is on the Internet.

WHOIS records have long been required for IP addresses and for Internet hostnames. When domain names became available for public consumption, the WHOIS controversy exploded. Criminals began deliberately falsifying WHOIS records, shady marketers exploited the publicly available contact information, and noncommercial domain owners feared for their privacy and safety.

The future of WHOIS is up in the air. There are parties who want to see it banned completely or have access severely restricted. Conversely, the demand and growth of the data is increasing, which calls for better management and more technical tools. Presently, we are at crossroads in the history of WHOIS.

While WHOIS existed in various formats for several decades, the formal documentation used for our current Domain Name System (DNS) was released in 2004 in Request for Comments (RFC) document number 3912.[3] This standards document admits to problems with the security and data formats with the expectation or disclaimer that the data is *intended to be accessible to everyone.*

It is important to understand how WHOIS fits in with the overall structure of the DNS.[4] WHOIS records are not "required" for the DNS, meaning there is no technical requirement for the WHOIS record to exist, be reachable, or be accurate for a domain name to resolve. However, a variety of networking services depend on WHOIS, for example, the firewall analyzing program **fwlogwatch**[5] calls WHOIS as one of its functions, the **-W** switch.

What does and does not have a WHOIS record:

example.com—Does
frediessubdom.example.com—Does not
example.com/utils/homepage.html—Does not
ns1.example.com—Does
fred@example.com—Does not

Email addresses do not have WHOIS records, but the domain name that serves the mailbox does. So for each email address, there is one unique WHOIS record for the attached domain, no WHOIS record for specific email addresses. Twitter addresses and Facebook pages do

---

[3] http://tools.ietf.org/html/rfc3912
[4] http://tools.ietf.org/html/rfc1034
[5] http://linux.die.net/man/8/fwlogwatch

not have WHOIS records but twitter.com and facebook.com do. The raw IP addresses behind domain names have WHOIS records as do nameservers and the major Internet providers who sponsor the architecture of the DNS. Specific services may have internal functions called "WHOIS." For example, Internet Relay Chat[6] (IRC) has the commands WHO,[7] WHOIS,[8] and WHOWAS,[9] which provide information about different account holders; these are not usually considered part of the common WHOIS lexicon. WHOIS has multiple definition and uses, including:

WHOIS *record*
WHOIS *service*
WHOIS *server*
WHOIS *database*
WHOIS *query*
WHOIS *program*

While registration data is casually referred to as "WHOIS," the more accurate term might be Domain Name Registration Data (DNRD), but few outside the industry use this.

I.1   CONVENTIONS USED IN THIS TEXT

All material is intended to be thoroughly sourced with examples and links to additional information or original material—but be warned; the source documents may even be more obscure and difficult to understand. The examples cited are meant to be simple and straightforward. *Italicized* sections are typically literal command strings intended to be typed at a terminal or shell prompt. While the term "WHOIS" is featured in many different ways (whois, WhoIs, etc.), the convention here is to use "WHOIS" for general concepts and "whois" for specific instructions and coding. In some instances, the capitalization may be from the original context of a cited document.

People tend to regard WHOIS as a single system, but nothing can be further from the truth. The results of a WHOIS query are limited by what the specific database has, what the specific server allows access to, the used account's level of access, and the functions of the WHOIS client being used.

The way domain owners are described varies within the industry. The official term is domain *registrant* as no one really owns a domain. Domains are leased for periods of 1 year typically and must be renewed. The colloquial term "domainer" is often used to describe the population of domain registrants in a political context, whereas "registrant" is used to describe their specific relationship with the registrar. Another simpler description is domain *customer*. All term may be used in this text, but generally refer to the same type of person or entity.

The official term describing what a registrar does for a registrant is *sponsorship*. However, domain name registrars do not like this term. "Sponsorship" is what appears in

---

[6] http://tools.ietf.org/html/rfc2812
[7] http://tools.ietf.org/html/rfc1459#section-4.5.1
[8] http://tools.ietf.org/html/rfc1459#section-4.5.2
[9] http://tools.ietf.org/html/rfc1459#section-4.5.3

the Internet Corporation of Assigned Names and Numbers (ICANN) Registrar Accreditation Agreement (RAA) contract, but registrars are concerned that this term implies a much more active type of oversight than they are required to provide.

Some records returned by WHOIS queries can be exceedingly long. If we have shortened the records for brevity in the text, it should be indicated clearly or terminated with an ellipsis (…). Specific commands list in the flow of discussion are in **bold**. Italicized block citations are typically from documentation, memorandum, or texts. If these italicized blocks are in quotes, they are usually from a single person or attributable to single person. Single italicized lines without quotes are literal command expression to be typed on a terminal or command prompt. Example system responses are indented in a different font.

I.2 FLOW OF THIS TEXT

The goal of this book is to provide a comprehensive overview, with a certain amount of depth through its coverage of WHOIS history and WHOIS use, as well as its greater role the DNS. The full picture is seen in WHOIS programming, WHOIS server details, the complex body of WHOIS policy development, and finally the future of WHOIS. All of these topics are deeply interwoven. The history helps explain why WHOIS has been structured as it is and why some of the problems are a result of those initial decisions. Historical issues have influenced how the services were developed technically and how they are used by various consumers of the data. The WHOIS imprint on the fabric of the Internet's DNS through the servers that implement policy and technical decisions are all dependent factors in the body of WHOIS.

I.3 WHOIS FROM VERSUS WHOIS ABOUT

It is important to understand that it is possible to both query WHOIS *from* a service and *about* a service. Registrars and registries are services that host WHOIS service but also have their own WHOIS records that provide contact information for the registrar or registry company itself.

The term WHOIS can refer ambiguously to a service program, a database that stores WHOIS records as well as the WHOIS records themselves:

- Contact/owner record for an Internet resource
- Database holding Internet contact/owner records
- Query of the database holding Internet contact/owner records
- Server hosting the database Internet contact/owner records
- Service listening for queries of the database Internet contact/owner records
- Client program querying the database Internet contact/owner records
- The entire scope of all services and policy concerning Internet contact/owner records

In the early days, a single failure on the network could stop all the data from moving. The immediacy of having a technical contact in WHOIS has shifted to security and policy needs. With multiple routes available on the Internet, and more coming all the time, this brings new threats of abuse on the network on even grander scales. The use of WHOIS may have shifted slightly, but its need has become greater.

I.4   ORIGIN OF THE TERM WHOIS

While we can trace the origin of the WHOIS protocol to specific people, events and code finding the exact origin of the term may prove a little difficult. The **who am i** command and related used is familiar to UNIX users,[10] but the use of WHOIS predates even UNIX. Different documents state that WHOIS was already in common use on systems prior to widespread UNIX deployment.[11] The use of whois as a command on Internet Relay Chat (IRC)does not appear until 1988.

Often capitalized, WHOIS is not an acronym. It literally means "who is." At one time, it was possible to type *whois* * (The asterisk "*" is a common wildcard system code, meaning it can be replaced with anything.) and retrieve all the profiles for everyone on the network. But where did it come from? *"Certainly someone coined the term,"*[12] wrote Ken Harrenstien about the origin of WHOIS. Harrenstien wrote the original WHOIS specification, and everyone I talked to said if anyone knew the origin, *"it would be Ken."* However, at the time, preserving the specific source of the term was not likely a priority. Ken surmised that his *"suspicion is that it first started being used at the MIT AI lab, which is where I first encountered the name."*[13]

The Artificial Intelligence (AI) Laboratory at the Massachusetts Institute of Technology was famous for the Incompatible Timesharing System (ITS). In the late 1960s, ITS was where great strides occurred in computing. One of the utilities on this system was called **who**. **who** could be used to call up a list of active usernames and the terminal names they were using, but nothing more. For those familiar with Windows NT administration, it would be similar to the **net view** DOS command, which retrieves a list of machine names connected to the network. **who** did not tell you anything about the account holder or even where the terminal was located. In 1971, another program called **finger** was paired with a database to extend the utility of **who** by providing information about the users found with **who**. **finger** would later be combined with the **name** program to create the precursor for today's WHOIS. The name/finger combination documentation in 1977 refers to the term "WHOIS" to describe the function, but the actual command switch was "/W".[14] Since this new process all ran on the ITS system, we must assume it was not new to developers at this point. Over time, WHOIS became the prevailing term for the function of seeing the record previously supplied by **finger**. To follow the logic, if **who** gave us a list active users but no further information, the follow-up question would likely be "who is" a particular user. Some RFCs assigning port number 43 refer to the service as "Who Is,"[15] but obviously the space in the command would cause problems, especially, in earlier systems, so it follows that the term would be contracted.

---

[10] http://linux.die.net/man/1/who
[11] http://tools.ietf.org/html/rfc742
[12] Harrenstien interview
[13] See note 12.
[14] See note 11.
[15] http://www.ietf.org/rfc/rfc1700.txt

Unlike many other early commands and future UNIX commands, "Who" is pretty straightforward, as compared to **grep**. There are some with the same sort of expected meaning like **which** (shows which version of a program is being used by virtue of the path-name), **whereis** (searches for files related to a utility), and **whatis** (describes a command). The one-letter command **w** combines features of who and finger with some additional features for more powerful searching on the local network. Even more specifically, **whodo** can retrieve a list of processes being run by which user. These commands check the system utmp[16] file (and others), which record user activity. There is also a **whom** command that is used for examining email headers.[17] However, most of these conventions appear long after WHOIS starts creeping into official Internet documents.

It would be difficult to make a direct connection with Internet WHOIS, but the first real use of the term in communication may have come from teletype machines as documented in the chapter on history. Long before the Internet sparked into being on October 29, 1968, remote signals were sent without electronics, and the recipients needed to identify the sender.

I.5   WHY WHOIS IS IMPORTANT (OR SHOULD BE) TO EVERYONE

Anyone who uses the Internet for any commerce or communication needs to understand there is an underlying record set documenting who controls websites and Internet resources. We all share and access the same Internet. How do we identify who controls a resource on this network? Specifically, within the context of a responsible party, for the purpose of addressing technical issues but also in the larger and more subtle context of ensuring a trust relationship on the shared network. Ensuring that a node on the network functions properly and is not passing traffic in a way that disrupts the network is part of that trust foundation. This becomes even more crucial when online transactions come into play. In this world, "transaction" has a few meanings, which need to be clarified. In networking, a *transaction* refers to a very literal transfer of data and has similar use in database programming. However, in the context of our trust relationship, transaction is used to refer to the exchange (sometimes unauthorized) of personal information or money. The fundamental reason for accurate and accessible WHOIS is to offer a layer of protection to users and consumers. WHOIS keeps the Internet democratic.

I.6   WHAT KIND OF USE AND CONTACT IS PERMITTED FOR WHOIS

There are concerns and accusations that WHOIS is being abused, or at least overused, but the records exist for a reason. WHOIS contact details may be used for "any lawful purpose,"[18] which would include research and questions related to online investigations. Registrars, ISPs, registrants, and users engaged in illicit activities may claim that storing or using WHOIS data is a violation of privacy or harassment, but this is merely a tactic. There are limitations on the use of WHOIS data, which includes mass marketing,[19] but this is inapplicable to data gathering in an investigation and contact in relation to the domain name. For example, contacting a domain registrant to ask if they have a valid pharmacy

---

[16] http://man7.org/linux/man-pages/man5/utmp.5.html

[17] https://www-01.ibm.com/support/knowledgecenter/#!/ssw_aix_61/com.ibm.aix.cmds6/whom.htm

[18] http://www.icann.org/en/resources/registrars/raa/ra-agreement-21may09-en.htm#3.3.5

[19] http://www.icann.org/en/resources/registrars/consensus-policies/wmrp

license for their domain is a completely legitimate use of WHOIS data. Illicit registrants will often accuse investigators of "spamming" them, but routine contact in connection to the use of a domain name is perfectly acceptable.

Registrars will often insert language into the headers of WHOIS records, which contain additional restrictions on the use of WHOIS. However, these conditions are frequently not supported by the registrar contracts. Specifically, the contract states: *"Registrar shall **not** impose terms and conditions on use of the data provided."*[20]

I.7   WHERE IS THE WHOIS DATA?

In terms of domain WHOIS data, ICANN does not accept or store WHOIS data. All data is stored in individual registrar or registry databases in addition to the WHOIS escrow at Iron Mountain. The Iron Mountain escrow is not a database that can be queried, and ICANN does not have access to it. The purpose of the Iron Mountain escrow is to provide a recoverable repository of WHOIS data in case of catastrophic failure or if a registrar refuses to turn over their database upon contract termination, which has happened. There is no single WHOIS database. Because of the number of possible office locations, virtual data storage, and off-site backups, the data exists in various states and levels of availability. Some registrar WHOIS servers are even run from small home offices. WHOIS records are not a single record; rather, they are field entries in a database, and in some cases, the results displayed in a query may have come from more than one database. This is why the records will appear different depending on how the record is retrieved or where it is retrieved from. The WHOIS files produced by queries are merely the text output of a database query.

I.8   IDENTIFYING REMOTE COMMUNICATION SOURCES

WHOIS is not a unique or new situation. The problem of identifying persons, devices, or broadcasts on a network predates even the creation of the modern Internet. We can point to the Imperial Wireless Chain[21] and the common telephone system.[22] Consider examples of communication and source identification, which predate even any kind of wired or wireless transmission, namely, lighthouses. In theory, every lighthouse has a different paint pattern for daytime identification and flash lights at different intervals in the dark.[23] While lighthouses keep ships from running aground, they also provide a critical navigational tool; the external stripes, color, or checkers are not just for quaint appearances. This is called a *DAYMARK* in sailor lingo.[24] Compare these two lighthouses from Bodie Island, NC,[25] and Cape Hatteras, NC,[26] respectively. They are very close to each other in terms of location and similar in construction. The variation in pattern distinguishes them for ships in the area.

Communication is not just about transmitting information but also validating the source of that information. The role of lighthouses in civilization stretches back to ancient times. Two

---

[20] See note 18.
[21] http://hansard.millbanksystems.com/commons/1913/aug/08/new-marconi-agreement
[22] http://www.thefreedictionary.com/Plain+old+telephone+service
[23] http://www.us-lighthouses.com/faq.php
[24] http://pharology.eu/Daymarks.html
[25] http://www.nps.gov/caha/planyourvisit/bils.htm
[26] http://www.nps.gov/caha/learn/historyculture/movingthelighthouse.htm

FIGURE I.1 Bodie Island Light Station. Courtesy of U.S. National Park Service.

FIGURE I.2 Cape Hatteras Light Station. Courtesy of U.S. National Park Service.

FIGURE I.3   Polybius Torch Signalling, Hulton Archive. Copyright Getty Images.

of the Seven Wonders of the Ancient World were lighthouses: the Colossus of Rhodes[27] and the Pharos of Alexandria.[28] Even more than sources of information, these structures were bold statements identifying the peoples who built them. The reference to lighthouses is not just a convenient comparison. Different types of signaling towers are directly related to the development of long-distance communication technologies that lead to the Internet. In the second century BC, the Greek statesman and historian Polybius created a tower-based signaling system, which employed an alphabet substitution system encoded on a grid, a *Polybius Square*.[29] The original purpose of the code was not encryption but to reduce messaging to a very simple character set that could be translated by the remote recipient. The square was a 5×5 grid with the letters of the (Greek) alphabet placed in ordered rows, here in English:

	1	2	3	4	5
1	A	B	C	D	E
2	F	G	H	I	K
3	L	M	N	O	P
4	Q	R	S	T	U
5	V	W	X	Y	Z

The ancient Greek alphabet only had 24 letters so we have omitted "J" to make it fit the 25 squares. Now, each letter can be represented by two digits, so 52 23 34 24 43 is "WHOIS." By using two sets of five torches on a tower, messages can be quickly transmitted.

[27] http://www.britannica.com/EBchecked/topic/501620/Colossus-of-Rhodes
[28] http://www.britannica.com/EBchecked/topic/455210/Pharos-of-Alexandria
[29] http://penelope.uchicago.edu/Thayer/E/Roman/Texts/Polybius/10*.html#45.6

Polybius was not just a communications scientist but also a political philosopher. For the purposes of this text, he serves as a kind of spirit guide on both counts.

An even better modern comparison in communications is radio. Like the Internet, radio waves are a shared public resource. IP addresses and domain names must be unique, just as specific radio frequencies can only be used by one broadcaster at a time within a specific range. Radio stations frequently give out the call letters (WXYZ or whatever) and broadcasting location. This is not just for promoting the station; it is a requirement of their license. In order to prevent clashing of signals, the airwaves are regulated; otherwise, the broadcast with the most powerful signal would simply control the frequency. This has serious implications beyond not being able to hear your favorite music. The frequencies of all radio emitting devices are regulated to keep them from interfering with other equipment or interrupting emergency frequencies of say the police. For example, there have been many cases over the years of military equipment interfering with remote residential garage door openers near air force or naval bases.[30] The Federal Communications Commission[31] (FCC), similar international agencies,[32] and private DXers[33] constantly try to track down unknown signals.

I.9 GETTING DOCUMENTATION

One of the main goals of this text is to bring together the rather large but disparate collection of information about WHOIS. Work on this book began out of a lack of texts dedicated to the topic. Much of the public information is incomplete or out of date. In researching, it was found that research for this text revealed that the the standard list of WHOIS servers, often embedded in extensively used code, was at-least 10 years old. The bug-reporting technical email in the VeriSign WHOIS client, info@nsiregistry.com, was rejected because the account address no longer exists. The ICANN has the largest oversight of WHOIS but a surprisingly thin webpage describing the subject.[34] However, the information does exist, often because of dedicated technical experts, noted in this text; have kept their own records; and are willing to share it. Here, we have pieced together a picture of WHOIS from a diverse selection of practitioners.

One series of documents that contain a wealth of information about WHOIS are the Internet development memorandums called RFC. This format of memos started in 1969 specifically for proposing Internet standards or creating discussions. The very first RFC, most appropriately, is called "host software" and describes the function of Interface Message Processors[35] (IMP), which was a gateway between networked machines. This first memo was written by Steve Crocker who has more recently been serving as board chairman of the ICANN. There are now over 7000 RFCs maintained by the Internet Engineering Task Force[36] (IETF). Many of these memos define or refer to WHOIS and form the basis for the current implementations. These documents also document proto-WHOIS implementations or WHOIS-like attempts to record and obtain network resource information.

---

[30] http://abcnews.go.com/blogs/headlines/2013/06/fort-gordon-radio-upgrade-causes-garage-door-havoc/
[31] http://www.fcc.gov/
[32] http://transition.fcc.gov/mb/audio/bickel/world-govt-telecom.html
[33] http://www.dxing.info/introduction.dx
[34] http://icannwiki.com/index.php/whois
[35] http://www.ietf.org/rfc/rfc1.txt
[36] http://www.ietf.org/download/rfc-index.txt

While considered the authoritative documentation for the Internet, RFCs were not the only standard documentation. Internet Experiment Notes (IEN) were documentation for a related Defense Advanced Research Projects Agency (DARPA) Internet project, which were eventually merged with RFCs. The last IEN was issued in 1982.

Some of the most interesting sources of information come from the WHOIS programs and servers themselves. These are the in the form of **Help** or **MAN** (for manual) files often stored within the WHOIS program itself. Calling these files may require experimentation since they are not all called the same way. In a Unix-based system, any native program can be detailed by typing *man <command-name>*; in our case, *man whois* would return a detailed and interactive instruction set for the program. Help files on various systems, and ones accessed on remote servers, may be retrieved with whois?, whois help, whois --help, or whois –h. This depends on the information source and software used. Some may have no help file, and the irony is that you need to access the help file to know how to access the help file. Sometimes, you can access the help file by making mistake and sending a bad query to the program. In the cases cited in this text, we will attempt when possible to demonstrate access to the help file. Unfortunately, many of the help files for WHOIS are out of date and poorly detailed. Many of the functions documented in WHOIS help files are 10–20 years old and have been disabled or are no longer accepted by the remote servers.

1

THE HISTORY OF WHOIS

Through the development of the Internet, in general, we see the development of WHOIS and its concepts as a necessary component. While the need for a clear record set for the network seemed a fundamental technical requirement, it was not simple to construct and manage. Throughout history, questions and discussions about the meaning and use of these resource records began to emerge. It is clear that various policy issues were on the minds of the early RFC authors, which sometimes portend future conflicts.

1.1 IN THE BEGINNING

In 1982, this dry sentence launched the Internet's model of record access for the next 30 years and beyond:

> The NICNAME/WHOIS Server is an NCP/TCP transaction based query/response server, running on the SRI-NIC machine, that provides net-wide directory service to ARPANET users.[1]

Where the SRI-NIC machine sits or what "SRI" stands for is not explained or footnoted in the document. Anyone reading it at the time would have common knowledge of its meaning. "NIC" of course stands for Network Information Center or Controller. Understanding what is behind these acronyms opens a door to the history of the Internet. SRI stands for Stanford Research Institute. In 1982, SRI-NIC, and its related machines, was the Internet. Many readers may be more familiar with the ARPANET as a precursor to the Internet.

---

[1] http://tools.ietf.org/html/rfc812

WHOIS Running the Internet: Protocol, Policy, and Privacy, First Edition. Garth O. Bruen.
© 2016 John Wiley & Sons, Inc. Published 2016 by John Wiley & Sons, Inc.

The ARPANET was a government-funded initiative to connect networks at the Massachusetts Institute of Technology (MIT), Harvard, Xerox, the RAND Corporation, The Pentagon, and a dozen other entities. However, we see from this memo that the location and coordination of the record set for this nascent network was at Stanford. The machine referenced would hold the contact information for all the hosts and directories on the ARPANET and respond to requests for that information. So what is the real difference between NICNAME and WHOIS, as they are used synonymously starting with the title of RFC 812? In the Unix services file (/usr/etc/inet/services), different ports are assigned for different network traffic. Port 43 lists "whois" as the service name and "nicname" as the process or program.[2] This is a common snapshot of that file with the Port 43 lines highlighted, compared to the entries for FTP and Telnet that have no alternate identities:

```
ftp         21/tcp
telnet      23/tcp
smtp        25/tcp          mail #Simple Mail Transfer
whois       43/udp          nicname
whois       43/tcp          nicname
. . .
```

It is in this context a subtle distinction. The *whois* accepts requests through Port 43 for *nicname*. The RFC from 1982 is often marked as the beginning of WHOIS by researchers like Milton Mueller,[3] a professor at the Syracuse University School of Information Studies and one of the major figures in the WHOIS policy debate. However, here we can push the origin back several years and may be even more.

1.2   THE SANDS OF TIME

In our introduction, we made a brief reference to lighthouses and the role they have played from ancient times, not just in warning ships of the coastline but also in the self-identification of the information source. The concepts in play in computing and networking have a long lineage. We often take our advance technology for granted, not understanding that generations past worked at these ideas long before they became real in our time. Our modern communication technology is an amalgamation of human achievements from prehistory, just out of reach, until now, due to a collision of mechanics and electricity in the last century.

The idea of building a network and passing information across the network did not spring into being 50 years ago. Humans have been tackling this problem since ancient times without computers or even electric power. The need to identify sources of information that could be passed through a network became a challenge as soon as the ancient networks began. Two of the best examples come from the Roman Empire and can still be seen (and even used), namely, roads and aqueducts. The Romans were distinguished from other ancient civilizations by the permanent lines linking cities and settlements. The testament to the Roman road was not just in its construction, but more so in its regulation, maintenance, and use. Roads had to be up to a certain size and standard and separated for specific use. Like modern network technology, the Roman road consisted of *layered* construction materials each with its own function.

---

[2] http://www.informatica.co.cr/linux-kernel/research/1993/0218.html
[3] http://faculty.ischool.syr.edu/mueller/Home.html

1.2.1 Seals

The Roman roads were of course used for travel, commerce, and messaging. Just like the Internet today, where any host can pass traffic, messages carried on ancient roads could come from anywhere. How would a recipient identify the source of a message? Since ancient times, systems of seals or impressions have been used. Older seals were made from clay and more recently wax. The sender would have a signet ring or special cylinder with an official mark impressed in the seal, which would serve as authentication.[4]

1.2.2 From Signal Fires on the Great Wall to Telegraphy

Another great construction feat of antiquity that can still be touched is China's Great Wall. Stretching over 8000 kilometers along China's northern border, its military defensive and border control are well known, but its use as a network is not. A system of fires, cannon, drums, and flags were used to pass information rapidly, not only up and down the wall but also to and from watchtowers outside the wall. Beyond simply warning of an impending attack, variations in the signals indicated enemy troop strength and position.[5]

FIGURE 1.1 Chappe optical telegraph from http://farm3.static.flickr.com/2174/3666825198_ a7ab2e6270_m.jpg. Mary Evans Picture Library.

---

[4] http://www.artofmanliness.com/2013/02/13/wax-seals-a-history-and-how-to/
[5] http://greatwall.shanghaifinance.com/greatwallmilitary.php

FIGURE 1.2   Telegraph Hill, San Francisco, California. http://www.superstock.com/stock-photos-images/1885-2819. Travel Library Limited.

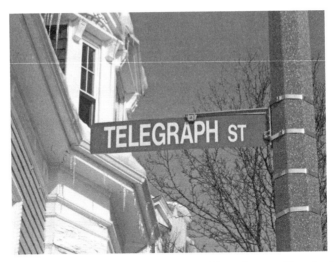

FIGURE 1.3   Telegraph Street, South Boston, Massachusetts. Photo by Author.

The use of optical signaling (telegraphy or semaphore) continued centuries on for message transmission until replaced by the telegraph. The term *telegraphy* itself was used initially to refer to long-distance optical signaling.

Many modern cities have locations or streets called "Telegraph Hill," which actually used to house these stations.

The eighteenth-century inventor of modern telegraphy, Claude Chappe [1], was inspired by the writings of the ancient Greek historian and politician Polybius [2].

Polybius is credited with creating one of the earliest coding systems by converting the Greek alphabet to numeric values and representing them with different numbers of torches on the top of a tower. Instead of fire, Chappe used mechanical arms at the top of towers to signal news across France. Prior to the twentieth century, the use of *heliographs*, mirrors reflecting the sun and transmitting the Morse code, was a concept also mentioned in ancient texts [3]. So, yes, the Internet, in thought, can be traced back over 2000 years.

1.2.3 The Eye of Horus

While we have established methods used by the ancients for conveying messages over long distances, there is still the matter of message compression and encoding. However, this was not much of a problem for our ancestors either.

The ancient Egyptians were obsessed with fractions, and one of their most interesting fractional sequences is wrapped up in a critical myth [4]. The god Horus lost his eye during a battle with his evil uncle Set. The broken pieces of the eye were collected and rebuilt. The Eye of Horus or *Wedjat* is a symbol of protection and royal power, which most would recognize. Few, however, know that the broken pieces of the eye each represent individually the fractions 1/2, 1/4, 1/8, 1/16, 1/32, and 1/64—each is one half the previous one. This fraction set was only used for measuring grain, which was a sacred resource.

This sequence appears again in representing our binary values 1, 2, 4, 8, 16, 32, 64, 128, 256, and 564—each one is twice the previous one. This sequence has played a role in limiting IP ranges (which are capped in their segments at 256) and the size of certain digital values (domain names have had a 64-character limit). Why? Because these values are mapped to the literal binary switches in a computer that enable them to "do math" by recognizing whether the switches are either active or inactive. With 10 binary operators each assigned with one of the values in the sequence, it is possible to combine them to create any number. The idea of binary numbers in particular could have originated over 2000 years

FIGURE 1.4 Wedjat, reproduced courtesy of The MIT Press, from Richard J. Gillings, *Mathematics in the Time of the Pharaohs.*

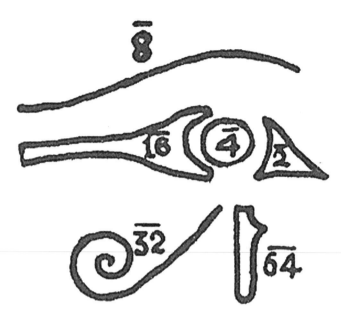

FIGURE 1.5   From mathisgoodforyou.com. http://www.mathsisgoodforyou.com/topicsPages/
egyptianmaths/horusfractions.htm. Reproduced courtesy of The MIT Press, from Richard J. Gillings,
Mathematics in the Time of the Pharaohs.

ago and was experimented with by mathematicians throughout the centuries searching for
methods to compress or encode information.

1.3   1950s: ON THE WIRES AND IN THE AIR

Everyone knows there was no Internet in the 1950s. Or was there? It could be said that
the Internet was *almost* there. The lines, coding, and terminals were all in place and had
been since the previous century, as explained later. WHOIS, the concept anyway, was
there too. There were a few pieces missing including ways to store and move large sets
of data as well as connections between real client and server networks. The Internet
needed a push.

1.3.1   Sputnik Changes Everything

The innovation drive that resulted in our Internet was sparked by the 1957 launch of the
USSR's Sputnik satellite.[6] US President Dwight Eisenhower pressed for the immediate
creation of a group advancing various technologies in the interest of national security. The
Defense Advanced Research Projects Agency (DARPA) was authorized in 1958 to expand
research and development beyond the existing military labs. Much of the work was
focused on communications and information processing as well as on military hardware
like missiles. One of the first projects released was TRANSIT, a satellite navigation

---

[6] http://tools.ietf.org/html/rfc2235

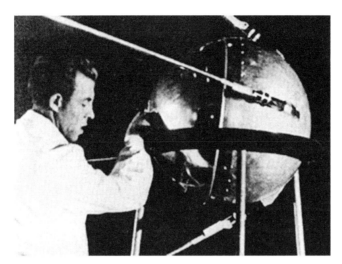

FIGURE 1.6   Sputnik, Courtesy of NASA.

system used for tracking US Navy ships and submarines.[7] This system was a precursor to our current Global Positioning System (GPS). The idea for this system came directly from the efforts to track Sputnik through *Doppler shifts*, which is in essence the change in waves between stationary and moving objects. So we see, wrapped up in the early development of the Internet, a need to identify a remote communication source. In fact, one of the things the US government was concerned about was the detection of nuclear explosions.

It was in part this need to get computers small enough to fit into satellites and submarines that required new thinking in the way computers functioned. For example, one of the early TRANSIT satellites began employing the concept of loading software into memory while orbiting the earth. Better computing and remote communication within DARPA projects of course led to the Internet, but not for another 10 years. Also, we indicate earlier that all of this occurred after *1957*. What happened before?

1.3.2   Telegraphs, Radio, Teletype, and Telephones

In *Victorian Internet*,[8] author Tom Standage explains how an electronic global nineteenth-century network spread news, delivered letters, and was even used for spam.[9] Text messages were converted to Morse code,[10] which consisted of varying electronic pulses representing letters of the alphabet and formatting codes circa 1837. Soon there was even competition in the coding from inventors like Jean-Maurice-Émile Baudot[11] whose code eventually replaced Morse. The text to code conversion was manual as was the retranslation on the receiving end. The telegraph cables ran over land and under the sea transmitting

---

[7] http://techdigest.jhuapl.edu/td/td1901/danchik.pdf

[8] http://www.smithsonianmag.com/history-archaeology/bookreview_jan99_a.html

[9] http://taint.org/2012/05/24/112415a.html

[10] http://www.history.com/topics/telegraph

[11] Baudot systems.

between North America and Europe in a matter of minutes.[12] The deployment of telegraph was often alongside another type of network, the railroads. The phone company SPRINT actually began as part of a railroad. The name SPRINT stands for Southern Pacific Railroad Internal Network Telecommunications. Telegrams continue to be an important part of global communications even in the Internet age.[13]

Of course, all of this wired technology got competition from the emerging *wireless* technology of the nineteenth century in the form of radio. Both telegraph and radio stations were identified by two-letter *call signs* that became longer as more stations started broadcasting. Since all stations in a telegraph network received all messages, the station codes were included to show who the transmission was intended for. This is not too different from peer-to-peer networks that pass traffic not intended for the intermediate machines. Ships and airplanes as well as ground stations have call signs.

While telegraph operators needed training in handling messages, the transmission and output were already automated, meaning it was not a far stretch to automate the translation of message and print the letters instead of a code. Teletype (TTY) took the existing mechanical typewriter model and connected its operations to the electric input. Pressing a letter key on the TTY would issue the same kind of code tapped manually by a code operator. On the receiving end, the electronic codes were mapped to the TTY keys that printed messages on paper. A 1932 *Popular Mechanics* issue contains this description:

> [AT&T] for the first time makes available to the public generally this means of transmitting messages electrically over the wires to any other subscriber, so that whatever is typed at one end of a circuit appears practically the instant at the other end, also in typewritten form.[14]

The first successful TTY transmission occurred in 1904 and commercial sales began in 1910.[15] Its use rapidly expanded for news transmission, law enforcement communication, and even hotel registration. By 1922, the US Navy had successfully used radioteletype (RTTY) to send printing instruction from an aircraft to a ground station.[16]

1.3.3   WRU: The First WHOIS

These devices were connected to the phone system and the combination made for amazing technology at the time. With multiple locations sending and receiving messages, the immediate questions become: where is the message coming from and who wrote it? The TTY machines had a hardcoded HERE IS key, a special code drum identifying the station.[17] Below is an excerpt from a TELETYPE Corporation A Teletype Model 33 ASR manual:

Here Is Answer-Back

2.1.39 The answer-back will cycle once when the HERE IS key is depressed.

---

[12] http://itelegram.com/telegram/Atlantic_Cable_150.asp
[13] http://www.theguardian.com/world/shortcuts/2013/jul/10/final-telegram-to-be-sent-india
[14] http://books.google.com/books?id=g_EDAAAAMBAJ&pg=PA577#v=onepage&q&f=true
[15] http://www.samhallas.co.uk/repository/telegraph/teletype_story.pdf
[16] http://www.princeton.edu/~achaney/tmve/wiki100k/docs/Radioteletype.html
[17] http://www.k7tty.com/development/teletype/model-32/index.html

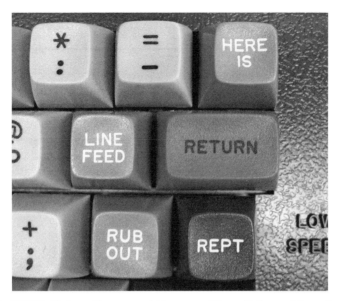

FIGURE 1.7   HERE IS key. Courtesy of Jessamyn West, flickr.com/photos/iamthebestartist/ 5559792267.

This encoding could be requested remotely by another terminal by issuing the WRU, which stands for "*WHO ARE YOU?*" This was not a question for the person operating the TTY; it was a question for the machine. Below is the WRU excerpt from the 33 ASR manual:

WRU Answer-Back

2.1.31 When WRU is sent from the keyboard or tape, the WRU function box mechanism operates at both sending and receiving stations. The answer-back at the sending station is mechanically prevented from responding, while the WRU function box mechanism trips the answer-back at the receiving stations.

The WRU command still exists in maritime communication.[18] This is the first real WHOIS, the first time an information source would respond automatically to a remote request for identification. The WRU would also be sent along with the end of a TTY message to confirm with the recipient that the transmission was unbroken. This command was also called the ENQ for "ENQuiry."[19] This is an excerpt from a TTY manual showing the location of the ENQ function:

Part of the drum encoding sequence included codes for Acknowledge (ACK), Carriage Return (CR), and Line Feed (LF), which are all part of the online WHOIS transaction that shows up later. Coding the answer drum involved a screwdriver and needle-nose pliers. Encodings were created by removing tiny tines in a sequence to indicate a specific American Standard Code for Information Interchange (ASCII) code.

---

[18] http://www.polaris-as.dk/wp-content/uploads/downloads/user_manuals/skanti/SKANTI_TRP_1000_Series_ Operators_Manual.pdf
[19] http://www.baudot.net/docs/smith--teletype-codes.pdf

FIGURE 1.8   HERE IS key. Courtesy David Gesswein pdp8online.com.

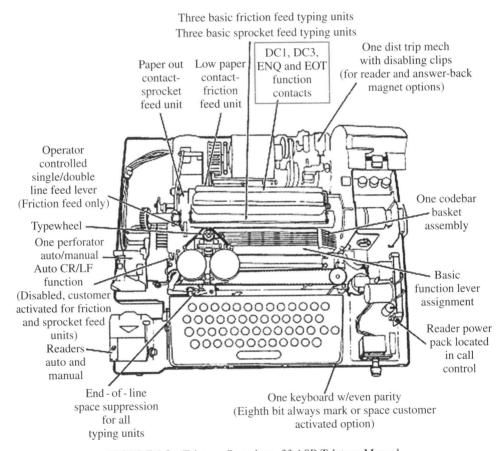

FIGURE 1.9   Teletype Overview - 33 ASR Teletype Manual.

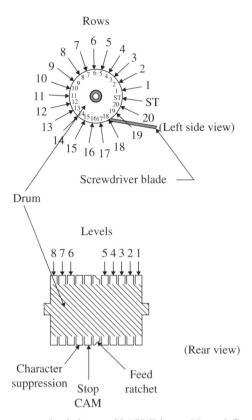

FIGURE 1.10   Teletype answer-back drum—*33 ASR Teletype Manual*. Courtesy of AT&T/Teletype Corporation.

Abbreviation	Key to abbreviation
ACK	Acknowledge
CR	Carriage Return
LF	Line Feed
RO	Rub Out
SP	Space
SUP	Character Suppression

FIGURE 1.11   Key to abbreviations—*33 ASR Teletype Manual*. Courtesy of AT&T/Teletype Corporation.

As telephones were becoming available throughout the United States and elsewhere, one might wonder, why bother? Why not just use the telephone? As the then Governor Ronald Reagan stated later in 1972 in one of the first test electronic email messages,[20] "*All this damned typing… Wouldn't you rather pick up the phone and call?*" Telephones of course were becoming the de facto remote communication standard, which is great as long as you are not deaf. The difficulty of using a telephone is not apparent to those with full hearing, but this actually plays directly into the creation of the Internet and WHOIS with

---

[20] http://www.arpanetdialogues.net/vol-i/

2.10   The number of rows available for actual station identification is less than shown above, because each coded message should begin and end with CARRIAGE RETURN and LINE FEED (this may be altered in specific applications). This assures that the transmitted message will appear at the beginning of a line of the receiving teletypewriter set and eliminates overprinting.

FIGURE 1.12   Section 2.10—*33 ASR Teletype Manual*. Courtesy of AT&T/Teletype Corporation.

USASCII code chart

b_7 b_6 b_5					0 0 0	0 0 1	0 1 0	0 1 1	1 0 0	1 0 1	1 1 0	1 1 1
b_4	b_3	b_2	b_1	Column → Row ↓	0	1	2	3	4	5	6	7
0	0	0	0	0	NUL	DLE	SP	0	@	P	`	p
0	0	0	1	1	SOH	DC1	!	1	A	Q	a	q
0	0	1	0	2	STX	DC2	"	2	B	R	b	r
0	0	1	1	3	ETX	DC3	#	3	C	S	c	s
0	1	0	0	4	EOT	DC4	$	4	D	T	d	t
0	1	0	1	5	ENQ	NAK	%	5	E	U	e	u
0	1	1	0	6	ACK	SYN	8	6	F	V	f	v
0	1	1	1	7	BEL	ETB	´	7	G	W	g	w
1	0	0	0	8	BS	CAN	(	8	H	X	h	x
1	0	0	1	9	HT	EM	)	9	I	Y	i	y
1	0	1	0	10	LF	SUB	*	:	J	Z	j	z
1	0	1	1	11	VT	ESC	+	;	K	[	k	{
1	1	0	0	12	FF	FS	,	<	L	\	l	|
1	1	0	1	13	CR	GS	–	=	M	]	m	}
1	1	1	0	14	SO	RS	.	>	N	∧	n	~
1	1	1	1	15	SI	US	/	?	O	—	o	DEL

FIGURE 1.13   USASCII code chart—*33 ASR Teletype Manual*. Courtesy of AT&T/Teletype Corporation.

Ken Harrenstien and Deafnet.[21] Harrenstien and Vinton Cerf are both hearing impaired and worked on various projects to promote text communication. We partially owe thanks for the Internet to people extending services to users who cannot hear.

Manufacturers of TTY introduced many innovations including data storage. Messages could be stored on punched tape and fed back into the device to be sent again. Eventually, TTY became the primary input devices for computers and time-sharing terminals. The WRU or ENQ remained part of the encoding set that moved into the new systems as part of the ASCII table in 1960.

The TTY continued to exist within the Internet even after the device itself was obsoleted by graphic terminals. Terminal software, Telnet, is actually designed to emulate a TTY.

[21] http://www.sri.com/work/timeline-innovation/timeline.php?timeline=health#&innovation=deafnet

```
To    |                    | Also    |Push  |   Or    |Code Sent |Upon receipt

Send| (Explanation)| Known as |Either|          |is (in hex)|Displayed as

----+--------------+----------+------+---------+-----------+------------

NUL |NULL          |    ^@    | [2]  |         |    00     |

    |              |          |      |         |           |

SOH |Start of      | [3]^A    | LS   |[4]CASE A|    01     |

    |      Heading |          |      |         |           |

    |              |          |      |         |           |

STX |Start of Text |    ^B    | ATAN | CASE B  |    02     |

    |              |          |      |         |           |

ETX |End of Text   |    ^C    | LOG  | CASE C  |    03     |

    |              |          |      |         |           |

EOT |End of        |          |      |         |           |

    |  Transmission|    ^D    | REFL | CASE D  |    04     |

    |              |          |      |         |           |

ENQ |Enquiry       |    ^E    | [4]  | CASE E  |    05     | [5] <ENQ>

    |              |          |      |         |           |

ACK |Acknowledge   |    ^F    | UP   | CASE F  |    06     | <ACK>

    |              |          |      |         |           |

BEL |Bell          |    ^G    | DOWN | CASE G  |    07     | <BELL>
```

FIGURE 1.14   TELNET Character Set.

Telnet actually stands for *Teletype Over Network Protocol*. The earliest RFC on Telnet makes the connection clear:

> *The TELNET protocol is based upon the notion of a virtual teletype, employing a 7-bit ASCII character set. The primary function of a User TELNET, then, is to provide the means by which its users can "hit" all the keys on that virtual teletype.*[22]

The **ENQ** command from ASCII, originally from the TTY WRU response, now becomes part of the TELNET character set[23] and can be invoked with **CTRL-E**, indicated by **^E**:
This function on Telnet is virtually identical to the previous TTY manual operation. Telnet uses ENQ to issue a "Who Are You" request to a remote station identification.[24]

[22] http://www.ietf.org/rfc/rfc0206
[23] See note 22.
[24] http://www.cs.tut.fi/~jkorpela/chars/c0.html

1.4   1960s: SPARKING THE INTERNET TO LIFE

Many of the Internet innovations occurred in the 1960s, especially the concept of *packet switching*, which breaks data into standard sizes for transmission [5]. This method permits large files to move and multiple users to access the network without consuming all the resources for one use. On early networks, the traffic was moved by *circuit switching*, which meant that only one use was permitted at a time.[25] The term "On-Line" also appears for the first time in the paper *ON-LINE MAN-COMPUTER COMMUNICATION* by J.C.R. Licklider and Welden E. Clark of Bolt, Beranek and Newman (BBN) Inc. The BBN continued to play a major role in Internet development, eventually becoming a part of Raytheon.[26] At the same time, the DARPA took a keen interest in networking technologies. This is an important point: many people and organizations were already developing networks and centralizing computing resources. The government did not create the Internet *ex nihilo*; rather, it coordinated existing concepts to expand their reach. In this new space, being able to identify which network was which became more and more important.

1.4.1   SRI, SAIL, and ITS

The proto-WHOIS RFC 742 stated the NAME/FINGER program:

> *Currently only the SAIL (SU-AI), SRI (SRI-(KA/KL)), and ITS (MIT-(AI/ML/MC/DMS)) sites support this protocol.*[27]

This is a list of three labs and seven host machines. SRI, as we saw, stands for Stanford Research Institute and SAIL the Stanford University Artificial Intelligence Laboratory.[28] The MIT system ITS in particular stands for "Incompatible Timesharing System" and was named to differentiate itself from the Compatible Timesharing System. "Timesharing" is something we all take for granted now in our systems and devices. Imagine the early computers that could only respond to one user, command, or process at a time. The idea that multiple processes or users could share a computer resource was a revolutionary concept. ITS was an operating system written in the assembly language MIDAS[29] on a DEC PDP-10 to support the development of artificial intelligence. Along with ITS at the MIT labs came a new concept: letting the public access the network. In order to address potential problems a policy was drafted: the *MIT AI Lab Tourist Policy*.[30] A *tourist* was a nonlaboratory person allowed in during off-hours under certain conditions, but more or less permitted to explore the system. Disruptive, abusive, commercial, and political activities were not permitted. Most importantly, tourists had to register as tourist through the ITS :INQUIRE program.[31]

---

[25] http://www.packet.cc/files/ev-packet-sw.html
[26] http://www.bbn.com/
[27] http://tools.ietf.org/html/rfc742
[28] http://ai.stanford.edu/
[29] ftp://publications.ai.mit.edu/ai-publications/pdf/AIM-238.pdf
[30] http://www.art.net/Studios/Hackers/Hopkins/Don/text/tourist-policy.html
[31] See note 30.

1.4.2   Doug Engelbart: The Father of Office Automation

On October 29, 1968, the ARPANET was born with the connecting of SRI and the University of California Los Angeles (UCLA). Being that there were only two hosts on the network, there was no need for a WHOIS record set just yet. Less than 2 months later, Doug Engelbart, the director of Augmentation Research Center (ARC) at SRI,[32] used this connection to run the "Mother of All Demos."[33] The key feature of the demonstration is that Engelbart conducted it remotely. In this single presentation, Engelbart did not predict, but showed many of the tools we are used to now including the word processing and hypertext. However, Engelbart did not simply focus on developing new tools; the tools were products of his visionary approach to collaborative work. He employed *bootstrapping* to promote existing resources and talent. With this explosion of innovation, he also saw the need to properly manage it with the right people. Anyone who has never seen the demonstration should be encouraged to watch it here: http://dougengelbart.org/events/1968-demo-highlights.html.

1.5   1970s: OK, NOW THAT WE HAVE AN INTERNET, HOW DO WE KEEP TRACK OF EVERYONE?

A link between two sites is not a network, but it is a private conversation. The ARPANET quickly went from two sites to three, and then all of the major sites within the United States that had their own networks began plugging in. The attendees at this growing gathering needed name tags.

1.5.1   Elizabeth "Jake" Feinler

We often hear about the "fathers" of the Internet, but there are mothers too, several in fact as we will see. Elizabeth "Jake" Feinler had been working at SRI since the 1960s but was asked by Doug Engelbart to draft the first ARPANET Resource Handbook[34] for SRI's ARC. Engelbart, who unfortunately passed away in 2013, may not be a household name but his inventions are, like the computer mouse and the term "On-Line." Feinler had an interesting task: to document this new concept that no one had heard of and few people understood. Having previously authored handbooks on complex chemicals, Feinler was certainly up to the job. Inventing the network was fantastic, but we will see over and over again the need for clear documentation to accompany this complex structure. The cited handbook ends at over 1000 pages. As Feinler shifted into evermore important roles, ensuring that specific files and documents were updated and shared properly became the focus of what made the network function.

1.5.2   The ARPANET Directory as Proto-WHOIS

WHOIS has often been compared to a phone book directory, which is exactly what it started out as a paper phone book called the ARPANET Directory. This hardbound directory was regularly updated and shipped to various project members and contacts. Publishing

---

[32] http://www.dougengelbart.org/about/cv.html

[33] http://www.dougengelbart.org/firsts/dougs-1968-demo.html

[34] http://www.computerhistory.org/collections/catalog/102714229

> The ARPANET DIRECTORY – A directory of users and
> hosts on the ARPANET. It gives the names, network and U.S.
> Mail addresses, phone number, and host affiliation of
> ARPANET users, as well as summary tables of host information.

FIGURE 1.15   The ARPANET Directory. Courtesy of Computer History Museum.

and distributing this ever-larger book was a burden, so as this new online system became available, the distribution of the ARPANET Directory went on it. The last hard copy of the directory was published in March of 1982,[35] after which the directory became completely digital. The following excerpt is from the April 1978 Defense Communications Agency ARPANET INFORMATION BROCHURE [6]:

This clarifies that the directory was for contacts and distinct from the HOSTS table. Morphing at different stages, the ARPANET Directory became WHOIS. While many may think WHOIS was created as a digital record to identify the owners of networked hosts, it was actually a record of persons, office locations, and phone numbers (and later emails) that merged with the new concept of virtual space.

When asked when WHOIS and the Internet became controversial, Feinler easily pointed to the influence of commercial interests. On the early network, there were no advertisements or commercial activity of any kind. Today, Feinler has little interest in the Internet Corporation for Assigned Names and Numbers (ICANN) and the commercialization of the network. She seemed concerned that the deployment of new generic top-level domains (gTLDs) might have negative consequences. The rush for commercialization was not on the minds of early pioneers like Feinler. She and her colleagues prided themselves on their open collaboration and general ethics. Like others interviewed for this book, she expressed a spirit of the time that guided the creation of the Internet, which now seems lost.

1.5.3   The Site Status List

SRI did not immediately provide routing and owner information for a network that was yet to exist. DARPA had contracted Cambridge, Massachusetts, company BBN, now part of Raytheon, to manage the ARPANET Interface Message Processors (IMPs). IMPs were the original Internet routers, packet-switching nodes that interfaced between internal networks and the external network. BBN assigned the IMP port number and collected the information about the entity connecting to the IMP. BBN employee Ellen Westheimer published a descriptive file of the IMPs and their owners called it the *Site Status List*. This was eventually renamed as the *Network Host Status List* [7].

In 1970, the Network Working Group (NWG), led by Steve Crocker, used the Network Control Protocol (NCP) to standardize the ARPANET network interface, which allowed more remote networks to join the new major network. In October 1971, the existing 15 ARPANET networks connected to each other through the NCP at a virtual meeting[36] at the MIT. But what

[35] Feinler interview.
[36] http://www.livinginternet.com/i/ii_ncp.htm

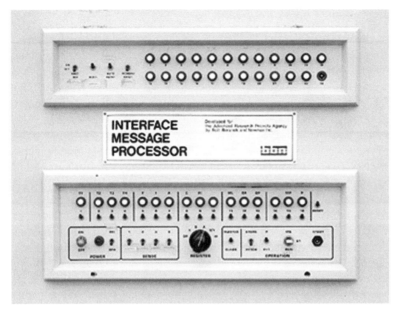

FIGURE 1.16   Interface Message Processor. Courtesy of Computer History Museum.

were the networks and how were they identified? The following is a list of the networks and their assumed hostnames[37]:

Bolt, Beranek and Newman	bbn
Carnegie Mellon University	cmu
Case Western Reserve University	case
Harvard University	harv
Lincoln Laboratory	ll
Massachusetts Institute of Technology	mit
NASA AMES	ames
RAND Corporation	rand
Stanford Research Institute	sri-nic
Stanford University	su-ai
System Development Corporation	sdc
University of California at Los Angeles	ucla
University of California at Santa Barbara	ucsb
University of Illinois at Urbana	illinois
University of Utah	utah

The BBN knew who everyone was because they issued the IMPs, but that was getting more complex as the next conference would connect 40 networks, and so on. The collection and maintenance of this list shifted to SRI-NIC and gradually merged with the paper ARPANET Directory.

[37] http://www.columbia.edu/~rh120/ch106.x08

1.5.4   Distribution of the HOSTS Table

In Andrew Blum's excellent book *TUBES* [8], the author cited Senator Ted Stevens in 2006 describing the Internet as a "series of tubes" as the source of his title. Blum showed us the physical Internet, the wires, and data centers in all of their strangeness. The text showed us that the Internet is real in the sense that it exists in fungible format. However, this is just the medium. The tubes, as they are, only exist to pass data and only have meaning because of the files that explain what each tube should do. The Internet is a series of tubes and a series of flat files that tell where everything is.

One of Feinler's important recruits was a hostmaster. There are an untold number of host-masters on the Internet today, but for a time Mary K. Stahl was *the* hostmaster for the Internet. Stahl sometimes had the tedious job of manually proofreading and distributing the ARPANET Hosts Table (HOSTS.TXT). This, of course, was the list of hostnames and associated IP addresses on the network that were passed around directly and later available on an FTP site. Today, this file is more to akin the root zone files and the related Domain Name System (DNS) files they point to. Along with the host table, Stahl also distributed what was called the Liaison File (LIAISON.TXT), which had the accompanying contact information for the hosts.[38] Liaisons had a number of duties and responsibilities concerning access granting and information collection.[39] For Stahl, this specifically technical task was a detour from her artistic passions, but when domains later replaced hosts, her job was eliminated, which was a bit of a blessing because working on the ARPANET burned people out. She now works on her painting,[40] having been out of the Internet industry for decades. Regardless, Stahl left her eternal fingerprint on WHOIS in the assignment of Port 43 to WHOIS in the RFC 1060,[41] which is called "MARY" because she had the oversight. The exact line is as follows:

```
43 NICNAME Who Is [55,MARY]
```

She also had the authority of the HOSTNAME server that responded at Port 101:

```
101  HOSTNAME  NIC Host Name Server [54,MARY]
```

1.5.5   Finger

The Finger protocol was developed by Les Earnest in 1971[42] to solve a specific problem while at SAIL. The DEC-10 system Earnest worked on with his colleagues had a utility called **who**, which would show the account names and terminal numbers of people currently logged into the system but none of the offline accounts. Earnest often observed people running their fingers down the output of the **who** command, so he created a database along with the program itself to provide information about all users regardless of their status. Upon request, Earnest added an "out of the office" feature for the database called "Plan," which could be updated to inform other users about vacations and other events. Issues of privacy and security did not yet come into place as Earnest, like many of the early pioneers, cited as the *"comradery of those gentler times."*[43] Finger itself has been the focus of some

---

[38] http://www.dtic.mil/dtic/tr/fulltext/u2/a482154.pdf
[39] http://www.rfc-editor.org/rfc/museum/ddn-news/ddn-news.n5.1
[40] http://www.marystahl.com/
[41] http://www.ietf.org/rfc/rfc1060.txt
[42] http://blog.djmnet.org/2008/08/05/origin-of-finger/
[43] http://www.djmnet.org/lore/finger-origin.txt

problems as most networks shut off finger now, especially for external users. In 1988, the Morris worm exploited the Finger daemon program, **fingerd**, and its access to the library system function **gets**, which was used to create a buffer overrun and execute the malicious code to keep spreading. The flaw has long since been plugged in **fingerd**, but the incident left a lasting impression on the Internet psyche showing how the network could be crushed by native software that was linked to personal contact information.

1.5.6   Sockets

Around the same time, Jon Postel began to standardize the most basic architecture of the ARPANET, assigning different functions to different *sockets* in RFC 349, *Proposed Standard Socket Numbers.*[44] There were only five specific assignments in this memo, but space was made for where NICNAME/WHOIS would eventually sit. Even more importantly, Postel insisted there be a central management of the system, proposing him to be the "czar" who hands out assignments to others on the network.[45] This power actually remained with Postel through the domain era until his death in 1998.[46] Postel gave out pieces of the Internet including top-level domain (TLD) assignments and even took control back briefly in 1998 from Network Solutions, the so-called DNS Root Authority incident.[47] This incident led to a larger role of Internet management by the US government.

In 1973, L. Peter Deutsch authored RFC 606, Host Names On-line.[48] Deutsch later developed the innovative Portable Document Format (PDF) software, but in 1973 he was part of the NWG. From RFC 606 came one of the best quotes behind the rationale for creating such centralized information services:

> *"Now that we finally have an official list of host names, it seems about time to put an end to the absurd situation where each site on the network must maintain a different, generally out-of-date, host list for the use of its own operating system or user programs."*

The frustration is clear in his tone. Having current and easily retrievable information about other nodes is critical for an interconnected network. He specifically proposed that the NIC (SRI) manage an online file listing names and host addresses. Deutsch insisted that the file be accessible to anyone. The group almost immediately responded in RFC 608:

> We at the NIC agree with Peter Deutsch's suggestion (in RFC# 606 / NIC# 21246) that the NIC maintain an online ASCII text file of Host names,[49]

The management went to Jake Feinler at SRI-NIC. In addition to hostnames and IP addresses, the file also included the Technical Liaison, which would be the contact for the hostname. It is from this moment on that the active search for a solution to tackling hosts and their owners began in earnest, but we were still 4 years away from the first WHOIS

[44] http://tools.ietf.org/html/rfc349
[45] See note 44.
[46] http://news.bbc.co.uk/2/hi/science/nature/196487.stm
[47] http://www.computerworld.co.nz/article/517378/internet_veteran_dns_test_causes_storm/
[48] http://tools.ietf.org/html/rfc606
[49] http://tools.ietf.org/html/rfc608

RFC. RFC 620 instructed the participating networks to begin monitoring the HOST table.[50] RFC 623 insisted that a different protocol from FTP be used to distribute the table and the file be stored in redundancy,[51] but RFC 625 pushed back against the notion of not using FTP.[52] The official deployment of HOSTS.TXT was announced in RFC 627.[53]

The need for tracking owners of hostnames was becoming apparent even with this comparatively small number of players on the Internet. Abuse had already started and was so concerning that Jon Postel devoted an RFC to the problem. *On the Junk Mail Problem* detailed the issue and possible solutions:

> *"It would be useful for a Host to be able to decline messages from sources it believes are misbehaving or are simply annoying."*

Postel proposed building the ability to refuse messages based on reputation right into the network interface (IMP) by *"measuring, per source, the number of undesired messages per unit time."*[54] Rapidly, being able to identify hosts and owners was about more than just management; it was about misuse of a host.

1.5.7   Into the VOID with NLS IDENTFILE

Before gradually and formally becoming WHOIS, the data was stored in Engelbart's oN-Line System[55] (NLS/AUGMENT) known as IDENTSYS. Each NIC user had an entry in the IDENT directory that contained their email address among other information.[56] These IDENTs had multiple purposes including authoring *ARC Journal* articles.[57] The protocol for managing IDENTs was documented in the "The Executive Package" file called EXEC. TXT at the SRI-NIC. The IDENT system was written in the NLS specific language, L10.[58] *"That didn't scale very well and was a beast to maintain,"*[59] related Ken Harrenstien in an email. Harrenstien's description was documented in the *ARC Journal* on November 13, 1972.[60] IDENT was noted in the journal as being a very important database but one that had no real room for growth and lacked controls for access and deletion of obsolete data.

Harrenstien has driven several updates of WHOIS over the years to handle the growing dataset. The first was called VOID DBMS. *"VOID stood for 'Vorxify ID File' which is a meaningless term I made up."*[61] VOID was developed in the assembly language MIDAS,[62] which was also used to develop the ITS system.

---

[50] http://tools.ietf.org/html/rfc620

[51] http://tools.ietf.org/html/rfc623

[52] http://tools.ietf.org/html/rfc625

[53] http://tools.ietf.org/html/rfc627

[54] http://tools.ietf.org/html/rfc706

[55] http://archive.computerhistory.org/resources/access/text/2013/05/102724043-05-01-acc.pdf

[56] http://sloan.stanford.edu/mousesite/Archive/Post68/augment-33076.htm

[57] http://tools.ietf.org/html/rfc543

[58] http://www.rfc-editor.org/rfc/rfc694.txt

[59] Harrenstien interview.

[60] *ARC Journal*, 12731 http://archive.computerhistory.org/resources/access/text/2013/05/102724029-05-01-acc.pdf

[61] See note 59.

[62] ftp://ftp.columbia.edu/kermit/dec20/assembler-guide.txt

Some of the data in VOID was entered to keep track of terminal access controller (TAC) data. TACs allowed registered remote users with terminals and modem couplers to dial into the host computers at the ARPANET. Once a user was registered in the database, they were issued a TAC card that provided credentials for logging in through a dial-up terminal. Previously, the phone numbers for remote access became a security risk. With the registration and TAC cards, only authorized users would be able to log on once dialled up.[63] Harrenstien eventually converted the MIDAS VOID program to C code using the TOPS-20 C compiler.

During this same period, Jon Postel wrote about the "Internet" in RFC 675, and some of the first electronic test chats occurred between people not directly involved in the network development, including the then Governor Ronald Reagan calling the technology "Neat stuff."[64] The ARPANET invited a series of people from different disciplines to engage in debates from remote locations using the new technology.

1.5.8 NAME/FINGER RFC 742 (1977)

While not called WHOIS officially yet, RFC 742 NAME/FINGER[65] marked the actual start of what we used for Internet WHOIS in 1977. The main author of 742 is Ken Harrenstien, but he noted in the background of the document that it would not have been possible without Brian Harvey, Les Earnest, and Earl Killian. Harvey in particular provided the spark of the idea that became WHOIS. *"We were just doing what made sense, what we thought had to be done,"*[66] Harvey related in our interview. As with many of the early Internet pioneers, he was remarkably humble about his contribution. It was Harvey's idea to provide a "simple" interface between the existing Name and Finger programs at different network sites.[67] The Finger program had existed since 1971 and provided information about users on a network, while Name identified remote hosts. Combining them actually created the first distributed WHOIS model. The term itself was referenced as a switch within the RFC:

> *the syntax for some servers can be slightly more elaborate. For example, if /W (called the Whois switch) also appears on the line given to an ITS server, much fuller descriptions are returned.*[68]

Harvey was in charge of the electronic mail services at the Artificial Intelligence Laboratory at MIT[69] when he worked with Harrenstien on 742. Managing the mail services between growing numbers of user accounts made the need for tying a person, account, and location important. *"The crux of early WHOIS was about finding someone physically,"*[70] Harvey noted as he recounted a specific story of a student who unleashed a process that

---

[63] http://www.oac.cdlib.org/findaid/ark:/13030/c8jw8fmx/entire_text/
[64] See note 20.
[65] See note 27.
[66] Harvey interview.
[67] See note 27.
[68] See note 27.
[69] http://www.csail.mit.edu/
[70] See note 66.

would delete every file on the server's disk. *"He didn't think it would actually work! It was curiosity and not malice."*[71] However, this clearly fits in with our ongoing themes of access, responsibility, and identification. At the time BBN knew who all the hosts were on the network,[72] they had to as a simple technical matter in order for the network to function. This rapidly became a challenge as the methods and sources of network connections changed. As Harvey stated, *"There are merits to equal knowledge of all hosts"*— meaning that everyone else on the network knows who controls all the other nodes. Dr. Harvey continued his contributions to technology as a lecturer at the University of California at Berkeley[73] and the development of SNAP!,[74] a visual drag-and-drop programming language. SNAP! was intended to be a teaching tool for children who can use graphic blocks of programming language to make things happen.

The various pieces are here, but it is not quite WHOIS yet. One of the first distinctions occurred at the beginning of the use instructions:

To use via the network: ICP to socket 117[75]

Instead of our familiar Port 43, we have socket 117. The immediate explanation is that since WHOIS does not yet exist as a named protocol, it cannot be assigned to a specific port. When Jon Postel created the socket list in 1972, the range of sockets from 64 to 127 was generically designated for "host-specific functions."[76] The ICP stands for Initial Connection Protocol,[77] a very basic and early network protocol. This connection should be followed by the specific request and the ubiquitous <CRLF> on the command line. At the time of writing, sending a blank command would return all of the available records, something incomprehensible in today's WHOIS. The list returned would specifically be *"the full names of each user and the physical locations of their terminals."*[78]

The makeup is also discussed in IEN 103[79] where the experiment of the name server is detailed. The first key detail is that the server will allow access to the data in the official Host Table rather than manually passing the host table around.[80] However, a more complex model emerged:

Work is in progress to investigate the feasibility of abstracting host related information from the NIC database management system via direct system calls.

Well beyond the simple task of serving up the Host Table, this is now about querying discrete information from more complex data structures through a specific protocol.

---

[71] See note 66.

[72] http://www.sri.com/newsroom/press-releases/computer-history-museum-sri-international-and-bbn-celebrate-40th-anniversary

[73] http://www.eecs.berkeley.edu/Faculty/Homepages/harvey.html

[74] http://byob.berkeley.edu/

[75] See note 27.

[76] See note 44.

[77] http://tools.ietf.org/html/rfc80

[78] See note 27.

[79] http://www.postel.org/ien/txt/ien103.txt

[80] See note 79.

1.5.9 Other Early Models

The need to identify and find contacts for remote resources was universal as the network grew. While one model emerged at the main one, surely other developers were thinking about the issue. RFC 724 stated that *"there are other systems with similar programs that could easily be made servers."*[81] It turned out that there were a number of concepts emerging to address identification of remote resources across the network. But what were they?

- IPHOST on TOPS-20. As various systems changed with constant improvements, utilities were created to provide information about machines and users. The TOPS-20 operating system was used on the DEC machines running at ARPANET. Many utilities had been developed for TOPS-20 including the NICNAME program,[82] which served WHOIS. Another utility in TOPS-20 was IPHOST, which gave information about ARPANET hosts. If the program had to be invoked on the command line with *IPHOST*, then this prompt would be IPHOST> awaiting commands. The ability to run multiple programs in separate sessions, threads, or windows was further down the road. In this environment, the programs had to be started, used, and exited before other programs could be invoked. The command within IPHOST was *NAME*. Entering *NAME?* would return a list of known ARPANET host. The command *NAME SRI-NIC* would return the IP address of the SRI-NIC server. To convert the other way, the command was *NUMBER* followed by an IP address that would return the hostname.[83]
- Online DIRectory SYStem (DIRSYS). This incremental search system was modeled after the pages in telephone directory. As a user typed a name in an interface like Emacs (Unix extensible text editor), the full pages available, with entries, would appear and become more specific as the user typed more letters. DIRSYS was specifically developed to help locate people at MIT. One interesting aspect was the ability of the users to request updates to their own records through the system, which is how WHOIS is updated now, by the domain registrants. Graduate student Kimberle Koile studied DIRSYS extensively in 1983 with the support of ARPA.[84] DIRSYS was developed with the CLU language (an ALGOG[85] based "CLUsting" code) and deployed two systems: a DEC-SYSTEM 20[86] and a VAX 11/750.[87] Within Koile's technical aspects, policy issues quickly came into play. Who should be in the directory? How will the directory be maintained? Who should access the directory? Specifically, Koile devoted a lengthy section to how access would be permitted for the outside world. The recommendation was to only allow nonincremental search and limit the number of queries permitted.
- Xerox Clearinghouse and Grapevine developed at the Palo Alto Research Center (PARC) [9] was a roaming profile system considered "ahead of its time" and allowed searches not only by name but also by closest printer.

[81] See note 27.
[82] See note 1.
[83] http://bitsavers.informatik.uni-stuttgart.de/pdf/dec/pdp10/TOPS20/arpanet/5221bm.mem.txt
[84] http://bitsavers.trailing-edge.com/pdf/mit/lcs/tr/MIT-LCS-TR-313.pdf
[85] http://www.softwarepreservation.org/projects/ALGOL/
[86] http://pdp10.nocrew.org/docs/ad-h391a-t1.pdf
[87] http://www.old-computers.com/history/detail.asp?n=20&t=3

- Postes, Télégraphes et Téléphones (PTT) Directory System allowed subscribers with terminals in France and public users at post offices to access online white pages. The system allowed reverse searches by telephone number.
- New England Bell Directory System specifically contained numbers in the 617 area code of the United States and used a Dvorak keyboard.
- Bell Labs SOUNDEX was a pattern matching search system triggered by sound.
- Computer Science Network (CSNET) WHOIS allowed online lookups of user email addresses.[88]
- Performance Systems International (PSI) White Pages Pilot Project[89] was an X.500 directory system allowing WHOIS lookups through telnetting to FRED.[90] It was also related to the NYSERNET X.500 Database project.[91]
- Knowbot Information Service (KIS) provided a single point for querying whois, finger, X.500, and other services.[92]

1.6   1980s: WHOIS GETS ITS OWN RFC

In 1982, Ken Harrenstien and Vic White released RFC 812 entitled NICNAME/WHOIS,[93] the first time WHOIS was used in the title of an RFC and the official call to make WHOIS a specific named service. The purpose of this RFC is to describe the service:

> The NICNAME/WHOIS Server is an NCP/TCP transaction based query/response server, running on the SRI-NIC machine, that provides netwide directory service to ARPANET users.[94]

This sentence highlights the basic function and intent, which is the same as what we are used to now. WHOIS continued to be a Transmission Control Protocol (TCP) transaction service intended for access across the whole network or Internet. This statement also makes it clear that this is the way to access the formerly paper-only ARPANET Directory:

> This server, together with the corresponding Identification Data Base provides online directory look-up equivalent to the ARPANET Directory.[95]

The next section details how users can access it (through programs or clients) and what they can find in it in terms of data:

> The server is accessible across the ARPANET from user programs running on local hosts, and it delivers the full name, U.S. address, telephone number, and network mailbox for ARPANET users.

[88] http://www1.chapman.edu/gopher-data/archives/Internet%20Information/cerfnet-users-guide-07-91.txt
[89] http://www.ietf.org/rfc/rfc1803.txt
[90] http://www.lights.ca/hytelnet/dir/dir009.html
[91] http://www.usucan.org/docs/affiliates/New%20York.pdf
[92] http://encyclopedia2.thefreedictionary.com/Knowbot+Information+Service
[93] See note 1.
[94] See note 1.
[95] See note 1.

As part of the introduction, it is made clear that everyone should be able to access WHOIS:

> DCA strongly encourages network hosts to provide their users with access to this network service.[96]

The question of who should be in the database is immediately following the introduction:

> DCA requests that each individual with a directory on an ARPANET host, who is capable of passing traffic across the ARPANET, be registered in the NIC Identification Data Base.[97]

This makes a clear distinction between hostmasters and simple users. As *hosts* became *domains* a few years later, the concept and intent remained the same. Having a host that can pass traffic on the network was a responsibility that required identification.

The 1982 RFC entitled *WHO TALKS TCP?* began to demonstrate the problems of a growing network. The RFC 834 by David Smallberg was a 13-page list of hostnames and IP addresses.[98] This was a dump of the NIC hostname table showing which ones accepted TCP connections and which nodes were dead. It may be difficult for people today to understand an Internet without domains. The following is an excerpt from the hostname table in 1982[99]:

```
coins-tas          10.0.0.36
src-ccp            10.0.0.39
utah-cs            10.0.0.4
office-1           10.0.0.43
mit-xx             10.0.0.44
collins-pr         10.0.0.46
wpafb              10.0.0.47
afwl               10.0.0.48
bbnb               10.0.0.49
bbnf               10.0.0.5
st-nic             10.0.0.51
ada-vax            10.0.0.52
afsc-ad            10.0.0.53
```

Manually reviewing and routing the growing table was clearly impractical. The memo is merely a list of servers with no contact data; if the contact data were included, this file would be enormous.

1.6.1 The DNS

This was all about the change as Paul Mockapetris drafted the RFC 882, "Domain Names: Concepts and Facilities," in 1983. The document starts off by indicating that the current scheme of mapping between HOSTNAMES and ARPA Internet address through the

[96] See note 1.
[97] See note 1.
[98] http://tools.ietf.org/html/rfc834
[99] See note 98.

ARPANIC HOSTS file on SRI-NIC was rapidly becoming unmanageable. One of the major concerns was mail delivery. Centralizing mail delivery on the expanding network would be impossible, but conversely the variety of emerging mail methods and routes was unwieldy. The fix was to create a consistent name space model that would be used for referrals in distributed authorities. The new model would have three main components: the Domain Name Space, Name Servers, and Resolvers. This RFC also introduces a database model for the DNS, the use Resource Records, and the "Dot" system we are all familiar with for domain names. As far as WHOIS goes, we get some very important concepts as well:

> There must be a responsible person associated with each domain to be a contact point for questions about the domain...and to resolve any problems[100]

The RFC also made it clear that data should expire and domains would have to be deleted under certain conditions and references NICNAME/WHOIS as the mechanism for accomplishing these tasks. With the structure documented, the flip from hosts to domain began with RFC 920 in 1984, which made first use of "The Dot" structure we are now accustomed to.[101]

1.6.2   WHOIS Updated for Domains (1985)

Now that the DNS has replaced the hostname system, it seems appropriate for WHOIS change as well. RFC 945 NICNAME/WHOIS was authored by Ken Harrenstien, Mary Stahl, and Jake Feinler who had all been working so closely at the lower levels of managing the practical aspects of the ARPANET. Some of the major differences in this update included dropping NCP from the protocol by strictly using TCP, but the major policy shift introduced the concept of a *registrar* who would handle the domain name entries and collect the WHOIS data. Domain registration was by email:

> To register, send via electronic mail to REGISTRAR@SRI-NIC.ARPA your full name, middle initial, U.S. mailing address (including mail stop and full explanation of abbreviations and acronyms), ZIP code, telephone (including Autovon FTS, if available), and one network mailbox.[102]

Autovon was a US military phone system,[103] aside from which the requirements for domain WHOIS data have not changed. Registration was required for anyone with a node capable of passing traffic on the network. With this new system, the concept of a Domain Name Administrator arose along with WHOIS being an important part of the toolkit. The Domain Administrator's Guide[104] from 1987 stated:

> VERIFICATION OF DATA: The verification process can be accomplished in several ways. One of these is through the NIC WHOIS server. If he has access to WHOIS, the DA can type the command "whois domain <domain name><return>". The reply from WHOIS will supply

---

[100] http://tools.ietf.org/html/rfc882
[101] http://www.rfc-editor.org/rfc/rfc920.txt
[102] http://www.ietf.org/rfc/rfc954.txt
[103] http://massis.lcs.mit.edu/archives/reports/autovon.instructions
[104] http://tools.ietf.org/html/rfc1032

the following: the name and address of the organization "owning" the domain; the name of the domain; its administrative, technical, and zone contacts; the host names and network addresses of sites providing name service for the domain.

The term NIC can be confusing since it stands for Network Information Center, an entity publishing Internet information, or it could also stand for "Network Interface Card," a specific device on a machine for accessing the network. For the most part in this text, we will use NIC to refer to the former.

1.6.3 Oops! The Internet Goes Public

The Internet started out as a US government-sponsored project with access restricted to the academic and private researchers as well as the US military. As we all know, access was eventually extended to the public. Few are aware that this was not a carefully thought-out process with considerations for identity and abuse. The Internet was opened quite suddenly and, some would say, without authorization. Barry Shein is an interesting character with quite a bit of Internet history under his name including that of becoming the world's first private Internet Service Provider (ISP) by accident.

Shein got his first ARPANET account in 1978 while working at Harvard University using his math skills to support medical research in pulmonary mechanics. *"In those days everyone was a super-user,"*[105] said Shein referring to a complete lack of access levels or distinction of roles, something unthinkable on large networks today. With the help of a grant to purchase computers and equipment, Shein moved to Boston University (BU) and built the university's machine rooms and connected them to what was called "The Triangle," a local high-speed network between Harvard, MIT, and BU. Information technology did not get the respect it does today as Shein used a reclaimed linen closet with a hijacked phone line to do his work. In putting things of that time in the WHOIS or identification context, I asked Shein how miscreants were dealt with. *"I went down to the patch closet and pulled their connection or we called them into the office and had a chat. It's clearly a little different now."*[106] Shein registered the first domain name for Boston University, BU.EDU, directly from Jon Postel. The backstory of BU.EDU tells an important lesson about who gets to register domain names. Apparently, some of the university fathers resented the abbreviation "BU" in general.

As Shein left the academic world for private sector software development as Software Tool and Die (STD) (std.com[107]), he started getting interesting requests from old colleagues. People who connected to the ARPANET at work wanted to be able to connect from home terminals too. They asked Shein if he could connect them from his new private office in Brookline, Massachusetts. So in the fall of 1989, he bought six 2400 baud[108] modems and installed them in a bookshelf with a router and a created link to the Internet in a nongovernment-sponsored location. This was all fine until the National Science Foundation Network[109] (NSFNET) and the Military Network[110] (MILNET) blocked his

---

[105] Shein interview.
[106] See note 105.
[107] http://www.std.com/
[108] http://www.linuxjournal.com/files/linuxjournal.com/linuxjournal/articles/010/1097/1097s2.html
[109] http://www.nsfnet-legacy.org/about.php
[110] http://www.computerhope.com/jargon/m/milnet.htm

access. The concern was fundamental to issues of access, responsibility, and identification: how to control abusive users.

After some back-and-forth with NSFNET, Shein was granted *permission* to allow others to access the network through his service, provided that they abide by the NSFNET Backbone Services Acceptable Use Policy,[111] which prohibited "*illegal or specifically unacceptable use*" and "*advertising of any kind.*"[112] Shein also offered to display such terms of use at the login and to drop any users who violated them. STD had contracts with its subscribers, which were enforceable as the point of entry for the Internet. Shein's brief spat with NSFNET became irrelevant as major changes were underway. Beyond the changes in network management, structure, and access, interaction was shifting from text to hypertext. The hypertext interface tuned the Internet into the *Web* and extended it to people not using a keyboard, forever changing its appeal.

1.7   1990s: THE INTERNET AS WE KNOW IT EMERGES

In 1989, domain registration and WHOIS updates were still being done through email,[113] but a major transition was seen at the beginning of the decade that expanded WHOIS drastically. The ARPANET was "decommissioned" in 1990 after 20 years of revolutionary development. The APRANET of course still existed, but the management changed, shifting to the National Science Foundation (NSF) that had been operating the *backbone* of the Internet since the mid-1980s. The backbone consisted of a collection of powerful networks that acted as national Network Access Points (NAP). The NSF filled the financial gap left by the Internet sponsorship shifting away from the Defense Department toward the Department of Commerce.

In 1992, the NSF awarded Network Solutions a contract to manage the DNS and register domain names. Network Solutions created InterNIC to handle the domain services, including WHOIS. The commercial sale of domain names was a disruption in the minds of many early Internet pioneers. Tim Berners-Lee, designer of the World Wide Web, wrote this arrangement:

> "*Network Solutions…made profits but does not have the reputation for accountability.*" [10]

This sentiment is reiterated in *Who Controls the Internet: Illusions of a Borderless World* by Jack Goldsmith and Tim Wu:

> "*Another was a widely detested corporation named Network Solutions that had taken over day-to-day administration of Internet domain registration. The community that invented the Net was losing control over its creation.*" [11]

Around this same time, web browsers, commercial ISPs, and a new method of traffic routing called Classless Inter-Domain Routing[114] (CIDR) all emerged to bring the Internet closer to general public use.

---

[111] http://w2.eff.org/Net_culture/Net_info/Technical/Policy/nsfnet.policy
[112] See note 111.
[113] http://tools.ietf.org/html/rfc1118
[114] http://tools.ietf.org/html/rfc1519

In 1994, the IETF Whois and Network Information Lookup Service (WNILS) Working Group reaffirmed the important role of WHOIS in RFC 1689.[115] The memo discusses the most commonly used contemporary search applications, here called *Networked Information Retrieval* tools. The memo explains the status of each along with proposals, spending considerable time on WHOIS. The authors noted that the use of WHOIS is spreading and being modified on different servers noting that the once central service is now *distributed*. It is also acknowledged that Port 43 is no longer the only method for accessing WHOIS records. Gopher, Wais, Archie, and Telnet are being used to get to WHOIS. They also note the growing presence of WHOIS clients in the exploding market of personal computers. The general conclusion of this review is that the service is important and in demand but completely lacks standards. They propose, among other things, to provide consistency for WHOIS and enhance its function. Part of this effort was geared toward the establishment of WHOIS++.

1.7.1 Referral WHOIS or RWhois RFC 1714 (1994)

Referral WHOIS was designed and proposed by the Network Solutions S. Williamson and M. Kosters through RFC 1714[116] in 1994. At this time, Network Solutions had the exclusive contract for registering domain names, so WHOIS services were a big part of their concerns. Within the RFC, the authors encapsulated the problems emerging from the development of WHOIS and proposed a method for addressing these problems. There had originally been one WHOIS database for everything. The database itself became fragmented as new registry authorities assumed control over different portions of the Internet under ICANN distribution. First, the authority over IP addresses that had been delegated to InterNIC was broken into three pieces with RIPE NCC gaining control over European IP space and APNIC for Asia-Pacific. With Network Solutions now registering domain names, there was no longer a single place for all WHOIS records, and someone performing a query would have to know where to look. Referral WHOIS was a plan to accept a query and perform a series of lookups through a hierarchical design until the query could be sent as close as possible to the maintainer of the WHOIS data. This of course is the *referral*. Rather than expecting all Internet users to know where to look or expecting every server to hold all data, we simply tell the client where the data really sits.

1.7.2 WHOIS++ RFCs 1834 and 1835 (1995)

In 1995, the WNILS Working Group and several technicians at BUNYIP Information Systems Inc. proposed an enhanced model for WHOIS services, hence the name "WHOIS-Plus-Plus." The "++" is also a reference to extensibility, something with added features and the ability to grow. The overall goal was to provide more structure to the WHOIS model, because as it was WHOIS had evolved in an ad hoc fashion that was not scalable for the growing Internet. Among other things, the proposal included a plan to create three classes of records—people, hosts, and domains—each with a specific structure. It sounded like a great plan, but it did not take off.

---

[115] http://tools.ietf.org/html/rfc1689
[116] http://tools.ietf.org/html/rfc1714

In speaking directly to one of the initial developers, Patrik Faltstrom,[117] we got a partial answer as to why. Faltstrom cited some missing pieces in WHOIS including a lack of updates to the existing protocol especially concerning standards.[118] *"XML needed to be born,"* said Faltstrom referring to Extensible Markup Language (XML), which would not be released until 1998.[119] One of the key features of XML is that it provides a bridge between human-readable language and machine-readable language. The development of WHOIS++ was also done with BUNYIP Information Systems who may have lacked the level of funding at the time needed to launch a project of this scope. As a result, Lightweight Directory Access Protocol[120] (LDAP) became the preferred model. The concepts of WHOIS++ however were solid, and he hoped the Web Extensible Internet Registration Data Service (WEIRDS) will deliver on the hopes of WHOIS++.

1.7.3 ICANN Takes over WHOIS (1998)

In 1998, the existing functions of the Internet including IP delegation, domain name registration, and DNS management were all reorganized under ICANN through a contract with the US Department of Commerce. This new body partly includes the existing Information Sciences Institute (ISI) and its Internet Assigned Numbers Authority (IANA) operations. The Network Solutions InterNIC operation becomes part of ICANN, and their domain registration monopoly ends with new registrars being given contract opportunities to sell domains. Under ICANN, the existing TLDs were also spun off from Network Solutions to be run by new registries. Much of this was done to expand market competition and bring more private money into the Internet. The authority of ICANN came directly from the US government through the Memorandum of Understanding.[121]

This major change generated an interesting artifact in WHOIS, which still exists today. This advertisement still appears in the WHOIS records returned by VeriSign through InterNIC:

> *Domain names in the .com and .net domains can now be registered with many different competing registrars. Go to* http://www.internic.net *for detailed information.*

For over 10 years, there have been hundreds of different registrars, and this message is a complete anachronism.

1.8 2000s: WHOIS STANDARDS

The ICANN is now in control. Domains are being sold by multiple registrars and new registries are emerging. In this new and growing space, the requirements for WHOIS were reaffirmed through updating the previous WHOIS RFC 954 and contractual obligations for WHOIS.

---

[117] http://tools.ietf.org/html/rfc1835
[118] Faltstrom interview
[119] http://www.w3.org/XML/
[120] http://tools.ietf.org/html/draft-hall-ldap-whois-01
[121] http://www.icann.org/en/about/agreements/mou-jpa/icann-mou-25nov98-en.htm

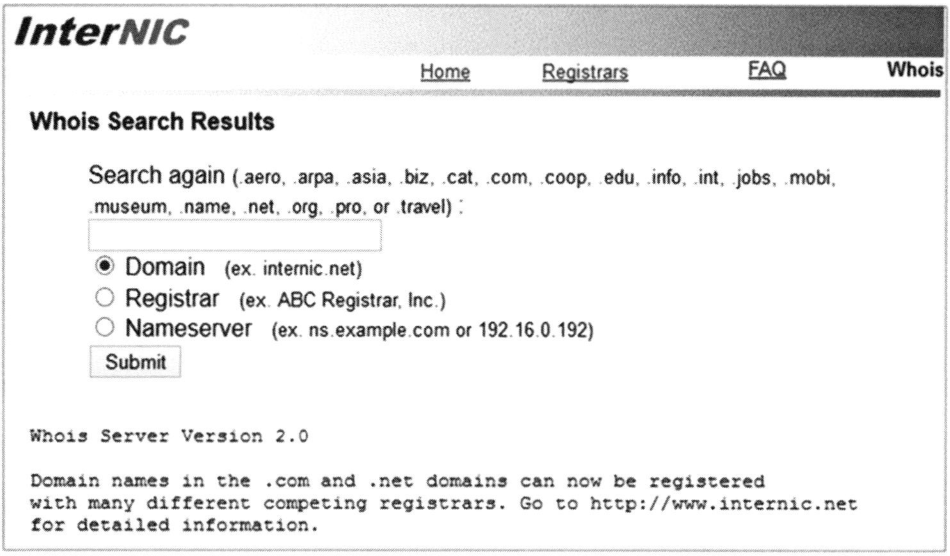

FIGURE 1.17 InterNIC WHOIS.

1.8.1 ICANN's Registrar Accreditation Agreement and WHOIS (2001)

The new nonexclusive registrar scheme included a contract with ICANN, which dictated standards for WHOIS service delivery and accuracy.[122] For all intents and purposes, a fairly large section of the contract is devoted to WHOIS topics and launched a number of controversies in the decade since it was put in place.

The ICANN's Registrar Accreditation Agreement (RAA) WHOIS requirements include the collection of the standard list of point of contact data as has always been part of WHOIS: name, address, email, phone number, etc. However, because the registration and data are now being held by third parties, there are additional obligations on the registrars in terms of WHOIS:

- A service level is expected of the registrar to provide access to WHOIS not only through public Port 43 but also through a webpage.[123]
- Registrars must also sell access to the WHOIS entire record for $10,000 or less.[124]
- And, in a very detailed section, registrars must enforce WHOIS accuracy and terminate domain agreement if the record is falsified.[125]

1.8.2 WHOIS Protocol Specification 2004 RFC 3912 (2004)

Authored by VeriSign's Leslie Daigle, more recently the chief Internet technology officer at the Internet Society[126] (ISOC), RFC 3912 is the Internet Official Protocol Standard for WHOIS[127] and has not been replaced or obsoleted as of 2015. While this document is fairly

[122] http://www.icann.org/en/resources/registrars/raa/raa-17may01-en.htm#3
[123] http://www.icann.org/en/resources/registrars/raa/raa-17may01-en.htm#3.3.1
[124] http://www.icann.org/en/resources/registrars/raa/raa-17may01-en.htm#3.3.6
[125] http://www.icann.org/en/resources/registrars/raa/raa-17may01-en.htm#3.7.7
[126] http://www.internetsociety.org/who-we-are/people/ms-leslie-daigle
[127] http://tools.ietf.org/html/rfc3912

brief and does not change the function of WHOIS, it is a critical part of WHOIS today. While many critics of WHOIS claim it is a dinosaur inherited by ICANN and no longer relevant, this RFC proves otherwise. First, it reaffirms the technical specification of WHOIS as TCP Port 43 transaction-based query-response service. By describing WHOIS in this way, it preserves the expectations of its functionality and the way clients call it and the way servers return information. The schematic of the transaction is spelled out:

```
3. Protocol Example

If one places a request of the WHOIS server located at
whois.nic.mil for information about "Smith", the packets on
the wire will look like:

client   server at whois.nic.mil
open TCP    ---- (SYN) ------------------------------->
            <---- (SYN+ACK) ------------------------
send query ---- "Smith<CR><LF>" -------------------->
get answer <---- "Info about Smith<CR><LF>" ---------
            <---- "More info about Smith<CR><LF>" ----
close       <---- (FIN) -----------------------------
            ----- (FIN) ------------------------------->
```

The meaning of these codes and sequences is spelled out in the chapter on WHOIS use.

Why the WHOIS protocol exists is clearly stated as an information service for Internet *users* to provide information about domain names.[128] There are no other target audiences or purposes stated. WHOIS exists to serve the Internet end user with domain name records and must do so in a *"human-readable"*[129] format. Further, in the RFC, it is even clarified that the data is *"intended to be accessible to everyone."*[130] One might think this is the end of the argument as to the purpose of WHOIS, but the debate is only the beginning.

Also of critical importance is the acknowledgment of problems within the WHOIS architecture, namely, language support and security. The *"WHOIS protocol has not been internationalised"* and *"lacks mechanisms for access control, integrity, and confidentiality."*[131] Internationalization and overall system integrity are two very real WHOIS problems that require addressing. However, the ongoing WHOIS debates focus on what data goes into the records with the most common, and unrealistic, recommendation being the elimination of the system altogether. Because of the notable security flaws, domain owners are admonished to only use *"non-sensitive information"*[132] in the records. Keep in mind as we move through the various debates within the text that RFC 3912 is the ruling principle.

1.8.3 Creaking of Politics

What happens next in the history of WHOIS defined its future for some time to come. Beyond the founding technical aspects of Internet development, its structure becomes defined by political difference as it crosses international borders, commercial interests emerge, and more

[128] See note 127.
[129] See note 127.
[130] See note 127.
[131] See note 127.
[132] See note 127.

ordinary people get domains. The potential problems of a global public Internet are no better encapsulated than in the 2002 paper *Tussle in Cyberspace: Defining Tomorrow's Internet*[133] by four eminent computer scientists. The "tussle" referred to is the various disputes destined to emerge between different Internet stakeholders. While the stakeholder disagreements may seem unfortunate, they are seen by the authors as critical to Internet maturity. This is the collision of predictable engineering principles and unpredictable societal movements. The architecture of the Internet passes bits of information that seems straightforward. The issues of what is in the bits, who gets to pass the bits, how many bits people get to move, and who handles the bits along the way make things much more complex. This is a shared space. Keeping the space open for everyone depends on trust, and trust comes from identity:

> *"One of the most profound and irreversible changes in the Internet is that by and large, many of the users don't trust each other… There are parties with adverse interests, and some genuine 'bad guys' out there. This implies that mechanisms that regulate interaction on the basis of mutual trust should be a fundamental part of the Internet of tomorrow."*[134]

This has clearly not improved since, and the authors point to the simple fact that

> *"if communication is to be mediated based on trust, then as a preliminary step, parties must be able to know to whom they are talking."*

The fundamental concerns of identity and trust pervade the real world as well as the digital and are not trivial problems to solve. This debate runs through the heart of WHOIS as a political matter and underlies the Internet development. Politics cannot be separated from technology once the technology crosses out of private space.

REFERENCES

1   Berloquin, P. 2008. Hidden Codes and Grand Designs. New York: Sterling.

2   Thornton, J. 2012. Polybius. The Encyclopedia of Ancient History.

3   Crabtree, J. 1901. The Marvels of Modern Mechanism and Their Relation to Social Betterment. Springfield, MA: San José The King-Richardson Company.

4   Gillings, R. 1972. Mathematics in the Time of the Pharaohs. New York: Dover Publications, P210.

5   Kleinrock, L. 1961. Information flow in large communication nets, http://www.lk.cs.ucla.edu/data/files/Kleinrock/Information%20Flow%20in%20Large%20Communication%20Nets0.pdf (accessed June 20, 2015).

6   Defense Communications Agency. 1978. ARPANET Information Brochure. Ft. Belvoir: Defense Technical Information Center.

7   Feinler, Elizabeth "Jake". 2011. Host Tables, Top-Level Domain Names, and the Origin of Dot Com, IEEE 33:74–79.

8   Blum, A. 2012. TUBES. New York: HarperCollins.

9   Kenyon, T. 2002. Data Networks: Routing, Security, and Performance Optimization. Amsterdam/Boston: Digital Press.

10 Berners-Lee, T. 1999. Weaving the Web. San Francisco: HarperSanFrancisco.

11 Goldsmith, J. and Wu, T. 2006. Who Controls the Internet: Illusions of Borderless World. New York: Oxford University Press.

---

[133] http://groups.csail.mit.edu/ana/Publications/PubPDFs/Tussle2002.pdf
[134] See note 133.

2

USING WHOIS

There are many uses for WHOIS data, a diverse set of sources, and a surprisingly large number of formats. Aside from the domain name registrar using WHOIS to contact a registrant, the most fundamental and most common use of WHOIS is to determine if a domain is already being used. If you perform a query for a name you want and there is no record, the domain name is likely available. Most registrars have this built in to their online shopping cart, and when you try to purchase a domain name, the registrar will tell you if the domain is already taken, which leads us to the next most common use. WHOIS is frequently used for contacting the current owner and offering to buy it. There is an entire industry around buying and selling domain names, but many never even deployed as a website, which leads us to the third common use. Because of the explosion in domain name sales in terms of speculation, there are a number of *domainers* who buy domain names that contain brand names or look like brand names in the hope of selling the domain to the brand owner at a higher rate. Because of this intellectual property, attorneys have taken to suing or filing dispute resolution claims against the domain owners. In most cases, the registered brand owner is awarded possession of the domain, but trademark investigators will use the WHOIS to track serial *cybersquatters*, often with considerable difficulty. Investigation actually makes up the bulk of WHOIS use, in terms of identifying abusers and criminals within the Domain Name System (DNS). WHOIS is also used illicitly by spammers, stalkers, and identity thieves, and that raises concerns within the privacy debate.

This is a hands-on chapter demonstrating basic WHOIS queries that any user on any platform may access. Using a variety of web-based and command-line queries, we review the WHOIS Port 43 interface, registrar WHOIS, registry WHOIS, InterNIC WHOIS, Internet Protocol WHOIS, and other sources with demonstrations. This chapter also helps the reader understand WHOIS record formats and data capture. This chapter will not only

WHOIS Running the Internet: Protocol, Policy, and Privacy, First Edition. Garth O. Bruen.
© 2016 John Wiley & Sons, Inc. Published 2016 by John Wiley & Sons, Inc.

teach someone to use WHOIS at an introductory level but also help experienced WHOIS users to understand why the system functions as it does, connecting the topics back to policy documents explained previously. This chapter also covers some advanced WHOIS topics including investigations and automated record parsing. Because the instructions make use of command-line instructions on various platforms, it is a good idea to have a background in using shells, terminal windows, or DOS. If you have never used them before, refer to this general command-line tutorial, http://lifehacker.com/5633909/who-needs-a-mouse-learn-to-use-the-command-line-for-almost-anything, mostly to get an idea of what you will be looking at and what to expect.

2.1 DOMAIN WHOIS DATA

For those who have been using Internet search engines to perform WHOIS lookups, there are better, more direct ways to obtain the data. WHOIS records returned in search results can be useful for comparison and research, but they are far from authoritative and current. The best way to start learning about WHOIS is to do lookups and review the responses. But first we should review some of the basic technical and policy concepts.

2.1.1 Record Terminology

WHOIS has its own terminology that may not always appear intuitive. Understanding the details and reviewing reference documents can help make WHOIS records more useful in investigations and research.

2.1.1.1 Required and Not Required Not all common data elements are required. Registrars may collect additional data, but the registrant does not need to supply it or ensure it is accurate. Only the required field data can be considered invalid or fraudulent. For example, the registrant name and postal address are required, but the registrant email and phone number are not. Fax numbers are not required.

2.1.1.2 Authoritative versus Nonauthoritative Nonauthoritative WHOIS servers do not have original WHOIS records. Instead, they have a secondary database or cache file that is constructed from all previous lookups for which it has gotten an authoritative response. When a nonauthoritative server queries an authoritative server and receives an authoritative answer, it passes that answer along to a WHOIS client as an authoritative answer. For example, while a registry like Afilias collects and distributes WHOIS data for .INFO domains, the specific registrar has the original data as collected from the registrant.

2.1.1.3 Character Sets WHOIS records for generic TLD (gTLDs) (.COM, .NET, etc.) must be in Latin character sets. This is not a language prohibition but rather a basic American Standard Code for Information Interchange (ASCII) parsing functionality of most information technology. Non-Latin characters simply cannot be stored or read in many existing systems. Arabic, Chinese, and other character sets are often found in WHOIS field entries but are technically in violation of the policy. There is a move to create internationalized WHOIS data to coincide with Internationalized Domain Names (IDNs), which are in non-Latin scripts. None of this prohibits the use of other languages as long as they are in the basic Latin alphabet. However, the business of the Internet (documents and correspondence) must be in English. This is a policy in transition as ICANN attempts to fulfill its commitment to working in local languages.

2.1.1.4 Look Up, Query, and Retrieve These terms are often used interchangeably but are slightly different in meaning. "Query" in particular refers to the specific technical process of requesting the data from a WHOIS service or database. A "Look Up" may refer not only to the overall concept but also to a WHOIS search, which does not involve a server or database but rather a static webpage.

2.1.1.5 Thin, Thick, and None A Thin WHOIS record is one that only has registrar and nameserver data, no owner, or contact data. Thick records contain all the registrant and administrative contact information, and sometimes without the Thin data. .COM and .NET registry records are only in Thin, and the thick records must be obtained from the registrar. All gTLDs are required to have WHOIS records, but some country code TLDs (ccTLDs) have no WHOIS records or have a single record for all domains. For example, every WHOIS record for .NU domains (the ccTLD for the tiny island nation of Niue) has the same information, which is the basic contact information for the technical administrator of the .NU registry. Then, we have .AD for Andorra,[1] which has no apparent WHOIS server for its domains. Some WHOIS queries will return the Thick record with the Thin record appended at the top or bottom. These records came from two locations.

2.1.1.6 WHOIS Formats Within the DNS, there are more than 1000 ICANN-accredited registrars, 26 gTLD registries (and growing), 256 ccTLD registries, and five regional Internet

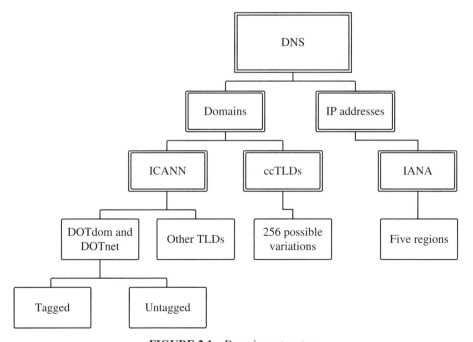

FIGURE 2.1 Domain system tree.

---

[1] http://www.nic.ad/index_eng.htm.

Protocol (IP) number registries. Each one of these entities has its own WHOIS format. Because there was never any true standard developed for WHOIS when ICANN established the registry–registrar system, we have a Babble Tower as the record set. Additionally, we have situations of cross-pollination of WHOIS record formats, for example, when a gTLD registry or registrar serves records for a ccTLD. The gTLDs that came after .COM and .NET generally have well-structured WHOIS formats, but they are still separate from each other. There are extreme inconsistencies within .COM and .NET because each registrar establishes its own format. While there are dozens of formats for .COM and .NET, they can be lumped into two broad subcategories: tagged records and untagged records. Tagged records return *labels* with the data, meaning each value is preceded by NAME:, ADDRESS:, EMAIL:, and so on. Untagged records just list the raw WHOIS data with little or no guidance. This chart shows the general breakdown of WHOIS formats.

Compare these to WHOIS results for the exact same domain, one from the registry and one from the registrar. First, use the .ORG WHOIS server at whois.pir.org:

```
Domain ID:D1504248-LROR
Domain Name:TELECO.ORG
Created On:31-Jul-1997 04:00:00 UTC
Last Updated On:09-Aug-2013 13:19:43 UTC
Expiration Date:30-Jul-2014 04:00:00 UTC
Sponsoring Registrar:Network Solutions, LLC (R63-LROR)
Status:CLIENT TRANSFER PROHIBITED
Registrant ID:23656023-NSIV
Registrant  Name:La Sociiti Iducative de l'nle-du-Prince-Idouard
Registrant Street1:ATTN insert domain name here
Registrant Street2:care of Network Solutions
Registrant Street3:PO Box 459
Registrant City:Drums
Registrant State/Province:PA
Registrant Postal Code:18222
Registrant Country:US
Registrant Phone:+1.5707088780
Registrant Phone Ext.:
Registrant FAX:
Registrant FAX Ext.:
Registrant Email:b94ds8xn63q@networksolutionsprivateregis-
tration.com
...
```

This is the same block but from whois.networksolutions.com:

```
Domain Name: TELECO.ORG
Registrar WHOIS Server: whois.networksolutions.com
Registrar URL: http://www.networksolutions.com/en_US/
Updated Date: 2013-08-09
Creation Date: 2002-09-18
Registrar Registration Expiration Date: 2014-07-30
```

```
Registrar: NETWORK SOLUTIONS, LLC.
Registrant Name: La Sociiti Iducative de l'nle-du-Prince-Idouard
Registrant Street: ATTN insert domain name here care of Network
Solutions PO Box 459
Registrant City: Drums
Registrant State: PA
Registrant Postal Code: 18222
Registrant Country: US
Registrant Phone: 570-708-8780
Registrant Phone Ext:
Registrant Fax:
Registrant Email:
...
```

It is the same domain, but the layout, field names, order, and even data are different. To further examine the differences, compare the records for two newspaper domains at two different registrars, the *Boston Globe* (boston.com)

```
Using WHOIS server whois.dyndns.com, port 43, to find boston.com

Registrant:
Scott, Damian Nigel  dns@boston.com
The Boston Globe Newspaper Company LLC
135 Morrissey Blvd
Boston, MA 02125
US

Domain name: BOSTON.COM
...
```

and the *New York Times* (nytimes.com)

```
Domain Name: nytimes.com
Registrar WHOIS Server: whois.markmonitor.com
Updated Date: 2013-11-25T17:37:09-0800
Creation Date: 2013-11-25T15:02:33-0800
Registrar: MarkMonitor, Inc.
Registrant Name: Domain Administrator
Registrant Organization: The New York Times Company
Registrant Street: 620 8th Avenue,
Registrant City: New York
Registrant State/Province: NY
Registrant Postal Code: 10018
Registrant Country: US
Registrant Phone: +1.2125561234
Registrant Phone Ext:
Registrant Email: hostmaster@nytimes.com
3...
```

2.1.1.7   Limits   All registrars and registries have query limits for WHOIS. These limits are ostensibly in place to prevent mass trawling of the data and or denial-of-service attacks against the WHOIS server; however, several registrars have placed arbitrarily low limits on WHOIS services, for example, some registrars block access after just one query. These limits are not supported by the contract. In this area, the registrars have to walk a fine line, as the contract states within the same section that

> *Registrar shall not impose terms and conditions on use of the data provided*[2]

But also not

> *"enable high volume, automated, electronic processes that send queries"*[3]

On the one hand, this service needs to be open to the public and not restricted, but on the other hand, the registrar must control the volume of queries. This is all for good reason, but there is little guidance on what constitutes high volume. However, the first step in avoiding limits is to use the methods listed in this book to determine which server is best to use. Never use a registrar WHOIS server for a domain they do not sponsor: not only is it possible to receive no results, but your IP may be blocked. For non-Thin TLDs (.INFO, .ORG, etc.), use the registry or InterNIC, not the registrar. There are additional tricks for getting full records from stubborn servers covered in this chapter.

2.2   DOMAIN WHOIS FIELDS

To start understanding the detail of WHOIS records, we need a sample to review. Perform the simplest query to get started, either on the command line

> *whois internetsociety.org*

or from a good web interface like geektools.com or domaintools.com. Either result should be similar to what we have displayed below. There are many options for queries covered in this chapter. Note: Record samples may be edited in the text. The first line containing *"Checking server"* is not part of the record but a command output that may or may not appear in the WHOIS display depending on how it is obtained. The bracketed server name ([whois.publicinterestregistry.net]) is the WHOIS server for the .ORG registry, Public Interest Registry (PIR):

```
Checking server [whois.publicinterestregistry.net]

Domain ID:D155729938-LROR
Domain Name:INTERNETSOCIETY.ORG
Created On:26-Mar-2009 14:30:56 UTC
Last Updated On:10-Feb-2012 09:12:42 UTC
Expiration Date:26-Mar-2017 14:30:56 UTC
```

[2] http://www.icann.org/en/resources/registrars/raa/ra-agreement-21may09-en.htm#3.3.5
[3] See note 2.

Sponsoring Registrar:2030138 Ontario Inc. dba NamesBeyond.
com and dba GoodLuckDomain.com (R117-LROR)
Status:CLIENT TRANSFER PROHIBITED
Registrant ID:NER2R-PERPG12039
Registrant Name:Peter Godwin
Registrant Organization:Internet Society
Registrant Street1:15 Galerie Jean-Malbuisson
Registrant Street2:
Registrant Street3:
Registrant City:Geneva
Registrant State/Province:Geneva
Registrant Postal Code:1204
Registrant Country:CH
Registrant Phone:+41.228071447
Registrant Phone Ext.:
Registrant FAX:+41.228071445
Registrant FAX Ext.:
Registrant Email:godwin@isoc.org
Admin ID:NER2R-PERPG12039
Admin Name:Peter Godwin
Admin Organization:Internet Society
Admin Street1:15 Galerie Jean-Malbuisson
Admin Street2:
Admin Street3:
Admin City:Geneva
Admin State/Province:Geneva
Admin Postal Code:1204
Admin Country:CH
Admin Phone:+41.228071447
Admin Phone Ext.:
Admin FAX:+41.228071445
Admin FAX Ext.:
Admin Email:godwin@isoc.org
Tech ID:NER2R-PERPG12039
Tech Name:Peter Godwin
Tech Organization:Internet Society
Tech Street1:15 Galerie Jean-Malbuisson
Tech Street2:
Tech Street3:
Tech City:Geneva
Tech State/Province:Geneva
Tech Postal Code:1204
Tech Country:CH
Tech Phone:+41.228071447
Tech Phone Ext.:
Tech FAX:+41.228071445
Tech FAX Ext.:

```
Tech Email:godwin@isoc.org
Name Server:NS-EXT.NLNETLABS.NL
Name Server:NS1.AMS1.AFILIAS-NST.INFO
Name Server:NS1.MIA1.AFILIAS-NST.INFO
DNSSEC:Signed
```

Now, we will walk through this record and explain what everything means. Remember that the record returned by a WHOIS query is from a database of individual fields and it is not a single text file. The record itself has several *blocks* that refer to the different parties or components attached to the domain name; each one has its own purpose.

2.2.1   Status

```
Status:CLIENT TRANSFER PROHIBITED
```

Status codes in WHOIS records generally refer to specific registry instructions and can vary from registry to registry. The lack of uniformity and the fact that records may have more than one code make status codes even more confusing. There are at least two official code sets: Extensible Provisioning Protocol (EPP)[4] for .ORG, .BIZ, .INFO, and .NAME and Registry Registrar Protocol (RRP)[5] used by VeriSign for .COM and .NET. Codes with "HOLD" in the name indicate a problem with the domain name. HOLD is an instruction from the registrar to not include the domain in the zone file, which means the domain should not resolve on the Internet. Status codes with "PROHIBITED" usually indicate that the WHOIS record cannot be changed and the domain cannot be moved. This type of status keeps domains from being stolen or hijacked. Registrars will sometimes put "suspended" in the WHOIS record, but unless a HOLD status is set and the nameserver fields are set to "No Nameserver," the domain is not actually suspended. This has been the case with many false suspensions in the past. Status cannot be set by the registrant, but can only be requested by the registrant. The full list of status codes and explanations is in the appendix.

2.2.2   Registrar

```
Sponsoring Registrar:2030138 Ontario Inc. dba NamesBeyond.
com and dba GoodLuckDomain.com (R117-LROR)
```

The registrar field is required in all gTLD WHOIS, but what name is listed is not always clear and not always easily identifiable. Some registrars have multiple entity names or doing business as (DBA) names, which causes confusion. Some registrars simply use their URL as the entity name, which is different from their actual corporate name. A good example is the registrar *URL Solutions, Inc.*, which commonly goes by the name *Panamanames* and uses the *Directi* platform LogicBoxes for registry services.

Another phenomenon is the prevalence of *shell* registrars or *cartel* registrars. There are five companies that own over 100 accreditations, each under various dummy corporations. There are various speculations as to why these extra accreditations are needed, especially

---

[4] https://www.icann.org/en/system/files/files/epp-status-codes-30jun11-en.pdf
[5] http://tools.ietf.org/html/rfc2832

when they are not actually used. Please refer to the appendix table "group codes" to see which registrars are connected.

2.2.3 Nameservers

```
Name Server:NS-EXT.NLNETLABS.NL
Name Server:NS1.AMS1.AFILIAS-NST.INFO
Name Server:NS1.MIA1.AFILIAS-NST.INFO
```

Nameservers are part of the very basic required record data. Nameservers make it possible for domain names to be resolved as websites. However, they vary in format and accuracy. It is possible to forge a nameserver in a WHOIS record. Records typically require at least two nameservers, but some have many more. Many registrations use the convention NS#. DOMAIN.TLD to denote a nameserver. Example.

The above comes from the *registry*—compare that format to the format provided by the *registrar* or the same domain:

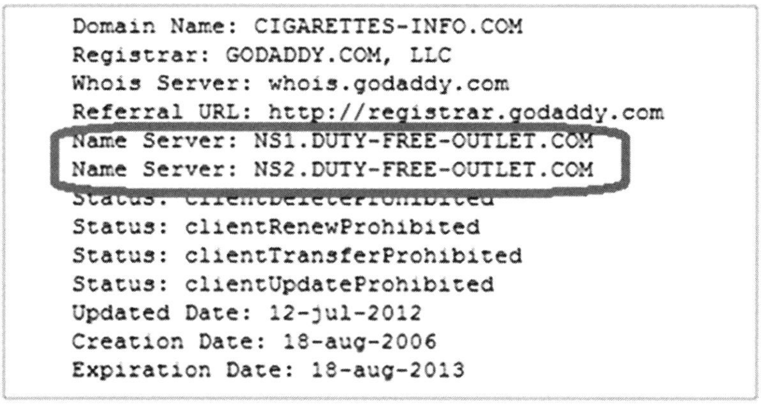

```
Domain Name: CIGARETTES-INFO.COM
Registrar: GODADDY.COM, LLC
Whois Server: whois.godaddy.com
Referral URL: http://registrar.godaddy.com
Name Server: NS1.DUTY-FREE-OUTLET.COM
Name Server: NS2.DUTY-FREE-OUTLET.COM
Status: clientDeleteProhibited
Status: clientRenewProhibited
Status: clientTransferProhibited
Status: clientUpdateProhibited
Updated Date: 12-jul-2012
Creation Date: 18-aug-2006
Expiration Date: 18-aug-2013
```

FIGURE 2.2   Nameserver portion of registry WHOIS record.

```
Domain servers in listed order:
NS1.DUTY-FREE-OUTLET.COM
NS2.DUTY-FREE-OUTLET.COM

Registry Status: clientDeleteProhibited
Registry Status: clientRenewProhibited
Registry Status: clientTransferProhibited
Registry Status: clientUpdateProhibited
```

FIGURE 2.3   Nameserver portion of registrar WHOIS record.

However, this is not a requirement and odd subdomains are frequently seen instead of the NS convention. Use the instructions in III B for obtaining more details on nameservers.

2.2.4 Registrant, Administrative, Technical, and Billing

```
Registrant Name:Peter Godwin
Registrant Organization:Internet Society
Registrant Street1:15 Galerie Jean-Malbuisson
```

For the registrant block, only name and postal address are required. Many WHOIS records have fields and data for registrant emails and phone numbers, but this information is not required; hence, it is not required for it to be accurate.

Administrative and other contact blocks have most fields required:

```
Admin Name:Peter Godwin
Admin Organization:Internet Society
Admin Street1:15 Galerie Jean-Malbuisson
Admin City:Geneva
Admin State/Province:Geneva
Admin Postal Code:1204
Admin Country:CH
Admin Phone:+41.228071447
Admin Phone Ext.:
Admin FAX:+41.228071445
Admin FAX Ext.:
Admin Email:godwin@isoc.org
```

Fake emails and phone numbers can only be considered invalid if they are in the administrative, technical, or billing field. Fax numbers are generally not required. Some WHOIS records have both billing and administrative blocks, while other registries consider the information redundant. Sometimes, the technical information refers to the hosting company or the registrar, and sometimes, it is the domain owner.

2.2.5 Names and Organizations

```
Tech Organization:Internet Society
```

Personal names are key required data but one of the most difficult for the investigator to verify. The only ones who truly know the legitimacy of a registrant name are the registrar and the registrant himself. While emails, addresses, and phone numbers can often be checked remotely, verifying the validity of a registrant name requires additional information. However, even fake names are useful to the investigator since illicit domain registrants may use them repeatedly or in variations that link various domains.

Name entries that are not valid include "HOST MASTER," "DOMAIN ADMIN," and similar generic titles. *Real* names must be provided only if a legal entity is also provided.

A registrant can be a person or a legal entity (a corporation). A WHOIS record with an entity name does not need an accurate personal name. The entity in the record must be a verifiable legal entity. Researching legal entity names can be time consuming due to the variations in record formats and unclear record location. In the United States, each Secretary of State manages the records and requirements for businesses registered there. Because of this, every state has a different search engine and format. Foreign registrations are entities existing in one state but listed in another. Some states have inexpensive and quicker incorporation systems as well as lower taxes, making them more attractive for registrations. Among these are Delaware, Florida, Nevada, and Wyoming. Some of these states also have lower disclosure requirements, making them more attractive for illicit operations. See the appendix for a list of more common states for business registrations along with the link for their query engines.

2.2.6 Emails

```
Admin Email:godwin@isoc.org
```

Emails are a quick source of record validation and often a path to additional information. By analyzing the domain name associated with a registration contact email, we can determine if the email address itself is valid and if the use leads to other illicit domains. If the domain associated with the email is not a generic service like Yahoo or Gmail, examine the WHOIS record behind that domain; it may be controlled by the same illicit operation as the primary domain being investigated and provide more details about the owners.

Beyond providing more information about an illicit operation, questions about the email address and its domain may show it as invalid without actually sending a test message to it. First, is it formatted correctly? There are a number of rules to email address formatting.[6] It must contain TEXT-ATSYM-TEXT-DOT-TEXT, in that order, or more specifically LOCALADDRESS@DOMAINNAME.TLDEXTENSION. The top-level domain (TLD) portion must be at least two characters and cannot contain numbers. Depending on the TLD, there may be a minimum number of characters in a domain name, and the maximum is generally 63. Domain names cannot start with certain characters or contain certain characters. Are there invalid characters in the email address? This may become more complex with internationalization. Also, some networks may allow special characters, even spaces, in the local part of the email address. Extended character sets are being used in various privacy protection schemes to thwart supposed spammers (see RFC 3696[7]). There may be more than one DOT on either side of the ATSYM, but not more than one ATSYM unless escaped with a backslash. The DOT cannot be the first or last character in the local part of the address. Special characters must be enclosed by double quotes. Is the TLD real? We have seen registrations that have been made with nonexistent TLDs in the administrator address. Is the TLD active? While a TLD may be in the Internet Assigned Numbers Authority (IANA) list, not all of them are sponsored or allocated or have active nameservers. Is the domain registered? With most registries, this is fairly trivial, but with some ccTLDs that employ wildcarding and block WHOIS queries, it may be more difficult. Is the domain active? Just because a domain is registered does not mean it can receive email; we must see if it is actually hosted in the DNS.

---

[6] http://tools.ietf.org/html/rfc5321
[7] http://tools.ietf.org/html/rfc3696

2.2.7 Addresses

```
Tech Street1:15 Galerie Jean-Malbuisson
Tech Street2:
Tech Street3:
Tech City:Geneva
Tech State/Province:Geneva
Tech Postal Code:1204
Tech Country:CH
```

Addresses are extremely complex datasets in terms of location and what determines accuracy of the data, even as it relates to other data elements. At a minimum, there must be a street name and number, a municipality, state or province, country, and postal code. Postal codes are difficult details in terms of accuracy. If the other address details are in fact accurate and verifiable, an incorrect postal code generally does not invalidate the record. However, erroneous postal codes that do not match the other record details are a legitimate reason for complaint. Google Maps now has an amazing amount of information on addresses; enter an address in the search and Google will easily find it if it is real. Many addresses used by illicit registrants are actually UPS mailboxes. Use the theupsstore.com site to look for an address and check if it is a UPS store. Scammers have also been using the UPS phone numbers as their contact number, which is against UPS policy.

2.2.8 Phone Numbers

```
Admin Phone:+41.228071447
Admin Phone Ext.:
Admin FAX:+41.228071445
Admin FAX Ext.:
```

Determining the accuracy of phone numbers in a WHOIS record can often be done without actually placing a test call. Understanding common phone number formats is the key. Accurate US and Canadian phone numbers have a three-digit area code, a three-digit exchange code, and a four-digit phone number. The +1 is the country code for the United States. So US phone numbers will always be 10 digits with the +1 usually not necessary. This does not just mean the United States, but is commonly called the North American Numbering Plan[8] (NANP). The NANP covers Canada and the Caribbean as well. There are a finite number of area codes, so it is easy to verify the location and authenticity. There are no area codes starting with 1, so "123" is a fake area code. "700" is a real area code but only used for obscure telecommunications functions so would unlikely be a real number in a WHOIS record. Similarly 600, 500, 533, 544, and 566 are real but do not represent locations and are for special "caller pays" services, the reverse of toll-free 800 numbers. For example, 544 is often used for home security alarm panels for the servicers to dial into; they are not normal phone numbers that can be answered. 710 is exclusively used by the US government; any WHOIS record with a "710" area code is fake. There are various services and maps to research area codes.[9]

---

[8] http://www.nanpa.com/about_us/index.html
[9] http://www.nanpa.com/number_resource_info/area_code_maps.html

International phone numbers can be more difficult to track but not impossible. Each country has its own dialing prefix that is required for the number in the WHOIS record to be accurate. This site will list them all: countrycode.org. The site will also list the city codes, example being Andorra: http://countrycode.org/andorra. A quick hint is the usage of zones for code sets: 2 is Africa, 3 and 4 are Europe, 5 is South America, 6 is Asia-Pacific, Russia is 7, 8 is East Asia, and 9 is Middle East and Central Asia. See this zone guide at http://www.wtng.info/wtng-cod.html. Each link will also state how many digits are in the number, for example, Tunisia: http://www.wtng.info/wtng-216-tn.html.

2.2.9   Record Dates

```
Created On:26-Mar-2009 14:30:56 UTC
Last Updated On:10-Feb-2012 09:12:42 UTC
Expiration Date:26-Mar-2017 14:30:56 UTC
```

WHOIS records commonly have three dates: Creation, Modified, and Expire. However, only the Creation and Expire dates are required. Hence, Modify dates do not always appear in every record consistently. It is also important to note that there are two (2) sets of record dates: registry and registrar. It is not always easy to determine which types of date you are looking at, and this accounts for why there may be discrepancies in the dates depending on where the query came from. For example, a registry Modified (updated) date may only change if there is a nameserver change but no change to the registrant data. Conversely, a change to a WHOIS record that does not change the hosting location may not be reflected in the registry Modified date. Also, because each registrar controls their database, it is unclear if these Modify dates are updated automatically or manually. Therefore, it is possible that WHOIS data may change and an update to the Modify date may not occur. These dates also come in many formats depending on the registry and registrar.

2.2.10   DNSSEC

```
DNSSEC:Signed
DS Created 1:23-Jun-2010 18:38:19 UTC
DS Key Tag 1:55956
Algorithm 1:5
Digest Type 1:1
Digest 1:07F305088A89349B34A82CCF218ACD3A3342EDAD
DS Maximum Signature Life 1:1814400 seconds
DS Created 2:23-Jun-2010 18:50:35 UTC
DS Key Tag 2:55956
Algorithm 2:5
Digest Type 2:2
Digest 2:C06D93103F046E056033CA1D47CCD31F60DC7CE8E1BF-
C381A1252879C98752EE
DS Maximum Signature Life 2:1814400 seconds
```

The sample record includes the field DNSSEC that stands for DNS Security Extensions. The overall point of DNSSEC is to add digital signatures to the root zones, which certify the source of DNS information as valid. It does not certify that the WHOIS record is valid. To be clear, it adds security to the *domain* itself. This is a new field not always present in records. The deployment of DNSSEC is new, while the concept has been in existence for some time. In our example, the DNSSEC field is marked as "Signed." A domain name without DNSSEC would display "Unsigned" in this field and not be followed by additional information. Signed domains have a number of additional fields that follow the signature field: DS Created, DS Key Tag, Algorithm, Digest Type, Digest, and DS Maximum Signature Life. The functions of these are described in RFC 4310.[10]

2.2.11   Other Information

```
Domain ID:D155729938-LROR
Registrant ID:NER2R-PERPG12039
```

Some registries have additional tracking fields like Domain ID and Registrant ID, which track information by number as well as character strings. This will become ever more important as more languages and character scripts are added:

```
Trademark Name:ICANNReserved
```

Trademark Name is another custom field added to declare that that domain name is a registered trademark and is held by the trademark owner.

2.3   GETTING RECORDS ABOUT VARIOUS RESOURCES

All levels of the Internet have some type of record set that indicates the source of accountability. Understanding the different pieces of the architecture, how to get their records, and what the records mean helps understand the actual Internet in its full context.

2.3.1   Starting at the Top: The Empty Domain

This may be a difficult concept, especially for people still grasping the general concepts of the Internet structure, but at the very top level of the DNS, there is an empty invisible domain. This is the unique root or *null* domain. You cannot see it, but it is there. It can be tested by entering a regular domain name with an extra dot on the end, such as "wiley.com." in a browser, and it should resolve just as it would without. The same can be done with a ping or other command-line instruction as well as WHOIS queries. Conversely, putting any other character at the end of the string will likely return an error. Internet resolver software assumes the invisible domain and the dot, so it is not needed but also ignored if entered. Examples of the null domain can be reviewed in the chapter on DNS. It is possible to perform a *dig* with no parameters and return the top-level root servers:

```
; <<>> DiG 9.6-ESV-R9-P1 <<>>
;; global options: +cmd
;; Got answer:
;; ->>HEADER<<- opcode: QUERY, status: NOERROR, id: 6318
```

---

[10] http://www.ietf.org/rfc/rfc4310.txt

```
;; flags: qr rd ra; QUERY: 1, ANSWER: 13, AUTHORITY: 0,
   ADDITIONAL: 14

;; QUESTION SECTION:
;.                              IN    NS

;; ANSWER SECTION:
.                       163813   IN    NS        k.root-servers.net.
.                       163813   IN    NS        d.root-servers.net.
.                       163813   IN    NS        g.root-servers.net.
.                       163813   IN    NS        b.root-servers.net.
.                       163813   IN    NS        f.root-servers.net.
.                       163813   IN    NS        i.root-servers.net.
.                       163813   IN    NS        c.root-servers.net.
.                       163813   IN    NS        a.root-servers.net.
.                       163813   IN    NS        j.root-servers.net.
.                       163813   IN    NS        m.root-servers.net.
.                       163813   IN    NS        e.root-servers.net.
.                       163813   IN    NS        l.root-servers.net.
.                       163813   IN    NS        h.root-servers.net.

;; ADDITIONAL SECTION:
d.root-servers.net.  163892   IN    A       199.7.91.13
d.root-servers.net.  164169   IN    AAAA    2001:500:2d::d
g.root-servers.net.  163841   IN    A       192.112.36.4
b.root-servers.net.  164038   IN    A       192.228.79.201
f.root-servers.net.  163833   IN    A       192.5.5.241
f.root-servers.net.  165869   IN    AAAA    2001:500:2f::f
i.root-servers.net.  164061   IN    A       192.36.148.17
i.root-servers.net.  165963   IN    AAAA    2001:7fe::53
c.root-servers.net.  164059   IN    A       192.33.4.12
a.root-servers.net.  163811   IN    A       198.41.0.4
a.root-servers.net.  163814   IN    AAAA    2001:503:ba3e::2:30
j.root-servers.net.  163891   IN    A       192.58.128.30
j.root-servers.net.  165702   IN    AAAA    2001:503:c27::2:30
m.root-servers.net.  163823   IN    A       202.12.27.33

;; Query time: 0 msec
;; SERVER: 192.168.1.1#53(192.168.1.1)
;; WHEN: Mon Aug 19 12:50:37 Eastern Daylight Time 2013
;; MSG SIZE  rcvd: 512
```

If you ever wanted to see the Internet, the previous text excerpt was it. This file makes the Internet work. The meaning of these records is explained in the chapter on DNS.

2.3.2 Query WHOIS for a TLD as a Domain

Most people understand the concept of a subdomain, for example, mail.yahoo.com contains the subdomain "mail" as part of the main domain "yahoo.com." What may be a slightly more obscure concept is that "yahoo" is actually a subdomain of "com" and that "com" is technically a subdomain of the empty root domain. This is the hierarchical model of the DNS: all dot-com domains are subdomains of com. com, edu, net, info, and all other TLD extensions are subdomains of the empty domain or unnamed root. So, does this mean we can perform a WHOIS lookup on a raw TLD as if it were a domain? Well, actually, yes.

The command

whois "domain com"

will produce this record:

```
Domain Name: COM
Registrar: INTERNET ASSIGNED NUMBERS AUTHORITY (2)
Whois Server: whois.iana.org
Referral URL: http://www.iana.org
Name Server: A.GTLD-SERVERS.NET
Name Server: B.GTLD-SERVERS.NET
Name Server: C.GTLD-SERVERS.NET
Name Server: D.GTLD-SERVERS.NET
Name Server: E.GTLD-SERVERS.NET
Name Server: F.GTLD-SERVERS.NET
Name Server: G.GTLD-SERVERS.NET
Name Server: H.GTLD-SERVERS.NET
Name Server: I.GTLD-SERVERS.NET
Name Server: J.GTLD-SERVERS.NET
Name Server: K.GTLD-SERVERS.NET
Name Server: L.GTLD-SERVERS.NET
Name Server: M.GTLD-SERVERS.NET
Status: serverDeleteProhibited
Status: serverTransferProhibited
Status: serverUpdateProhibited
Updated Date: 12-apr-2011
Creation Date: 01-jan-1985
Expiration Date: 31-dec-2099
```

2.3.3   WHOIS for A Registrar or Registry

The IANA is the top-level registry. This is their WHOIS record:

```
Registrar Name: INTERNET ASSIGNED NUMBERS AUTHORITY (2)
Address: 4676 Admiralty Way, Suite 330, Marina Del Ray, CA
90292, US
Phone Number: +1-310-823-9358
Email: iana@iana.org
Whois Server: whois.iana.org
Referral URL: www.iana.org
Admin Contact: RCC . Command Registry Center
Phone Number: 1-310-823-9358
```

```
Email: iana@iana.org
Admin Contact: RCC Registry Command Center
Phone Number: 1-310-823-9358
Email: iana@iana.org
Billing Contact: RCC Registry Command Center
Phone Number: 1-310-823-9358
Email: iana@iana.org
Technical Contact: RCC Registry Command Center
Phone Number: 1-310-823-9358
Email: iana@iana.org
```

Getting this record is tricky, for reasons explained further in the chapter, but this is the command to retrieve it:

whois –h whois.internic.net "INTERNET ASSIGNED NUMBERS AUTHORITY (2)"

2.3.4 Nameservers

The nameserver WHOIS query will retrieve data for nameserver strings and IP addresses used for nameservers.

Domains used as nameservers are listed with their IP addresses in the registry zone files. There is a certain amount of room for forging nameserver locations in WHOIS records. This is one way to verify nameservers in conjunction with the nslookup or DiG tool. For example, if a particular domain is listed in a WHOIS record as the nameserver, use this query to see if the domain is actually listed as a nameserver. For example, the

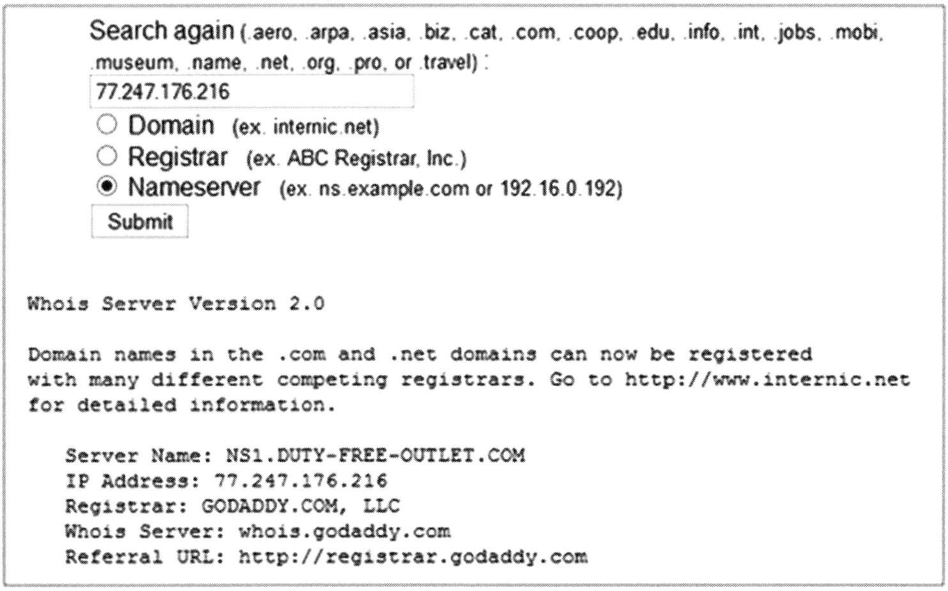

FIGURE 2.4 InterNIC WHOIS record results.

WHOIS record for cheap-cigarette-shop.com claims that the nameserver is NS3. WEBCONTOLCENTER.COM. The following nslookup will verify this:

nslookup –query=ns cheap-cigarette-shop.com

The query confirms the claimed nameserver along with a number of IP addresses that can also be investigated. That query asks for the nameserver name, and the following query will check the actual nameserver to see if the domain name is listed there:

nslookup cheap-cigarette-shop.com NS4.WEBCONTROLCENTER.COM

This query returns the IP address 216.119.102.5. Take this address back to the internic.net query for nameservers, and it should return a list of nameservers using this address including NS4.WEBCONTROLCENTER.COM. To test this run, the query with a nameserver we know is not associated with the domain:

nslookup cheap-cigarette-shop.com YNS2.YAHOO.COM

This query returns the message "Unknown can't find cheap-cigarette-shop.com." A very useful nslookup switch is –**d**, which returns all record types available:

nslookup –d cheap-cigarette-shop.com

A full list of options and instructions can be found here.[11] It is also useful to combine nameserver and IP findings with tools like Passive DNS Replication and other tools explained in this text.

2.3.5   Registrar and Registry

Registrars and registries have their own special WHOIS records and query engines. These records are difficult to obtain but have additional information often not publicly available. The trick is that the engine has to be queried with the *exact* registrar name string that is in the database, which does not always match what is publicly available. For example, go to http://www. internic.net/whois.html, select Registrar, and enter ZIGZAGNAMES.COM LLC. The engine will return contact information that is not publicly displayed including the names *Rhonda Richey, John Pariury,* and *Bill Greenseth* along with their email addresses and phone numbers. This information is not published anywhere else on ICANN websites. However, this can only be obtained by entering the registrar name as it exactly appears in the database, which is unknown.

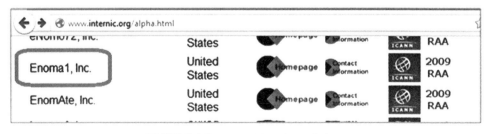

FIGURE 2.5   InterNIC registrar listing.

[11] http://support.microsoft.com/kb/200525

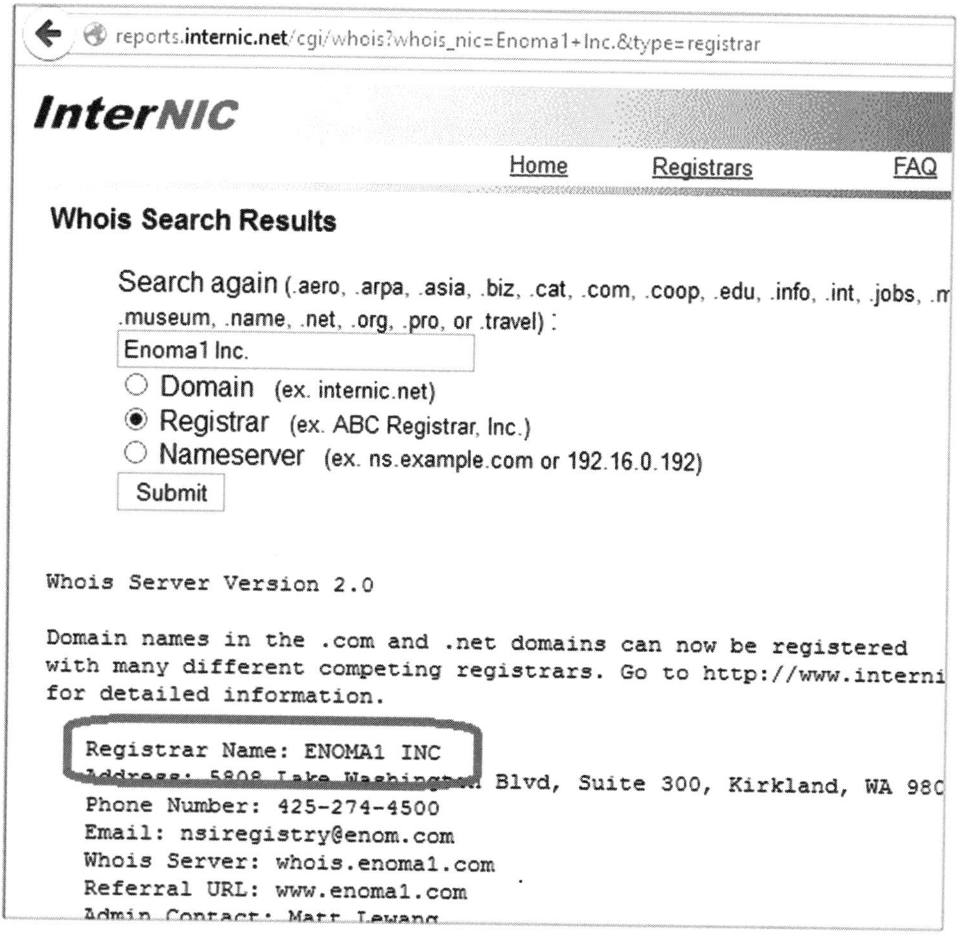

FIGURE 2.6 Registrar name in WHOIS record.

Take the published registrar name "! #1 Host Australia, Inc.", the exclamation point is an invalid query character and will produce an error. The hash tag is an invalid character too. This database is not searchable by other terms and wildcards are not accepted. In some cases, a comma is part of the official name but apparently not in the WHOIS database name, for example, "Enoma1, Inc." However, using the command line, we can get the full results.

There is a list of active registrars found at http://www.internic.org/alpha.html and a list of every company that has ever been accredited at http://www.iana.org/assignments/registrar-ids/registrar-ids.xml. This list also includes dummy and test registrars. Registries are also listed here. Enter the literal string "VeriSign Global Registry Services" in the query, and it will return contact details that are different from information publicly available.

2.3.6 Special Cases

There are a number or registries and registrars that have created their own standards and formats. For the purposes of conducting WHOIS queries, these nuances should be noted along with ways to work around the limitations.

2.3.6.1 Godaddy   Godaddy is the largest single gTLD domain registrar. It is also one of the few registrars that are a household name, especially from its celebrity endorsements and NFL Super Bowl commercials. Like many leaders in other industries, it does things a little differently, and this extends to WHOIS as well. Godaddy's Port 43 does not return thick WHOIS records for any of its domains even ones that commonly have Thick registries like .INFO and .ORG. Godaddy's WHOIS server returns the registrant name with an entity, the two primary nameservers, and preformatted HTTP string with instructions to paste this into a web browser. Upon entering the string in a browser address field, you will be directed to Godaddy's website and asked to enter a CAPTCHA code to receive the full WHOIS record, for example,

```
Copy and paste the link below to view additional details:
http://who.godaddy.com/whoischeck.aspx?domain=GODADDY.COM
```

2.3.6.2 NAME   VeriSign, who runs .COM and .NET, also is the registry for .NAME, which is supposed to be only for personal use, but is easily exploited, for example, cheapviagra.name, which redirects to trycheapviagra.com. This is problematic because as .NAME is intended for personal use only, there is a lower level of WHOIS disclosure; hence, the typical WHOIS record only contains the following.

Even the registrar and nameservers are unlisted. More details can be obtained from Internic.net.

```
Domain Name ID: 9875877DOMAIN-NAME
Domain Name: CHEAPVIAGRA.NAME
Domain Status: clientTransferProhibited
```

FIGURE 2.7   .NAME WHOIS results.

```
Domain Name ID: 9875877DOMAIN-NAME
Domain Name: CHEAPVIAGRA.NAME
Sponsoring Registrar ID: 243REGISTRAR-NAME
Sponsoring Registrar: DomainContext, Inc.
Domain Status: clientTransferProhibited
Registrant ID: 2206460CONTACT-NAME
Admin ID: 2206460CONTACT-NAME
Tech ID: 2206460CONTACT-NAME
Billing ID: 2206460CONTACT-NAME
Name Server ID: 2331660HOST-NAME
Name Server: NS1.FERENSNAMES.COM
Name Server ID: 2331661HOST-NAME
Name Server: NS2.FERENSNAMES.COM
Created On: 2012-06-14T02:52:32Z
Expires On: 2013-06-14T02:52:30Z
Updated On: 2012-12-14T00:08:23Z
```

FIGURE 2.8   Expanded .NAME WHOIS results.

The WHOIS server is at whois.nic.name, and the graphic interface is at https://webwhois.nic.name/DotNameWhois/pages/Query.jspx and allows a number of different results and search types. The difference between the two above examples is *summary* versus *standard*. There is a third option called *detailed* that requires a password. You may request *extensive* access at https://webwhois.nic.name/DotNameWhois/pages/Register.jspx, and the conditions can be found at https://webwhois.nic.name/DotNameWhois/pages/pdf/extensiveagreement-2010.pdf. The query also allows for record requests by DOMAIN, REGISTRAR, NAMESERVER, CONTACT, and BLOCKED. The purpose of BLOCKED is unclear but may apply to string that cannot be registered.[12]

This is critical when running a command-line Port 43 lookup of a .NAME site

whois –h whois.nic.name CHEAPVIAGRA.NAME

will only reveal the summary information, but

*whois –h whois.nic.name **domain**=CHEAPVIAGRA.NAME*

will return the standard WHOIS with more information. If we obtain the full record for the domain nic.name, we will see that the nameserver is A1.VERISIGNDNS.COM; this can be queried with

*whois –h whois.nic.name **nameserver**=a1.verisigndns.com*

What should be returned is a list of individual records at several registrars where this particular nameserver has an account to serve as a .NAME nameserver. In the record, we also see that the registrar for nic.name is "RPT Internal," for which we can get more information with

*whois –h whois.nic.name **registrar**= "RPT Internal"*

Various entries in the .NAME database also have ID numbers that can be queried with "registrar ID=".

2.3.6.3   .PRO Second-Level Domains

.PRO is a gTLD created for "professionals" and uses different subdomains to dedicate to different industries. It may be necessary to query .PRO domains on the second level. These are the second-level .PRO extensions: AAA.PRO, ACA.PRO, ACCT.PRO, ARC.PRO, AVOCAT.PRO, BAR.PRO, BUS.PRO, CFP.PRO, CHI.PRO, CHIRO.PRO, CPA.PRO, DDS.PRO, DEN.PRO, DENT.PRO, ED.PRO, ENG.PRO, JUR.PRO, LAW.PRO, MED.PRO, MIN.PRO, NTR.PRO, NUR.PRO, NURSE.PRO, OPT.PRO, PA.PRO, PHA.PRO, PHARMA.PRO, POD.PRO, PR.PRO, PROF.PRO, PRX.PRO, PSY.PRO, PT.PRO, RECHT.PRO, REL.PRO, TEACH.PRO, and VET.PRO.

For example, the WHOIS record for "med.pro:" is not the same as the record for "apc.med.pro".

whois –h whois.registrypro.pro med.pro

returns

```
Domain ID:D6389-PRO
Domain Name:MED.PRO
Created On:18-Aug-2004 00:00:00 UTC
```

[12] http://www.rwgusa.com/biz/_name_information.htm

```
Last Updated On:25-Jun-2012 14:56:23 UTC
Expiration Date:26-Jan-2016 00:00:00 UTC
Sponsoring Registrar:Afilias Limited (R2331-PRO)
Status:DELETE PROHIBITED
Status:TRANSFER PROHIBITED
Status:UPDATE PROHIBITED
Registrant ID:RSC-1
Registrant Name:Afilias Limited
Registrant Organization:Afilias Limited
Registrant Street1:2 La Touche House
Registrant Street2:IFSC
Registrant Street3:
Registrant City:Dublin
Registrant State/Province:IL
Registrant Postal Code:1
Registrant Country:IE
Registrant Phone:+353.14310511
Registrant Phone Ext.:
Registrant FAX:+353.14310557
Registrant FAX Ext.:
Registrant Email:domainadmin@afilias.info
```

But

whois –h whois.registrypro.pro apc.med.pro

returns

```
Domain ID:D5838-PRO
Domain Name:APC.MED.PRO
Created On:30-Sep-2005 00:00:00 UTC
Last Updated On:19-Aug-2013 19:39:22 UTC
Expiration Date:30-Sep-2014 00:00:00 UTC
Sponsoring Registrar:Corporation Service Company dba CSC
  Corporate Domains, Inc (R2338-PRO)
Status:OK
Registrant ID:c-86576
Registrant Name:Jose Lopez-Zeno
Registrant Organization:
Registrant Street1:1000 Johnson Ferry Rd., NE
Registrant Street2:
Registrant Street3:
Registrant City:Atlanta
Registrant State/Province:Georgia
Registrant Postal Code:30342
Registrant Country:US
Registrant Phone:+1.7708158080
Registrant Phone Ext.:
```

```
Registrant FAX:+1.7708158080
Registrant FAX Ext.:
Registrant Email:jalz@mac.com
```

Two different registrars and two different registrants.

2.3.6.4 CentralNIC Domains CentralNIC[13] is not an ICANN registrar. CentralNIC sells specialized subdomains that reverse the typical ccTLD domain convention, for example, website.uk.com instead of website.co.uk. In the traditional ccTLD, "uk" is the TLD, "co" is a second-level (country code second level) domain, and the rest is the customer's domain. In the case of a CentralNIC domain, "com" is the TLD, "uk" is the domain, and the rest is a subdomain. This type is not an actual ccTLD but what is called a "domain hack." Subdomains typically do not have WHOIS records, but CentralNIC provides them for their product. The web-based WHOIS is at https://manage.centralnic.com/support/view_whois, and the WHOIS server is whois.centralnic.com. CentralNIC also offers the EPP[14] as a service to registrars.

Starting with the website webhosting.uk.com, we run into some potentially confusing record trail. Knowing that this looks like a gTLD subdomain, we assume that "uk.com" is the actual domain and perform a typical thin lookup at InterNIC to get the actual registrar that returns

```
Domain Name: UK.COM
Registrar: NETWORK SOLUTIONS, LLC.
Whois Server: whois.networksolutions.com
Referral URL: http://www.networksolutions.com/en_US/
```

Attempting to perform an InterNIC WHOIS on "webhosting.uk.com" returns an error, as would be expected. Running the WHOIS lookup at Network Solutions for "uk.com" returns this record:

```
CentralNic Ltd
domains@centralnic.com
35-39 Moorgate
London,  EC2R 6AR
UK
Phone: +44.8700170900
Fax: +44.8700170901
```

Performing a lookup for "webhosting.uk.com" at Network Solutions does not return any data, as would be expected. However, performing this lookup through CentralNIC returns a completely different record for webhosting.uk.com:

```
Domain ID:CNIC-DO265661
Domain Name:WEBHOSTING.UK.COM
Created On:2003-02-15T15:47:20.0Z
```

---

[13] https://www.centralnic.com/
[14] https://www.centralnic.com/registry/technical/epp

```
Last Updated On:2013-07-01T11:49:51.0Z
Expiration Date:2014-02-15T23:59:59.0Z
Status:OK
Registrant ID:c69961b2da086e4d
Registrant Name:DNS Admin
Registrant Organization:Webhosting UK Com Ltd
Registrant Street1:Suite 1, 7 Commercial Street,
Registrant Street2:Morley
Registrant City:Leeds
Registrant State/Province:West Yorkshire
Registrant Postal Code:LS27 8HX
Registrant Country:GB
Registrant Phone:+44.1916450385
Registrant Email:andrew@webhosting.uk.com
```

This is interesting in and of itself, but what is more curious is the sponsoring registrar section of this special subdomain record:

```
Sponsoring Registrar ID:7065-EN
Sponsoring Registrar IANA ID:48
Sponsoring Registrar Organization:eNom, Inc.
Sponsoring Registrar Street1:5808 Lake Washington Boulevard
Sponsoring Registrar City:Kirkland
Sponsoring Registrar State/Province:WA
Sponsoring Registrar Postal Code:98034
Sponsoring Registrar Country:US
Sponsoring Registrar Phone:425-274-4500
Sponsoring Registrar FAX:425-974-4796
Sponsoring Registrar Website:http://www.enom.com/
```

This record claims that the "registrar" is eNom, which is a completely different company than Network Solutions. So how can eNom be the registrar for webhosting.uk.com? The answer is that since webhosting.uk.com is not a domain, it does not have a registrar and is not required to have a WHOIS record. So it follows that whatever data is placed in such a record would not be authoritative. But it is in fact authoritative in this context. eNom is a *registrar*[15] of CentralNIC under the system they have created within their domains. So, to clarify the real hierarchy here, Network Solutions is the ICANN gTLD registrar for uk.com, and CentralNIC is the registrant. eNom is the CentralNIC *registrar* for webhosting.uk.com, and Webhosting UK is the *registrant*. CentralNIC acts as a top-level accrediting organization within their subdomains. While eNom is an ICANN registrar, they are not acting as one in this case. eNom includes these in their TLD sales pages[16] and discloses that they are second-level domains. The domain keyword lookup produces the same results discussed earlier;

> *whois –h whois.centralnic.com "domain whois.centralnic.com"*

---

[15] https://www.centralnic.com/portfolio/registrars/overview
[16] http://www.enom.com/help/faq-tlds.aspx

It is also possible to use the same method with "nameserver" and "contact." Searching for "registrars" through CentralNIC is interesting. Using *whois –h whois.centralnic.com "registrar CentralNic Ltd"* produces

```
Using WHOIS server whois.centralnic.com, port 43, to find registrar
centralnic ltd This whois service is provided by CentralNic Ltd
and only contains information pertaining to Internet domain names
we have registered for our customers. By using this service you
are agreeing (1) not to use any information presented here
for any purpose other than determining ownership of domain
names, (2) not to store or reproduce this data in any way, (3)
not to use any high-volume, automated, electronic processes to
obtain data from this service. Abuse of this service is monitored
and actions in contravention of these terms will result in being
permanently blacklisted. All data is (c) CentralNic Ltd https://
www.centralnic.com/

Registrar Name:CentralNic Ltd
Address:35-39 Moorgate, London, EC2R 6AR, United Kingdom
Phone Number:+44 8700 170 900
Email:hostmaster@centralnic.net
Admin Contact:Hostmaster
Last Updated On:2009-09-09T16:56:24.0Z
```

So, within their own WHOIS database, CentralNIC lists itself as a registrar under a structure that it has created over which it has the authority. Querying the server similarly for eNom shows a variation:

```
Registrar Name:eNom, Inc.
Address:5808 Lake Washington Boulevard, Kirkland, WA, 98034,
United States
Phone Number:425-274-4500
Email:regnotify@enom.com
Referral URL:http://www.enom.com/
Admin Contact:Domain Administrator
IANA ID:48
Last Updated On:2013-08-22T15:02:28.0Z
```

Here, there is an IANA field that provides eNom's ICANN accreditation account code[17] as "48."

It is also possible to query by contact ID (*whois –h whois.centralnic.com "contact c69961b2da086e4d"*). But one would assume that a full WHOIS lookup had already been conducted to get the ID already.

The full CentralNIC WHOIS help file can be found with this query:

whois -h whois.centralnic.com help

---

[17] http://www.internic.org/registrars/registrar-48.html

The full list of their second-level domain offerings are EU.COM, KR.COM, DE.COM, US.COM, AE.ORG, QC.COM, GR.COM, GB.COM, BR.COM, GB.NET, SA.COM, NO.COM, SE.COM, HU.COM, SE.NET, JPN.COM, UK.COM, UY.COM, UK.NET, ZA.COM, RU.COM, and CN.COM.[18]

This is not a system without controversy. It may seem to anyone reading this that CentralNIC has essentially set itself as another ICANN within the DNS. A *pro se* litigant named Graham Schreiber filed a suit against ICANN, CentralNIC, and a number of registrars for allowing domains to be registered with CentralNIC, which violated his trademark.[19] The problem is that the processes created by ICANN to handle various disputes do not address the issues experienced by Schreiber.[20] However, the dispute involves parties contracted to ICANN selling "domains". This is an example showing how problematic the domain marketplace can be for consumers from different sectors. Also, in 2011, all of the third-level domains[21] in CentralNIC's GB.COM registry vanished one day as a result of a legal dispute.[22] CentralNIC is structured like ICANN but does not have the protection or transparency of ICANN.

2.3.6.5 ZA NiC ZA NiC offered free domains within za.net and za.org until 2012.[23] They do not accept any new registrations, but existing ones can be queried as below:

$$whois\ -h\ whois.za.net\ <domain>.za.net$$

$$whois\ -h\ whois.za.org\ <domain>.za.org$$

2.3.6.6 puntCAT (.CAT) .CAT represents the Catalonia region in Spain, but it is not a ccTLD. While Catalonia is technically part of Spain, it has always had a strong cultural identity and cites a history of repression within the county.[24] Catalan is not Spanish and represents a cultural community not determined by borders as its speakers live in Andorra, France, and Italy as well as in Spain. This is one of ICANN's sponsored anomalies. In 2011, the registry Fundacio puntCAT requested a change to its WHOIS policy[25] to conform to European privacy law allowing registrants to opt out of WHOIS disclosure. Their Port 43 WHOIS server is at whois.cat, but protected records will not display any contact information; rather, it displays instructions to use one of the registries' several forms for law enforcement and trademark contacts. Here is a query response:

```
%
% This domain has chosen privacy settings according to the European
% data protection framework provisions.
%
% Should you need to contact the registrant, please see
% http://www.domini.cat/contact-registrant
```

[18] http://srv.alphadivision.net/kb/servlet/KBServlet/faq1262.html

[19] http://www.icann.org/en/news/litigation/schreiber-v-dunabin/schreiber-notice-of-appeal-24jun13-en.pdf

[20] http://www.wipo.int/amc/en/domains/gtld/

[21] http://www.linfo.org/third-level_domain.html

[22] http://domainincite.com/5607-fight-over-gb-com-claims-thousands-of-victims

[23] http://www.za.net/

[24] http://firstmonday.org/ojs/index.php/fm/article/viewArticle/1305/1225

[25] http://www.icann.org/en/news/public-comment/cat-whois-changes-18jan12-en.htm

```
%
% For law enforcement and trademark protection purposes, see
% http://www.domini.cat/whois-access
%
% In case of technical problems, please see
% http://www.domini.cat/report-problem
%
```

2.3.7 Dealing with Weird Results

Anyone who has tried to run a WHOIS lookup of major, well-known brand sites like Amazon, Google, Microsoft, Sony, IBM, Facebook, Apple, or YouTube would have seen something very strange and confusing in the results. Instead of a thick or thin response, you may have seen something like this displayed:

```
MICROSOFT.COM.ZZZZZ.MORE.DETAILS.AT.WWW.BEYONDWHOIS.COM
MICROSOFT.COM.ZZZZZ.GET.LAID.AT.WWW.SWINGINGCOMMUNITY.COM
MICROSOFT.COM.ZZZOMBIED.AND.HACKED.BY.WWW.WEB-HACK.COM
MICROSOFT.COM.ZZZ.IS.0WNED.AND.HAX0RED.BY.SUB7.NET
MICROSOFT.COM.WILL.BE.BEATEN.WITH.MY.SPANNER.NET
MICROSOFT.COM.WAREZ.AT.TOPLIST.GULLI.COM
MICROSOFT.COM.THIS.IS.A.TEST.INETLIBRARY.NET
```

There are in fact over 30 entries like these that are returned for the WHOIS query. Run queries of the other big Internet names and similar items will be returned. None of the displayed addresses have anything to do with Microsoft. This has been called DNS Spam, DNS Pollution, or WHOIS Spam. The last term can cause confusion with the issue of unsolicited email sent to WHOIS contacts so we will avoid using it here. Take "MICROSOFT.COM.THIS.IS.A.TEST.INETLIBRARY.NET" and break off everything before "INETLIBRARY.NET." What is left is the real domain name—everything else is a subdomain. In this example, "MICROSOFT" is the final subdomain and "COM" is the subdomain just above. This is caused by people creating bogus host records for their domains with a well-known site in the string. Domain names are supposed to be unique, but the WHOIS server is confused because there are several potential matching entries.

Some of these domains actually serve content. The ones that will not be listed (they do not need more free advertising) lead to a pornographic site. The motivation for these funky hosting records is that some are pranks, some are political statements, and others are attempts to divert Internet traffic. Some WHOIS clients will properly handle the issue and ignore the junk listings. There are also a few ways of dealing with this. The query

whois =microsoft.com

will return a specific IP and registrar listing for each of the listings, expanding the dataset and displaying where each bogus host is hosted and sponsored. For the specific correct Microsoft entry, the registrar WHOIS server will be displayed, which can be queried directly. The query

whois "domain microsoft.com"

will only return the domain record, because the rest of the strings are not *domains* but are hosts. Now, if you were to perform a query in the form "*whois nameserver <bogus-host>*", it would return the information about one of the pollution hosts. There are much more serious cases and impacts of DNS Pollution.[26]

2.4 IP WHOIS

There are two sides of the DNS, one we usually see (domain names) and the other we do not pay attention to or even know is there (IP addresses). IP addresses are literal host machine addresses that serve websites and route traffic on the Internet. Domain names are mapped to IP addresses through the DNS, which only traffics by IP. The Internet Routing Registry[27] (IRR) coordinates the worldwide routing policy databases that use the Routing Policy Specification Language[28] (RPSL). IRR is run by Merit Network, Inc.[29] and provides a list of all routing registrars at irr.net/docs/list.html. Beneath this registry are five regional registries or Network Information Centers (NICs), which each have their own formats and policies. Merit runs the Routing Assets Database[30] (RADb), which is intended to improve routing on the Internet. Instructions for using the RADb WHOIS service and its special options can be found at http://www.radb.net/faq.

There are 256 slash-8 Internet Protocol version 4 (IPv4) address blocks. Each one of these blocks contains about 16.7 million IP addresses. The total number of possible addresses is approximately 4.3 billion, but not all of these addresses are available for public use and not all of the addresses are even being used. Most of the blocks are assigned to regional registries and redelegated to one of a variety of service providers. However, in the early days of the Internet, some of the blocks were assigned to private companies and to the US military who do not lease the addresses into the public space. More curious is the fact that many of these ranges do not have WHOIS records beyond the one of the top-level assignment. However, it is unlikely that the normal Internet user would stumble across many of these networks as there are no reachable domains hosted on these ranges nor are there known routes to them. Also, within the top-level block list are numbers intended to be used in local private networks. For example, your computer sees itself internally as 127.0.0.1. This entire range is called the *loopback*—meaning any address will loop back to the machine itself instead of going to the network.[31] There are also other address ranges designated for use inside of private networks as defined in RFC 1918.[32] These addresses have no WHOIS records. Explorers of WHOIS and IP hosting may have seen the term *lame delegation*; this is where networks go to die. A lame delegation assignment occurs when an authoritative nameserver stops responding and becomes unreachable. Regional Internet Registries (RIRs) have procedures for attempting to contact the administrators of failed servers before marking them as lame.[33]

[26] https://breakwall.net/2012/04/simple-explanation-to-dns-dns-pollution-and-solution/
[27] http://www.irr.net/
[28] http://www.ietf.org/rfc/rfc2622.txt
[29] http://www.merit.edu/
[30] http://www.radb.net/
[31] http://tools.ietf.org/html/rfc3330
[32] https://tools.ietf.org/html/rfc1918
[33] https://www.arin.net/policy/proposals/2002_1.html

2.4.1   Five Regional NICs

The five NICs represent North America (ARIN), Latin America/Caribbean (LACNIC), Europe/Central Asia/Middle East (RIPE), Africa (AfriNIC), and Asia-Pacific (APNIC). These NICs issue subblocks of IP addresses to Internet Service Providers (ISPs) who lease them to smaller providers and companies. They are collectively called RIRs. Africa only recently obtained control over its IP space. By 1990, it became critical to begin dividing the IP space for regional and international administration to cope with the potential for growth [1]. Up until a few years ago, the continent was divided between the European and American networks. Even now, some parts of North Africa still use European space. At one point, North and South America had one IP network. While the name "LAC" reflects the Caribbean as well as Latin America, some Caribbean locations are still part of ARIN. RIPE NCC stands for Réseaux IP Européens Network Coordination Centre; the Europeans of course had to change from the English-based naming convention. Different regions have started varying initiatives to improve WHOIS, for example, LACNIC started the JOINT WHOIS,[34] now administered by the Number Resource Organization[35] (NRO), which has influenced the WHOIS-based Extensible Internet Registration Data Service (WEIRDS) project described in the previous chapter. Each region has its own server and database:

ARIN, North America: whois.arin.net

APNIC, Asia-Pacific: whois.apnic.net

AfriNIC, Africa: whois.afrinic.net

RIPE NCC, Europe: whois.ripe.net

LACNIC, Latin America/Caribbean: whois.lacnic.net

Each region, of course, uses slightly different record formats, and not every source supplies the same type of data nor have they all fully embraced the Autonomous System Number or Network (ASN) method. Below is a table that compares the data tags in the formats of the different regions; note that the AfriNIC is missing as many records still have RIPE or ARIN designations.

	RIPE	ARIN	LACNIC	APNIC
CIDR	route:	CIDR:	inetnum:	route:
ipRange	inetnum:	NetRange:	inetrev:	inetnum:
ASN	origin:	OriginAS:	aut-num:	origin:
orgName	descr:	OrgName:	owner:	descr:
admin2	abuse-mailbox:	OrgNOCEmail:	e-mail:	e-mail:
admin3	abuse-mailbox:	OrgTechEmail:	e-mail:	e-mail:
admin4	abuse-mailbox:	RTechEmail:	e-mail:	e-mail:
streetAdd	address:	Address:	address:	address:
cityAdd		City:		
stateAdd		StateProv:		
postalCode		PostalCode:		
Country		Country:	country:	country:
phoneNum	phone:	OrgAbusePhone:	phone:	phone:
contactName	person:	OrgTechName:	person:	person:

[34] ftp://ftp.registro.br/pub/gter/gter20/02-jwhois-lacnic.pdf

[35] http://www.lacnic.net/documents/10834/295010/whois_en.pdf

2.4.1.1 Exploring ARIN   ARIN in particular has a great interface at http://whois.arin.net/ui, which allows you to look up by IP address, and even better an advanced search at http://whois.arin.net/ui/advanced.jsp, which has lookups for Classless Inter-Domain Routing (CIDR), ASN, organizations, customers, and most data points in the records. ARIN also offers RESTful (Representational State Transfer) services for their WHOIS, which are HTTP-based rather than database calls requiring WHOIS clients.[36] Overall, RESTful models are being offered as the future of WHOIS services as explained in the previous chapter.

It is not unusual to see strange responses with WHOIS lookups. Queries to ARIN will sometimes return results like this:

```
Internap Network Services Corporation PNAP-12-2002
(NET-69-25-0-0-1) 69.25.0.0 - 69.25.255.255
Bare Metal Cloud INAP-MIA003-BAREMETAL-57261
(NET-69-25-188-0-1) 69.25.188.0 - 69.25.189.255
```

Clearly, this is not a WHOIS record. The original query was *whois –h whois.arin.net 69.25.188.49*. This happens because the IP address queried has one ASN number but two CIDR announcements that calls for a more specific query. Whenever two providers appear in a list instead of a single WHOIS record, the second listing is a subset of the first listing. This is clear as the range 69.25.188.0–69.25.189.255 is contained within 69.25.0.0–69.25.255.255.

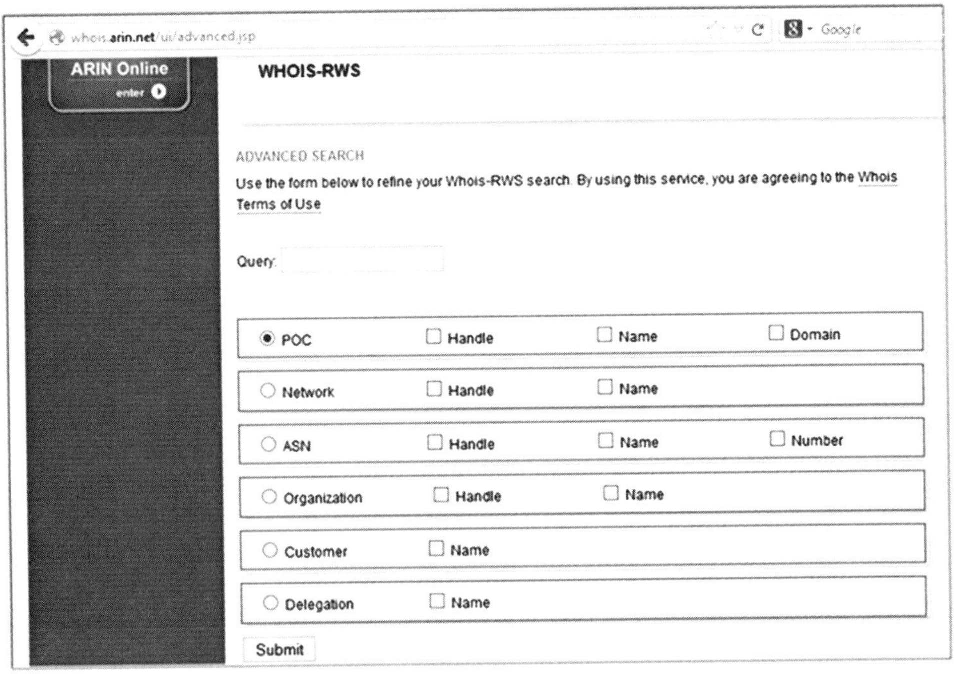

FIGURE 2.9   ARIN WHOIS.

[36] https://www.arin.net/resources/whoisrws/whois_api.html#whoisrws

Internap Network Services Corporation is the owner of the network, and Bare Metal Cloud is their customer.[37] Basically, because there are two records, ARIN does not know which one to return. To get both WHOIS records, use this query:

whois –h whois.arin.net "+ 69.25.188.49"

The quotes are critical as it separates the WHOIS client from the query. WHOIS clients typically look for a specific number of parameters and do not understand additional information, returning an error. By encapsulating the ARIN server switch with the IP address, we can overcome the limitations of the client. The + switch or option would not work on other WHOIS servers. The client here reads in the –h switch, then the server, and then what is being passed to the WHOIS server. Without the quotes, the client will assume the + symbol is the query and return an error.

2.4.1.2 *RIPE Extensions and the RIPE Client* RIPE has an extensive command-line instruction manual[38] with additional switches and detailed definitions for RIPE record fields. It is possible to browse the RIPE ftp site at ftp://ftp.ripe.net for a variety of useful documents as well as their document library[39] that has a number of guides for using their WHOIS and related services. RIPE of course has terms and conditions for use.[40] The RIPE database uses RPSL,[41] which is yet another instance where a deployment of a new standard is accused of "breaking" WHOIS.[42] In 2001, RIPE switched to the new format, and users noted that their old queries no longer worked.

LACNIC and AFRINIC use the same structure and switches as RIPE does, while APNIC uses a slightly modified model of RIPE. An extensive help file of current commands can be obtained from RIPE with this command:

whois –h whois.ripe.net help

RIPE issues its own client,[43] which is extremely useful for looking up IP addresses. Rather than having to specify an RIR server on the command line, the RIPE WHOIS client will assume it is being passed an IP address, and queries for domain names will actually fail. RIPE has issued a comprehensive document describing their database structure called the RIPE Database Query Reference Manual[44] and even has a test database that can be used to learn from[45] as well as training courses.[46] Review the RIPE terms[47] before experimenting with the client or server.

RIPE WHOIS server has an extensive set of options that can be obtained with *whois –h whois.ripe.net "help"* or by visiting http://www.ripe.net/data-tools/support/documentation. It would in fact be difficult to demonstrate all of the options, so we will cover them in

---

[37] whois.arin.net/rest/nets;q=69.25.188.49?showDetails=true&showARIN=false&ext=netref2
[38] ftp://ftp.ripe.net/ripe/docs/ripe-157.txt
[39] http://www.ripe.net/data-tools/support/documentation
[40] http://www.ripe.net/db/support/db-terms-conditions.pdf
[41] http://tools.ietf.org/html/rfc2280
[42] http://lists.debian.org/debian-user/2001/11/msg00154.html
[43] ftp://ftp.ripe.net/tools/ripe-whois-latest.tar.gz
[44] http://www.ripe.net/data-tools/support/documentation/query-ref-manual
[45] http://www.ripe.net/data-tools/support/documentation/ripe-database-user-manual-getting-started
[46] http://www.ripe.net/lir-services/training
[47] See note 40.

categories and cite some examples. The most straightforward query would be to retrieve a record for a RIPE IP address:

whois –h whois.ripe.net 193.0.6.139

More complex queries should be enclosed in quotes on the command line; this one will just retrieve the record for an entire range:

whois –h whois.ripe.net "-l 193.0.0.0 - 193.0.7.255"

In reviewing the results of RIPE queries, and IP queries in general, it is obvious that the records are more organized and thorough than domain WHOIS records. Additionally, it is possible to perform certain queries no longer possible in domain WHOIS: *inverse* queries. Inverse queries allow lookups on all records with a particular data point. For example, the query

whois –h whois.ripe.net "-i abuse-mailbox abuse@ripe.net"

will return every record with the same abuse email address. The **–i** switch is the inverse switch and can be used with several *attributes* of a RIPE record but not with all elements of the record. Names, addresses, and phone numbers cannot be used in this kind of search, but various *handles* can be used. The following are RIPE field names that can be used for inverse lookups; not all are required fields, so depending on the record, they may not find results. Some fields may only appear once in a record, while others may have more than one instance:

- org—Organization: a single optional inverse key that represents the entity holding the address space, for example, ORG-RIEN1-RIPE.
- admin-c—Administrator contact: a mandatory inverse key with multiple instances possible, for example, JDR-RIPE.
- tech-c—Technical contact: a mandatory inverse key with multiple instances possible, for example, OPS4-RIPE.
- notify—Change notification email address is an optional inverse key with multiple instances possible. This is where notifications of changes to the record should be sent.
- mnt-by—Maintained By: a mandatory inverse key with multiple instances possible, for example, RIPE-NCC-HM-MNT
- mnt-lower—In a hierarchical administration, this is an optional secondary record maintainer with multiple instances possible.
- mnt-domains—A maintainer authorized for authenticating reverse domain lookups.
- mnt-routes—A maintainer authorized to create routing objects. This is documented in RFC 2622 RPSL.[48]
- mnt-irt—A Computer Security Incident Response Team maintainer.

Some fields cannot be inversed because they are unique like **inetnum** and **netname**. These are the IP range and name for the range, respectively. **source** specifies where the record is registered as there are a number of sources where query results can be pulled from. Below is the full list of sources, where GRS stands for Global Resource Service and synchronizes

---

[48] http://tools.ietf.org/html/rfc2622

the data with the other global resources. To see the list, use *whois –h whois.ripe.net* *"-q sources"*:

- AFRINIC-GRS—African Network Information Center
- APNIC-GRS—Asia-Pacific Network Information Center
- ARIN-GRS—American Registry of Internet Numbers
- JPIRR-GRS—Japan Network Information Center
- LACNIC-GRS—Latin American and Caribbean Network Information Center
- RADB-GRS—Merit Routing Assets Database
- NTTCOM—Nippon Telegraph and Telephone

These are additional routing registries, which may provide data to the records presented, but the data itself is not held by RIPE. See the RIPE Queries Reference Card for quick summaries of the various options at http://www.ripe.net/data-tools/support/documentation/queries-ref-card and download the RIPE client at http://whois.sourceforge.net.

2.4.1.3   APNIC Detailed Query Options   APNIC[49] has an excellent guide to their WHOIS found at http://www.apnic.net/apnic-info/whois_search/using-whois/searching/query-options.

To obtain the help file with switches, use this command:

whois –h whois.apnic.net "help"

A simple WHOIS query on an APNIC address is structured like this:

whois –h whois.apnic.net 202.12.29.175

This, of course, returns a long record. If we only wanted the abuse contact, we can simplify the query using the *–b* switch:

whois –h whois.apnic.net "–b 202.12.29.175"

This should simply return one line of the record:

```
abuse-mailbox:    helpdesk@apnic.net
```

Some switches can be called with abbreviated options or a full-string option. By using the *--abuse-contact* switch, the same data will be returned as with *–b*:

whois –h whois.apnic.net "--abuse-contact 202.12.29.175"

Some searches of the APNIC WHOIS may return this result:

```
No entries found in source APNIC,CHINANET,IRINN,JPNIC,KRNIC,TWNIC.
```

Clearly, here the APNIC is redirecting a query to five other sources in addition to its own database. So what and who are these five other entities? Unlike the other regions,

---

[49] http://www.apnic.net/apnic-info/whois_search/using-whois/searching/query-options

Asia-Pacific further breaks their IP administration up into national registries. Here is the list decoded with the specific WHOIS servers if available:

- China Telecom Corporation Limited (CHINANET)
- Indian Registry for Internet Names and Numbers (IRINN)—192.168.1.88
- Japan Network Information Center (JPNIC)—whois.nic.ad.jp, whois.jprs.jp, whois.jp
- Korea Network Information Center (KRNIC)—whois.kisa.or.kr, whois.krnic.net
- Taiwan Network Information Center (TWNIC)—whois.twnic.net.tw

2.4.2 CIDR and ASN

In the simplest context, a CIDR is a specific sequential range of IP addresses owned or controlled by a single entity (which in turn can be subleased). An ASN is a collection of CIDRs that, while not contiguous, form a single network. These collections have their own records that will be returned for individual IP WHOIS queries, but sometimes more information is available by querying the whole CIDR or ASN. Each region may have its own format for these queries.

2.4.2.1   CIDR   CIDR[50] refers in part to the slash "/" notation, which indicates the size of a block of IP addresses. The IP address before the slash is the first address in the noted range, and the number that follows the slash determines the limit of the range; the smaller the number following the slash, the larger the count of addresses in that range. For example, 0.0.0.0/8 has more IP addresses than 0.0.0.0/20. The slash 8 would have 16 million addresses, or "hosts," and the slash 20 would have 4000.

An ARIN CIDR query

whois –h whois.arin.net "r 192.149.252.0/24"

returns

```
ARIN Operations ARIN-NET (NET-192-149-252-0-1) 192.149.252.0
- 192.149.252.255
Various Registries (Maintained by ARIN) NET192 (NET-192-0-0-0-0)
192.0.0.0 - 192.255.255.255
```

These details can be further queried by network name and organization. Understanding how the IP ranges work can be difficult; for a little help from ARIN in calculating CIDRs, use this interface: https://www.arin.net/public/cidrCalculator.xhtml.

2.4.2.2   ASN   ASN[51] is a notation for aggregating IP ranges into a single "network" for an ISP. It is a way of grouping multiple CIDR ranges under one name especially when they are not adjacent or "peers." A *downstream* ISP may lease IP ranges from different mega ISPs in different regions of the world. An ASN starts with "AS" and is followed by varying numbers of digits. The table found at http://www.iana.org/assignments/as-numbers/as-numbers.xml

---

[50] http://tools.ietf.org/html/rfc4632
[51] http://tools.ietf.org/html/rfc1930

maintained by IANA is a list of the allocated numbers. The table only provides regional allocation information, not ISP data. For ISP data on an ASN, use the query found at http://www.radb.net/index.php; this will return all the ISP contact data for an ASN. To see all the CIDR delegations for an ANS, try this query at the CIDR report: http://www.cidr-report.org/cgi-bin/as-report?as=. Put the ANS after the equal sign, for example, http://www.cidr-report.org/cgi-bin/as-report?as=as2707. This information changes constantly as networks are created and destroyed.

To query ARIN for an ASN, use this format, substituting the sample AS with any number to get that record:

whois –h whois.arin.net "a AS10745"

which returns, in part,

```
ASNumber:      10745
ASName:        ARIN
ASHandle:      AS10745
RegDate:       1997-11-14
Updated:       2012-09-07
Ref:           http://whois.arin.net/rest/asn/AS10745
OrgName:       ARIN Operations
OrgId:         ARINOPS
Address:       3635 Concorde Pkwy
Address:       Suite 200
City:          Chantilly
StateProv:     VA
PostalCode:    20151
Country:       US
RegDate:       2012-09-07
Updated:       2012-09-19
Ref:           http://whois.arin.net/rest/org/ARINOPS
...
```

2.4.3   IPv4 and IPv6

The Internet is not running out of addresses, despite what you may have heard. IPv4 refers to the numbering scheme for network addresses: 0.0.0.0 through 255.255.255.255. This address range allows for around 4.3 billion unique locations, and while that is a big number, the addresses have been used up quickly. This is what many refer to as "the Internet running out of space," which sounds like a dire prophecy, but the size of the Internet is virtually unlimited. While all addresses have been *allocated* or *assigned*, many are still unused, and each IP address can serve many websites. The problem really only refers to the numbering scheme. Internet Protocol Version 6 (IPv6) allows for 340 undecillion (a number with 36 zeros; a million times a million 11 times) addresses. In addition to being a longer number set, the IPv6 also uses hexadecimal digit sets that include the letters A–F to represent the values 10–15, creating a 16-digit numbering system (0–F). Instead of the four quads being separated by dots (#.#.#.#), as in the IPv4 sequence, IPv6 addresses are separated by colons in eight tuples (#:#:#:#:#:#:#:#). The display and notation of IPv6 addresses may vary as leading zeros and tuples with only zeros can be omitted. For example, "2607:f8b0:4006:801::1000" is the same as "2607:f8b0:4006:0801:0000:1000:0000:0000."

IP WHOIS lookups may be done on these addresses just as IPv4 addresses. The query

whois –h whois.arin.net 2607:f8b0:4006:0801:0000:1000:0000:0000

should show the same owner as

whois –h whois.arin.net 173.194.43.7

The records will be slightly different but will have the same ASN and contact information. This is a good introduction article for IPv6.[52]

2.5 ccTLDs AND IDNs

ICANN and various Internet authorities are under a mandate to expand the use of the Internet in local languages and cultures. There are two umbrella structures for addressing the true global expansion: (1) ccTLDs that are issued to governments and (2) IDN that are TLDs and domain strings in local languages. ccTLDs are distributed by ICANN, but ICANN does not oversee the policy, only governments do. IDNs could be gTLDs or ccTLDs which can cause confusion over which entity is responsible.

2.5.1 ccTLDs

There are 256 ccTLDs (at the moment), and because each represents a different sovereign nation, there are 256 different sets of policies and legal systems. The delegation of ccTLDs is based on ISO 3166, which assigns the codes for various international purposes[53] as specified in RFC 1591.[54] Many ccTLDs, in fact, have no stated WHOIS policies.[55] This is complicated by the fact that many are not sponsored or hosted within the sovereign nation, but rather outsourced to private companies in the United States and elsewhere. Additionally, the status of some "nations" is in question, examples being .BV (Bouvet, an inhospitable and uninhabited island) and .SU (Soviet Union, a defunct government and now a dozen independent countries). Some ccTLDs have become known havens for cybercrime and also have little or no WHOIS disclosure. Other ccTLDs have strict policies, but there is difficulty in monitoring or enforcing them. For example, .US (United States) requires a US nexus for registrations, that is, either citizenship or business location. However, reviews of illicitly used .US domains show that foreign registrants can easily obtain domains. It is an open question as to whether the policies of each country and ccTLD are in fact or even can be communicated to domain customers. The complexities of international code assignment can be seen in the ISO 3166-1 decoding table (http://www.iso.org/iso/iso-3166-1_decoding_table).

Several ccTLDs issued to sovereign governments have been redelegated to private companies and repurposed for sale in the domain name market, and the original meaning of the ccTLD becomes lost. For example, the extension intended for Moldova (.MD) is managed by Max.md that handles domain registration and is in Fort Lee, NJ, and has been marketed

[52] http://arstechnica.com/gadgets/2007/03/ipv6/
[53] http://www.iso.org/iso/country_codes/iso_3166_code_lists/country_names_and_code_elements.htm
[54] http://tools.ietf.org/html/rfc1591
[55] http://www.icann.org/en/about/agreements/cctlds

for medical professional websites. For several years, Laos's ccTLD, .LA, had been managed by CentralNic USA Ltd. in Woodland Hills, California, and marketed exclusively as the "Los Angeles" TLD. There was no mention of Laos anywhere on the ccTLD website; they even posted the current weather for Los Angeles on the home page. In 2011, the government of Laos demanded their ccTLD back. In the case of .PR, the entire ccTLD, and presumably the WHOIS database, was removed from the public university space to a private company when the manager retired from the university, an issue that has moved to litigation.[56]

Reviewing the WHOIS policies of every ccTLD could be contained in a book of its own. Here, we review some typical and contrasting situations. It is important to note that none of these registries are administered by ICANN; enforcing policy on WHOIS for these TLDs is completely within the sovereign governments.

2.5.1.1   .EU, European Union   A Port 43 query of the .EU WHOIS server, whois.eu, returns some data excluding the registrant information replacing with instructions:

```
Registrant:
  NOT DISCLOSED!
  Visit www.eurid.eu for webbased whois.
```

The disclaimer part of the record contains this further information:

```
% The EURid WHOIS service on port 43 (textual whois) never
% discloses any information concerning the registrant.
% Registrant and onsite contact information can be obtained through
use of the
% webbased whois service available from the EURid website
www.eurid.eu
```

2.5.1.2   CN, China   China has instituted what is called by some the strictest registration policy and by others a grave intrusion of privacy. The Chinese national registry requires a photographic identification to register a .CN domain name along with a "Letter of Commitment" declaring the registrant responsible for any misuse of the domain name.[57] It is not clear if this actually helps WHOIS accuracy or reduces abuse but is one being adopted by other ccTLDs.

2.5.1.3   NU, Niue   Niue is a tiny island nation in the Pacific,[58] which had granted an American company the authority to manage its registry and sell domain names around the world,[59] but the technical management is provided by the Swedish Internet Infrastructure Foundation.[60] The Port 43 WHOIS at whois.nic.nu does not return any contact information, but rather a list of handles. Prior to coming under the management of .SE, all of the .NU domains had a single WHOIS record that pointed to the registry for all contacts.

[56] http://domainsafrica.blogspot.com/2011/07/university-of-puerto-rico-files-lawsuit.html
[57] http://www.asiaregistry.com/domains/domains_cn.html
[58] http://www.gov.nu/wb/
[59] https://nunames.nu/who-we-are/
[60] https://www.iis.se/english/news/se-completes-successful-transition-of-the-nu-domain/

2.5.1.4   IT, Italy   In our discussions with Ruby-Whois developer Simone Cartelli, we reviewed the .IT WHOIS policies. Cartelli believes that .IT is one of the better registries for WHOIS accuracy and privacy. He claims that the "*Italian bureaucracy*" is effective within the .IT space to ensure valid information is collected and the information of individuals is protected. Personal sites have a limited amount of WHOIS details, no emails, addresses or phone numbers, only names and contact handles. Conversely, commercial domains have full disclosure.

2.5.1.5   US, United States   US prohibits WHOIS proxies and requires registrants to have a US nexus, meaning they must be a US citizen or a business or have some clear relationship to the United States. This is intended to cut down on fraud but has proven difficult to police. Illicit pharmacies from outside the United States have been easily registering domains for spamming with non-US details,[61] and some registrars openly offered privacy services within .US. This demonstrates that the policies of a registry are only as good as the enforcement at the registrar level. This is an example of an eNom-sponsored .US domain with private WHOIS:

```
Domain Name:                            GLURL.US
Domain ID:                              D33280669-US
Sponsoring Registrar:                   ENOM, INC.
Registrar URL (registration services):  whois.enom.com
Domain Status:                          clientHold
Registrant ID:                          B17E6C8A1BA44731
Registrant Name:                        James  Brown
Registrant Address1:                    Privite
Registrant City:                        Private
Registrant State/Province:              Private
Registrant Postal Code:                 Private
Registrant Country:                     United States
Registrant Country Code:                US
Registrant Phone Number:                +1.3167782233
Registrant Email:                       Private@private.org
```

2.5.2   IDNs

Domain name TLDs are now available in non-Latin character sets. Some of the major ones are Cyrillic, Chinese, and Arabic. However, IDNs are being deployed for dozens of different character sets and even have variations, for example, Traditional versus Standard Chinese. Many of the not-yet-deployed IDNs may be listed as being in test mode or under IDN evaluation.[62] This process impacts not only two-character ccTLDs but also standard gTLDs like .COM, .NET, and others that now have a variety of IDN equivalents.[63] The availability of different character sets grows constantly. Some of the available IDNs beyond

---

[61] http://www.circleid.com/posts/20100922_policy_failure_enables_mass_malware_part_i_rx_partners_vipmeds/
[62] http://www.icann.org/en/resources/idn
[63] http://www.iana.org/domains/idn-tables

the ones mentioned above include Devanagari, Hindi, Urdu, Telugu, Gujarati, Punjabi, Tamil, Bengali, Sinhalese, Hangul, and still more. The full list can be found at http://www. iana.org/domains/root/db.

2.5.3 Language versus Script

Some IDNs are designated as scripts and others as languages, and there is a subtle difference that is important to recognize. Where Russian is a language, it uses the Cyrillic, but so does Ukrainian. Compare this to Greek, which is both a language and a script.

The Russian country code is "RU." The equivalent characters in the Cyrillic alphabet are "Er" (which looks like a Latin P but is more akin to the Greek letter Rho) and "U" (which looks like a Latin Y but is derived from the Greek letter Upsilon). This combination would appear as "**РУ**." However, РУ is not the Russian IDN. The Russian IDN is "**РФ**" with the Cyrillic **Ф**—"Ef" character being equivalent to the Latin F. The IDN RF in fact stands for "Russian Federation" (Российская Федерация, or transliterated to "Rossiyskaya Federatsiya"). The ".RF" is not a ccTLD in the Latin script, but only in the Cyrillic. If you are not confused yet, further study in the IDN world eventually will confuse since the subtle changes in language, alphabet, character set, and TLD variations add layers of complexity to an already complex system. Then, add to this, languages that do not use atomic characters but rather logograms or syllable combinations to express words and ideas. Furthermore, we are discussing the technical underside, which is a study in and of itself.

2.5.4 ASCII

ASCII is an encoding set that matches our human-readable alphabet to numeric values that computers can process (notice the avoidance of "understand" since computers do not understand the way humans do, but rather they process values). The character set contains all 26 letters of the English alphabet (in upper- and lowercase), the numerals 0–9, and punctuation codes—basically anything that could be typed on an old manual typewriter, from which much of our data-entry technology evolved. This encoding also contains numerical values for basic instructions like line feed (LF) or vertical tab (VT). The development of this encoding was for early Teletype machines that would accept a key press of the letter A and convert it to the number 65. The numeric code would be processed by a local or remote device, which then printed the letter "A" on paper. On a manual typewriter, pressing the A key would mechanically move an arm with the letter A to an ink ribbon pressing it up against the paper manually. Electric typewriters and teletypes had to flex the "virtual arm" through code processing. As ingenious as this mapping from human letters to numeric codes and then back into human-readable printed letter was, the rapid application of this coding methodology to remote teletypes and then the early Internet left little room for foreign languages. Even European languages that use the Latin alphabet have additional characters and accent marks. While it is possible to write French, German, and Spanish using the English alphabet, there are severe limitations. One word with an accent mark over a vowel has a completely different meaning than one without. In a basic example, the Spanish word for "yes" is "sí" with an accent mark. Without the accent mark, "si," it actually means "if." The phrase "Yes, I am going" becomes "If I am going," which has completely different connotations. The difference here in terms of the Internet can cause a variety of difficulties including the basic problems of browsing the wrong website or delivering email to an incorrect location. The character set for the Internet has long been exclusively US-ASCII[64] but is changing due to innovation and cultural demand. IPs and various programming languages were developed using the most basic character set of the standard 26-letter English Alphabet, which has been met with varying degrees of frustration throughout the world.

2.5.5   Unicode

Unicode not only expands the available character sets for languages but also enables cross-platform communication as many legacy systems used character sets that were English based but not ASCII as developers adopted and created varying standards. The ASCII table itself only had 128 slots, which was itself limiting even for English-only processing. The Unicode Standard[65] is an internationally used set with room for one million different characters. Unicode is not only intended to be used for current languages but for historical ones as well including Egyptian hieroglyphics.[66] Unicode values are represented by a four-digit hexadecimal number (0–F) preceded by a capital U and plus sign, so Latin capital A is "U+0041" and value for the standard Arabic "Alef" is "U+0670". The Arabic Alef also has a corresponding HTML code of "ٰ", so compliant Internet browsers will interpret that code and display the appropriate character.[67] However, these encodings are specific to machine and software processing, and the Internet has an additional code set for domain names in non-Latin scripts. IDN conversions are discussed in RFC 3490,[68] 3491,[69] 3492,[70] and 3454.[71]

Punycodes allow the Unicode characters to be translated as domain name strings as the underlying structure of the Internet mostly continues to work from ASCII characters. So the IDN domain name must be converted into an ASCII string before being routed by the DNS. First, all IDN domain names are preceded, in their ASCII state with "xn--", to indicate that it is an IDN. Next, any Unicode characters within the domain name are removed from the string and appended at the end of the string with their punycode format. For example, we shall start with a very simple Swedish example, "besök.se", which has one non-Latin character. It would be displayed in punycode as

xn--besk-7qa.se

Entering this into a compliant browser converts this string and returns the website besök. se. This punycode version is what a WHOIS lookup would be performed on through any WHOIS client or command line that does not accept the Unicode characters. Sending a ping to besök.se will likely fail, but pinging xn--besk-7qa.se will return an IP address. Breaking this string up, we find that

xn-- is the IDN prefix

besk is the string without the Unicode character

---

[64] http://tools.ietf.org/html/rfc2046
[65] http://www.unicode.org/standard/principles.html
[66] http://www.iana.org/domains/idn-tables/tables/name_egyp_1.1.txt
[67] http://unicode-table.com/en/#control-character
[68] http://www.ietf.org/rfc/rfc3490.txt
[69] http://www.ietf.org/rfc/rfc3491.txt
[70] http://www.ietf.org/rfc/rfc3492.txt
[71] http://www.ietf.org/rfc/rfc3454.txt

-*7qa* is the encoding for ö and its placement in the order of the preceding string
.se is the Swedish TLD

The -*7qa* is the crucial part of the string. The leading hyphen indicates the beginning of the punycode encoding, and *7qa* is what needs to be calculated and converted. How this value is converted is through a fairly complex algorithm described in RFC 3492.[72]

2.5.6   Getting WHOIS Records for IDNs

IDN domain records lookup should start with obtaining the *punycode*. There are a number of punycode/Unicode converters available. In terms of referring to a standard authority, some of the registry websites are good especially when dealing with particular TLDs, for example, the PIR (.ORG), which offers through its registrars IDNs in Danish, Hungarian, Korean, Lithuanian, and other languages.[73] Using their punycode,[74] converter may be useful since the registry WHOIS is available on the same page. However, now that we can query on the IDN punycode, we may encounter a problem in parsing the WHOIS record itself, which could also contain Unicode characters. Many WHOIS parsers cannot properly translate or display these characters. Ram Mohan, CTO of the registry Afilias, presented the issue clearly in 2009 to ICANN's Security and Stability Advisory Committee[75] by quoting directly from RFC 4690,[76] which describes various issues concerning IDNs:

> …the whois protocol itself [RFC3912] has no standard capability for handling non-ASCII text: one cannot search consistently for, or report, either a DNS name or contact information that is not in ASCII characters.

The RFC Mohan refers to goes on to suggest moving to a proposed system called Internet Registry Information Service (IRIS), which is proposed in RFC 3982.[77] The WHOIS issues emerging from IDN deployment are used by Mohan as an example of the overall limitations of the existing WHOIS system. Mohan asks the audience: Can we deliver a better WHOIS service? He insists that this should be an ICANN board-level priority, but is not moving very quickly. WHOIS in other languages and character sets is not just a "nice to have." The lack of it presents dire consumer concerns in many countries, which requires policy and technical solutions.

2.6   WHOIS SERVICES

WHOIS can be queried by and from many services. The primary lookup tools are via command-line WHOIS clients and web-based WHOIS clients. This is partly because these two services are required by ICANN's contract with gTLD registrars. However, other options are available.

---

[72] http://tools.ietf.org/html/rfc3492
[73] http://www.pir.org/why/global/idn#q3
[74] http://pir.org/help/knowledge/punycode
[75] http://mex.icann.org/files/meetings/mexico2009/ssac-whois-usage-display-02mar09-en.pdf
[76] http://www.ietf.org/rfc/rfc4690.txt
[77] http://tools.ietf.org/html/rfc3982

2.6.1   Port 43 Command Line or Terminal

Computers (and now mobile device) users have become very comfortable with and actually expectant of graphic user interfaces (GUI). The use of visual tools in technology makes their function fast, accessible, and simple, but they are a relatively new invention in the world of computer and network technology. The command line still pervades our use even on the Internet. The search field on Google or Yahoo is technically a command line, as is the address bar in an Internet browser.

Command-line environments employ a prompt that is different on every system but usually reflects the environment, directory, or current user. The prompt is a space for you to enter instructions for the computer and usually sits there waiting. Commands typed in will appear next to the prompt. Press Enter or Return to execute the command. The results will be displayed as text in the window commonly followed by a new blank prompt.

All ICANN registrars are required to have an open WHOIS service open at Port 43.[78] Web services have traditionally been assigned to different ports, for example, web HTTP is assigned to port 80; port 25 is the SMTP port. However, this terminology is rapidly becoming archaic as most registrars have a dedicated subdomain called "whois" rather than simply an open port at their operational domain. We tend to think about web-based WHOIS versus command-line WHOIS, but most web queries are actually scripts that call on the command line and parse the results to a webpage.

When using command-line WHOIS, it is best to direct the query to a specific registrar or registry using the –h option, for example,

whois –h whois.dynadot.com dutyfreedepot-group.com

This example uses the –h option to specify whios.dynadot.com as the server to query for the domain dutyfreedepot-group.com. The results will be returned in machine-parsed text, which is important as some web-based WHOIS services will convert the text to image to prevent copying. Simply using

whois dutyfreedepot-group.com

may return the correct results depending on the WHOIS program used. As described earlier, using specific registrar servers is best for .COM and .NET, and registry servers are best for other gTLDs, for example,

whois –h whois.pir.org discountcigarettes24.org

will return results for the .ORG domain in the same tagged format each time, whereas using at the specific registrar

whois –h whois.publicdomainregistry.com discountcigarettes24.org

will return an untagged version that is harder to parse. Compare the two versions for the same domain below.

---

[78] http://www.icann.org/en/resources/registrars/raa/ra-agreement-21may09-en.htm#3.3.1

```
Domain ID:D160798149-LROR
Domain Name:DISCOUNTCIGARETTES24.ORG
Created On:30-Nov-2010 09:01:07 UTC
Last Updated On:05-Dec-2012 12:27:09 UTC
Expiration Date:30-Nov-2013 09:01:07 UTC
Sponsoring Registrar:PDR Ltd. d/b/a PublicDomainRegistry.com (R27-LROR)
Status:CLIENT TRANSFER PROHIBITED
Status:AUTORENEWPERIOD
Registrant ID:PP-SP-001
Registrant Name:Domain Admin
Registrant Organization:PrivacyProtect.org
Registrant Street1:ID#10760, PO Box 16
Registrant Street2:Note - All Postal Mails Rejected, visit Privacyprotect.or
Registrant Street3:
Registrant City:Nobby Beach
Registrant State/Province:
Registrant Postal Code:QLD 4218
Registrant Country:AU
Registrant Phone:+45.36946676
Registrant Phone Ext.:
Registrant FAX:
Registrant FAX Ext.:
Registrant Email:contact@privacyprotect.org
```

From the registry

```
Domain Name: DISCOUNTCIGARETTES24.ORG

Registrant:
     PrivacyProtect.org
     Domain Admin            (contact@privacyprotect.org)
     ID#10760, PO Box 16
     Note - All Postal Mails Rejected, visit Privacyprotect.org
     Nobby Beach
     null,QLD 4218
     AU
     Tel. +45.36946676

Creation Date: 30-Nov-2010
Expiration Date: 30-Nov-2013

Domain servers in listed order:
     ns1.dtrec.net
     ns2.dtrec.net
```

From the registrar

FIGURE 2.10   Command-line WHOIS.

2.6.2   Clients

Running your own WHOIS client is critical for testing and learning about WHOIS. WHOIS can be run on all the common platforms in a variety of ways. Installing a WHOIS GUI client will often give you access to a command-line WHOIS as well.

2.6.2.1   Apple/Mac   Apple computers typically come with a WHOIS command-line program. The command line is called Terminal and can be found in the Applications/ Utilities folder. Click the Terminal icon and a special window should open. Enter *whois* and a domain name. Entering *whois help* will produce an extended instruction set, and *whois?* will return a brief version. Unfortunately, the standard WHOIS client on MAC is fairly old

(1993) and has not been updated in new distributions. Calling help returns this, which is short and cryptic in comparison to other WHOIS help:

```
usage: whois [-aAbdgiIlmQrR6] [-c country-code | -h hostname]
[-p port] name ...
```

Our –h (hostname) switch is familiar, the –p (port) switch is self-explanatory if you need to switch from the default Port 43. However, –c (country) does not refer to ccTLDs but rather to the national location of the WHOIS server being queried, which is somewhat obsolete. Many of the -c servers are no longer operational. The -**aAbdgiIlmQrR6** options need more explaining, which unfortunately is not found by using *man whois* instead of *whois –help*. However, we were able to get the meaning from the source code[79]:

-a	whois.arin.net	host = ANICHOST;
-A	whois.apnic.net	host = PNICHOST;
-b	whois.abuse.net	host = ABUSEHOST;
-d	whois.nic.mil	host = DNICHOST;
-g	whois.nic.gov	host = GNICHOST;
-i	whois.networksolutions.com	host = INICHOST;
-I	whois.iana.org	host = IANAHOST;
-l	whois.lacnic.net	host = LNICHOST;
-m	whois.ra.net	host = MNICHOST;
-Q	.whois-servers.net	flags |= WHOIS_QUICK;
-r	whois.ripe.net	host = RNICHOST;
-R	deprecated use "-c ru" instead	
-6	whois.6bone.net	host = SNICHOST;

The default is NICHOST whois.crsnic.net. There were also three unreferenced server variables:

BNICHOST whois.registro.br

NORIDHOST whois.norid.no

GERMNICHOST de.whois-servers.net

Simone Cartelli,[80] an Italian software developer who has developed custom WHOIS tools in Ruby, was consulted about the outdated Mac WHOIS. Cartelli's Ruby-Whois 3.0[81] can be loaded onto MAC by using the terminal.

There are a few ways of opening the terminal window on a MAC. One is to press the command button and space bar at the same time, which will bring up the Spotlight search; type Terminal and it should appear in the list. Terminal can also be found in Finder under Applications in the Utilities folder. Once you have found it, you can drag a copy to the Desktop or the Dock:

gem install whois

Or use this version if you are not logged in as root:

sudo gem install whois

---

[79] http://www.opensource.apple.com/source/adv_cmds/adv_cmds-149/whois/whois.c?txt

[80] http://www.simonecarletti.com/

[81] http://www.simonecarletti.com/blog/2013/03/ruby-whois-3-0/

You will be prompted for the **su** or super user root password. Cartelli's full instructions can be found here: http://ruby-whois.org. This is a quick convenient way to upgrade your MAC WHOIS, but it will only work if certain dependencies are in place. Ruby WHOIS requires 1.9.2. or higher. Run the terminal command **ruby --version** to find out for sure. If your MAC does not have the latest version of Ruby, you may have to update a number of dependencies to proceed, including gem, **dvm**, command-line tools, Xcode, and the MAC OS. If your MAC is a few years old and has not been configured for code development, you will likely have to update all of them, but it is worth the time and investment if you want to use your MAC as an advanced WHOIS engine. Follow these steps:

1. Upgrade the MAC OS: OS X costs about $20 from the Apple Store.
2. 2. Install Xcode: This is a free add-on from the Apple Store.
3. Install Command Line Tool: This should also be free from the Apple Developer site.
4. Run this command to download Ruby:
   \curl -L https://get.rvm.io | bash -s stable --ruby
   (complete instructions: http://stackoverflow.com/questions/3696564/how-to-update-ruby-to-1-9-x-on-mac/14182172#14182172).
5. Run this command to load Ruby: **rvm reload**.
6. Finally run this to install Ruby WHOIS: **sudo gem install whois**.

The results should be this displayed like this:

```
Thank you for installing the whois gem!
If you like this gem, please support the project.
http://pledgie.com/campaigns/11383
Does your project or organization use this gem? Add it to the
apps wiki.
https://github.com/weppos/whois/wiki/apps

Are you looking for a quick and convenient way to perform
WHOIS queries?

Check out RoboWhois WHOIS API.
https://www.robowhois.com/
Successfully installed whois-3.3.1

Parsing documentation for whois-3.3.1
Installing ri documentation for whois-3.3.1
1 gem installed
```

To verify the installation, type **ruby-whois** with no arguments to see the instructions. It is also possible to install the WHOIS client on Mac by Marco d'Itri using Debian.

MAC Utilities from the App Store
- Whois by Paul Chatwin/The Apps Pod[82]
- QuickWho by Kevin Walzer/WordTech Communications, LLC[83]

---

[82] https://itunes.apple.com/us/app/whois/id447588653
[83] https://itunes.apple.com/us/app/quickwho/id495380540

- nsCherry by Tomoyuki Okawa/MacHouse[84]
- iVerify by Tomoyuki Okawa/MacHouse[85]
- GUI Dig by Ranko Rodic EmbeddedSoft[86]

2.6.2.2 Microsoft/Windows Windows computers do not have a command-line WHOIS bundled. However, there are plenty of options. Coding and compiling your own client are covered in the chapter on WHOIS code. These examples are downloadable installations of WHOIS clients.

Windows Sysinternals Whois by Mark Russinovich Created by Mark Russinovich, technical fellow at Microsoft and author of *Windows Internals*,[87] this precompiled executable can be downloaded from the TechNet site,[88] which is a common support site for Windows systems. Russinovich, like many developers, has a passion for this analysis, so he wanted a WHOIS with good functionality, but could not find a simple, free, reliable tool for Windows. This client is a completely clean creation not based on previous versions. His passion expands to speculative concepts as well as the author of the fictional novels *Zero Day*[89] and *Rogue Code*.[90] These books bring technology dangers to life in ways dry technical texts often cannot.

Unzip the compressed file and place it in a convenient folder and then navigate to that directory from the command line. If you are running and testing multiple WHOIS versions, it is a good idea to put them in different folders and use unique names for each EXE. Just be sure to use that custom name instead of *"whois"* when calling the program from the command line.

To open a command line in Windows prior to version 8, open the Start menu, select Run, and enter *cmd* in the field. In Windows 8, the Start menu has been removed, so we have to do a little extra work. To simply open the command line, press the WIN button and X (or WIN+R to open the Run field), and a menu should open with one of the options being "Command Prompt." One method is to create a simple batch file that will allow us to access the command line on demand. Create an empty text file on the Desktop and edit it. Enter "CMD.EXE" as the only line in the file and save it as "commandline.bat". Be sure there is no ".txt" on the end of the file; it must end in ".bat". Double-clicking on this file should open a DOS command-line terminal window. If you prefer using the new Windows Apps, you can conduct a search for "CMD"; right-click the icon and select "Pin to Taskbar" to make it available there.

To move to the directory where the whois.exe is, use this command:

$$cd <full\text{-}directory\text{-}name>$$

cd stands for "change directory" and the easiest way is to copy and paste the full directory name from the Windows Explorer folder.

Unlike other versions of WHOIS, the order of the command is *whois <domain-name> <whois-server>* instead of *whois –h <whois-server> <domain-name>*. If this client is

---

[84] https://itunes.apple.com/us/app/nscherry/id653424760

[85] https://itunes.apple.com/us/app/iverify/id439169757

[86] https://itunes.apple.com/us/app/dig/id527447387

[87] http://www.amazon.com/Windows-Internals-Part-Covering-Server/dp/0735648735

[88] http://technet.microsoft.com/en-us/sysinternals/bb897435

[89] http://www.amazon.com/Zero-Day-Novel-Mark-Russinovich/dp/1250007305

[90] http://www.amazon.com/Rogue-Code-Novel-Mark-Russinovich/dp/1250035376

queried without a WHOIS server designation, the program will first check whois-servers. net for the correct server. whois-servers.net is run by CenterGate Research.[91] This version has a –v switch that allows for redirections to be displayed.

GNU-whois for Win32   This more extensive GNU-whois for Win32 client created by Yuyunwu[92] can be downloaded from sourceforge.net.[93] GNU is a free software Unix-variant operating system.[94] Unlike the zipped executable program from Sysinternals, it must be complied, but Yuyunwu made this process simple. Download and extract the file whois-for-win32.zip from http://whoiswin.sourceforge.net or http://sourceforge.net/p/whoiswin/wiki/Home/. Within the extraction folder, there are two batch files: make_vs.bat and make_mingw32.bat. Double-clicking these will create two versions of a WHOIS client in a subdirectory called "output."

Intelligent WHOIS Client[95] by Marco d'Itri   This is a command-line client available through debian.org,[96] which parses queries and finds the correct server. Marco d'Itri also maintains the library for Ruby-WHOIS.[97] He has commented on WHOIS development and stated in a brief email exchange that he believes that Port 43 may not exist for much longer and that the continued lack of consensus in ccTLD WHOIS has created a "jungle" within the DNS architecture. He is considered an authority among other WHOIS programmers as source comments make reference to whether or not d'Itri lists this or that WHOIS server.[98] The d'Itri WHOIS documentation is found at http://www.unix.com/man-page/Linux/1/whois.

WhoisCL v1.58 by Nir Sofer   The main WHOIS client can be downloaded at http://www. nirsoft.net/utils/whoiscl.html and has two interesting options. The –r switch will remove remark text from the returned WHOIS record, and –n will find the correct server for your query from xx.whois-servers.net, instead of using the internal WHOIS servers list.
   Sofer offers other WHOIS-related clients with varying objectives:

- IPNetInfo[99] is a graphic tool for examining IP records.
- WhosIP[100] is a command-line utility that queries IP address information from WHOIS.
- WhoisThisDomain[101] is a graphic interface for retrieving registration data.
- IPInfoOffline[102] lets you check IP information from an offline database rather than making an actual connection.

---

[91] http://www.centergate.com/rjoffe.html
[92] http://sourceforge.net/u/yuyunwu/profile/
[93] http://whoiswin.sourceforge.net/
[94] http://www.gnu.org/
[95] http://packages.debian.org/sid/whois
[96] See note 95.
[97] http://ruby-whois.org/about/
[98] http://www.phpschool.com/gnuboard4/bbs/board.php?bo_table=tipntech&wr_id=34606&sca=%C1%A4%BA%B8&page=20
[99] http://www.nirsoft.net/utils/ipnetinfo.html
[100] http://www.nirsoft.net/utils/whosip.html
[101] http://www.nirsoft.net/utils/whois_this_domain.html
[102] http://www.nirsoft.net/utils/ip_country_info_offline.html

2.6.2.3   Unix/Linux   In the history section of this text, we reviewed early host systems like ITS written in assembly languages. In the 1970s, AT&T (Bell Labs) developed the Unix operating system[103] and the higher-level programming language C.[104] These two innovations would forever change computing and Internet technology. The Unix would become the standard for running various network services, and Ken Harrenstien would use C to convert early Internet software from assembly language, including WHOIS. In 1991, Linus Torvalds developed a free operating system that could run a variety of systems but functioned like Unix. Today, there are dozens of different implementations of Linux.

JWhois   Common distributions of Linux come bundled with JWhois, which can be called either *jwhois* or *whois* in a Linux shell. This, like the MAC WHOIS version, is old, even though your Linux may have the most recent version, which is 4.0. To check your JWhois version on Linux, open a terminal shell window and run this command:

jwhois --version

Even if you have JWhois 4.0, it is worth trying to see if there is an update by running

sudo yum install jwhois

The system will prompt for the root password and then attempt an update. However, this response may be displayed:

```
Package jwhois-4.0-8.fc10.i386 already installed and latest version
Nothing to do
```

One might think that the J in "JWhois" stands for Java®, but it does not; it was actually originally written in Perl and represents the author Jonas Oberg. Oberg originally wrote his version of the WHOIS to handle ccTLD calls properly, referring them to the proper registry. Because his bug-reporting email address for the client is imbedded in the code, he still regularly receives abuse reports from people who do not understand that his email is not part of the WHOIS record. Given JWhois is free GNU[105] software, Oberg has been looking for a new maintainer, which can be difficult to recruit. "*I think the general problem here is that it seems difficult to find people today that have an interest in contributing to core infrastructure tools,*" wrote Oberg in our email interview. "*The amount of people who'd like to work on such a rudimentary project is quite limited. While there's been quite a bit of interest from people employed at registrars around the world in contributing changes to the configuration files, no one has generally felt that they had enough time to devote to taking over the role as maintainer.*"[106] What does it mean to be a GNU maintainer? GNU is run by the Free Software Foundation[107] and promotes a collaborative and

---

[103] http://www.unix.org/what_is_unix/history_timeline.html
[104] http://www.nytimes.com/2011/10/14/technology/dennis-ritchie-programming-trailblazer-dies-at-70.html?hp&_r=0
[105] http://www.gnu.org/gnu/about-gnu.html
[106] Oberg interview
[107] http://www.fsf.org/

volunteer approach to system development. The project is supported by people who like to code, share ideas, and volunteer their time. If you want to become a GNU maintainer, contact the project coordinators at maintainers@gnu.org.

Some JWhois Options

- Help: *jwhois –help*
- Use a configuration file: *jwhois –c <filename>*. This optional file can be used to create your own list of WHOIS servers, as a way of extending or updating the static list of servers. The file accessed by default is called "jwhois.conf". This contains a list of regular expressions that parse the domain or IP and determine the best server to use. These are four lines from the file as a sample:

```
"\\.org$" = "whois.publicinterestregistry.net";
"\\.pe$" = "whois.nic.pe";
"\\.pk$" = "pknic.net.pk";
"\\.pl$" = "whois.dns.pl";
```

It is within this file that you would add new gTLDs or modifications to existing servers. A sample version of the config file can be seen at http://linuxmafia.com/pub/linux/network/jwhois.conf.

- Specify server: *jwhois –h whois.ripe.net*. This overrides the config file settings.
- Specify a port: *jwhois –p 43*. While Port 43 is assumed, it is not always the port used.
- Force a new lookup as opposed to using a cached WHOIS response: *jwhois –f* or use *jwhois –d* to disable the cache.
- Block a redirection in lookup, *jwhois –n*, or display redirections, *jwhois -i*
- Keep client from altering your query as typed: *jwhois –a*
- Use RWhois, *jwhois –r*, and display the RWhois results, *jwhois –rwhois-display=DISPLAY*

There is additional documentation for UBUNTU Linux here maintained by Marco d'Itri at http://manpages.ubuntu.com/manpages/lucid/man1/whois.1.html.

Linux Shell   Linux has very powerful shell scripting utilities that can be combined with the WHOIS stream output. Developers and administrators like Luke Sheppard[108] prefer the power of the Unix-based command-line environment. The WHOIS command-line utility is fast and concise and can be scripted for automated lookups. Sheppard has published tutorials[109] demonstrating the use of **alias**,[110] **head**,[111] and **grep**[112] to extract WHOIS data. "Grep" stands for *globally search a regular expression and print* and matches strings and patterns. He points out that not only can WHOIS lookups be augmented on the fly, but

---

[108] https://www.tcpiplab.com/things-ive-written-or-co-authored/
[109] http://answers.oreilly.com/topic/408-how-to-use-and-understand-whois-in-its-many-forms/
[110] http://www.computerhope.com/unix/ualias.htm
[111] http://www.computerhope.com/unix/uhead.htm
[112] http://www.computerhope.com/unix/ugrep.htm

system settings can be used to empower WHOIS in Linux. *"You can make your life easier by putting things like this in your **.bash_profile**:"*[113]

alias arin= "whois -h whois.arin.net"

alias afrinic= "whois -h whois.afrinic.net"

These alias assignments allow for lookups like

arin "electronic frontier foundation" | grep NET | awk "{print $(NF-2), $(NF-1), $NF}"

which should return

```
64.147.188.0 - 64.147.188.31
209.237.230.64 - 209.237.230.79
```

Then you can quickly look up the IP address that sent a suspicious looking email message about your bank account in North America:

arin 41.205.188.2 | head -3

```
OrgName:    African Network Information Center
OrgID:      AFRINIC
```

It is not from North America at all, but somewhere in Africa. Continue with

afrinic 41.205.188.2 | grep -i -B 1 country

to see

```
descr:      Assigned to Lagos dial-pool customers
country:    NG
```

So this is not from your bank. You should alert the network operator, who can be found with

afrinic 41.205.188.2 | grep mail

returning

```
e-mail: navneets@starcomms.com
e-mail: adminit@starcomms.com
```

To warn your actual bank, find their contacts with

whois bofa.com | grep -i -e abuse -e mail:

This returns

```
Registrar Abuse Contact Email: compliance@markmonitor.com
Registrar Abuse Contact Phone: +1.2083895740
```

[113] Sheppard interview

```
Registrant Email: Domain.Administrator@bankofamerica.com
Admin Email: Domain.Administrator@bankofamerica.com
Tech Email: hostmaster@bankofamerica.com
```

Sheppard understands the importance of identifying remote sources of information, not only for online communications but also for wireless communication as a shortwave radio enthusiast. Call signs are a critical component of radio communication. When sharing a public communication space, there is a mutual responsibility to follow procedures and not abuse channel access. Without remote identification and respect, the network falls apart.

2.6.3 Representational State Transfer (RESTFul) WHOIS

RESTful is a very fancy term for building a dynamic web-based structure for data delivery rather than directly accessing the database. RESTful puts an interface between the client and the data source, which is not new and is the way most web services work. As we have covered, WHOIS has not quite caught up with the times, and applying this model to WHOIS may solve many of its inherent problems. IP registries like ARIN and RIPE are already offering RESTful services. The RIPE RESTful database is at rest.db.ripe.net and their API is explained at https://github.com/RIPE-NCC/whois/wiki/WHOIS-REST-API. As this applies to WHOIS, rather than using some of our clunky WHOIS clients with potentially incompatible options for different servers, we use just URLs to retrieve data in this kind of format:

```
http://rest.db.ripe.net/{source}/{objecttype}/{key}
```

A source is one of the RIPE databases, an object type is all the field types in a RIPE record, and the key is specific information. You will note these functions just like a directory structure within the URL, which is the point. The WHOIS data can be accessed through XML or JavaScript Object Notation (JSON). As for applying this to domain names, this is the goal of the WEIRDS, which is explained in the previous chapter. A good example of the application is RoboWhois, a RESTful WHOIS API that uses the cloud (https://www.robowhois.com/).

2.6.4 Web-Based WHOIS

Using Web-Based WHOIS has benefits especially having the access to proxy, which records the server's IP address instead of yours when performing queries. We have covered the InterNIC web-based WHOIS in several examples earlier. Here, we focus on third-party WHOIS sites and registrar interfaces.

2.6.4.1 What Happened to SamSpade.org? One of the earliest and most popular Internet record research tools was called SamSpade after the Dashiell Hammett detective from the *Maltese Falcon* novel and film of the same name starring Humphrey Bogart. Developed by Steve Atkins, the site handled WHOIS and DNS queries of various kinds but went dark around 2004 and has displayed the message "Back soon" ever since. The site had quite a following among the antiabuse and investigative crowds. The SANS

Institute even released a guide to SamSpade in 2003.[114] tcpiputils.com offers the same kind of multiple lookup facilities.[115]

2.6.4.2   Geektools.com by CenterGate Research   The site uses a CAPTCHA code[116] entry per submission and limits the number of queries allowed. The GeekTools service is reliable and one of the best available. GeekTools will often return results when other methods have failed.

In an effort to combat the increasing abuse of this system, you must now enter the text shown in the image below in the **Key** field before submitting a query. There are no spaces. Lynx users (and others with a standard whois client) may wish to point their client at whois.geektools.com.
Why did we do this?

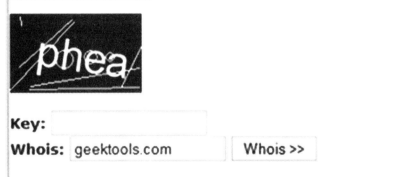

Key:

Whois: geektools.com   **Whois >>**

FIGURE 2.11   GeekTools WHOIS with CAPTCHA code entry.

[114] http://www.sans.org/reading-room/whitepapers/tools/sam-spade-934
[115] http://www.tcpiputils.com/
[116] http://www.captcha.net/

2.6.4.3 DomainTools DomainTools.com is actually a domain name registrar who specializes in collecting and selling WHOIS records. They allow a number of free lookups and offer tiered services for various rates. Their historical services are covered in more detail later in this chapter.

2.6.5 Telnet to WHOIS Server

The VeriSign HELP response at InterNIC.net contains this instruction:

```
Q, QUIT, or hit RETURN    Exits WHOIS.
```

If all the examples of WHOIS we have looked at so far are set up to issue a query and then disconnect, why would we need a *QUIT* command to exit? These are instructions to use when directly connecting through *Telnet*.

Today, we have Internet browsers and personal computers, which are luxuries. In the days of old, computer systems were accessed through *dumb terminals*, which merely passed instructions from the keyboard to the network and then displayed the results on the screen, usually in one color only. There were no processor and no disk drives, just the command line and the response from the server. Because there were different terminal manufacturers and different host software running on individual networks, a common virtual interface was needed to interface between various types of equipment. First discussed in RFC 15, *Network Subsystem for Time Sharing Hosts*[117] (1969), Telnet constantly evolved as a standard. Its function was formalized by Jon Postel in 1972[118] and updated by Postel in 1983.[119] In general, Telnet represents a critical concept of computing: a platform-independent interface, which, in many ways, is a precursor to web browsing.

As disk drives and local processing were integrated with these terminals, the personal computer began to emerge. However, even as the computing power moved to our desktops, we still needed to be able to access remote servers through a terminal emulator. Telnet is a protocol that allows us to access a server remotely and interact with it as if we were using a terminal directly connected to it. While our WHOIS calls from clients only connect long enough to submit a query and receive a response, early WHOIS services were done through a direct connection with the WHOIS server and the database through Telnet. It is still possible to connect to some WHOIS servers with Telnet, but the interaction is limited and fewer servers offer it. Being able to connect directly to a server at the command-line level is a security threat. WHOIS through Telnet is simply not practical for current use because of display and capture limitations. For most of the current needs of WHOIS, Telnet is not suitable, but remains a historic curiosity with a clear fingerprint in current systems, which link back to teletype. However, this is how the procedure would have gone, starting with this command:

telnet whois.internic.net 43

The Telnet port is commonly 23, but here we use the WHOIS Port 43. Once connected, at the prompt a user would type 'WHOIS' to connect to the registry services (rs) database. The terminal prompt would change to 'whois:' which would be used to query a domain name.

---

[117] https://tools.ietf.org/html/rfc15
[118] https://tools.ietf.org/html/rfc318
[119] http://tools.ietf.org/html/rfc854

Now, InterNIC allows telnet connections to Port 43 but will immediately disconnect after issuing the requested record.

Trying to create a telnet connection to IANA.ORG produces interesting results. The server will allow a connection but disconnects after one query. Attempting detailed queries will often produce the message "*use –h for help.*" However, entering **–h** produces the message "*For query help and examples please see* http://www.iana.org/whois_for_dummies." The IANA page no longer exists. Efforts to track down the archived content of this guide were not successful. IANA's telnet connections only return top-level data for queries, for example, it will return the PIR root servers for "iana.org". This is to be expected since the IANA database would only have top-level data.

According to the most recent RIPE guide,[120] they still allow Telnet connections to Port 43. There is no login for the connection and the prompt is blank. Simply type an IP address like 193.0.6.139, and the record will be returned and then the connection will be terminated. RIPE has a mirroring database accessible through Telnet at nrtm.db.ripe.net via Port 4444, but it requires an account[121]. More documentation is available[122].

Telnet should be available on Unix-based systems. On Windows, it may be necessary to turn the service on as it is typically no longer loaded by default. Use the instructions from Microsoft TechNet[123]. There are also several GUI Telnet clients available, which may be easier to use than Windows Telnet[124]. There are still a number of open Telnet servers available for testing and experimentation (http://www.telnet.org/htm/places.htm).

2.6.6   More Services, Software, and Packages

- Whois v1.36 by Jeroen Kessels : http://www.kessels.com/whois/
- net.demon Windows tools used on Unix systems, such as Whois, Ping, and Traceroute, and over 35 other tools: http://netdemon.net/
- DomainPunch Domain Name Portfolio Management: http://www.domainpunch.com/
- PingPlotter: http://www.pingplotter.com/manual/standard/undocftrswhois.html
- Perl WHOIS (pwhois): A Perl-based[125] WHOIS client for Linux or platforms running Perl. This client has additional switches:

  -s Copyright and disclaimer strip

  -c Return an empty answer for search failures

  -e Drop connection if rate to server has been exceeded

  -T Timeout for connection attempts

  -t Turn on caching

  -a Specify an IP address for source

  –d Debug mode

  -F Display first result in recursive calls (or -L for the last)

  -A Return all recursive results

---

[120] See note 44.

[121] http://www.ripe.net/data-tools/support/documentation/nrtm-agreement-and-terms-conditions-of-use

[122] http://www.ripe.net/data-tools/support/documentation/mirroring

[123] http://technet.microsoft.com/en-us/library/cc771275%28v=ws.10%29.aspx

[124] http://www.putty.org/

[125] http://search.cpan.org/~dhudes/Net-Whois-1.9/Whois.pm

- RIPE Client: Download at http://sourceforge.net/projects/whois/files/. Be sure to call this version with "whois3" from the command line. Available options are:

-h Change WHOIS sever queried

-p Specify port number other than 43

-4 Use IPv4

-6 Use IPv6

-k Request persistent connection for batch lookups

-R Turn off referral lookups on domains

-r Turn off recursion

-a Specify sources available with -q source query

-s List sources to be used in queries separated by commas

-F Output using short hand notation for attribute names.

-K Return only primary keys

-k Persistent connection for batch lookups

-g Near Real Time Mirroring (NRTM) service[126]—This is only available with a RIPE account

-l First-level less specific IP objects

-L Returns all IP objects

-m First-level more specific IP objects

-M All level more specific IP objects

-x Exact matches

-d Use the switches -**m**, -**M**, -**l**, and -**L** for reverse delegation domain lookups

-i Inverse queries on record objects, invoked with –*i xx* "*abc123*" where –**i** calls the switch, **xx** is the specific call code, and "**abc123**" is the string searched for:

    ac admin-c, a nic-handle or person-name. nic-handle is a person or role object that matches a nic-handle attribute query.

    ah author, a nic-handle or person-name.

    pn admin-c, tech-c, zone-c, author or cross-nfy.

    ct cross-mnt or mntner-name "Maintainer".

    cn cross-nfy, could be nic-handle or person-name.

    la local-as, an as-number. as-number is an ANS.

    mr mbrs-by-ref, an mntner-name.

    mo member-of, a set-name. set-name is a primary key that matches the query argument.

    mb mnt-by, a mntner-name.

    ml mnt-lower, lower-level mntner-name.

    mn mnt-nfy, an email.

    mu mnt-routes, a– returns all aut-num, inetnum by mntner-name.

    ny notify, an email.

    ns nserver, domain-name or ip-lookup for nameservers.

    i an as-name.

---

[126] http://www.ripe.net/data-tools/db/nrtm-mirroring

rb referral-by, a mntner-name.

rz rev-srv, a domain-name or ip-lookup, returns inetnum and inet6num network names. ip-lookup is an IPv4 address prefix, range, or single address.

sd sub-dom, domain-name as a subdomain.

tc tech-c, a nic-handle or person-name.

dt upd-to, an email.

zc zone-c, nic-handle or person-name.

2.6.7 WHOIS Functions, Switches, and Tricks

Because of the variety of WHOIS servers, databases, formats, permission, and clients, there is no single list of WHOIS commands that will work universally. There are, of course, some powerful lookups that can be used on the greater population of WHOIS record:

- Getting more from VeriSign: For .COM and .NET, use a specific command-line query via InterNIC to get both the Thin and Thick record: *whois –h whois.internic.net "domain amazon.com"*. Does not work in every instance; apparently depends on the registrar availability since it is a referral from VeriSign.
- Stripping the Disclaimer: Many WHOIS clients have the built-in ability to remove disclaimers, copyrights, and advertisements from the registrar. This is the first step in efficiently parsing WHOIS records. Since there is a lack of standards in WHOIS, it is important to check the help file of any WHOIS client being used to see if it is supported and what the specific switch is, for example, the Perl WHOIS switch is **–s**.
- Breaking the output into pages to scroll in Windows DOS (using the pipe "|"):

whois example.com|more

Or on Linux:

whois example.com|less

- It is possible to use WHOIS wild cards "**...**" to find domain names and return lists of similar names. For example, it is possible to find all the domains that start with "cosmic" in .NET and .COM with

whois –h whois.internic.net cosmic...

This will return up to 50 alphabetical results (partial results example):

```
Aborting search 50 records found .....
COSMIC-AVIATORS-AND-THE-GOLDEN-STONE-OF-ETHOS.COM
COSMIC-AVIATION.COM
COSMIC-AURA.COM
COSMIC-AUDIO.COM
COSMIC-AUCTION.NET
COSMIC-AUCTION.COM
```

```
COSMIC-ATTRACTION.COM
COSMIC-ASTROLOGY.COM
COSMIC-ASLONGAS-RESPECTABILITY.COM
COSMIC-ASCENSION.COM
...
```

By adding the **full** keyword to the search, the actual records can be retrieved. Keep in mind this could be a lot of data, so it is useful to narrow the search based on what is being sought:

whois –h whois.internic.net "full cosmic-angel…"

This should return a list of the domains with details (again, briefed here):

```
Using WHOIS server whois.internic.net, port 43, to find full
cosmic-angel...

Whois Server Version 2.0

Domain names in the .com and .net domains can now be
registered
with many different competing registrars. Go to http://www.
internic.net
for detailed information.

    Domain Name: COSMIC-ANGELS.COM
    Registrar: TUCOWS DOMAINS INC.
    Whois Server: whois.tucows.com
    Referral URL: http://domainhelp.opensrs.net
    Name Server: NS.NAMESPACE4YOU.COM
    Name Server: NS2.NAMESPACE4YOU.COM
    Status: clientTransferProhibited
    Status: clientUpdateProhibited
    Updated Date: 06-jul-2013
    Creation Date: 13-apr-2008
    Expiration Date: 13-apr-2014

    Domain Name: COSMIC-ANGEL.NET
    Registrar: GMO INTERNET, INC. DBA ONAMAE.COM
    Whois Server: whois.discount-domain.com
    Referral URL: http://www.onamae.com
    Name Server: 01.DNSV.JP
    Name Server: 02.DNSV.JP
    Status: ok
    Updated Date: 24-feb-2011
    Creation Date: 03-oct-2003
    Expiration Date: 03-oct-2014
    ...
```

2.6.8   Obscure, Archaic, and Obsolete WHOIS Services

- WHOIS By email was once possible by sending a message to mailserv@ds.internic. net with the *whois* and the domain name in the subject line. RIPE document 157 in Section 2.1.5 provides instructions for sending WHOIS queries to whois@ripe.net,[127] but this address is no longer active. RFC 1032, *Domain Administrator's Guide* by Mary Stahl, lists similar instructions for service@sri-nic.arpa,[128] but this no longer responds either.

- HORTON provided a method for creating a directory of email addresses. Users can look up email addresses knowing only a fragment of the name or username of the person in question, with the command *whois -h horton_server search_key* where horton_server is the name of the computer running Horton and search_key is the fragment of the name. All people whose names or usernames match the pattern are listed, one per line.[129]

- UWHO simple tool for accessing the many whois servers on the Internet. It lets you look for somebody's email address without knowing the details of where such information is kept.[130]

- California State University Sacramento Name Lookup Service: A mail service that allowed an email to be sent to a person at an organization without knowing their exact email address, which would perform a database lookup on the fly.[131]

- LDAP-WHOIS++ Lightweight Directory Access Protocol[132] (LDAP) is an extensible protocol for accessing an X.500 directory service.[133] The UC Davis uses LDAP for its personnel lookup directories.[134]

- BUNYIP Information Systems WHOIS++ server "whoisd" implements the basic WHOIS++ protocol and functionality as described in the draft RFC from the WNILS Working Group of the IETF.[135]

- KTH whois++ Server: Prototype implementation of the whois++ protocol in Perl code.[136]

- LUT whois++ Server: Generates an inverted tree of whois++ template data.[137]

- Wide Area Information Servers (WAIS): A client–server text searching system[138] using the Z39.50-1988 protocol for information retrieval.[139] RIPE document 157 in Section 2.1.3 provides instruction for connecting and querying through WAIS.[140]

---

[127] http://ftp.ripe.net/ripe/docs/ripe-157.txt
[128] http://tools.ietf.org/html/rfc1032
[129] Matt Power List of publicly available whois-server source code, 7 November 1993 "whois-servers.source."
[130] See note 129.
[131] See note 129.
[132] http://tools.ietf.org/html/rfc4510
[133] See note 129.
[134] http://directory.ucdavis.edu/PeopleSearch.htm
[135] See note 129.
[136] See note 129.
[137] See note 129.
[138] http://www.ietf.org/rfc/rfc1625.txt
[139] http://www.loc.gov/z3950/agency/markup/01.html
[140] See note 127.

- RADAR: The ICANN Registrar Database is at radar.icann.org. This is ICANN's system for updating contact listings specifically for communication between ICANN and for the public directories at InterNIC. This has also started to include Transfer Emergency Action Contact (TEAC), which is intended to improve domain transfers between registrars. Emails sent to the registrar TEAC address must be responded to by a human.
- WHOIS on fred via X.500 [2]: Not to be confused with the Forensic Registry EDitor,[141] this was FRont End to Directories that had WHOIS[142] with very flexible functionality.

REFERENCES

1   Karrenberg D., Ross G., Wilson P., and Nobile L. Development of the Regional Internet Registry System, http://www.cisco.com/web/about/ac123/ac147/archived_issues/ipj_4-4/regional_internet_registries.html (accessed June 20, 2015).
2   Gilster, P. 1994. Find it on the Internet. New York: John Wiley & Sons, Inc.

---

[141] http://epyxforensics.com/node/41
[142] http://robmorton.20m.com/software/prognotes/intdum/index.htm

3

RESEARCH AND INVESTIGATIONS

As Dr. Hank Brightman, Director of Applied Research and Analysis at the United States Naval War College, says in *Today's White Collar Crime*, "*Computers afford criminals a wide range of tools to engage in everything from credit card fraud to blackmail and espionage.*"[1] However, so much of digital forensics, for good reason, is particularly focused on actual computers and not as much on the global network. Computer crime, as it is, moved off the desktop a long time ago. Illicit traffic and crime can be wholly conducted without a home computer, that is, over the Internet from changing locations, making the investigator preoccupation with seizing hard disk data only one piece of the puzzle. A new discipline in Internet forensics is emerging with a variety of opportunities and pitfalls. WHOIS is an enormous part of this endeavor, but in this author's experience, otherwise competent investigators are oblivious to the depth of WHOIS.

Domains are simply another criminal tool, a platform for launching attacks, deceiving consumers, and collecting money. In *Crimeware*: *Understanding New Attacks and Defenses* by Markus Jakobsson and Zulfikar Ramzan, the authors lay out a multitude of ways by which domain names can be used in cybercrime but cited specific cases emerging around the 2008 US presidential election. An explosion of domain speculation, cybersquatting, campaign fund phishing, and other abuses occurred during one of the most competitive national elections in decades. As part of Jakobsson and Zulfikar's research, they created some custom tools that included WHOIS queries to determine if various election-related domain names were malicious. By conducting proper WHOIS analysis, they were able to confirm that certain sites were malicious or registered in bad faith including domains intended for syphoning off political contributions from unsuspecting voters. Here is an excellent example of the Domain Name System (DNS) being used as a weapon against

[1] Today's White Collar Crime

---

consumers and WHOIS analysis being the potential tool for defending the consumer. For criminals, domain name abuse is a ripe opportunity. With no verification of WHOIS, with the partnership of rogue registrars, and with no enforcement from ICANN, there exists an unholy trinity that locks cybercrime victims out of the process.

3.1 COMPLETELY DISASSEMBLING A WHOIS RECORD

Conducting Internet investigations means using WHOIS, and even if the WHOIS record is falsified or privacy protected, it can still yield useful clues. Every piece of the WHOIS record can potentially lead to more information, additional domains, hosting companies, commercial entities, and illicit suspects.

3.1.1 A Normal, Safe Domain: cnn.com

Starting with simple example, the news domain cnn.com, we will completely deconstruct and verify the details. The analysis here is extremely detailed because in tracking domain activity, every minor detail is important. The point of the exercise is to demonstrate that every detail can be verified. We will do the same with a few malicious sites to compare the difference. First, we perform a generic WHOIS query by using either our command-line client with *whois cnn.com* or the main web WHOIS at Internic.net, selecting the "Domain" radio button.[2]

Because the VeriSign .COM registry is thin, we will likely receive this record, which does not have the registrant contact data but has important details nevertheless:

```
Domain Name: CNN.COM
Registrar: CSC CORPORATE DOMAINS, INC.
Whois Server: whois.corporatedomains.com
Referral URL: http://www.cscglobal.com
Name Server: NS1.P42.DYNECT.NET
Name Server: NS1.TIMEWARNER.NET
Name Server: NS2.P42.DYNECT.NET
Name Server: NS3.TIMEWARNER.NET
```

Whois Search

cnn.com

◉ Domain (ex. internic.net)
○ Registrar (ex. ABC Registrar, Inc.)
○ Nameserver (ex. NS.EXAMPLE.COM or 192.16.0.192)

Submit

FIGURE 3.1 WHOIS domain request.

---

[2] http://www.internic.org/whois.html

```
Status: clientTransferProhibited
Status: serverDeleteProhibited
Status: serverTransferProhibited
Status: serverUpdateProhibited
Updated Date: 29-aug-2013
Creation Date: 22-sep-1993
Expiration Date: 21-sep-2018
```

From the thin record, we learn the sponsoring registrar's name, the registrar's WHOIS server, the nameservers, the status, and registration dates. In order to get the full thick WHOIS record, we need to query the registrar's WHOIS server directly, but we should keep the thin record handy for comparison. At this point, we can use the command-line client with the specific server, *whois –h whois.corporatedomains.com cnn.com*, or visit the CSC CORPORATE DOMAINS, INC. website at http://www. cscglobal.com. These are important details because the registrar is required to have both a Port 43 WHOIS server and a web-based WHOIS page.[3] It would seem to make a lot more sense if InterNIC or VeriSign parsed this query on the server end and retrieved the thick record or at least provided a hyperlink to the CSC CORPORATE DOMAINS website within the results, but these are issues for discussion. Before we query the server, it is useful to verify the registrar as some registrars go by many names and sometimes false information appears in the "registrar" field.[4] There are a few things we can do: first cut and paste the registrar name string ("CSC CORPORATE DOMAINS, INC.") into the InterNIC WHOIS form and select the "Registrar" radio button.

Because this name was retrieved directly from the InterNIC/VeriSign database, it should be the same name used for the registrar record itself. In this case, this correct registrar WHOIS record is returned, but this does not happen all the time due to apparent inconsistencies in the database. We can also verify the registrar name at the InterNIC Registrar Directory (http://www.internic.net/alpha.html), the ICANN Registrar Contact list (http://www.icann.org/registrar-reports/accreditation-qualified-list.html), or the IANA Registrar ID list (http://www.iana.org/assignments/registrar-ids/registrar-ids.xhtml). For CSC

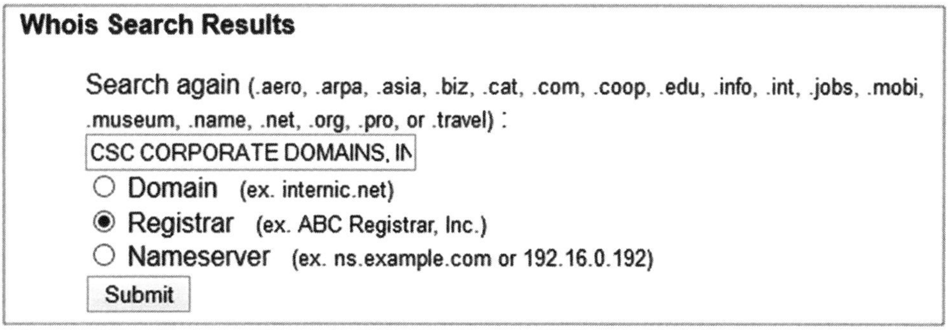

Whois Search Results

Search again (.aero, .arpa, .asia, .biz, .cat, .com, .coop, .edu, .info, .int, .jobs, .mobi, .museum, .name, .net, .org, .pro, or .travel) :

| CSC CORPORATE DOMAINS, IN |

○ Domain   (ex. internic.net)
◉ Registrar   (ex. ABC Registrar, Inc.)
○ Nameserver   (ex. ns.example.com or 192.16.0.192)

Submit

FIGURE 3.2 WHOIS registrar request.

---

[3] http://www.icann.org/en/resources/registrars/raa/ra-agreement-21may09-en.htm#3.3
[4] http://www.circleid.com/posts/20120327_fake_bank_site_fake_registrar/

Corporate, all three entries have the same name and spelling for the registrar, which is not the case for some. All of these locations have varying degrees of information about the registrar presented in different formats by separate groups that are all under the ICANN structure. For the sake of convenience and transparency to the Internet user, all relevant registrar information should be available in one location, but this does not appear to be a priority for ICANN.

Now, in reviewing the thick WHOIS record for cnn.com, we find that both the Port 43 and web WHOIS at CSC Corporate work flawlessly, but with slight variations. It is also important to note that the CSC Corporate web WHOIS was easy to locate, which is linked directly from the home page. The Port 43 for CSC Corporate appears to query the registrar WHOIS directly, while the web-based script checks InterNIC.net first for the correct server and then queries its own WHOIS database:

```
[QUERYING WHOIS.INTERNIC.NET]
[REDIRECTED TO WHOIS.CORPORATEDOMAINS.COM]
[QUERYING WHOIS.CORPORATEDOMAINS.COM]
[WHOIS.CORPORATEDOMAINS.COM]
```

Registrars are only required to WHOIS server data for domains they sponsor, so there is no need to return data for domains at other registrars, but there are a few ways by which this can be done. On the CSC Corporate Port 43 query, a request for a domain not sponsored by CSC Corporate, say, foxnews.com instead of cnn.com, returns "No match for foxnews.com." Conversely, the CSC Corporate web WHOIS checks InterNIC for the correct registrar and then retrieves that record from that server. CSC Corporate is not required to do this; they do so as a courtesy. Regardless, this demonstrates that different methods are available for checking domain data and redirecting queries. In the Port 43 method CSC Corporate WHOIS process simply checked its own database and finding nothing went no further, making no referrals. The full thick cnn.com record follows below, the terms and disclaimer have been removed. We will analyze the record line by line:

```
Registrant:
    Turner Broadcasting System, Inc.
    Domain Name Manager
    One CNN Center 13N
    Atlanta, GA 30303
    US
    Email: tmgroup@turner.com

Registrar Name....: CORPORATE DOMAINS, INC.
Registrar Whois...: whois.corporatedomains.com
Registrar Homepage: www.cscprotectsbrands.com

Domain Name: cnn.com

    Created on..............: Wed, Sep 22, 1993
    Expires on..............: Fri, Sep 21, 2018
    Record last updated on..: Thu, Nov 01, 2012
```

```
Administrative Contact:
    Turner Broadcasting System, Inc.
    Domain Name Manager
    One CNN Center 13N
    Atlanta, GA 30303
    US
    Phone: +1.4048275000
    Email: tmgroup@turner.com

Technical Contact:
    Turner Broadcasting System, Inc.
    TBS Server Operations
    One CNN Center 13N
    Atlanta, GA 30303
    US
    Phone: +1.4048275000
    Email: hostmaster@turner.com

DNS Servers:

ns1.p42.dynect.net
ns1.timewarner.net
ns2.p42.dynect.net
ns3.timewarner.net
```

The first line indicates that this is the registrant block of the record. The next six lines refer to the required registrant data for this domain. The fields in this block are untagged, so we have to make some assumptions about what data denotes what. The first entry, "Turner Broadcasting System, Inc.," appears to be a company or entity name, followed by the generic "Domain Name Manager," which would be invalid as registrant name if an entity name were not also provided. The next three lines appear to be the street address, city/state/zip code, and country, respectively. The last line is an email address that is useful, but not required for the registrant block. Phone numbers are not required in the registrant block either. Because they are not required, there is no requirement for them to be valid either.

For the purposes of this analysis, we will focus on the names and physical addresses in the registrant block, starting with the company name. Because the address given is in the US state of Georgia, we will check their business registration with the Secretary of State of Georgia Corporations Division at http://www.sos.ga.gov/corporations/. Every state has a different interface, services, and requirements. Some US states only issue entity information for a fee. In the case of Georgia, they require you to create an account. It is a good idea to start with the exact name and spelling of the entity in the WHOIS record first and then use variations if the record cannot be found. In the case of Turner Broadcasting System, Inc., the record is in Georgia under the same spelling, and the street address in the corporate filing is exactly the same as the address in the WHOIS record. So, now we have an official document that validates the entity and address. The business filing has a number of officer names and a filing agent, which could be useful if we need further verification. The record also has a long history of filings and tells the consumer that the company is in good standing. Just to be absolutely sure, we can also check the address in online maps to see if the street and building actually exist. A general search of the address returns a multitude of information about the location, company, and the building itself. While there is no need to do so in this case so far, it is possible to further verify correct zip codes, street names, and proper municipal names within states.

Being fairly satisfied with the validity of the registrant information, we can move on to the next three lines that display the registrar name, WHOIS server, and website. This information is identical to the data provided in the InterNIC thin record, and we have already verified the website and WHOIS server with our additional queries. The next line is a confirmation of the queried domain itself, which is of note but does not need further examination. The three lines with the domain dates give us our first inconsistency, which needs explaining. Compare these dates in the thick record from CSC Corporate

```
Created on.............: Wed, Sep 22, 1993
Expires on.............: Fri, Sep 21, 2018
Record last updated on..: Thu, Nov 01, 2012
```

with the dates from the thin InterNIC record

```
Updated Date: 29-aug-2013
Creation Date: 22-sep-1993
Expiration Date: 21-sep-2018
```

The first obvious difference is that the dates are displayed in a different format. The InterNIC/VeriSign version uses an international DAY-MONTH-YEAR format, while the registrar version uses the US MONTH-DAY-YEAR order. The more interesting difference is between the two updated dates. The registry has an updated date of August 29, 2013, while the registrar has an updated date of November 1, 2012. The simple answer for this discrepancy is that the data came from two different databases, one from the registry and the other from the registrar. The most likely explanation is that the registry date of August 29 is the last time the data supplied by the registrar was written to the registry database, while the record held by the registrar simply has not changed since November of the previous year. It is also possible that the registrar requested a change to the registry data, which did not include any changes to the fields in the registrar version of the record, for example, a change to the domain status field. There are reasons to closely examine domain record dates, but in the case of cnn.com, nothing seems out of the ordinary.

The next block is the administrative contact details. We note that most of the information is identical to the registrant block, which we have already verified. However, it contains the additional phone number and email contact fields that are required for the administrative contact but not for the registrant. In verifying the phone number, we can take a few simple steps. First, the company claims to be in the United States, and we know that US phone numbers have 10 digits plus the "1" for international dialing to the United States. The first three digits, 404, are the area code, which we can verify through a number of services as being the area code for Atlanta, GA. The next three digits, 827, are the local exchange or prefix, which we can also verify as a valid local exchange within the area code.

The last four digits, 5000, is the actual local phone number. A number of this format is usually the front end of a large corporate switchboard with a number of different numbers and extensions behind it. In conducting a search for the whole phone number, we find various documents relating to CNN, Turner Broadcasting, and other domain names held by Turner. This seems to give us further verification. Finally, call the number. Calling CNN is not particularly dangerous, but calling WHOIS phone numbers of malicious sites could be. Here, the number connects immediately, and we are greeted by a recorded voice belonging to none other than CNN's Wolf Blitzer[5] requesting we stay on the line until an operator is available.

Verifying the email is our next step. First, is it properly formatted as an email with account-name@host-name.tld (that is in compliance with RFC 1035[6] or 2822[7])? Seeing that it is, we check to see whether the TLD used is valid. Yes, .COM is a valid TLD. Next, let us perform another WHOIS lookup on the email domain since it is different from the original domain name we are researching. For several reasons, one can and should use the same procedure performed earlier on cnn.com as turner.com. First, the WHOIS lookup will tell us if the domain name even exists (is registered); if not, then the email address is forged or inaccurate. In an investigation, this may also tell us about some of the operators of the initial domain and provide additional contact details. In the case of turner.com, the record has virtually the same contact information as cnn.com, so there is not much more to do in terms of WHOIS research on that record. However, because it purportedly handles email, there are more checks to perform. We ping turner.com to see if it is online; if not deployed in the DNS, it likely cannot receive email, but in this case it is online. Now, we perform a DNS lookup on turner.com to see if it has valid MX (mail exchange) records; while not required to receive email, it makes our verification job easier if they do: *dig turner.com mx* returns several MX entries, and pinging any of them shows us they are online. At this point, we know the domain turner.com can receive email, but we still do not know if the address exists. There are options we can try before actually testing mgroup@turner.com by sending an email to the address.

The natural flow of the DNS from the user perspective is for a domain name to be translated into an Internet Protocol (IP) address that is used by the network software to locate a resource. It is possible to conduct a *Reverse Lookup* that takes an IP address and returns a domain or domains. This is done through retrieving *pointer* records (PTR). This does not always work because the PTR does not always exist.[8] However, the relationship can be tested with services like dnsqueries.com.[9]

Before testing the email address itself, it is useful to conduct a basic search on the Internet for other references to the email address. For tmgroup@turner.com, we find numerous references to the address in other WHOIS records and posting from Internet users about their experiences using it. From this, we know the address has history or footprint, so it is not a one-time-use address or blatantly forged. This still does not mean it actual works, but if this were an illicit domain, we would want to record all other uses or instances of the address including its appearance in abuse or antispam logs. The local portion of the address "TMGROUP" is likely an abbreviation of "Turner Media Group" or

[5] http://www.cnn.com/CNN/anchors_reporters/blitzer.wolf.html
[6] http://www.ietf.org/rfc/rfc1035.txt
[7] http://www.ietf.org/rfc/rfc2822.txt
[8] http://technet.microsoft.com/en-us/library/ff796197%28v=exchg.80%29.aspx
[9] http://www.dnsqueries.com/en/reverse_lookup.php

"Turner Management Group." Among their brand names are "Turner Media Innovations" and "Turner Media Solutions." This is a case where a local email portion probably has a meaning or relates to a specific name, but many email addresses do not have a discernible meaning. On a more specific level, it is possible to conduct a search of the use of the email address within actual domain with "tmgroup@turner.com *site:cnn.com*" in most standard search engines. The results of this search show public posting of the email address on FAQ pages. Again, although not proven, it is still additional verification.

We now move into more technical spaces, which may or may not work in all cases. It is possible to make an email connection without actually sending an email. Many servers do not allow this type of activity because spammers and phishers may use it to test for potential target emails. Scripts can be used, which throw "dictionary" attacks to test for various names or combinations of possible accounts to target, but we are only checking one email address, so hopefully, we will not get flagged by their abuse team. Basically, we want to connect to one of the **MX** servers found in a previous step and create a connection through **SMTP** to the mailbox without actually sending any message and then disconnect. There are a number of methods for doing this. An email is basically a text file with a number of tagged fields like **FROM**, **TO**, **SUBJECT**, and **MESSAGE**. Exchanges send and accept these files using the different fields for various purposes. By engaging the server directly through a Telnet client, it is possible to manually input their field values for specific responses. The first **STMP** command is called **HELO** for which we insert our sending domain. The remote server may or may not accept your connection. If it does, you can then initiate the next set by manually entering the **FROM** field with a valid address with **MAIL FROM:** and a return address. If the remote server responds with OK, you can then enter the address to be tested with the command **RCPT TO:**, for example, *RCPT TO*: <tmgroup@turner.com>. In our test, the server responded with "Recipient ok." There are a variety of services online that will perform this kind of check through a web script including verify-email.org, validmail.org, and verifyemailaddress.org. It may be a good idea to use more than one to verify the results. While our checks of this example do not raise any red flags, it is not an absolute proof. A final test is to send a polite test email to the address. Some servers may also accept a **VRFY** command that checks addresses.[10] If you are addressing an abuse issue, sending email to the WHOIS contacts is a completely legitimate use of the data, but keep in mind that dealing with malicious Internet players may result in retaliations.

In looking at the technical contact block, we see the details are identical, so they do not need additional verification. The differences in contact details between different blocks can vary widely. In many cases, they are the same; in others, the registrant, administrator, and technical contacts are three completely independent persons or entities that operate the site. Regardless of who the administrative or technical parties are, the registrant is ultimately responsible for the domain and the completeness of the WHOIS data.

The final lines are a list of nameservers or "DNS servers" as they are called in the record. A primary and a secondary nameserver are required in the record, while many may have more; for purposes of accuracy, only the first two values need to be accurate. For the purposes of investigation, it may be necessary to analyze all the cited nameservers for more details. Start by pinging the primary nameserver to see if it responds and to record the IP address. *ping ns1.p42.dynect.net* returns the IP address of 208.78.70.42—save this for later. Next, check the nameserver with the InterNIC web form.

---

[10] http://cr.yp.to/smtp/vrfy.html

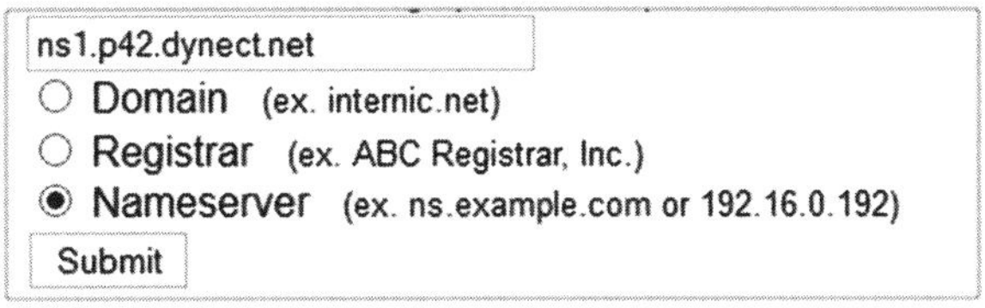

```
ns1.p42.dynect.net
○ Domain   (ex. internic.net)
○ Registrar   (ex. ABC Registrar, Inc.)
◉ Nameserver   (ex. ns.example.com or 192.16.0.192)
Submit
```

FIGURE 3.3   WHOIS nameserver request.

The query returns the following information:

```
Server Name: NS1.P42.DYNECT.NET
IP Address: 208.78.70.42
Registrar: DYNAMIC NETWORK SERVICES,  INC
Whois Server: whois.dyndns.com
Referral URL: http://www.dyn.com
```

This means the server is a valid nameserver, also noting that IP address matches our ping from earlier. While this form is still open, conduct the same search on the IP address. That query returns the identical information, so we have verified the nameserver string and IP address as valid for a nameserver. Now, we perform a DIG query on cnn.com for nameservers: *dig cnn.com ns* returns "ns1.p42.dynect.net" as one of the nameservers. Believe it or not, it is possible to forge these records, and illicit Internet players do so all the time. So what we need to do is check the claimed nameserver directly for our domain with *nslookup cnn.com ns1.p42.dynect.net*. If the nameserver in the WHOIS record is not the actual nameserver for the domain, it will respond with "REFUSED," "Unknown," or "Can't Connect..." depending on the configuration.

In terms of hosting, cnn.com resolves to the IP address 157.166.226.25. An IP WHOIS lookup (*whois –h whois.arin.net 157.166.226.25*) reveals that this address is held by Turner Broadcasting System, Inc. along with 65,000 other IP addresses. A quick Border Gateway Protocol (BGP) check of the addresses shows that they are all used for Turner channels, shows, brands, and various corporate operations. The street address for the IP WHOIS record is the same as the domain WHOIS record, and the phone number is in the same system. A traceroute of the IP address suggests that it is located in the Atlanta area.

For the purposes of investigation and abuse tracking, retrieving the nameserver WHOIS and putting it through the same procedure can yield useful information. In many cases, the nameserver is operated by a third-party Internet Service Provider (ISP), host, or registrar with the domain registrant as a customer. In other cases, nameservers are operated by the spammers themselves or other illicit networks. In the case of cnn.com, everything checks out. The registrar they use, CSC Corporate, offers a suite of online trademark protection products and other business services, not considered a problem registrar. However, the last three examples may not be so simple and straightforward. We will look at a spammed domain, a malware domain, and an illicit drug domain. For obvious reasons, we may encounter interesting details and problems while retrieving certain information.

3.1.2   Deconstructing the WHOIS for a Spammed Domain

Spam means different things to different people. Some may classify messages from in-laws or obnoxious coworkers as spam, although this is not the real definition. According to SPAMHAUS, spam is *"Unsolicited Bulk Email."*[11] Unsolicited is the key word as it means that a recipient did not grant permission to the sender. However, many email messages are unsolicited especially the first time one person contacts another. Spam is frequently sent to many recipients at once in an indiscriminate fashion and repeatedly even after the recipient has requested it to stop or has "opted out." Unsolicited email of a pornographic nature may be illegal in certain jurisdictions.[12] Spam can also lead to virus deployment, browser hijacks, and attempts at identity theft. Protection is getting better, but the mailbox has long been a vector to crack open a variety of attacks and will continue to be as long as it is effective for the attackers. This is why using WHOIS to track spam is a critical tool.

Unfortunately, antispam is a growing field with lots of opportunities for analysis and threat response. There are many good people in this business who have developed amazing tools, and it is a subject that is sadly known to every Internet user. Because of the diversity of the subject, this text focuses on the WHOIS aspect of "spamvertised" domains and the resources behind message sending and content hosting. Spammers are mercenaries who largely advertise products and services they have little connection to. The relationships between actual spam senders and what they advertise can be nebulous, yet they are not doing it for free, and the entities that end up getting the traffic are paying for spam as a service. The parties funding spam should be named and shamed.

Starting with a spam message promising methods for using "mind control" to meet women is an age-old pitch now on the Internet. The email subject is: "Make women WANT you (finally)." The email links to the domain suzbo.com, but this is just the advertising site run by what is called an affiliate who gets paid to drive traffic to a shopping domain. The displayed webpage has a link to attractiontracker.com and an opt-out or unsubscribe link to lntag.com. Clicking on the attractiontracker.com link, we only briefly pass through that domain before loading the domain puatrainingcheckout.com with other content and links loaded from puatraining.com. Passing through attractiontracker.com has two purposes: one is to track the source of clicks so the spammers can get paid according to how much traffic they drive from their domains, and the second is to provide an additional buffer between the spammer and the merchant. Because these are all .COM domains, we will have to check InterNIC for the specific registrar and then query those servers for details:

suzbo.com: BIZCN, whois.bizcn.com

lntag.com: BIZCN, whois.bizcn.com

attractiontracker.com: MONIKER, whois.moniker.com

puatrainingcheckout.com: ENOM, whois.enom.com

puatraining.com: GODADDY, whois.godaddy.com

This is interesting for our exercise, because for five domains we have four different registrars; each will give us varying results and tell us something about the structure of this

---

[11] http://www.spamhaus.org/consumer/definition/

[12] http://www.gpo.gov/fdsys/pkg/PLAW-108publ187/html/PLAW-108publ187.htm

spam campaign. Running these lines, we use the specific registrars sponsoring each domain (there are various methods for batching lookup, covered in Chapter 5):

> *whois -h whois.bizcn.com suzbo.com*
>
> *whois -h whois.bizcn.com lntag.com*
>
> *whois -h whois.moniker.com attractiontracker.com*
>
> *whois -h whois.enom.com puatrainingcheckout.com*
>
> *whois -h whois.godaddy.com puatraining.com*

As explained, the linked domain from the spam message and the unsubscribe link are probably not directly operated by the party selling the final product. So in looking at the records for the two BIZCN-sponsored sites, we find identical registration information. Note also that the record results are untagged, so we have to work from some assumptions. First, at the spam landing site, just look at some sections for the sake of brevity:

```
Domain name: suzbo.com
Registrant Contact:
   zhang neng
   neng zhang sdrfsfsdfs@msn.com
   01052412566 fax: 01052412566
   beijingshichangyangqudongshanhuan33hao
   beijing beijing 021411
   cn
   ...
```

Then look at the unsubscribe site:

```
Domain name: lntag.com
Registrant Contact:
   zhang neng
   neng zhang sdrfsfsdfs@msn.com
   01052412566 fax: 01052412566
   beijingshichangyangqudongshanhuan33hao
   beijing beijing 021411
   cn
   ...
```

A few things may jump off the page immediately including the very long string underneath the presumed phone number. Believe it or not, this may be a valid address format. First, we recognize that a registrant in China formats street addresses differently and then has to translate the address from Chinese to Latin characters. In the United States, postal addresses usually start with the most specific information first (street number) and then move to less specific information (street name). In many countries, this information is displayed in the opposite direction, and actually the entire address is often written with the recipient's name on the last line. In China, it is typical to include additional sublocations in an address, not just the city and state, comparable to including a county and neighborhood name in a US address. This is further complicated by the fact that there are no spaces in the string, so we will have to make further assumptions about the meaning. Remember also that just because someone has put the phonetic spelling of a location into the record, it does not mean it is the *common* phonetic spelling. It is clear that this is not easy to parse without some help from an expert. The string starts with "beijing," which we already know is the larger city location in the address (Beijing is often displayed as "Bei Jing" as well). The string "hao" at the end of the string after the number transliterates to the Chinese word for "number," which is somewhat redundant but often appears in other country's addresses (e.g., "Number 10 Downing Street"). That leaves us with "shichangyangqudongshanhuan," which has to be broken into substrings that correspond with the Chinese names, and then we have to reverse the order. "dongshanhuan" is likely Dong San Huan Road in Beijing, leaving us now with "shichangyangqu." Dong San Huan Road is in the Chao Yang District of Beijing. To completely restructure the format in a Western sense, we end up with a best guess of "Hao 33 Dong San Huan Chao Yang Qu Beijing."

Does the phone number look correct? "01052412566" is definitely missing China's international dialing code of *86*, but while we assume the number is in China, this may not be the case. Mobile telephone numbers in China have 11 digits as this number does, but this could also be an eight-digit landline number with the Beijing area code of *10* and the required zero prefix. The phone number passes a basic visual test. The email sdrfsfsdfs@msn.com looks suspicious because "sdrfsfsdfs" appears to be a string of characters all next to each other on a standard keyboard. msn.com is a free, public email service like Yahoo, so that part is real at least. However, in testing our suspicions, an email sent to the address was rejected. This means the two BIZCN domains have false WHOIS. A little research on various Internet abuse lists like Artists Against 419 (aa419.org) shows that this registration is used in many deceptive advertising campaigns. Further attempts to verify these details or directly link them to the sites being advertised may prove fruitless, so we will focus on the other three domains.

The WHOIS record for the MONIKER site gives us a little more useful information; once again, the fields are untagged:

```
Domain Name: ATTRACTIONTRACKER.COM
Registrar: MONIKER

Administrative Contact [3794130]:
   Richard La Ruina gulliver@puatraining.com
   PUA Training
   22 canterbury close
   Cambridge
   england
   cb4 3qq
   UK
   Phone: +44.7941299366
```

Immediately, we see that the email contact uses the domain puatraining.com, which was also collected from the spammed purchasing webpage; verifying that domain as well will be doubly important. The fact that the registration contains a company name and consistent location information for the United Kingdom gives us details to investigate. Verifying people and entities of a public nature can be done today using available records and social media, but for the sake of brevity, we will point other resources for conducting additional investigations or intelligence gathering.

Richard La Ruina is a real person who trains men in the "pickup arts," and research found complaints about his marketing tactics,[13] so it seems we are on the right track. A check of the UK's Companies House online registry[14] shows that PUA Training LTD is duly registered at the same address as the WHOIS record.

In checking the GODADDY domain puatraining.com, we run into a minor delay. GODADDY does not provide WHOIS details through Port 43; rather, they supply a direct link to their web-based WHOIS at http://who.godaddy.com/whoischeck.aspx, which requests a CAPTCHA code before displaying the full WHOIS record. The details are the same as the MONIKER domain, so additional verification of the details is not needed.

The record of puatrainingcheckout.com at ENOM is interesting because it is behind a privacy shield:

```
Domain name: puatrainingcheckout.com

Administrative Contact:
    WhoisGuard, Inc.
    WhoisGuard Protected
(45f01ceb9de24a01a64ee88294515072.protect@whoisguard.com)
    +507.8365503
    Fax: +51.17057182
    P.O. Box 0823-03411
    Panama, Panama NA
    PA
```

According to their website, they also go by the name RLR Media Ltd. (assuming that RLR stands for "Richard La Ruina"), which leads us to a number of related websites like pick-up-artist-forum.com:

```
Domain Name: PICK-UP-ARTIST-FORUM.COM

Tech Street: 56 my address
Tech City: My city
Tech State/Province:
Tech Postal Code: wv12678
Tech Country: Afghanistan
Tech Phone: +93.0000000000000
Tech Fax: +93.0000000000
```

There are a number of problems with this record as it is generally false and obfuscated, so it is appropriate to file a complaint with the sponsoring registrar. According to our research, RLR Media Ltd. is registered in the country of Mauritius,[15] which may raise eyebrows as it has been accused of being an offshore tax haven.[16]

[13] http://www.puafraud.com/tag/puatraining/
[14] http://www.companieshouse.gov.uk
[15] https://portalmns.mu
[16] http://www.ifcreview.com/viewarticle.aspx?articleId=6263&areaId=32

We may also want to analyze the WHOIS records found in the headers of spam emails, being sure to extract the right data from the header. Headers should be read backward or from bottom to top. The header tells a story of where a message started, went, and landed. By reading it backward, we can easily identify the destination, our mailbox, and then within the "Received" field, there could be more than one where we want to find the earliest non-local IP address. Most emails start at 127.0.0.1 ("local-host"), which is the local IP address of every machine. The point of this analysis is to eliminate irrelevant and possibly forged header data ("spoofed") in the search for the true origin of an email. Most spam has forged headers or is sent from hijacked machines (and often both); in either case, finding the real source is important. Email header forgery is easy because an email is basically a text file with certain tagged fields that tell mail transfer agents (MTA) where to route the email. The situation is quite similar to dropping a letter in postal mailbox; the return address could be any address, and bad return addresses are only discovered if the letter is returned or responded to by the recipient. The sender of an email effectively has that kind of control over the sender fields in the email, but little control over what happens when it leaves the spammers' network. Once it leaves the network, other networks along the way add legitimate IP and domain information to the email, which is verifiable. The depth of the forgery demonstrates how much control the spammer has. In case where they control a network or even an ISP, the layers of obfuscation can be thick.

In one example of a phishing email from "WELLS FARGO," the sender and return path domain is amc.org, but the Originating-IP is 213.182.126.47. WHOIS lookups on 213.182.126.47 and amc.org find they are completely unrelated, specifically that the address 213.182.126.47 has no mail service or hosting relationship with amc.org. Furthermore, the spoofed domain is hosted in the United States, but spam itself came from an ISP in Germany. Additionally, a blacklist check of 213.182.126.47 finds it in seven different databases for spam. Every email is supposed to have a unique Message-ID that can be forged if the spammer has control of the network. In dealing with these issues, you are not alone. There are a number of WHOIS databases and services that offer special WHOIS services to track spam and abuse. The Network Abuse Clearinghouse WHOIS service at whois.abuse.net accepts domain queries and returns *only* the abuse contact email address, cutting to the chase, which is also available through a web interface.[17] This is a project by John Levine author of *The Internet for Dummies*.[18]

3.1.3   Illicit Domain WHOIS

If you have not noticed, there is quite a bit of criminal activity occurring on the Internet. Due to the proliferation of illegal good, knockoff products, and outright scams, it is necessary for consumers, law enforcement, and intellectual property attorneys to be able to retrieve WHOIS records. Just getting the records is half the battle. One of the most prevalent types is the rogue pharmacy site,[19] which pretends to be a licensed pharmacy but in reality sells drugs from unknown sources without a prescription. For this example, we have

[17] http://www.abuse.net/lookup.phtml
[18] http://net.gurus.org/toc-i4d11.html
[19] http://www.usatoday.com/story/news/nation/2013/07/10/stateline-online-pharmacies/2505379/

examined a site flagged by the National Association of Boards of Pharmacy (NABP) for being out of compliance—33drugs.com:

```
Checking server [whois.joker.com]
Results:
domain: 33drugs.com
owner: - -
organization: 33 DRUGS LTD
email: domains@33drugs.com
address: Slington House, Rankine Road
address: Office 6
city: Basingstoke
state: Hampshire
postal-code: RG24 8PH
country: GB
phone: +44.2081338455
admin-c: CCOM-1283149 domains@33drugs.com
tech-c: CCOM-1283149 domains@33drugs.com
billing-c: CCOM-1283149 domains@33drugs.com
nserver: ns1.drugcustomer.com 85.25.71.252
nserver: ns2.drugcustomer.com 124.217.252.93
nserver: ns3.33drugs.com 85.25.71.252
nserver: ns4.33drugs.com 124.217.252.93
status: lock
created: 2007-09-23 14:23:33 UTC
modified: 2012-01-26 21:29:32 UTC
expires: 2015-09-23 14:23:33 UTC
```

The first item of concern is that the owner or registrant field is blank, but this is permitted as long as a valid entity (organization) is provided instead. The name of the organization is "33 DRUGS LTD," and since this entity purports to be in the United Kingdom, they must be registered with the Companies House. A review of their public database shows that 33 DRUGS LTD is not registered. Just to be sure, we also verified whether this was not a former or dissolved entity. Right off, this record appears to be invalid. Within the record, we also found a different domain in the top nameserver, drugcustomer.com, which in the WHOIS record claims to be a Danish company. We checked with the Danish Commerce and Companies Agency[20] (DCCA) and could not find a record for this either. For an extensive list of national corporation databases, visit this site: http://www.rba.co.uk/sources/registers.htm.

3.1.4 Virus Domain WHOIS

Now, we are stepping into really dangerous territory. Do not actually visit any malware dispensing domains; there are a number of online services that will test websites on the fly for malware, one of which is sitecheck.sucuri.net. Some of these domains are registered by

---

[20] http://www.virk.dk/home.html

malicious users for the purposes of spreading malware, and others are completely innocent victims of an intrusion or hijack. Even government websites have been hacked to spread malware.[21] If fact, from the attacker's perspective, it is even better to infect a legitimate site because it increases the likelihood of victims becoming infected. In either case, it is important to be able to review the various records and figure out whom to contact to report the issue to. Using sites like stopbadware.org[22] can help domain owners keep clean.

Tracking WHOIS for virus cases can be extremely complicated due to the number of different domains or IP addresses used, the behavior of malware in terms of multiplying and using compromised machines, the deliberate obfuscation of malware-related WHOIS records, and the specific collusion of rogue service providers. The problems are so complex that many security services have developed their own WHOIS engines. A great example is the WHOIS utility provided by Team Cymru (team-cymru.org), which pairs queries with checks of malware *hashes*[23] to provide a more detailed view of where infections exist on the Internet (see http://www.team-cymru.org/Services/MHR/#whois). A hash is a fixed-length code that corresponds to varying values for quick reference. Hash functions speed up searching and have a variety of applications beyond virus tracking. Cymru has other critical tracking services like mapping IP addresses to BGP and ASN.[24] Here is the full list of options:

Default options (always on)
　-b Disable allocation date
　-d Disable country codes
　-e Enable column headings
　-q Disable matching prefix
　-s Disable registry display
　-n Include ASN
　-t Truncate ASN
　-w Include ASN column

Additional options

　-c Include country code
　-o Disable ANS
　-r Display registry
　-a Enable allocation date
　-u Disable ANS truncate
　-v Verbose mode, enable all flags: -c -r -p -a -u -a -e -w
　-f Disable column headings
　-p Include prefix
　-x Disable ASN column

[21] http://www.securityweek.com/department-labor-website-hacked-distribute-malware
[22] https://www.stopbadware.org/webmaster-help
[23] http://www.team-cymru.org/Services/MHR/
[24] http://www.team-cymru.org/Services/ip-to-asn.html

Cymru has some great assets in its staff including Steve Santorelli who used to work for Scotland Yard.[25] Santorelli sees the damage of cybercrime first hand and cannot underestimate the importance of WHOIS in tracking criminals. Because subpoenas, especially international ones, can take months, having accurate and responsive records up font is critical and serves to limit the threats presented by criminals. While he notes serious issues with some service providers, he also sees positive changes in the way law enforcement and industry are working together with data sharing to develop a trust relationship that ultimately benefits the consumer. Santorelli also cites the success of computer emergency response teams (CERTs) around the globe but sees a growing need for more support in emerging economies. Africa, for instance, is expanding its Internet access but at the same time seems woefully unprepared to deal with the wave of cybercrime that comes along with it. Santorelli wants the community to know that Cymru is here to be used as a resource and it is not about the money, but the independent security group wants information and collaboration.[26]

3.1.5 Tracking Cybersquatters and Serial Trademark Violators

The true battlefield of WHOIS and the source of much of the policy controversy concern intellectual property in terms of domain strings. The trade in domain names themselves has warped the original intent of the DNS and WHOIS record set.[27] The use of private business, as opposed to government funding, to expand and innovate on the Internet throughout the 1990s was largely successful in terms of improving technology and increasing access. Free market principles work fine in most cases, but the domain market aspect of the Internet is a strange animal. In the free market, an apple company does best when as many consumers as possible can get their apples at the lowest cost. Apples are plentiful and everyone can have one, but other substances like gold are rare, which makes them more expensive, but even still gold can be purchased by people of various classes. Domains on the other hand are *unique*, and only one party can own a particular domain. This makes the domain market completely different from any other market and abnormally competitive. Domain names rapidly became a commodity, some selling for millions of dollars. Suddenly, having a domain name was no longer about posting content; it was simply about reselling the domain name. In the early days of the DNS, no one was issued a domain name without a network to serve it from. Once it was possible to simply stockpile idle domain names, an Internet marketplace emerged, which had nothing to do with communications or technology. Money was the only goal in the new domain trade, and WHOIS became an innocent casualty. The ICANN registrar system is seen both for lowering the general price of domains and for bringing corruption into the Internet. Tim Berners-Lee,[28] creator of the World Wide Web, made this critical statement in his 1999 book *Weaving the Web*:

> *"One problem is that the better domains will wind up with the people with the most money... the ability to charge for a domain name, which is a scarce, irreplaceable resource, has been given to a subcontractor, Network Solutions, which not surprisingly made profits but does not have the reputation for accountability, or meeting its obligations."* [1]

---

[25] http://www.tomsguide.com/us/9-tips-scotland-yard-detective,review-1841.html
[26] Santorelli interview
[27] http://www.buchalter.com/wp-content/uploads/2013/06/summer-2006-patents.pdf
[28] http://www.w3.org/People/Berners-Lee/

The massive single-sale profits in domain speculation were largely driven by the capturing of generic terms like "sex" and "business." However, the legal issues and problems with WHOIS arose from the speculation of trademarked terms and product names. While the breakup of Network Solutions monopoly brought more competition to the domain market, many of the new registrars were not in the market to sell domains to the consumer; they were selling domains to themselves for speculation. These more specifically are cybersquatted names, which contain actual trademarks, and typsquatted names, which contain strings that can be perceived as trademarks.

The *Wall Street Journal* reporter David Kesmodel[29] penned *The Domain Game* in 2008 to cover the world of domain name speculation. In Chapter 8, he details how WHOIS obfuscation and registrar shenanigans turn the domain market into a den of thieves, particularly citing the registrar Doster:

> "*From at least the second half of 2005 until March 2006 [Dotster] didn't list any Whois information in its public Whois computer server for any of the names it registered through tasting, which is a violation of Icann rules...Dotster instructed [staff] to tell any third party that inquired about a name that is was registered to a Doster customer...even though [the name] was owned by Dotster.*" [2]

So, here we have an example of WHOIS being manipulated from the authority itself and not simply falsified by the registrant. The complete absence of WHOIS makes the investigator's job extremely difficult. This is actually more the norm than the exception as we will see as the subject is covered further in the chapter on WHOIS policy.

3.1.6 Network Security Administrator Issues

Network administrators have the duty of keeping unauthorized and unauthenticated users off the network. Networks are under constant attack from various outside sources as well as vulnerabilities created by malicious outgoing traffic. Administrators need to know where traffic is coming from and going to outside the firewall. Using WHOIS needs to be part of the admin's toolkit. One of the areas of concern for administrators is *Secure Shell (SSH) Attacks*. This section was developed in conjunction with security researcher Dr. Robert Bruen who, for the purposes of full disclosure, is the author's father.

ssh is the standard method for remote logins. Traffic is encrypted using public key cryptography. It has been shown to be the most secure way to communicate between hosts and is ubiquitous, thus making it a desirable target for attack.

A weak point in ssh is the password chosen by the user. A weak password defeats the purpose of strong encryption. Using *key exchange* instead of passwords between hosts helps protect hosts generally, but uses still need to login to some host to get started. That host is the main target of attacks.

One attack is called the ssh dictionary attack, because the attack is automated, trying to login to an account using a list of passwords, as well as a list of accounts. Accounts on systems include generic privileged accounts, such as root or admin, plus many user accounts for applications, such as MySQL, Nagios, and so on. Other user account names are in a list, including the names of people and words of all kinds.

---

[29] http://thedomaingame.org/bio.html

The programs simply try to login using an account and password, running through the lists until they are successful. The programs are generally part of a broad scan of a site, with many sites being scanned. A run keeps going until the perpetrator decides to stop it.

Log files indicate a failed login, as when legitimate user mistypes or forgets a password, resulting in a loss of access to the account, until a systems administrator fixes it or an automatic process handles a password reset. This attack mode will show lots of failed attempts in that same way. The attack log entries are different, because many account failures will come from the same IP. A legitimate user failure will come, most of the time, from one source, without attempts made on numerous accounts.

If a user has a weak password, the probability that the account will be breached increases; otherwise, the attacks will fail. The attacks can become annoying when large numbers of attempts are made, especially when the same attacks are repeated from multiple sources.

One of the best ways to mitigate the attacks is to use DenyHosts,[30] a free, open-source program, with configurable parameters. It will prevent access to a host IP after some number of attempts, as a firewall does. It keeps a list of IPs that have been blocked. It also provides an option to share your list with anybody else willing to share their list. This creates a large, global list of IPs known to be generating ssh attacks.

Going beyond this approach, the list of IPs recorded can be used to determine sources. Useful information can be obtained by a WHOIS lookup of the IP. This provides the registrant (owner of the IP), the country of origin, the registrar, and a contact for abuse reporting.

Once a list of attack sources has been gathered over a period of time, an analysis of these sources is easily done. The analysis can be of the country of origin, showing, for example, that 75% of the sources were from China. The registrars can be determined as well, showing which ones allow more of the abusive IPs and domain names.

3.1.7 Protecting Your Domain with Accurate WHOIS

In all of the discussion about criminals deliberately obfuscating WHOIS and lawful users trying to protect their privacy, it is easy to forget the practical reasons for having accurate WHOIS. There are a number of really bad things that can happen to your domain if you are not contactable, most notably malware infection, hijacking, and domain theft. Do not expect your ISP or registrar to protect you; sometimes, they are the culprit. If there is an intrusion on your site and malware is installed or the content is vandalized, a vigilant member of the public may try to contact you and let you know but will fail if your information is not valid. It is possible, and has happened numerous times, that a hacker can maliciously take control of your domain by changing the WHOIS contact information, and if your contact information is not accurate, this makes the task much easier for them. In addition to taking control of your domain and using it to conduct illicit activity, redirect it to another domain, send spam, or spread malware, an attacker can transfer your domain to another registrar or even sell it to a third party. Getting the domain back at this point is nearly impossible. However, most registrars will allow domain owners to turn on WHOIS or registration *locks*. The lock prevents any changes to the WHOIS record without the owner's permission, but in order for this to work best, the contact information must be accurate in the first place.

---

[30] http://www.denyhosts.net

3.2   MORE TOOLS

While not strictly WHOIS, many of these programs and protocols can be used to obtain additional network information, which in turn can be used to query WHOIS or support other WHOIS results.

3.2.1   Ping

Ping is a basic and fundamental networking tool. Invented in 1983 by a US Army Research Scientist Mike Muuss[31] to help resolve a specific network problem, it is still used to troubleshoot and analyze network connections decades later. Ping uses the Internet Control Message Protocol[32] (ICMP) to send test packets to remote hosts and to record the time it takes, the IP address behind a domain name, and other useful information. It can tell us on a basic level if a domain is online and assigned to an IP address, which can then be passed to WHOIS, for example, by the command:

ping example.com

Will return:

```
Pinging example.com [93.184.216.119] with 32 bytes of data:
```

The data in the brackets is the IP address, which can now be queried for additional information. Ping has a number of options that can be viewed with *ping/?* with Windows or *man ping* on Linux. There are also a number of online Ping utilities like network-tools. com or just-ping.com, which will allow you to ping from other locations. Pinging from other locations is critical for comparison to see if sites are unavailable globally or for verifying traceroutes.

3.2.2   Traceroute

Traceroute[33] (called tracert in Windows[34]) is a very important tool for determining where an Internet resource is truly located. IP geolocation can be erroneous as records are easily forged or even reflect office locations instead of literal server locations. Sometimes, this is for security reasons as ISPs try not to give out actual equipment locations. However, in investigations, we often find that maliciously used IPs have fake or misleading record locations. A fuller explanation of tracerouting can be found in the chapter on DNS and WHOIS.

3.2.3   Secondary Sources, Historical Data, and Additional Tools

- DomainTools (domaintools.com) of course has great historical data on WHOIS records but restricts cross-referencing with paid reports. They have varying levels of paid access, which can be affordable or expensive depending on the need. It is important

[31] https://news.ycombinator.com/item?id=5030309
[32] http://support.microsoft.com/kb/170292
[33] http://linux.die.net/man/8/traceroute
[34] http://support.microsoft.com/kb/162326

to note that DomainTools records are not live, so they should be used in conjunction with fresh records.

- Archive.org Wayback Machine at archive.org captures historical web content. This service often misses fly-by-night spam site content but provides many clues about other websites.
- BGP helps Internet traffic route better by finding the shortest and most stable path for communication. To aid this, organizations like Hurricane Electric (HE) Internet Services publish vast amounts of data on IP address use. The BGP Toolkit (bgp.he.net) allows you to review entire IP ranges and see which domains are hosted or served from a particular network along with detailed network owner information and access to WHOIS records. When investigating a domain name, search for it in the HE BGP to find all domains hosted in the same place in addition to who owns the network. The screenshot below shows the HE BGP interface. An IP address search can yield quite a bit of information. The standard tabs show WHOIS records, other domains hosted at the IP, and ratings for the address on 50 blacklists.
- Domain Information Groper (DIG) is covered in more depth in the section on DNS, but this tool that comes bundled with BIND allows DNS records to be retrieved in various ways. The command *dig example.com* will return default DNS records that can be analyzed and requeried with more specific options.
- For simple host information, HOSTgets *host example.com*; for detailed host information, *host –v example.com*; and for reverse lookup, *host 97.74.144.105*.
- DNS server fingerprinting tool (fpdns) reveals DNS server versions by sending queries and comparing responses against known server versions.[35]
- Network Mapper (NMap) is a powerful utility[36] for network security auditing.[37] It will test ports on the target machine to see which are open or closed and attempt to determine the operating system type. Download http://nmap.org/download.html and reference http://nmap.org/book/man.html.
- Wget allows the download of web content from the command line:

wget http://example.com

To download an entire site, use the –r (recursive) and –l (level) switches to get all pages and pages of at least five subdirectories:

wget –r –l 5 http://example.com

To get the wget help file, use *wget –h* or use stored copies.[38]
- cURL is a more automated command-line downloader, which can be scripted to operate without interaction and to download entire websites. cURL is not just for website, but it can also be used for ftp, ldap, etc. In its simplest use,

curl http://example.com

---

[35] http://linux.die.net/man/1/fpdns
[36] https://svn.nmap.org/nmap/COPYING
[37] http://nmap.org/
[38] http://linux.die.net/man/1/wget

This command will grab the source code of the index or default page of a domain but simply display it to the terminal window. Dumping this to a file is more useful with

> *curl http://example.com > example_com.txt* or
> *curl http://example.com -o "example_com.txt"*

Some sites are slow to download or use tricks to block downloading of content, in which case we might want to limit the amount of time for attempting to download:

> *curl -m 1800 http://example.com -o "example_com.txt"*

The (lowercase) m switch here is set to 1800 seconds, after which the process will be terminated. This is useful especially in batch downloading. Get all curl instructions with this command, *curl –M*, or review online copies.[39]

- Passive DNS Replication at the University of Stuttgart (cert.uni-stuttgart.de/dienste/dns-replication.en.html) is an interface that allows you to query by IP and domain name to navigate through all the related records. Also use Dedicated Or Not (dedicatedornot.com), which determines how many other domains are served from a particular IP or nameserver. None of the services have *all* the information, so it is important to check several of them and cross-reference. Many of the nslookup functions have been combined and enhanced in the DiG.

- The Shadowserver Foundation is another security project, which runs its own WHOIS service to assist in incident tracking.[40] The Shadowserver WHOIS service has special functions for batching WHOIS and obtaining origin information.

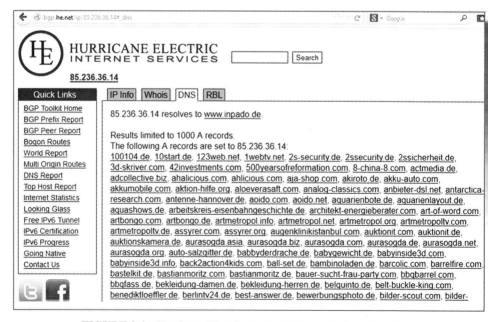

FIGURE 3.4   Hurricane Electric Border Gateway Protocol Interface.

---

[39] http://linux.die.net/man/1/curl
[40] http://www.shadowserver.org/wiki/pmwiki.php/Services/IP-BGP

- badwhois.info publicizes various illicit online activity and ties it back to various WHOIS issues including access and falsification.
- hostexploit.com is a focal point for open-source resource research and publication and for creating awareness of cybercrime activity.
- httrack is a graphic interface web content downloader.[41]
- **diff** ("difference") is a Mac[42] and Linux command that finds the difference in two files.[43] **fc** ("file compare") is the Windows/DOS version.[44] This can be used to compare two versions of a WHOIS file for changes or webpages on similar sites. The Linux command **diff3**[45] allows comparisons between three files and **cmp**[46] is used for binary files.
- MXToolBox (mxtoolbox.com/diagnostic.aspx) is used for SMTP diagnostics.
- SNORT (snort.org) and WIRESHARK (wireshark.org) are types of packet sniffers for network traffic analysis.
- Proxy WHOIS (extremeexploits.com/tools/whois.ee).
- Dmitry is an extended host information gathering tool (linux.die.net/man/1/Dmitry).
- BW WHOIS (whois.bw.org) is a modern WHOIS client with a lot of features
- Is It Down Right Now? (isitdownrightnow.com) checks the status of websites without loading them locally.
- Dedicated Or Not (dedicatedornot.com) determines if a nameserver or IP address serves just one site or several sites.
- DNSStuff (dnsstuff.com) has various lookup tools.

REFERENCES

1 Berners-Lee, T. 1999. Weaving the Web, The Original Design and Ultimate Destiny of the World Wide Web. San Francisco: HarperSanFrancisco.
2 Kesmodel, D. 2008. The Domain Game.

---

[41] http://www.httrack.com/
[42] https://developer.apple.com/library/mac/documentation/Darwin/Reference/ManPages/man1/diff.1.html
[43] http://linux.about.com/library/cmd/blcmdl1_diff.htm
[44] http://www.computerhope.com/fchlp.htm
[45] http://osr600doc.sco.com/en/man/html.C/diff3.C.html
[46] http://osr600doc.sco.com/en/man/html.C/cmp.C.html

4

WHOIS IN THE DOMAIN NAME SYSTEM (DNS)

WHOIS records and systems fit into the greater context of the Internet Domain Name System (DNS). DNS is a topic widely documented but not always from the viewpoint of WHOIS record retrieval. This chapter will also discuss other Internet records like zone files, resource records (RRs), and hint files. While these are technically not WHOIS records, they provide more information and context to the Internet record structure. One of the simplest explanations of the DNS came from Jon Postel in RFC 971 from 1981:

> "*A distinction is made between names, addresses, and routes. A name indicates what we seek. An address indicates where it is. A route indicates how to get there.*"[1]

None of it would work without an accompanying record set. The quality and availability of that identifying record set determines the quality and availability of the network as a whole. Where the records exist or do not exist defines the problems we experience.

4.1 THE BIG MISTAKE

WHOIS records are required by *policy*, but they are not required by *technical* function. In the opinion of this author, not integrating WHOIS into the DNS is one of the biggest mistakes in the current Internet model. Registrars of domains and Internet Protocol (IP) addresses are required to collect WHOIS data from customers, but the accuracy and availability of those records are not required before a host can be deployed or a domain resolves. In the early Internet, valid registration had to be provided before a host could be

[1] http://www.ietf.org/rfc/rfc791.txt

WHOIS Running the Internet: Protocol, Policy, and Privacy, First Edition. Garth O. Bruen.
© 2016 John Wiley & Sons, Inc. Published 2016 by John Wiley & Sons, Inc.

added. Because of the complete lack of validation standards of WHOIS data and the Internet Corporation of Assigned Names and Numbers' (ICANN) poor track record of effective compliance, the general policy requiring WHOIS records for domain names is a functional failure. A technical requirement for accessible and valid WHOIS integrated with the DNS would preclude many problems and much fraud on the Internet. There are a variety of ways this could work. For example, simply before a domain could resolve a special resource record would certify the WHOIS behind the domain. WHOIS checks could also be done on the fly. These checks would include accessibility of the registrar or registry WHOIS service and at a minimum some standard of validity of the record itself. The details of validation are subject to different discussion, but the fact is that the technical ability exists to integrate this into the DNS. Consumers should be able to retrieve WHOIS records of domains they conduct commerce with, but they should be expected to in every instance. As an example, consider the case of DATTATEC, a registrar who allowed completely blank WHOIS records to be stored for illicit domains;[2] see example below:

```
Using WHOIS server whois.dattatec.com, port 43, to find
nobledrugstore.com
Datttatec.com - Registration Service Provided By: Dattatec.com

Registrant contact:
Name:
Company:
Email:
Address:
- ( zip: )
Phone : -
```

DATTATEC had already been breached by ICANN 5 months earlier for not correcting WHOIS inaccuracies, so it should not have been a surprise.[3] Other registrars like Best Bulk Register had been cited for blocking access to their WHOIS.[4] In these cases, the domains sponsored by these companies simply would not resolve on the Internet until the issues were fixed if WHOIS was integrated as a technical requirement. This would be a big incentive for registrants and providers to ensure WHOIS was valid and functioning. The additional concerns over registrant privacy could be addressed within this architecture as well. In fact, WHOIS certification integrated within the DNS could enhance privacy while protecting Internet users. If part of the basic function of DNS resolution was the presence, accessibility, and validity of WHOIS, there would be fewer requests for WHOIS records and fewer copies created by other parties. As an example of function, a domain would resolve if (i) the relevant WHOIS server was operational, (ii) the record existed, and (iii) the record passed some validity test. This function could be performed by certification. In the opposite case, if the WHOIS record had a bad validity score or was not accessible, the Internet user would be presented with a warning in their browser or email client indicating that there was an issue

[2] http://www.circleid.com/posts/20131006_registrar_allows_completely_blank_whois/
[3] http://www.icann.org/en/news/correspondence/serad-to-irazoqui-07may13-en.pdf
[4] http://www.icann.org/en/correspondence/burnette-to-gurung-09feb11-en.pdf

with the record. So, if someone clicks on a spam link or is redirected by a browser hijack, the final destination domain would not resolve immediately due to a problem with the record. The point would be to use the WHOIS record as an additional piece in the trust chain.

This is not to say that attempts have not been made to integrate WHOIS with the DNS on a technical level. In 2004, David Venable proposed a Cryptographic Domain Ownership Verification (CDOV) Protocol[5] that would leverage the WHOIS database to assist certificate authority validation. The author acknowledges some pitfalls at the beginning of the document:

```
1.1  Assumptions

This protocol assumes that the registrars' whois servers are
secure and that only authorized persons have access to the
individual records.
```

Any plan that relies on secure servers and records will fail in the current environment. These areas have been the major problems with a distributed model that also lacks enforcement from the top-level authority, ICANN.

4.2 BASICS OF THE DNS

Instead of using binary strings, programs refer to hosts and mailboxes by American Standard Code for Information Interchange (ASCII) strings while the network itself only understands binary addresses; therefore, a mechanism is required to map ASCII strings to binary addresses. The early ARPANET used a file called hosts.txt, which listed all the hosts and their associated IP address. Every night, all the hosts would copy the updated hosts.txt from the site that maintained it. This worked when there were only a few hundred machines in the network. As the number of attached machines increased, the method needed updating. The hosts.txt file would simply become too large to distribute each day, and the number of potential address conflicts would increase if the list was not centrally managed. Having a centrally located list for an international network becomes problematic. The solution was the creation of the DNS under RFC 1034[6] and 1035.[7] Essentially, the DNS is a hierarchical system that maps hostnames (domains) to IP addresses. Under the DNS application, programs access a library procedure called a *resolver* that accepts the domain name ASCII string. The resolver sends a User Datagram Protocol (UDP[8]) packet to a local DNS server that looks up the name and returns the IP address to the resolver that passes it back to the requesting program. Once the IP address is obtained, the program begins a Transmission Control Protocol (TCP) connection or sends more UDPs.

4.2.1 TCP/IP, Layers, and Resolvers

As indicated by the name, TCP and IP are two protocols. Working together, these two pieces of code make it possible for our computers to pass data to the network and have it arrive at a remote machine. This protocol is flexible, not proprietary, and free. The essence

---

[5] http://tools.ietf.org/html/draft-venable-cdov-00
[6] http://www.ietf.org/rfc/rfc1034.txt
[7] http://www.ietf.org/rfc/rfc1035.txt
[8] http://tools.ietf.org/html/rfc768

of TCP/IP is that it breaks our various data into small pieces (packets) that are reassembled by the destination devices. This model can be compared to the BITNET model that stored and forwarded[9] digital files in their entirety, which for obvious reasons can cause traffic problems as more machines and data are added to the network. RFC 1180[10] by Theodore Socolofsky and Claudia Kale provides a comprehensive overview of the protocol suite.

Layers are an important part of the networking model; these are essentially the different phases information passes through between your software and the literal hardware of the network. TCP runs on the transport layer, which is where packets move back and forth. This is right in the middle of the layered model with the application layer on one end and the physical layer on the other end. Application layer software is what users interact with directly such as web browsers (Hypertext Transfer Protocol (HTTP)) and email (SMTP) where the physical layer refers to the actual methods for passing data through the wires. There are seven standard layers in all with dozens of different protocols. It is clear from reviewing the layers that WHOIS is not included. Some in the industry refer to "Layer 8" as being the political layer,[11] which concerns things beyond the bits. However, there is no practical reason why WHOIS could not be integrated within the layers as a matter of security.

A resolver is a program or procedure that translates domain names into IP addresses. Resolvers exist in various pieces of software and actually do the work of walking the DNS structure to find the correct location of a host. However, there are various ways resolvers can be misled to load the wrong host. If WHOIS were better used in resolution, it could prevent certain malicious resolution and redirection. In general, there are multiple opportunities of WHOIS to be better used for comprehensive Internet security and assurance.

4.2.2   How a Domain Becomes a Website

It starts with a registrant purchasing a domain name from a registrar. As part of the process, the registrant must supply WHOIS information and agree to the registrant agreement. The registrar then submits the domain name, paired with a nameserver (NS) that holds the domain's specific IP address, to the top-level domain (TLD) registry for insertion in the applicable zone file. The zone file should already have the NS information and its IP address listed. The registry refreshes the zone file in the live DNS, making the domain name resolvable to the IP address. After this is completed, content loaded on the IP address associated with the domain name will become retrievable through HTTP and any other network protocols. So, here at the very beginning of the process, we have an opportunity to ensure that the WHOIS is valid, probably the best time, since some abusive domains do not remain online long after being deployed. Validating the WHOIS record at any point after insertion in the zone file is missed opportunity to prevent abuse of a domain name.

4.2.3   WHOIS Pervades the DNS

In order for a domain to resolve on the Internet, the registrant must submit data to the registrar, which becomes the WHOIS record for the domain. The registrar associates the domain name with an NS and an IP address through the nameserver. This data is submitted

---

[9] http://www.livinginternet.com/u/ui_bitnet.htm
[10] See note 8.
[11] https://blogs.rsa.com/engineering-security-solutions-at-layer-8-and-above/

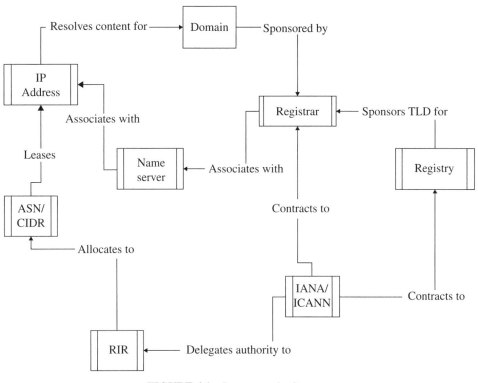

FIGURE 4.1 Internet authority map.

to the registry for insertion in the zone file, which makes the domain resolvable in the DNS. In addition to the domain itself, the registrar, registry, nameserver, and IP address all have WHOIS records. Also, the NS may have its own IP with a unique WHOIS record. There can be even more records behind backup nameservers, content hosts, mail services, and other components attached to the domain. While WHOIS is not a functional requirement for the DNS, each portion has its own record. To make things even more interesting, the related WHOIS records also have the same elements with their own WHOIS records. Obtaining each record and analyzing the details can provide a full picture of how the website operates and who controls it. The following chart shows the relationships between all the entities that make it possible for a website to resolve on the Internet.

Compare the chart above to the one below, which shows the same structures but defines the relationships in terms of WHOIS.

4.2.4 ICANN, IANA, Registries, and Registrars

The ICANN[12] administers contracts with registry companies who sponsor TLD extensions. Registrars sell individual domain names within the TLDs administered by registries. The Internet Assigned Numbers Authority[13] (IANA) is responsible for the IP side of the Internet

[12] http://www.icann.org/
[13] http://www.iana.org/about/

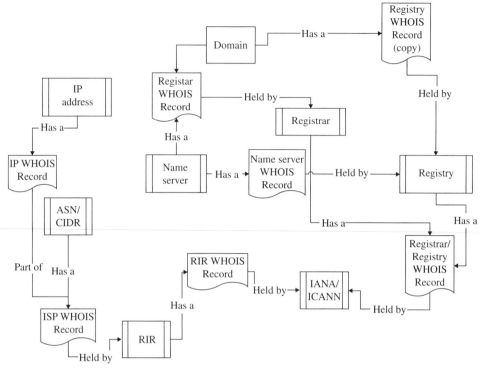

FIGURE 4.2   Internet WHOIS record map.

through the five regional RIR NICs.[14] In theory, ICANN and IANA are separate, but ICANN runs IANA through a contract issued by the US Department of Commerce. Additionally, IANA is the registry for .ARPA and .INT. InterNIC[15] is an older technical function that is now part of ICANN but initially had the responsibility of the original Network Solutions contract to issue domain names. The WHOIS thread in all of this exists with the Registrar Accreditation Agreement[16] (RAA), which is a contract between the registrar and ICANN. The contract governs how WHOIS data is collected and presented. These data standards (or lack of standards) within ICANN's administration of WHOIS are the subject of considerable debate and criticism.

Within the registry structure, there are a diverse number of TLDs with different rules, populations, and uses. The country code top-level domain (ccTLD) structures are basically registries that operate TLDs that represent the two-letter code of a nation or region. ccTLDs are obviously completely separate from generic top-level domains (gTLDs), but even within the gTLDs, there are divisions especially in terms of WHOIS data and access. There is a subset of what are called sponsored TLDs (sTLDs). sTLDs are ones that require some kind of community identification for use. For example, .CAT is exclusively for the use of the Catalan language and cultural community. A governing body usually

[14] http://www.iana.org/numbers/

[15] http://www.internic.org/

[16] http://www.icann.org/en/resources/registrars/raa/ra-agreement-21may09-en.htm

authenticates the registrants on a level not found in the other gTLDs, and hence, the WHOIS is much more reliable. There are two sponsored TLDs specifically reserved for the United States: .GOV for government agencies and .MIL for the military. Neither serves WHOIS through InterNIC. Different registries have different formats and options, for example, the .MUSEUM (museums) WHOIS server will allow for different character sets for the input and the output with –C switch, and .JOBS (human resource managers) uses the VeriSign WHOIS server. The rest of the following are organized by their WHOIS server formats.

These TLDs all use Afilias WHOIS servers: .MOBI (providers and consumers of mobile products and services), .POST (postal services), .XXX (pornographic sites), .ASIA (Asia-Pacific region), .AERO (air transport industry), and .COOP (cooperative associations). Within this model, there are features like searching for specific registrar:

whois –h whois.dotmobiregistry.net "registrar CSC Corporate Domains, Inc"

or by contact handle (a numbered ID string)

whois –h whois.dotmobiregistry.net "contact 6653942g1db97743"

You can use wildcard searches with "…"; the following will find all .MOBI domains with "phone" in the name:

whois –h whois.dotmobiregistry.net phone…

This is also possible with ID numbers:

whois –h whois.dotmobiregistry.net "ID D45…"

and contacts:

whois –h whois.dotmobiregistry.net "contact 665…"

.TEL (originally telecom, now open for other uses) and .TRAVEL (travel agents, airlines, hoteliers, tourism bureaus) permit wildcard searches of various types, for example,

whois –h whois.nic.tel "domain w…"

will return a list of .TEL domains starting with "w" and

whois –h whois.nic.tel "domain wa…"

will return a list starting with "wa." A powerful variation will return all *records* for a wild-card search:

whois –h whois.nic.tel "partial full wa…"

.EDU (accredited institutions) allows searches by emails and names that are no longer available in other WHOIS engines:

whois –h whois.educause.net "ma noc@bu.edu"

Wildcard searches are possible on names:

whois –h whois.educause.net "person jones%"

.INT is used for international treaty organizations and administered by IANA. Attempting to get help from whois.iana.org produces this message:

```
Using WHOIS server whois.iana.org, port 43, to find -h

% For query help and examples please see
% http://www.iana.org/whois_for_dummies
%
```

But the webpage http://www.iana.org/whois_for_dummies does not exist. After contacting IANA about this, they redirected the dead link.

4.2.5 .ARPA: Special Architectural TLD

.ARPA is a strange TLD. Unlike other TLDs that represent broad categories or geographical locations, .ARPA stands for an organization that technically no longer exists. Since the ARPANET was "decommissioned" in 1990, .APRA is a kind of ghost in the machine, directly sponsored and managed by IANA. If you review enough DNS records and follow them up the chain eventually, you will see in-addr-servers.arpa or in-addr.arpa. The use of special in-addr.arpa for private address and reverse mapping is documented partially in RFC 6761.[17] There are exactly nine .ARPA domains including the two mentioned above as well as e164.arpa[18] (for telephone number mapping), ip6-servers.arpa,[19] ip6.arpa,[20] iris.arpa,[21] uri.arpa,[22] and urn.arpa. Of course, "ARPA" stood for "Advanced Research Projects Agency," but the acronym has been reengineered since ARPA no longer exists. Now, in the DNS, "ARPA" now stands for "Address and Routing Parameter Area."[23]

When the DNS was switched, starting in 1983 [1], in place of the existing ARPANET scheme, a decision was made to append ".arpa" to all the existing hostnames as check on the functionality of the new model. The other organizations connected to the network protested because they had no specific organizational relationship with ARPA, and these hosts insisted they receive their own TLDs for each organization. Instead, Feinler developed the scheme to have generic categories for the TLD extensions. The specific origin of .COM is a curious accident. When SRI-NIC staff was considering the generic domains, they picked .BUS for "business" over .COM for "commercial." When Ken Harrenstien, author of the original WHOIS RFCs, set about to do the actual work of configuring the DNS, he realized that various hardware controllers ended in ".bus" and might create a conflict, so he made the quick choice of using .COM instead. So the most popular TLD so far was actually a last-minute default. .COM ("company/commercial"), .INFO ("information"), and .NET ("network") have all lost their original meaning and are now publicly accessible for a variety of commercial and noncommercial uses.

---

[17] http://tools.ietf.org/html/rfc6761
[18] https://www.ietf.org/rfc/rfc3761
[19] https://www.ietf.org/rfc/rfc5855.txt
[20] https://www.ietf.org/rfc/rfc3152.txt
[21] https://www.ietf.org/rfc/rfc4698.txt
[22] https://www.ietf.org/rfc/rfc3405.txt
[23] http://www.iana.org/domains/arpa

4.2.6   Setting the Example with Reserved Domains

Throughout this text, we use example.com or example.org in different demonstrations, which are real domains created for testing. example.info is registered but not deployed. The Internet is a project forever in development, so spaces for testing are necessary. example. com is deployed in the DNS and has a website displaying this message:

```
Example Domain

This domain is established to be used for illustrative examples
in documents. You may use this domain in examples without
prior coordination or asking for permission.
```

There is single link on the page that leads to a list of other special domain names found at http://www.iana.org/domains/reserved. These are called Reserved Top Level DNS Names and documented in RFC 2606[24] from 1999. This is a partial WHOIS record for example.org:

```
Domain ID:D2328855-LROR
Domain Name:EXAMPLE.ORG
Created On:31-Aug-1995 04:00:00 UTC
Last Updated On:27-Jul-2010 20:57:51 UTC
Expiration Date:30-Aug-2010 04:00:00 UTC
Sponsoring Registrar:Internet Assigned Numbers Authority
(IANA) (R193-LROR)
```

While example.org can give us a model structure of the .ORG WHOIS record structure, example.com is a *bad* example for learning about WHOIS. The entire WHOIS record response is this (with *whois –h whois.iana.org example.com*):

```
% IANA WHOIS server
% for more information on IANA, visit http://www.iana.org
% This query returned 1 object

domain:        EXAMPLE.COM

organisation: Internet Assigned Numbers Authority

created:       1992-01-01
source:        IANA
```

This record does not even provide the nameservers, let alone any registrant or technical information. It is telling because .COM has no standard WHOIS format.

RFC 2606 also documents reserved TLDs for testing:

.test is used for testing DNS code without impacting an active TLD space

.example is used in documentation and demonstration.

.invalid is used for domain names in records intended not to resolve making it obvious.

.localhost is a TLD used for local testing—anything here points back to 127.0.0.1.

[24] http://tools.ietf.org/html/rfc2606

These TLDs are not registered, so they have no WHOIS records. Special-Use Domain Names are further documented in RFC 6761.[25]

4.2.7   DNS RFCs 882, 883, 1033, and 1034

RFC 882[26] (1983) by Paul Mockapetris establishes the DNS as a mapping between hostnames and ARPA Internet addresses. 882 introduces the critical concepts for the DNS still in use: a database model, timeouts, nameservers, resolvers, datagrams versus virtual circuits, recursive versus iterative, and the "DOT" system. However, for our purposes, the most important part of this standard is on page 14 in reference domain registration (RFC) 882 and administration:

> There must be a **responsible person associated with each domain to be a contact** point for questions about the domain, to verify and update the domain related information, and to resolve any problems (e.g., protocol violations) with hosts in the domain.

This requirement for a responsible person to be contactable could not be clearer. The reason is obvious: on the global network, every domain can impact every other domain. This is a shared resource, and responsibility is the trust framework that the hardware and software cannot provide. This information is held within the various WHOIS records associated with the domain. Domain ownership is a *responsibility* which is assured by the owner being *contactable*. The purpose of this contact is specifically to "resolve any problems" with technical issues only being one example. So issues of spam, infringement, and illicit activity are completely legitimate. RFC 883 *Domain Names—Implementation and Specification*,[27] also by Mockapetris, supports the theory of RFC 882, with specifics, and references the early WHOIS RFC 812. The issue of owner contact information was clearly on the minds of the original developers. An update came 5 years later in the RFC 1034[28] with 20 additional pages and a number of separate RFCs to address specific issues within the growing Internet; one is 1033,[29] which is dedicated to the responsibility of domain administrators. This guide clarifies the requirements stated in 882:

> The administrator of a domain must be a **responsible person** who has the **authority to either enforce these actions** himself or delegate them to someone else.

What the administrator is responsible for is specified just above in the same paragraph:

> He must **be aware of the behavior of the hosts in domain**, and **take prompt action on reports of problems**, such as protocol violations or other serious misbehavior.

The document details the procedures for domain registration and how contact data will be displayed in WHOIS.

---

[25] See note 17.
[26] http://tools.ietf.org/html/rfc882
[27] http://tools.ietf.org/html/rfc883
[28] See note 6.
[29] http://www.ietf.org/rfc/rfc1032.txt

4.3   DNS RR

While not commonly called WHOIS records, these are nevertheless information records that provide important information about providers, operators, and owners. Some of the data in RRs is intended to match what is in related WHOIS records and provide a fuller perspective on an Internet site. In many cases, when the RR details do not match the WHOIS record, it indicates a problem. Like WHOIS records, RRs can be falsified and manipulated. Details in RRs are also additional data points that can in turn be passed to WHOIS for more information.

Just as the Internet may be a "series of tubes," the DNS may be a series of files. At the top of the file order is the root zone. The root zone may sound mysterious, but it is simply a listing of where further information can be obtained about TLDs and primary Internet servers. The file is even viewable.[30] The list of top-level Internet root servers is also viewable.[31] Each one of the registries for TLDs runs a *zone* and deploys a zone file, which is a listing of the domains submitted to the registry by the registrars to resolve on the Internet. Each domain name in the zone file is matched to a nameserver. At the top of the zone file is a list of the nameservers and their IP addresses. This is what makes a registry or registrar special, that is, the authority to add entries to the zone file. Each entry in the zone or root file, no matter how high it goes, has a WHOIS record.

4.3.1   Berkeley Internet Name Domain

The Berkeley Internet Name Domain (BIND) is the most common open-source software for implementing various DNS protocols. There are a number of utilities and functions bundled with BIND, but its main functions are (i) running a DNS server, (ii) as a resolver library, and (iii) as a diagnostics for servers.[32] BIND was first developed under a DARPA contract at the University of California at Berkeley by graduate students Douglas Terry, Mark Painter, David Riggle, and Songnian Zhou in the early 1980s.[33] BIND has evolved over the years and is now on its 10th version and sponsored by the Internet Systems Consortium (ISC) (isc.org). ISC also operates one of the Internet's redundant root servers.[34] For our purposes, BIND comes with an excellent DNS analyzing tool called the Domain Information Groper (DiG).

4.3.2   Shared WHOIS Project

Shared WHOIS Project (SWIP) is a way, within the IP space, to ensure the various WHOIS databases are consistent and complete, since records are located in many places. It was started in the early 1990s[35] with the concern that as the network became distributed, the ownership data would be fragmented. SWIP is one of the options offered by ARIN for submitting WHOIS data.[36]

---

[30] ftp://ftp.rs.internic.net/domain/root.zone
[31] http://www.internic.net/domain/named.root
[32] https://www.isc.org/downloads/bind/
[33] http://www.eecs.berkeley.edu/Pubs/TechRpts/1984/5957.html
[34] https://www.isc.org/services/
[35] http://tools.ietf.org/html/rfc1491#page-7
[36] https://www.arin.net/resources/request/reassignments.html

4.3.3   Using the DiG

dig is easy to remember because we are DiGging up information. DiG comes bundled with BIND, which can be downloaded for Windows at http://www.isc.org/downloads/ if not already installed. DiG options can be displayed with *dig –help*. Running DiG on the command line like this on the domain for the National Oceanic and Atmospheric Administration

dig noaa.org

should yield this record:

```
; <<>> DiG 9.6-ESV-R9-P1 <<>> noaa.org
;; global options: +cmd
;; Got answer:
;; ->>HEADER<<- opcode: QUERY, status: NOERROR, id: 4373
;; flags: qr rd ra; QUERY: 1, ANSWER: 0, AUTHORITY: 1, ADDITIONAL: 0

;; QUESTION SECTION:
;noaa.org.                      IN      A

;; AUTHORITY SECTION:
noaa.org.            5813   IN     SOA    dns02.woc.noaa.gov.
hostmaster.noaa.gov. 2010061002 10800 3600 604800 86400

;; Query time: 19 msec
;; SERVER: 10.33.2.8#53(10.33.2.8)
;; WHEN: Wed Oct 09 17:16:03 Eastern Daylight Time 2013
;; MSG SIZE   rcvd: 91
```

This record has four clearly separated sections, but some may have more. The first section starting with "**DiG 9.6-ESV-R9-P1 <<>> noaa.org.**" is a summary section, which tells us what to expect in the rest of the data. The initial line prints the DiG version number and the domain we asked about. The "global options" line tells us which DiG options are set by default; in this case, the **+cmd** means the command-line response will be displayed. So far, this output is all about the software and not a DNS record. "Got answer:" simply informs us that the process worked; it does not mean it retrieved records or it is the best answer. Note that all the domain names in the results end in an extra dot; this is the presence of the invisible or null domain. The various fields are defined in RFC 1035.[37]

The **HEADER** block contains information about the quality of the returned record and again is not record data itself. **opcode:** is the operation performed, in this case a query for records. The next field, **status:**, is critical as it tells us if the lookup succeeded. In this case, "NOERROR" means exactly what it says. If the status had been "NXDOMAIN" instead, this would indicate that the domain queried does not exist, but we have to be careful with this because it is not absolute. The **id:** will change every time the query is run to help

---

[37] http://www.networksorcery.com/enp/rfc/rfc1035.txt

compare results; this number links the actual query to the result. The **flags:** field in the next line is critical for telling us about the quality of the results in terms of the way we asked for it. The two-letter codes that follow—**qr**, **rd**, and **ra**—could be read as "these are the query results from a server where recursion was available and recursion was desired." However, there is an important flag missing: **aa**, which means "authoritative answer." This is because we used the default DNS to retrieve this record instead of using the authoritative server, getting this, and designating the server to use for a DiG, which is explained in the following text. Not having **aa** as a flag does not necessarily mean the record is bad, but it is just not the source record.

The **QUESTION SECTION** is a confirmation of our request. By default, we asked for the Internet (**IN**) host (**A**) record for **noaa.org**. Again, this is not record data, but it is important to match it to our request.

It is the **AUTHORITY SECTION** that actually has the information we want. This is a start of authority (**SOA**) record that has two server domains that mark the start of a DNS zone of authority. The record class displayed here is IN, which simply means "INTERNET," and this is the only class that is likely to be seen in an active domain record. There are other codes from defunct standards like CSNET (CS), CHAOS (CH), and HESIOD (HE).

It is important to be aware that there are dozens of DNS record types and not all are displayed by default. Use DiG to query the specific records and test the results. The order of the answer line will usually be in this order:

<Domain_name> <Time_to_live> <Class> <Type> <Value>

The domain name is what we are querying about. Time to live (TTL) indicates how long the information will be valid for. Class, as we explained, should always be IN. The type is the RR we are asking about and the value is the answer we seek.

SOA record is the top-level record in the zone file for this domain.[38] The SOA should contain information about the source host, a contact email, a serial number, and a number of time-related values. It is the SOA that determines how the zone reaches the secondary nameservers:

dig example.com soa

This should return

```
3351 IN SOA sns.dns.icann.org. noc.dns.icann.org. 2013102177
```

The first part is a TTL value. The "IN SOA" indicates it is an Internet SOA record. The next string "sns.dns.icann.org" is the top-level source host who created the record. Believe it or not, "noc.dns.icann.org" is the email address of the administrator, which can be converted to "noc@dns.icann.org" for contact purposes; the at-symbol is removed to avoid automated harvesting of the email addresses. The first numerical value is a serial number. The different number sequences that follow (not shown in the example) mark the Refresh, Retry, Expire, and Minimum times in seconds. Abuse.net has a DNS utility for handling these records for the purposes of dealing with spam.[39]

---

[38] http://support.microsoft.com/kb/163971
[39] http://www.abuse.net/using.phtml

The host record (A) is the IP address of a host. This is a critical piece of information for researching domain name records and their validity. This value should, most importantly, match the result returned by **ping**. To get the host address, use

dig example.com a

This should return

```
1648 IN A 93.184.216.119
```

Compare this to the IPv6 (AAAA) address record, obtained with

dig noaa.org aaaa

This should return

```
1570 IN AAAA 2606:2800:220:6d:26bf:1447:1097:aa7
```

The Mail Exchange (MX) is a domain waiting to accept mail for the domain in the record, which is not required and does not have to be the same domain. There may be more than one MX record depending on how mail centric the particular site is. If there is no MX record, the query will return the SOA record. The command

dig microsoft.com mx

should return

```
MX 10 microsoft-com.mail.protection.outlook.com.
```

The numeric value between "MX" and the mail server is the *preference* value, which can be from 0 to 65535. The lower the number, the more preferred the server is, dictating which server is selected once the primary one fails.

NS records are required if the name is deployed, and we may assume that the nameservers returned by DiG would be the same as the NS in the WHOIS record, but they do not always match. This is important to note as the WHOIS and the DNS records are different and not explicitly linked. To get the NS, run this query:

dig example.org ns

Canonical name (CNAME) is a domain name that is a variation or extension of a domain name that functions in place of the domain. The most common example is "www.", which precedes most domain names but more or less points to that domain name:

dig www.google.com cname

However, CNAME can be used to redirect content from one domain to another:
Pointer (PTR) alias for an IP address:

dig noaa.org ptr

Host description (HINFO) CPU and OS in ASCII:

dig noaa.org hinfo

Text (TXT)—uninterrupted ASCII text:

dig noaa.org txt

Just because various record types exist does not mean every domain has the record type. If the domain does not have the record type, there will be no ANSWER SECTION in the response. See the full DiG MAN for all options.[40] One operation that may be useful for research and investigation is the *zone transfer*. This procedure can copy all subdomains attached to a domain with the AXFR protocol.[41] However, fewer and fewer servers allow open access to this bulk information. The point of the process is to allow zones to be easily copied from one server to another, but this can be useful in analyzing malicious activity remotely.

4.3.4   Graphic DNS Software and Websites

As we know, the various records that underlie the Internet are textual and often obscure in their makeup. Clearly, there is considerable time devoted in this text to deciphering the language of these records. There are various facilities available that present the data and relationships in graphic form. The Hurricane Electric BGP interface is one of many that produce *route propagation* maps. These graphics show how particular networks and endpoints on the Internet obtain their access to the Internet from upstream providers. The arrows in the map indicate the direction of access obtained, not access granted, that is, the arrows point to the network above in the chain.

There are a variety of graphic ping and traceroute sites available. For example, Computer Associates CloudMonitor[42] will allow traceroutes from global proxies.

Not all services are web based: NirSoft offers software like DNSDataView.[43]

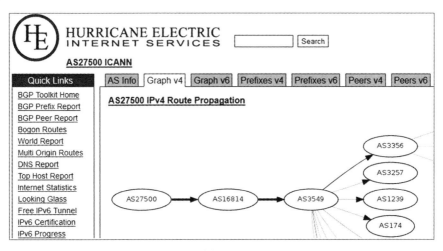

FIGURE 4.3   ASN routing.

---

[40] http://linux.die.net/man/1/dig

[41] https://tools.ietf.org/html/rfc5936

[42] http://cloudmonitor.ca.com/en/traceroute.php

[43] http://www.nirsoft.net/utils/dns_records_viewer.html

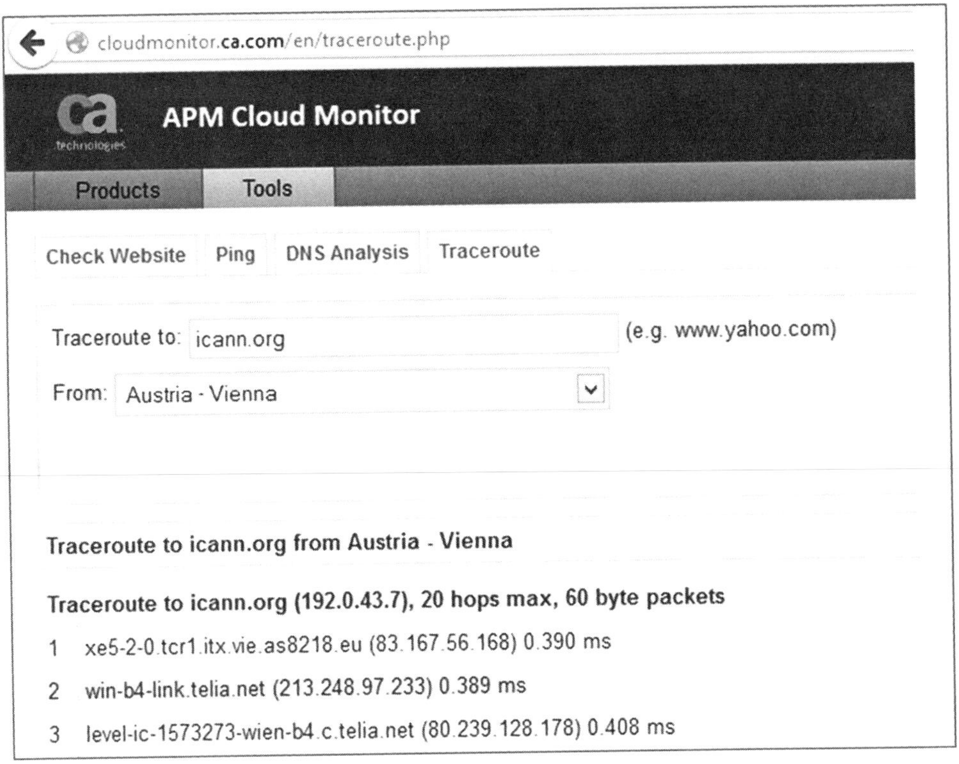

FIGURE 4.4   Web traceroute window.

4.3.5   Finding Hidden Registrars and Tracking Roots

As above, so below. If the WHOIS record set in general is messy for the broad population of domain names, it is in part because of the lack of consistency throughout the system. Because registrars and registrants are also recorded in WHOIS, we can look at their entries and the related record sets available from ICANN, IANA, and InterNIC (which frequently do not match). Additionally, each dataset only has fragments of a complete record. The InterNIC directory has website and general contact listings. The ICANN registrar contact page has specific names of registry operators. The IANA page has registrar account numbers. The VeriSign database has specific technical contacts and real business addresses. There is no single place for a consumer to go to get everything they need to know about a registrar. This is likely due to a decade of information fragmentation and generally poor administration of critical data as opposed to anything malicious. However, if the upper record set for the contracted parties (around 1000) is confusing, can we expect the lower record set for 200 million domains to be any better? There are several locations for registrar data within ICANN's sphere of control that can be in conflict. For example, the IANA list[44] of registrar IDs has an accredited registrar called "Affinity Internet, Inc." with an IANA number of 280. However, the InterNIC Registrar Directory[45] and the ICANN Descriptions

---

[44] http://www.iana.org/assignments/registrar-ids/registrar-ids.xml
[45] http://www.internic.org/alpha.html

and Contact Information for Accredited Registrars[46] list no such company. So, in order to get more information, we query the WHOIS database with

> *whois –h whois.internic.net "registrar Affinity Internet, Inc."*

which returns

```
Registrar Name: AFFINITY INTERNET, INC.
Address: 16607 S. Vermont Ave., Gardena, CA 90247, US
Phone Number: 310-426-2402
Email: TKUNZE@AFFINITY.COM
Whois Server: whois.affinity.com
Referral URL: www.affinity.com
Registrar Contact: No Contact
```

So it seems we have found a hidden registrar. To start collecting all the hidden registrars, we use wildcard WHOIS lookups just like domains, for example,

> *whois –h whois.internic.net "registrar a..."*
>
> *whois –h whois.internic.net "registrar b..."*

and so on. This is a partial output for the letter "C" wildcard lookup:

```
CRAZY8DOMAINS.COM INC.            whois.kudo.com
CRAZY DOMAINS FZ-LLC              whois.syra.com.au
CPS-DATENSYSTEME GMBH             whois.cps-datensysteme.de
COOLHOSTING.CA INC.              whois.coolhosting.ca
COOLHANDLE HOSTING, LLC           whois.moniker.com
COOL OCEAN, INC.                  whois.coolocean.com
CONDOMAINIUM.COM INC.             whois.epik.com
COMPUGLOBALHYPERMEGA.COM LLC whois.compuglobalhypermega.com
COMPANA, LLC                      whois.budgetnames.com
COMMERCE ISLAND, INC.             whois.commerceisland.com
COMFYDOMAINS LLC                  whois.comfydomains.com
COLUMBIANAMES.COM LLC             whois.columbianames.com
. . .
```

The brief output is in registrar WHOIS server pairs. This is actually the source of server names provided in InterNIC Thin WHOIS lookups.

What we find by examining all of the entries in the database is a series of inconsistencies and anomalies. In general, the IANA has over 1700 entities listed, whereas ICANN has fewer than 1000. For example, the IANA list has dozens of unknown registrar entities not listed in the ICANN version, including 11 simply entitled "*Unassigned*."[47] There are of course various test entries like #8 "Test Registrar" and the unnumbered "#TEST ACCOUNT 123!#." One can understand that test entries are needed or mistakes

---

[46] http://www.icann.org/registrar-reports/accreditation-qualified-list.html

[47] See note 44.

may occur, but the "Unassigned" accounts are all listed as *accredited* and active. One strange entry is #500 called "Terminated Registrar" but is actually accredited. There is also the issue of missing entries in the form of skipped account numbers, for example, after "Terminated Registrar," 100 accreditations are missing from the count. Since even terminated registrars continue to be listed in the database, there is no obvious reason for the skipped numbers. One example of an unlisted but obvious technical entry is "NOC PING UTILITY," which has a corresponding WHOIS server of "xxx.xxxxx.net" that does not exist. The same is true for "REGY_DIAGNOSTICS(1)," which simply has "whois" as the WHOIS server. What follows is a sampling of possible misentries and test registrars found in the database:

```
ASF
ICANN PDT 1
ICANN PDT 2
ICANNPDT
MALDETECTOR INTERNAL - VERISIGN, INC
MB TEST
NAME SUGG REST API
NAMESUGGESTION WIDGET REST API
TDRS TEST
TEST 15
TEST BONNIE REGISTRAR
TEST JESUS REGISTRAR
TEST REGISTRY OPERATOR
TT
VERISIGN CUSTOMER PILOTS
VERISIGN DIAGNOSTICS AND MONITORING
VERISIGN DOMAIN HASHLINK PRODUCT
VERISIGN EMT MONITORING
VERISIGN IDEFENSE SERVICES
VERISIGN LISP INTERNAL ACCOUNT
VERISIGN MALWEB TEAM
VERISIGN MOBILEVIEW
VERISIGN SARL
VERISIGN SECURITY AND STABILITY
VERISIGN ZONE SCANS
VERISIGN NETSEC MONITORING
VERISIGN ROOT NAMESERVER DIRECTORY
```

There are also these three that are likely some kind of test:

```
whois.dummy.com     ENIC (DIRECT DUMMY)
whois.dummy.com     NETWORK SOLUTIONS (DIRECT DUMMY)
whois.dummy.com     SRSPLUS (DIRECT DUMMY)
```

ICANN has at times had difficulty tracking its registrars. Many of the business addresses disclosed publicly, especially by registrars accused of contact violations, have proven false. In 2009, ICANN terminated the registrar Parava Networks,[48] which investigators had been trying to contact about illicit steroid sales,[49] but postal notices were returned as undeliverable. OnlineNIC is a registrar that has been sued by Microsoft,[50] Yahoo,[51] Verizon,[52] and others[53] for various online trademark violations. OnlineNIC purported to be in Oakland, California, but turned out to be located in China.[54] The ongoing issue is one of identification of sources of information. Part of the problem is that until 2009 ICANN did not require registrars to disclose their addresses to the public.[55] Additionally, before 2011, ICANN did not perform extensive criminal history checks of registrar applicants.[56] If this kind of verification had been in place from the beginning, it could have prevented the debacles of EST Domains[57] and Dynamic Dolphin,[58] two registrars with convicted felons in their leadership. Those two registrars had been noted for their illicit activity and high spam volumes. The problem becomes even more complicated when a difficult-to-locate registrar extends its authority to other parties who are difficult or impossible to locate. For example, the registrar Internet.BS claims to be *"based in the Commonwealth of The Bahamas,"*[59] but an undercover investigation in 2012 could not locate an office present in the Bahamas, and it was later shown that their principals were in Panama.[60] As a registrar, they have control over and source all of their WHOIS records. Like many registrars, they use *resellers* who often have direct access to update the WHOIS database. A reseller of Internet.BS named Jolis Intercom registered imposter "Bank of Switzerland" domains (phishing) and inserted themselves as the registrar in the WHOIS record.[61] So we have a situation where the entire chain of identification and accountability has been compromised. Where would the consumer even begin to sort this out, especially when the WHOIS record itself is useless?

This goes back to the proper identification of the contracted parties as foundation for the trust relationship of the network. IANA is supposed to track the Internet roots, but their tracking appears to be problematic. Following the controversial and legally challenged[62] redelegation of Puerto Rico's TLD (.PR) from a public institution to a private company, IANA Vice President Elise Gerich was asked in a public session how IANA tracks the operators of various TLDs. Gerich replied, *"You're going to laugh at our process…We send out holiday cards and we send them out to the addresses that we have in the database, and then the ones that don't respond, we contact them."*[63] This would appear

---

[48] http://www.icann.org/en/news/correspondence/burnette-to-valdes-09apr09-en.pdf
[49] http://www.legitscript.com/download/Steroid%20Report.pdf
[50] http://www.thedomains.com/2009/03/12/onlinenic-settles-with-microsoft-appeals-verizon-decision/
[51] http://blog.ericgoldman.org/archives/2009/01/onlinenic_loses.htm
[52] http://www.nytimes.com/2008/12/25/technology/companies/25verizon.html?_r=0
[53] http://dockets.justia.com/docket/california/candce/3:2009cv05612/222027
[54] http://www.esecurityplanet.com/news/article.php/3794661/Verizons-Cybersquatter-Based-in-China.htm?mchk=1
[55] http://atlarge.icann.org/node/1987
[56] http://www.icann.org/en/news/announcements/announcement-01jun11-en.htm
[57] http://voices.washingtonpost.com/securityfix/2008/09/estdomains_a_sordid_history_an.html
[58] http://krebsonsecurity.com/2013/11/spam-friendly-registrar-dynamic-dolphin-shuttered/
[59] https://internetbs.net/en/domain-name-registrations/aboutus.html
[60] http://krebsonsecurity.com/2012/03/half-of-all-rogue-pharmacies-at-two-registrars/
[61] http://www.circleid.com/posts/20120327_fake_bank_site_fake_registrar/
[62] http://domainincite.com/docs/Exhibit-3-LETTER.JohnJeffrey.pdf
[63] http://dakar42.icann.org/meetings/dakar2011/transcript-naralo-monthly-24oct11-en.pdf

as impractically naïve tracking system on which the global Internet user depends. ICANN in general seems to lack an understanding of the importance of tracking critical resources, which trickles down to the domain level.

4.3.6   Traceroute

A traceroute is supposed to show the path taken from one network to another. When you send email, transfer files, establish connections, or browse the web, the data packets are passed through a series of routers at different networks before reaching the destination. The packets leave your network and passed to the service provider, and Internet routing algorithms attempt to use the shortest path possible to the destination. In theory, every network or *hop* is identifiable and recordable. The program works by sending data packets to one hop at a time, breaking the connection, measuring the time, and then starting over with the next hop. Traceroutes have many applications including network troubleshooting[64] and of course tracking Internet abuse. Not only can we find out where abuse is originating from, but we can also use traceroute to see if various WHOIS records have been forged. The original program was created by Van Jacobson in 1987.[65] The traceroute utility is on most systems at the command line (*tracert* in Windows, *traceroute* elsewhere) and can take domain names or IP addresses as parameters:

tracert yahoo.com OR traceroute yahoo.com

A partial extraction of the results is given below (your results may be different):

```
he-2-7-0-0-cr01.newyork.ny.ibone.comcast.net [68.86.95.29]
23-30-206-166-static.hfc.comcastbusiness.net [23.30.206.166]
po4-20G.ar7.SEA1.gblx.net [67.16.153.210]
YAHOO-TRANSIT.Te3-3.1189.csr2.SEA1.gblx.net [207.138.112.162]
ae-5.pat2.gqb.yahoo.com [216.115.101.197]
ae-1.msr1.gq1.yahoo.com [66.196.67.5]
xe-5-0-0.clr1-a-gdc.gq1.yahoo.com [67.195.0.21]
et-18-25.fab3-1-gdc.gq1.yahoo.com [98.137.31.174]
po-16.bas2-7-prd.gq1.yahoo.com [206.190.32.43]
ir1.fp.vip.gq1.yahoo.com [206.190.36.45]
```

This is a list of network locations along the route to yahoo.com, at least from one location. The address at the top of the list is the closest to the network that initiated the traceroute. As we move down the list, the servers listed are progressively closer to our destination.[66] Each point along the route can be queried through WHOIS. Using the related locations available through IP WHOIS, we see a general path from New York to Colorado and then to California, which makes geographic sense. A route may not always be that straightforward. Many websites and browser features will often state that a *server* or an *IP address* is a particular country or city, but this is not exactly correct. There are malicious and

---

[64] http://customer.comcast.com/help-and-support/internet/run-traceroute-command/
[65] http://www.ieeeghn.org/wiki/index.php/Van_Jacobson
[66] http://www.cisco.com/en/US/products/sw/iosswrel/ps1831/products_tech_note09186a00800a6057.shtml

completely ordinary reasons for this. Some records are simply outdated, and IPs may be transferred from one company to another but the records may not have been changed. IP record locations likely reflect the *office* location of an ISP and not the data center; this is for security reason and also simply for the practical reason that the servers themselves are in ugly remote buildings. Then you have the issue of rogue ISPs and customers altering records to conceal their location. However, someone altering records or concealing their real location can only control so much of the network. The closest hops to the end of the trace are the most critical in determining the authenticity of the route. A great example can be found in the Pirate Bay case.[67] Pirate Bay is a *torrent* site that openly permits downloads of pirated media. For obvious reasons, the operators have taken steps to conceal their location. In 2013, traceroutes to their sites showed Pirate Bay to be in North Korea,[68] which is impossible for several reasons, but the one most critical for our analysis is the impossible jump in hops documented in the traceroute from New York to Asia. In our yahoo.com example, there are multiple hops between New York and California. In the Pirate Bay traceroute, there are no intermediate routers between New York and the supposed destination. The point is to look for inconsistencies and verify the WHOIS records of hops in the route until clearly false or impossible information appears.

Traceroutes can also be conducted from proxy services like TCPIPUTILS (tcpiputils. com). Proxy services will allow you to conduct traceroutes from a location other than your own and output all the hops in a graphic image with ISP details. Use this in conjunction with services like just-ping (just-ping.com), which will ping the same address from multiple locations around the world. Network Tools (http://network-tools.com) also has a great interface for using multiple lookups. Using a number of sources helps verify the validity of the supposed location of an IP address; resources like traceroute.org list over 1000 traceroute sites. However, there are more advanced tools, for example, the concept of *traceback*, which discovers the origin of data and not just the general path of connection.[69] The Locator/Identifier Separation Protocol is another architecture that was created to improve routing but also maps equipment to specific locations.[70]

4.3.6.1 Prefix WHOIS and Layer Four Traceroute by Victor Oppleman

Victor Oppleman, coauthor of *Advanced Defenses Against Hardcore Hacks (Hacking Exposed)*,[71] has developed a number of advanced tracerouting and WHOIS-related services. "*No one cares about traceroute, but they should*," related Oppleman in a phone interview. "*Everyone should understand the Internet better to protect themselves and their businesses.*"[72] He started in the industry with General Telephone & Electronics Corporation (GTE) as well as BBN Technologies.[73] As to what drew him to WHOIS in particular, he noted the simplicity of the function paired with the importance of its role. One of his projects is the Prefix WHOIS Project[74] (pwhois.org). Pwhois is a RIPE service[75]

---

[67] http://www.zdnet.com/pirate-bay-and-four-more-torrent-sites-get-blocked-in-italy-7000022115/
[68] https://rdns.im/the-pirate-bay-north-korean-hosting-no-its-fake
[69] http://www.circleid.com/posts/20131106_ip_addresses_and_traceback/
[70] http://citeseerx.ist.psu.edu/viewdoc/download?doi=10.1.1.125.8411&rep=rep1&type=pdf
[71] http://www.extremeexploits.com/
[72] Oppleman interview.
[73] http://www.extremeexploits.com/authors.ee
[74] http://pwhois.org/
[75] http://www.ripe.net/data-tools/stats/ris/riswhois

at riswhois.ripe.net, which will return prefixes and ASN origins for IP addresses. The main point is to obtain routing information from a number of peers rather than from registrar-oriented network information, which is often wrong or limited. *"The domain WHOIS world is a mess, IP is much better."* Oppleman likes the way IPs are divided by global regions with the five RIRs but is concerned about national subdivisions in the Asia-Pacific region. While he appreciates the organizational advantages IPs have over domains, he acknowledges a problem the public is generally unaware of, *"we are still mostly routing by rumor,"* meaning there is no real map of the Internet and even attempts to clarify the global routing are met with skepticism.[76] The amount of work that goes into making the Internet work by people like Oppleman is largely unknown and unappreciated. The information used by PWhois is the most recently collected routing table data from Remote Route Collectors[77] (RRC). This can all be accessed with the RIPE WHOIS client[78] and offers additional switches.

Layer Four Traceroute (LFT) displays route packets[79] and is a kind of an advanced version of traceroute. Layer four is the transport layer as explained earlier that handles TCP and UDP, By examining routing at the packet level, collecting additional information, and testing hops more thoroughly, LFT provides a more comprehensive view of routing. In one example, compare these results below from LFT with the results from a standard traceroute to yahoo.com discussed earlier in this section:

```
[226]   [LOS-NETTOS] ln-usc3-acg303.ln.net (130.152.181.81)
[226]   [LOS-NETTOS] ln-cit2-citusc2037.ln.net
(130.152.181.187)
[292]   [TELEHOUSE-IIX] laix.bas1.lax.yahoo.com
(198.32.146.28)
[10310]  [A-YAHOO-US2] xe-4-0-2.pat2.sjc.yahoo.com
(216.115.96.46)
[10310]  [A-YAHOO-US2] ae-3.pat2.swp.yahoo.com
(216.115.96.57)
[10310]  [A-YAHOO-US2] ae-5.pat2.gqb.yahoo.com
(216.115.101.197)
[10310]  [INKTOMI-BLK-3] ae-0.msr2.gq1.yahoo.com
(66.196.67.23)
[36647]  [A-YAHOO-US6] xe-8-0-0.clr1-a-gdc.gq1.yahoo.com
(68.180.253.131)
```

The LFT version includes ASNs and network names. LFT will also indicate when it has reached a firewall. You can download LFT,[80] try it online,[81] or even buy the graphic version of Path Analyzer Pro.[82]

---

[76] http://bgpmon.net/?p=140

[77] http://www.ripe.net/data-tools/projects/faqs/faq-ris/what-is-a-remote-route-collector-rrc

[78] ftp://ftp.ripe.net/tools/ripe-whois-latest.tar.gz

[79] http://linux.die.net/man/8/lft

[80] http://pwhois.org/lft/

[81] http://www.extremeexploits.com/tools/lft.ee

[82] http://www.pathanalyzer.com/?ad=pw

Within LFT, there is an incorporated function called **WhoB**, which was once its own program, but can still be called independently. WhoB queries various sources of WHOIS,[83] especially for IP, ASN, and hosts.[84] The program can be accessed from the C or PHP code. WhoB can access ASN origins by connecting to RIPE, Cymru, and the Internet Routing Registry (IRR) Routing Arbiter Database (RADb). While these improved methods pull additional reputational information, the major advantage of regular traceroute is that it helps explain when the tracing fails or what kind of obstacles it encounters.

4.4 OUTSIDE THE DNS: AN INTERNET WITHOUT WHOIS

There is no need to speculate about a world without WHOIS records because it exists. So, are there other *Internets?* Yes, but it is not considered a polite conversation at ICANN. ICANN's motto has been *"One World, One Internet,"*[85] but this is more wishful thinking than anything else. While there is a common Internet accepted by the public, there have been alternatives, even in the beginning. There are hundreds of known alternative TLDs and possibly more unknown ones. A future in which there are several different "gated" global Internets is a very real possibility.[86] How is this possible? It is actually fairly simple. We have seen in this chapter on DNS that the domain system is a series of files and software that reads the files. Our browsers and other network utilities route through a single root because that is the accepted standard. To get to the other DNSs, we need to know where the other roots are and the software that reads those roots. In a world with multiple roots, ICANN's role becomes diminished or even irrelevant.

4.4.1 The Onion Routing

The Onion Routing (TOR) uses the same IP space as the normal DNS but does not use the ICANN/IANA DNS. TOR is not another Internet; it is a different map to the existing space. Beyond permitting access to other domain structures, TOR also has mostly anonymous browsing by bouncing traffic through multiple different routes and specifically longer routes. Standard Internet browsing is designed to use the shortest path possible and keep track of where content came from. TOR does not cache like the standard DNS, thus obscuring where content was originally retrieved from. TOR, in essence, gives you directions to locations within the current IP space that are not listed in the public DNS. Imagine there is map of Route 66, which is available publicly. I am having an illegal party in the woods somewhere off of Route 66. So I take my friends' maps and mark "The Old Cemetery Road" with an "X" halfway through on all of their maps and distribute them. Could someone find the party by driving down every side road off Route 66? Possibly, but it would take a very long time to find it and the party would probably be over by then. The key is that you need the map because there are also no signs and you might not even know you are driving on the right road until you get there. The company that makes the maps will never put "The Old Cemetery Road" on their maps and will

---

[83] http://linux.die.net/man/8/whob

[84] http://pwhois.org/lft/whob-manpage.html

[85] http://www.icann.org/en/about/learning/factsheets/ecosystem-06feb13-en.pdf

[86] http://www.computerworld.com/s/article/9228200/Chinese_operators_hope_to_standardize_a_segmented_Internet?pageNumber=1

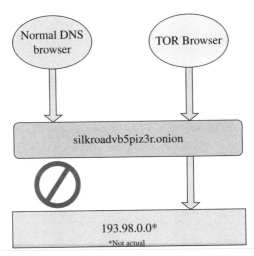

FIGURE 4.5   Onion routing versus DNS.

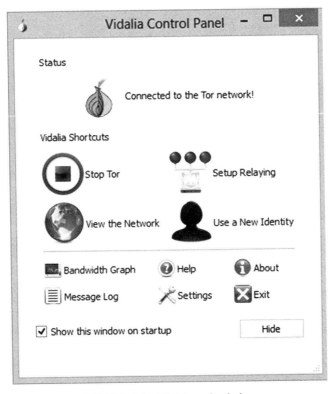

FIGURE 4.6   TOR launch window.

even refuse to talk about it. The bottom line is that the normal DNS cannot find TOR's
.ONION sites because it does not know how.

The DNS is often compared to a phone book with good reason. A phone book allows us
to look up names and find addresses and phone numbers. TOR provides an expanded phone

book to the same space with special hash encoding that functions differently than standard DNS. To access, you will need to install the TOR browser[87].

This is a complex story because while the controversial face of TOR concerns the illicit, the Tor Project (http://torproject.org), which maintains the software and network, has a completely different agenda. The Tor Project considers itself a community that has no intention to replace the existing DNS. Rather, the project helps activists, journalists, stalking victims, law enforcement, and anyone wishing to preserve their anonymity. The system is very much in response to the fact that the Internet was not built with privacy in mind.

4.4.2 .ONION and Other TLDs

The TLD extension used for sites on TOR is .ONION, but it is not a TLD in a normal sense; it is called a *pseudo-TLD*. There is no registrar to buy a .ONION site; rather, the URL is generated when the TOR package is run on your webserver. Without a central registry, there are no WHOIS records. There are a *directory protocol*, *directory documents*, *router descriptors*, and the *hash values*[88] that allow the site content to be retrieved but no other records beyond that. While it is not a DNS, there is a *structure* linking domain strings to machine numbers, and it would not work without one. However, the structure is designed to not store any information about the *owner* of a domain. So what happens in this WHOIS-less world? Anything you can imagine.

4.4.2.1 Silk Road
The Silk Road was/is a *Dark Web* marketplace accessible through TOR. The site allowed vendors to sell cocaine, heroin, crystal methamphetamine, ecstasy, and explosives and offered money laundering services, phishing and spamming services, document forgeries, knockoff merchandise, and a host of other illegal products. Even more troubling was the access provided to additional dark web locations that openly sold military-grade weapons and child exploitation material and that were involved in human trafficking and murder-for-hire services.

The URL for the Silk Road was silkroadvb5piz3r.onion, which is the generated locator of the server and not a registered domain name in the typical sense. This scheme allowed the operator, known only as the Dread Pirate Roberts, to operate anonymously handling billions of illicit dollars through the site and hiring assassins to kill people who threatened his business.[89] In the normal DNS, any concerned Internet user could report this to law enforcement that would use WHOIS to track suspects and issue court orders to the service providers for more information. The operator of Silk Road was eventually caught through extensive, old-fashioned detective work.[90] This only happened after more murders were sanctioned. The site was seized and shut down on October 1, 2013, after operating with impunity for several years.[91] Even though Silk Road's operator was incarcerated, the marketplace was back in operation 1 month later under new operators at a new .ONION site.[92]

---

[87] https://www.torproject.org/download/download-easy.html.en

[88] https://gitweb.torproject.org/torspec.git/tree/dir-spec.txt

[89] https://www.cs.columbia.edu/~smb/UlbrichtCriminalComplaint.pdf

[90] http://www.huffingtonpost.com/garth-bruen/the-last-twist-on-the-sil_b_4164184.html

[91] http://www.forbes.com/sites/andygreenberg/2013/10/02/end-of-the-silk-road-fbi-busts-the-webs-biggest-anonymous-drug-black-market/

[92] http://silkroad5v7dywlc.onion

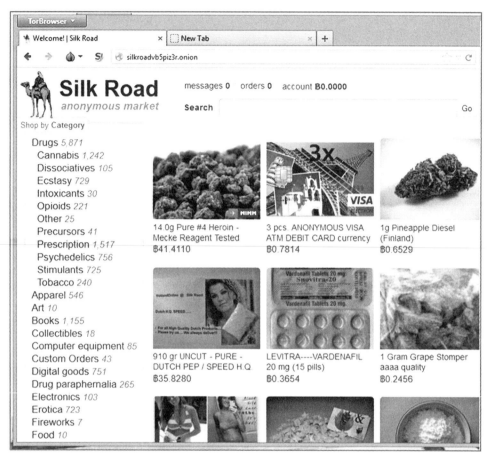

FIGURE 4.7   Silk Road webpage.

Silk Road is just one of many illicit marketplaces on TOR, and TOR is just one of many alternate DNSs. This is what complete Internet anonymity looks like; it is the dangers offered by a complete lack of accountability and absent WHOIS record set. There are many who will say that there are legitimate uses for TOR, especially by those who fear for their privacy and safety. However, the argument against an alternate DNS is not an argument against privacy and safety; it is an argument for ICANN to better address various issues of abuse in the DNS with proper balance. Otherwise, the dark web becomes more attractive to mainstream and brings its cabinet of horrors along with it.

4.4.2.2   The Other Roots   While TOR refers to its .ONION identifiers as "domains," TOR is not a true DNS as it has no hierarchy like the DNS. There are other completely separate roots and many with conflicts or *collisions* in the ICANN hierarchy. Some of these other roots do in fact have WHOIS records for domains. This is only a select list of the better known alternate roots:

- Cesidian Root is a naming system run from a fictitious country, United Micronations Multi-Oceanic Archipelago (UMMOA) (http://cesidianroot.net).

- name.space (namespace.us) was founded in 1996 by Paul Garrin because he felt the existing domain system was arbitrarily limiting. The entity would actually sue ICANN for infringement as ICANN's "new" gTLDs already existed in the name.space system.[93]
- New.Net was an alternate root that seems to have disappeared after a number of controversies and legal issues.
- New Nations (new-nations.net) focuses on creating alternate ccTLDs for underrepresented peoples like Kurds, Tamils, and Uighurs who have no countries but nevertheless exist as distinct populations.
- OpenNIC (opennicproject.org) claims to be a truly democratic DNS and free, free in terms of government control and free in terms of cost.

There may be hundreds of alternate roots in existence as the known ones are so because they are published and want to attract users. Other alternate roots like .JAQ are more obscure, created as a kind protest of ICANN attempts to solidify the single unique root.[94]

4.4.2.3   *Dotless Domains*   Just to make things even more confusing, there is the concept of a dotless domain.[95] Since we are now used to a DNS based on the "dot," it is difficult to imagine websites without them. However, this is of course the way the ARPANET used to operate: the original hostnames did not have dots. Resurrecting this concept was seen as problematic by ICANN's Security and Stability Advisory Committee (SSAC), which issued a report on dotless domains in 2012 that stated in part:

> *"SSAC stated that dotless domains would not be universally reachable and recommended strongly against their use"*[96]

This sentiment was reinforced by another body, the Internet Architecture Board, which issued a statement claiming that dotless domains are "harmful."[97]

REFERENCE

1   Feinler, Elizabeth "Jake". 2011. Host Tables, Top-Level Domain Names, and the Origin of Dot Com, IEEE. 33:74–79.

---

[93] http://www.icann.org/en/news/litigation/namespace-v-icann
[94] http://kernel-panic.org/pipermail/kplug-newbie/2000-October/002602.html
[95] http://tools.ietf.org/html/rfc7085
[96] https://www.icann.org/en/groups/ssac/documents/sac-053-en.pdf
[97] http://www.iab.org/documents/correspondence-reports-documents/2013-2/iab-statement-dotless-domains-considered-harmful/

5

WHOIS CODE

This chapter provides source code examples for querying WHOIS systems so it can be used as a reference as well as an opportunity to provide a step-by-step tutorial. Deploying and executing these programs may require C/C++, Perl, or other coding skills. The basics of coding and the tools required are not covered here; rather, we focus on the components of the code that apply to WHOIS. The full source code is provided at the end and through links along with recommendations for compliers and tutorials. Editing, compiling, and deploying code are not covered at length. Concepts like string handling, pointers, functions, and data structures may be referenced but not detailed.

5.1 AUTOMATING WHOIS WITH BATCHING AND SCRIPTING

There are a variety of ways to perform lookups on large lists of domains or addresses. Conducting mass searches manually is not practical for large system operations or on-the-fly analysis. To handle large lists, we need to understand batching, looping, iteration and recursion.

5.1.1 DiG Example

In DiG using the –**f** switch allows for the passing of a list in a file to the process. This is a built-in option for DiG that opens a designated file and runs each line against DiG. If we use

dig –f domainlist.txt >>digout.txt

WHOIS Running the Internet: Protocol, Policy, and Privacy, First Edition. Garth O. Bruen.
© 2016 John Wiley & Sons, Inc. Published 2016 by John Wiley & Sons, Inc.

and the file domainlist.txt contains the entries:

google.com
yahoo.com
bing.com

the process will call for the DNS records of all these domains and dump the results to a file called "digout.txt." See the sections on using WHOIS and DNS for more details about DiG.

5.1.2 DOS Batch File Example

While Unix-based shells are much more powerful, Windows is not completely without its built-in functions. Unix/Linux shell scripting is covered in the chapter on WHOIS use.

Believe it or not, you can process a massive list of domains through a WHOIS client and put the results into individual files with one line:

```
FOR /F %%i in (domlist.txt) DO whois.exe %%i > %%i.txt
```

If "domlist.txt" is a raw text list of domain names, the DOS batch **FOR** command, using the **/F**, which indicates the data source is external, that is, a file, will cycle through the values and pass them to our WHOIS client. Each item in the text file is assigned, one at a time, to the variable **%%i**. If the file contained the values "amazon.com" and "yahoo.com," the computer will actually process *whois.exe amazon.com > amazon.com.txt* and then *whois.exe yahoo.com > yahoo.com.txt*. There is certainly room for this process to become complex and dynamic. However, this single line is a quick way to expand the scope of WHOIS collection. For more comprehensive process, it is preferable to use real code, which is less intimidating than it sounds for nonprogrammers. There are platforms with more powerful tools that are actually more accessible and more intuitive than DOS batch scripts.

5.1.3 VBScript Example

VBScript can actually be used to create a standalone WHOIS client, but here, we simply use VBScript to batch process lookups with an existing external client. These three lines create a *shell scripting object* that allows access to the command line from within the VBScript, calls the command, and puts the results in a file:

```
Set WshShell = WScript.CreateObject("WScript.Shell")
WIExeString = "whois nytimes.com > nytimes.com.txt"
WSHShell.Run WIExeString, 2, true
```

In a modified version, we replace the specific domain name in the command line with a *variable*:

```
domainName = "nytimes.com"
Set WshShell = WScript.CreateObject("WScript.Shell")
```

```
WIExeString = "whois " + domainName + ">" + domainName + ".txt"
WSHShell.Run WIExeString, 2, true
```

Once the specific string is replaced with a variable, we can change the variable in a loop with values extracted from a file. Single quotes in VBScript indicate a line of comment that is not treated as code:

```
'The scripting object allows us to access files
Set objFSO = CreateObject("Scripting.FileSystemObject")
'Our raw list of domains assigned to a stream object
txtFileindex = "domfile.txt"
Set objTextFileindex = objFSO.OpenTextFile(txtFileindex, 1)
'Read first line of file
domainName = objTextFileindex.ReadLine
Set WshShell = WScript.CreateObject("WScript.Shell")

''Loop through file until the end
While Not objTextFileindex.AtEndOfStream
        WIExeString = "whois " + domainName + ">" + domainName + ".txt"
        WSHShell.Run WIExeString, 2, true
        domainName = objTextFileindex.ReadLine
Wend
```

5.2   WHOIS CLIENT CODE

Writing your own WHOIS client is an extremely useful way to learn how the process works and eventually add features that support your specific needs. There are several examples provided in different languages. In each case, we explain what the language is, where you can get a compiler as well as coding tutorials. Wherever a specific developer is cited, we attempt to discuss their WHOIS experience.

5.2.1   What a WHOIS Client Should Do

There are a number of fundamental principles involved in developing WHOIS client code. On one level, you will need the software to manage input and output locally but also the core function of WHOIS as a *protocol*. A protocol in the network world is a technical method for communicating. HTTP is a protocol for requesting web pages, and STMP is a protocol for email delivery. There are many protocols for different Internet functions. The WHOIS standard in RFC 3912[1] describes the basic protocol option as this:

```
open TCP      ---- (SYN) ------------------------------->
              <---- (SYN+ACK) -------------------------
```

---

[1] http://tools.ietf.org/html/rfc3912

```
send query  ---- "Smith<CR><LF>" -------------------->
get answer <---- "Info about Smith<CR><LF>" ---------
           <---- "More info about Smith<CR><LF>" ----
close      <---- (FIN) ------------------------------
           ----- (FIN) ------------------------------>
```

These seven lines show the complete *transaction* of a WHOIS query. The column on the left shows the fundamental operations, and the column on the right shows the specific commands and the direction of the data flow. The --> indicates data going to the server, and <-- shows data being returned to the client. This is a classic client–server relationship where local client software requests a service from a remote host.

The first line "open TCP" refers to opening a TCP connection, initiating what is called the TCP "three-way handshake." The "SYN" is a synchronize packet sent to the remote WHOIS server—basically indicating your computer wants to talk to it. When this is received by the remote server, it returns a "SYN+ACK" that is a synchronization and acknowledgement packet—which tells your computer that it is okay to send a query. The send query is the third part of the handshake that consists of the query itself plus "CR" and "LF," which are carriage return and line feed, the command combination that makes the ENTER button or instruction execute some operation. In the sense of a terminal instruction, ENTER indicates "do this" or "end this" as opposed to a line feed by itself, which just moves the cursor down. Visually, CR+LF or ENTER also creates a new line in a terminal session. The term "carriage" archaically refers to manual typewriters. A carriage controlled where the letters would strike the paper through the ink ribbon. When the carriage came to the end of the paper margin on the right, the mechanism of the typewriter would return the carriage to the left side margin and then roll the paper up one line (line feed). This combined operation was mimicked on teletype machines later. A teletype machine receiving data would print letters until it received the CR+LF instruction. As teletypes were replaced with monitors and digital storage, this convention remained imbedded in the system.

At the other end, the remote server performs its lookup internally within the WHOIS database and responds with the "get answer," which is the WHOIS data itself, which is also followed by CR+LF telling your computer the information has ended. The WHOIS query response will also contain (hopefully) formatting line feeds that are not read as CR+LF instructions but rather are used to properly display the data.

When the transfer is complete, the remote server will send a close connection request: "FIN," which stands for finished. Your computer responds with its own FIN acknowledgement and the transaction is done. However, this is the operation of the transaction itself; before we can get to that point, our WHOIS client should be able to:

1. Accept a domain name as a string (with options if appropriate)
2. Identify the WHOIS server host (either in the code or as another parameter)
3. Format the query with any host-specific options in mind
4. Use the network to connect to port 43 on the remote server
5. Direct the data it receives from the remote host to the terminal, file, or database

There are specific coding pitfalls to be aware of when creating more advanced WHOIS versions that check various servers. Some versions of WHOIS have had the *infinite loop* bug,[2] which sends the query forever searching when it cannot find the correct server. It is important to establish a limit of the number of attempts, referrals, and searches.

5.2.2 Early Versions

The original NICNAME WHOIS was written in assembly language. Assembly language is one step above pure machine code. The FAIL and MACRO assemblers were common on the early DEC Systems[3] used by SRI and others working on the ARPANET. The Incompatible Timesharing System (ITS) at MIT was developed on the MIDAS assembler language.[4] Ken Harrenstien supplied one of the oldest versions of the MIDAS WHOIS, which is 1555 lines long on 39 printed pages. Compare that to the Berkeley WHOIS code, which around 300 lines. Assembler code is cumbersome because the very basic functions of the system and memory management have to be included to run a process, whereas higher-level languages like C have libraries that handle these concerns. What follows is a small section of the MIDAS WHOIS code provided by the courtesy of Harrenstien who dutifully archives and organizes much of this information. The code segment is part of the terminal input handling for the early WHOIS:

- ;; TNXRD -- Read a line from the terminal, allowing some editing functions
- ;; (delete character, delete word, delete line, retype line). The routine
- ;; assumes a printing tty only for greatest correctness, since it would be
- ;; difficult to determine what display functions, if any, the terminal has.
- ;; String is ended with a CRLF or EOL (octal 37) and input of the line is
- ;; aborted by control-Q or control-X.   Control-A, control-H and DEL will
- ;; delete one character; control-W deletes a word; control-U flushes the

```
;; line (but doesn't abort); control-R retypes prompt and line.
;; Takes:
;;      A/      pointer to prompt string (<-1,,addr> is ok)
;;      B/      pointer to destination (<-1,,addr> is ok)
;;      C/      RH has max number of chars to read
;; Returns:
;;      +1      Overflow (C>max), or aborted with ^Q or ^X (C=0)
;;      +2      Success, ASCIZ string (if null fits) in buffer.
```
- ;; Updates B to point at last byte read, C to number chars read.

---

[2] https://rt.cpan.org/Public/Bug/Display.html?id=73050
[3] ftp://ftp.columbia.edu/kermit/dec20/assembler-guide.txt
[4] http://bitsavers.trailing-edge.com/pdf/mit/rle_pdp1/memos/PDP-1_MIDAS.pdf
• The bullet point represents the code breaks

```
tnxrd:  tlc     B,-1            ; Complement LH of presumed BP
        tlcn    B,-1            ; Was a 'HRRO' ptr (<-1,,addr>)?
        hrli    B,440700        ;  Yes, change it to a BP
        aos     C               ; Bump max count for AOBJP checks
        add     P,[E+1,,E+1]    ; Adjust the stack in order to
        movem   E,(P)           ;  save some ACs
        movei   E,-E(P)         ;  ...
        blt     E,-1(P)         ;  ...
;;;     psout                   ; Output the prompt -- ** NOT
                                HERE **
        move    D,B             Copy dest pointer to D
        movni   E,(C)           ; Negative of max count to E
        movsi   E,(E)           ;  into left half for AOBJ
                                counter
        movei   A,.priou        ; The controlling tty
        rfcoc                   ; Read control char output flags
        push    P,B             ; Save these words so that
        push    P,C             ;  we can restore things later
        tlz     B,140003        ; Turn off control-A, control-H
        tlz     C,606300        ;  control-R, control-U and
                                control-W
        sfcoc                   ; Do it
```

Anything following a semicolon is a *comment* and not read by the assembler. **tnxrd:** is the name of the function, and everything that follows are instructions within that function. The items in the left columns like **move**, **push**, and **add** are common assembler *instructions* that process variables in the right column.[5]

5.2.3   C/C++

The C language was developed by Dennis Ritchie at Bell Labs in 1969 as a general-purpose language. Previously, computer code was authored directly with specific machine instructions and later assembly language, which allowed access to the machine instructions. C uses more natural language that is then *compiled* into machine code behind the scenes. C has been extended with C++ and is the foundation for many other languages like Perl and Java.

Before getting started with C, it is critical to learn about the structure of the language and experiment with compiling simple programs before attempting a WHOIS client. There are a number of free C tutorials available online; here are just a few:

- C++ language tutorial: http://www.cplusplus.com/doc/tutorial/
- The C++ tutorial: http://www.learncpp.com/
- Multiple links on different C topics: http://www.cprogramming.com/tutorial.html

Given C's long history, finding used textbooks at fair prices is not difficult. Even older C books are still useful for leaning, and it is not necessary to buy the newest, most expensive guide. Unfortunately, there is not enough room in this book to explain functions, pointers, streams and data structures!

[5] http://pdp10.nocrew.org/docs/instruction-set/pdp-10.html

A C compiler is of course required to convert your C code into machine language. A good place to start is with the tutorials listed previously to follow their suggestions. Linux installations should have the GNU C++ compiler[6] **gcc** installed. If it is not installed, try *sudo yum install gcc* from the command line; the same should work on MAC too. There are other options for both Linux and MAC. GNU gcc can run on Windows with modifications.[7] Microsoft does offer a free express development studio.[8] Embarcadero offers free trials of its C++ Builder.[9]

There are three common blocks in a C program: Declarations, which establish parameters; Main, which initiates and controls the program; and Functions, which do all the work. C, like other languages, uses a series of *libraries* called in the declarations that contain code already written and tested to handle different pieces of common programming. For example, rather than writing the process from scratch each time to send output to the terminal (screen) and accept input from the keyboard, we simply *include* libraries in the declarations of our program, which then allow access to that code within our code. For a WHOIS program, we will need to access network utilities, specifically code to open *sockets* for our query. The most common library for this is called "socket.h." The *.h* notation denotes a *header* file, and header files are added to your code by using the preprocessor directive *#include*. The full path of this library is "sys/socket.h" because this library is part of underlying system functions shared by a number of processes on a computer. This header library gives us access to several built-in functions: **socket()**[10] and **connect()**.[11] The **socket()** function creates an endpoint for communication, *a socket*, and then **connect()** accepts the socket to create that connection. Windows does not use the Unix **sys/socket.h**; it has its own C libraries called **winsock.h** and **winsoc2.h**.[12] Using some existing C WHOIS sources, we will review the basic components of a WHOIS client and how they work. For comparison, we have supplied several versions with different models. Full source of these programs are in the appendix and available for download under different distribution licenses.

5.2.3.1 *Processing Input*   The Main section of our sample C program starts with

```
int main(int argc, char *argv[])
```

This is a completely routine opening that indicates that our program will accept parameters from the command line. The ***argv[]** represents a collection of parameters from the command line, and **argc** is the count of those parameters. It is exactly this format that allows us to use the client like this:

whois –h whois.internic.net yahoo.co

The program *whois* takes zero or more parameters in the main function. The main function proceeds to examine each parameter, and finding the –h option, our case will assign the variable **host** to the server we entered and then pass the host variable with the domain and any flags to the **whois()** function.

---

[6] http://gcc.gnu.org/

[7] http://www.mingw.org/

[8] http://www.microsoft.com/visualstudio/eng/products/visual-studio-express-products

[9] http://www.embarcadero.com/products/cbuilder

[10] http://pubs.opengroup.org/onlinepubs/009695399/functions/socket.html

[11] http://pubs.opengroup.org/onlinepubs/009695399/functions/connect.html

[12] http://research.microsoft.com/en-us/um/redmond/projects/invisible/include/winsock.h.htm

5.2.3.2   Identify the Best WHOIS Server   If we had not identified the WHOIS server to use, the program will help select one. First and foremost, we should check if the query entered is a domain name or an IP address. Since there are no TLDs that contain numbers, it is easy to tell the difference between a domain and an IP by looking at the string that follows to the right of the dot (e.g., ".COM" is a domain and ".123" is an IP). Once we have established that, the rest is as complex as we want to make it. We could pass all domains to whois.internic.net and all IP addresses to whois.ripe.net, but that will not always get us the results we need. We need structures and functions that look at the query value and decide the best WHOIS host. This, of course, can be hardcoded into the program using a number of methods including functions, arrays, and switches. A function would take the domain or even better just the TLD and return a hostname. For example,

```
static char get_wi_server(char tld)
{
        char *wiserver = NULL;
        if(strcmp(tld, "org") != 0){
             strcpy(wiserver, "whois.pir.org");
        }
        if(strcmp(tld, "us") != 0){
             strcpy(wiserver, "whois.neustar.us");
        }
        return (wiserver)
}
```

This is fine if WHOIS servers never changed. However, the code would really need to be constantly updated as WHOIS servers were deployed, changed, or removed, and then, the program would have to be recompiled. It is better to look to an external source for a server list, either a local file that can be updated or service on the Internet with the most updated list of servers. The **JWhois** program uses an external configuration file called **jwhois.conf**, which can be updated and called from the program without recompiling the whole code. The Berkeley **whois.c** code calls different subdomains at whois-servers.net, for example, de.whois-servers.net for Germany (.DE) domains or uk.whois-servers.net for United Kingdom (.UK). This service provided by CenterGate Research[13] acts as an alias for the correct registry servers.

   This presents a much more complex problem for .COM and .NET, which do not have a reliable central database with the full set of WHOIS data. If we cannot get the full record from whois.internic.net, we will have to conduct two queries, one to get the registrar WHOIS server and a second to send a query to that server.

5.2.3.3   Prepare a Socket for the Query   With the correct, or closest to, server in hand, we can prepare the query. This is an extraction of the very top of the **whois** function from the Berkeley version:

```
whois(const char *query, const char *hostname, int flags)
{
   FILE *sfi, *sfo;
   struct addrinfo *hostres, *res;
```

---

[13] http://www.centergate.com/

```
char *buf, *host, *nhost, *p;
int i, s;
size_t c, len;

hostres = gethostinfo(hostname, 1);
```

The function accepts a domain (***query***), the target WHOIS server (***hostname***), and any additional query flags. The function **gethostinfo()** creates a **struct** *data structure*[14] for our query.

5.2.3.4 Connect to the Remote Server

The **socket()** function creates the socket and assigns it to the variable **s**:

```
s = socket(res->ai_family, res->ai_socktype,
res->ai_protocol);
```

The **connect()** function actually does the work of establishing our socket link:

```
connect(s, res->ai_addr, res->ai_addrlen)
```

5.2.3.5 Direct the Response

Our query results are placed in a buffer, which is an extremely brief memory space, before the data is sent to a stream, which outputs to the display. It is at this point that the program can be altered to send data to file or a database or further parse the results. The function used is called **printf()**[15]:

```
printf("%.*s\n", (int)len, buf);
```

Several full client code examples are in the appendix.

5.2.3.6 WHOIS Protocol Library from Catalyst SocketTools

Dynamic link libraries (DLLs) are files that contain functions that can be called by other programs. This scheme makes programs smaller and easier to update. Instead of compiling large amounts of code into one program and using up lots of memory, the DLLs sit outside waiting to be used if needed.[16] This also makes it possible to update software without replacing the entire program. Catalyst Development Corporation has created a WHOIS protocol function set as part of its SocketTools Library. There are 25 different functions[17] that can be called as part of the WHOIS set. These are all made available in a program by first installing then including (specifically meaning the standard C/C++ #include directive) the cstools8.h header file:

---

[14] http://www.cplusplus.com/doc/tutorial/structures/

[15] http://www.cplusplus.com/reference/cstdio/printf/

[16] http://msdn.microsoft.com/en-us/library/windows/desktop/ms681914%28v=vs.85%29.aspx

[17] http://www.catalyst.com/support/help/sockettools/library/index.html?page=html%2Fwhois%2Flibrary%2Findex.html

WhoisAsyncConnect	Asynchronously connection
WhoisAttachThread	Attach a client handle to a different thread
WhoisCancel	Cancel a blocking operation
WhoisConnect	Connect to a server
WhoisDisableEvents	Disable event notifications
WhoisDisableTrace	Disable logging
WhoisDisconnect	Disconnect from a server
WhoisEnableEvents	Enable notifications
WhoisEnableTrace	Enable logging
WhoisEventProc	Callback function for client events
WhoisFreezeEvents	Stop or start event handling
WhoisGetErrorString	Get error code description
WhoisGetLastError	Return last error code
WhoisGetStatus	Return client status
WhoisGetTimeout	Get operation timeout in seconds
WhoisInitialize	Initialize the library
WhoisIsBlocking	Check if process is ready for input
WhoisIsConnected	Check server connection
WhoisIsReadable	Check for data on server
WhoisRead	Read response data
WhoisRegisterEvent	Register callback function
WhoisSearch	Search for a record
WhoisSetLastError	Set last error code
WhoisSetTimeout	Set operation times out in seconds
WhoisUninitialize	End access to the library

5.2.4   Perl

Known to some people as the "duct tape that holds the Internet together,"[18] Perl is a powerful C-based language with powerful text and file processing created by Larry Wall[19] that is also surprisingly useful for network programming as well. Perl can be downloaded for the major platforms here: http://www.perl.org/get.html. Tutorials can be found here: http://www.perl.org/learn.html. Within Perl, there is a module (**Net::Whois::Raw**[20];) that attempts to strip WHOIS records of their copyright and disclaimer text, just returning the actual record. Here are three variations to experiment with:

1. WP.cgi Whois Proxy by John Bro: http://wp-whois-proxy.sourceforge.net or http://directory.fsf.org/wiki/Whois_proxy
2. Perl Net-Whois-1.9 by Chip Salzenberg and Dana Hudes: http://search.cpan.org/~dhudes/Net-Whois-1.9/Whois.pm
3. Pwhois[21] by Ariel Brosh and Walery Studennikov: http://search.cpan.org/~despair/Net-Whois-Raw-2.48/pwhois

---

[18] http://www.infoworld.com/article/2625767/data-center/whatever-happened-to-perl-.html
[19] http://learn.perl.org/faq/perlfaq1.html#What-is-Perl-
[20] http://search.cpan.org/~despair/Net-Whois-Raw-2.46/lib/Net/Whois/Raw.pm
[21] http://linux.die.net/man/1/pwhois

5.2.5 Java

Created by Sun Microsystems in 1995, the Java language is imbedded in many web services and mobile devices.[22] Denis Migol, Senior Java Developer at Luxoft,[23] has developed several Java packages for WHOIS called jwhois (**com.googlecode.jwhois**[24]), but not to be confused with the standard Linux WHOIS called JWhois. This is not a WHOIS program so much as a Java library that can be called by other Java programs, giving that program access to the WHOIS functions. Deron Eriksson[25] explains how to create a socket to a WHOIS server in this tutorial: http://www.avajava.com/tutorials/lessons/how-do-i-query-a-whois-server-using-a-socket.html.

Erik C. Thauvin created a java-based[26] WHOIS as part of the GeekTools[27] package. This code is available under GNU General Public License and provided for testing in the appendix. To run java code, you will need the Java development kit (JDK), which can be downloaded here: http://www.oracle.com/technetwork/java/javase/downloads/index.html. There are many free tutorials including this one: http://www.javacoffeebreak.com/tutorials/. The text *Java Network Programming* by Elliotte Rusty Harold also features a Java WHOIS Parser.[28]

5.2.6 Recursive Python WHOIS by Peter Simmons

Python is a powerful and user-friendly open-source language that runs on all major platforms. You can learn about and download Python at python.org.

The Peter Simmons source called rwhois.py not only finds the correct server but also attempts to parse the returned record in a common format. The straightforward Python source can be downloaded here: http://sourceforge.net/projects/rwhois/. Python has a socket library[29] with a socket() function that is similar to the C version. The function accepts three parameters—family, type, and protocol number—and then returns the socket object. This is the socket line from the Simmons source:

```
s = socket.socket(socket.AF_INET, socket.SOCK_STREAM)
```

5.2.7 Lisp WHOIS by Evrim Ulu

Several of the nurseries that birthed the Internet were in fact Artificial Intelligence (AI) Laboratories. One of the core languages of AI is the List Processing language or Lisp, developed by John McCarthy in 1958.[30] Lisp was one of the first higher-level programming languages and introduced many critical concepts used in coding today including tree-based data structures, recursion, and functions. It seems only fitting that we include a Lisp

[22] http://www.java.com/en/download/faq/whatis_java.xml

[23] http://www.luxoft.com/

[24] http://code.google.com/p/jwhois/source/browse/trunk/jwhois/src/com/googlecode/jwhois/

[25] http://www.avajava.com/about.jsp

[26] https://github.com/ethauvin/Whois/blob/master/Whois.java

[27] http://www.geektools.com/tools.php

[28] http://www.javafaq.nu/java-example-code-591.html

[29] http://docs.python.org/2/library/socket.html#socket.socket

[30] http://conservancy.umn.edu/handle/107476

version[31] of WHOIS developed by Evrim Ulu and released under a GNU General Public License. Ulu wrote his WHOIS service to query and sell domains within his Coretal.net site. He chose Lisp due to its *homoiconicity* and ability to metaprogram. He built a core server using common Lisp with SMTP and IMAP protocols implemented as well as WHOIS. In order to run the Lisp code sample in the appendix, you will need to download a Lisp interpreter like the one available for Common Lisp at CLISP[32] and learn the basics of the language.[33]

5.3 WEB WHOIS FORMS

There are a number of examples in the WHOIS use chapter of web-based interfaces. If you have a webserver or an editable website, you can create your own WHOIS form and process. Some of the options available include Active Server Pages[34] (ASP) and Perlscript.[35] However, one of the most popular is PHP.

5.3.1 Creating a WHOIS Web Interface with PHP

PHP Hypertext Processor is a server-side code, meaning the code runs on the server and produces results for the client, which is used mostly to display web content but is really a more powerful scripting language than many web script tools.[36] PHP can be used in place of HTML, to produce HTML, or within HTML. In essence, PHP can be used to create a front-end on a webpage that accepts and processes WHOIS queries. You must have administrator access to a webserver that allows PHP content to run these pages and check with webmasters and service providers. It is also to run PHP in standalone modules for development and testing. PHP.net has tutorials, manuals, and all the information needed to run PHP: http://www.php.net/.

The following PHP example is an extremely stripped-down version of a WHOIS script that performs a basic lookup. The variables here are hardcoded for demonstration. A real WHOIS PHP would have input fields, error checking, formatting, and server selection, but this is intended to demonstrate the basic process:

```php
<?php

$wicall = fsockopen("whois.internic.net", 43);
fputs($wicall, "iana.net\r\n");
while(!feof($wicall)) {
      echo fgets($wicall);
}
fclose($wicall);

?>
```

[31] https://github.com/evrim/core-server/blob/master/src/services/whois.lisp
[32] http://www.clisp.org/
[33] http://www.cs.sfu.ca/CourseCentral/310/pwfong/Lisp/1/tutorial1.html
[34] http://www.planet-source-code.com/vb/scripts/ShowCode.asp?lngWId=4&txtCodeId=6499
[35] http://stackoverflow.com/questions/23690866/perl-script-to-serve-whois-data-as-requested-on-port-43
[36] http://php.net/manual/en/intro-whatis.php

The first code line **$wicall = fsockopen("whois.internic.com", 43);** assigns our WHOIS lookup to the variable "$wicall." The function **fsockopen()** is a built-in PHP function that accepts a *hostname* and a *port number* as the parameters and opens a socket at the remote host.[37] The second line calls the PHP function **fwrite()** with our set socket variable and the example domain name to query. Note that the domain name parameter also contains a carriage return ("\r") and a line feed ("\n")—the ENTER command. The **fwrite()** function passes our domain and ENTER command to the socket stream.[38] The next three lines constitute a while block that loops through the stream returned by the remote server until the end of the stream, which is determined by the **feof()** condition.[39] The last function **fclose()** closes our socket.[40] Note that this sequence completely follows the conventions in RFC 3912.[41] There are some variations available to experiment with including one by Mark Jeftovic available at SourceForge[42] under a GNU license and a simpler version by Marty Khoury at internoetics.com.[43]

5.4 PARSING WHOIS RECORDS

Ok, so I have WHOIS records. What do I do with them? Various figures in the ICANN world say that what Simone Carletti does is "impossible," too difficult, or not scalable in terms of parsing diverse WHOIS records. Ingenious coders constantly overcome the odds. Carletti, like many in this field, has diverse interests and passions, which help in overcoming complex technical problem. As a professional wine taster and certified SCUBA diver, Carletti may end up thinking about the DNS in ways others do not. He has developed two important products: RoboDomains,[44] which can be used to manage domain portfolios, and RoboWhois,[45] a cloud-based application program interface (API) service that provides access to RESTful WHOIS. Like this author, he has taken the time to share information about WHOIS and draft guides for using it[46] in addition to software development. Carletti has developed his own custom WHOIS client in Ruby that not only retrieves records but also parses the results regardless of the source.

5.4.1 Ruby WHOIS by Simone Carletti

Carletti chose the Ruby[47] environment for specific reasons: *"Ruby is an amazing programming language with elegant syntax and efficient time management."*[48] Furthermore, *"There is Ruby philosophy which attracts developers with a similar mindset."*[49] He recommends

[37] http://php.net/manual/en/function.fsockopen.php
[38] http://www.php.net/manual/en/function.fwrite.php
[39] http://www.php.net/manual/en/function.feof.php
[40] http://www.php.net/manual/en/function.fclose.php
[41] See note 1.
[42] http://sourceforge.net/projects/phpwhois/
[43] http://www.internoetics.com/2010/01/12/simple-whois-php-script/
[44] https://dnsimple.com
[45] https://www.robowhois.com/
[46] http://www.simonecarletti.com/blog/2012/03/whois-protocol/
[47] http://ruby-whois.org/
[48] Carletti interview.
[49] See note 48.

the text *Eloquent Ruby* by Russ Olsen for people wanting to get into Ruby. Ruby is an open-source,[50] object-oriented development language created by Yukihiro "Matz" Matsumoto and released in 1995.[51] To code and compile Ruby, you will need to download and install one of the options listed here: https://www.ruby-lang.org/en/downloads/. For Windows, try Ruby Installer: http://rubyinstaller.org/. There are free tutorials attached to each website, but Elegant Ruby is a good resource: http://eloquentruby.com.

Aside from the benefits of using Ruby, Carletti has created a library to deal a problem discussed in previous chapters: inconsistent WHOIS formats. He commented that it is bad enough when registrars have their own formats, but some registrars even have different formats within their own holdings. Immediately, this reminded me of the registrar Tucows who relies largely on resellers for domain registrations. In 2013, Tucows was breached by ICANN for failing to maintain WHOIS records as required by Section 3.4.2 of their contract,[52] suggesting someone other than the registrar controlled the records. If resellers of registrars can create their own WHOIS formats, this complicates matters even further. Country code top-level domain (ccTLD) formats also are a problem, but the ever expanding Ruby WHOIS library makes the situation scalable. The code handles domains, TLDs, as well as both IPv4 and IPv6. There is also support for IDNs and CentralNIC domains. The query is treated as an object and tested for validity and whether or not it is actually registered. The library dictates which server to check and how the results are parsed, so with this version, there is no need to know the specific server or use a regular expression to extract the data. The Ruby code dumps query results into a **Whois::Record** object that encapsulates a WHOIS record[53] and passes it to a parser. Each known WHOIS format has its own parser library with a series of specific properties and methods.[54] The concept is that regardless of how many WHOIS formats exist in the wild, they more or less contain the same types of information, albeit with different tags and in different orders. A proper parsing mechanism acts as a proxy between the record objects and output, making the results appear the same regardless of the source. These are two excerpts from two library files dealing with the same type of data but from two different WHOIS sources. The first one is for VeriSign[55]:

```
property_supported :created_on do
  node("Creation Date") { |value| Time.parse(value) }
end
```

This one is for the registrar ASCIO TECH[56]:

```
property_supported :created_on do
  if content_for_scanner =~ /Record created: (.+)\n/
    Time.parse($1)
  end
end
```

---

[50] https://www.ruby-lang.org/en/about/license.txt
[51] https://www.ruby-lang.org/en/about/
[52] http://www.icann.org/en/news/correspondence/burnette-to-eisner-22jun12-en.pdf
[53] https://github.com/weppos/whois
[54] http://ruby-whois.org/manual/parser/properties/
[55] https://github.com/weppos/whois/blob/master/lib/whois/record/parser/jobswhois.verisign-grs.com.rb
[56] https://github.com/weppos/whois/blob/master/lib/whois/record/parser/whois.ascio.com.rb

In this record data, there are actually formatting problems. One is obviously that the tags are different ("Creation Date" and "Record Created"), and the second problem is that the format of the dates themselves can be different. The VeriSign date looks like this:

```
Creation Date: 02-jun-1995
```

And the ASCIO date is formatted this way:

```
Record created: 2005-03-01 14:11:50
```

The ASCIO version also has a 24-hour time stamp with seconds in addition to being in the reverse order. Are we also to assume the second value in the date is the month? This is just one example, so parsing on the fly is a great utility but one that must be added to as new registrars and registries are deployed or even as some parties change their formats randomly. There is neither a right nor wrong way to display the date stamps since there is no standard.

5.4.2   Regular Expressions

Regular expressions (or "regex") are syntax code tools geared at manipulating text in powerful ways. With regular expressions, we can do very fast comparisons, extractions, and edits of text on the fly within our code. For extracting WHOIS data from the diverse record set we are dealing with, this provides excellent methods for overcoming the challenges presented. These matching codes can become very complex and may look like hieroglyphics to people who have never seen them before. The following is an example of a regular expression that matches IP addresses:

```
\d{1,3}\.\d{1,3}\.\d{1,3}\.\d{1,3}
```

Breaking this down, we actually have four sets of the same matching, which is **\d{1,3}**, where **\d** indicates numbers and not letters, which is followed by the two digits in the braces that indicate that the number must be at least 1 digit but not more than 3. The four sets are separated by **\.** that indicates that the dot is supposed to be treated as a literal dot character.

This expression matches email addresses and is a little more complex:

```
[\w-\.]{1,}\@([\da-zA-Z-]{1,}\.){1,}[\Da-zA-Z]{2,4}
```

Brackets indicate character classes for which we have three: **[\w-\.]**, **[\da-zA-Z-]**, and **[\Da-zA-Z]**. Character classes are encapsulated sets dictating what is permitted within a string or substring. The first class **\w-\.** means this section of the string is a word made up of numbers and letters (not a single character), which may contain a hyphen or a dot. This is followed by the **{1,}** that indicates this portion must be at least one character long. This is followed by the literal character **\@**, thus ending the user name portion of the email string. The next portion, **[\da-zA-Z-]**, indicates this section can contain numbers, letters, and hyphens of more than one character and ends with a literal dot. The second braced digit indicates this substring type can occur more than once. This is our hostname. The last section **[\Da-zA-Z]** may only contain letters, no numbers or special characters, and must be at least two characters but not more than four. This is not the only way or the best way to build the expression. Expressions can become very complex, but they do not have to be. Expressions can be literal matches too. For example, we can simply search for and remove terms like "Registrar Name:," "Phone Number:," "Created On:," etc. to purely extract the data and sort it correctly. Regular expressions are available in several languages, but one of the best is Perl.

6

WHOIS SERVERS

This chapter gives an overview of WHOIS servers and their components with specific examples of installing and configuring a WHOIS server. Here, we describe the theory of listening on ports and conducting transactions with a database. This is also a policy discussion concerning basic requirements of contracted service providers in terms of their responsibility to provide WHOIS data to the public and will contain brief case studies when service providers failed to meet their obligations. Not all servers are created equal; some do not source the data and are just referrals. Check the appendix for an extensive list of different WHOIS servers.

The client–server relationship is the basis of Internet function. Clients (your browser and other software) make requests across the network and servers respond to the requests. When you visit a webpage, the actual process is a request for a copy of a file, which is displayed in your browser. For email, your email client requests copies of the email stored on the server. A WHOIS server is just that, a hot machine that responds to requests for Port 43 connections and returns data. There are different types of servers for different functions, and special functions are often designated within dedicated subdomains in common formats that clients and other processes expect to be present. For example, name servers are usually designated by *ns1.<domain-name>* and *ns2.<domain-name>*, while mail servers are often structured as *mail.<domain-name>* or *smtp.<domain-name>*. This is a way different services can be distributed throughout a domain on different machines at different addresses more efficiently. With WHOIS, the convention is *whois.<domain-name>*, but not every provider follows this.

The topics of server configuration and administration are professional disciplines, which are complex and diverse beyond the limits of this text. Here, we focus mostly on the specifics of WHOIS services which are port listening and basic database administration.

WHOIS Running the Internet: Protocol, Policy, and Privacy, First Edition. Garth O. Bruen.
© 2016 John Wiley & Sons, Inc. Published 2016 by John Wiley & Sons, Inc.

6.1 HISTORICAL SERVERS

While we have previously examined RFC 812,[1] NICNAME/WHOIS, as the definition of an early WHOIS process, it is also a document about a server. In fact, the document begins:

> "The NICNAME/WHOIS Server is an NCP/TCP transaction based query/response server, running on the SRI-NIC machine, that provides netwide directory service to ARPANET users."

The early WHOIS story is very much about the hardware with software only later becoming powerful enough to take the spotlight. The current WHOIS RFC completely omits discussions of hardware and merely describes what servers should do. Prior to the creation of RFC 812 and following the deployment NAME/FINGER,[2] we can see the growing need to have adequate resources backing a potentially intensive process. John R. Pickens, Elizabeth "Jake" Feinler, and James E. Mathis collaborated on RFC 756,[3] which establishes the requirements for a robust NIC server in 1979. Above being the simple control center for the network, it is anticipated that the numbers and types of services will expand:

> "Extensions to the service are suggested that would expand the query functionality to allow more flexible query formats as well as queries for service addresses."[4]

This document also introduces the concept of the *name* server, which becomes a critical component of the Domain Name System. At the time, retrieving verbose WHOIS-type records through the native system would have been difficult due to the size limits of the packets. Within the document, the **MORE DATA Protocol**[5] is described, which would allow the use of more than one datagram in query reply. It is difficult for us now to comprehend the very small data limits in computing, not just in network transmission. Earl Killian is credited along with Harrenstein and Harvey with creating NAME/FINGER,[6] and when asked about his role, he responded, "*there isn't a lot to tell*," which is right in line with the other pioneers who just did what was needed or what made sense and are still quite humble about the impact.

The original WHOIS server was a DEC PDP running TOPS-20. Starting in 1959, the Digital Equipment Corporation (DEC) began developing a series of Programmed Data Processors (PDP), later known as "minicomputers" because they were smaller than the traditional massive computers of the time. The TOPS-10 had a number of inherent utilities[7] including **IPHOST** and **ACCOUNT**. **IPHOST** gets information about hosts and **ACCOUNT** identifies user accounts at remote sites. The **IPHOST** program would have to be loaded and then access to the subcommands would be allowed. The subcommands which begin to show the formats that become our common WHOIS and DNS tools. The **NAME** command returned information about ARPANET hosts, specifically the IP (called

---

[1] http://www.ietf.org/rfc/rfc0812.txt
[2] http://tools.ietf.org/html/rfc742
[3] http://tools.ietf.org/html/rfc756
[4] See note 3.
[5] See note 3.
[6] See note 2.
[7] http://bitsavers.informatik.uni-stuttgart.de/pdf/dec/pdp10/TOPS20/arpanet/5221bm.mem.txt

FIGURE 6.1 Digital PDP 10. Image from http://www.computerhistory.org/collections/catalog/102621832. Courtesy of Computer History Museum.

a "decimal octet number" earlier), host name, status as user or server, and type of server software. The **NUMBER** command returned the same information but based on the IP address. Interestingly, within **IPHOST**, there was a privileged command called ARPANET, which was used to load the host table.[8] There wee various operating system platforms being tested on the PDPs, including TENEX, a time-sharing system implemented on a DEC PDP-10, which had special paging hardware developed at BBN.[9] The NICNAME/WHOIS worked on both platforms.[10] However, it has been a long time since there was just one WHOIS server with a single platform or hardware.

6.2 SERVER STANDARDS AND ICANN REQUIREMENTS

Contracted parties, like ICANN registrars, are required to have WHOIS servers for the domain they sponsor. Specifically, they have to have a Port 43 WHOIS service and a web-based WHOIS service. The concepts of Port 43 are briefed here; refer to the chapter on WHOIS code for examples of WHOIS web forms. This is an important consideration as a WHOIS server is also a *web server* or at least a web server must have access to the WHOIS database server. In order to comply with ICANN requirements, the WHOIS server must be available and functioning 24 hours per day. For this, competent administrators are required with professional technical training as their business model depends on it. Many registrars have fairly dynamic websites that use the existing WHOIS data to offer additional services. While WHOIS is an open system, there are still security concerns. First, data should only be *read* from the WHOIS server. No one outside of the registrar should have write access to the database; updates and insertions should only pass through a controlled process. Typically, domain registrants have accounts that allow them to submit WHOIS data updates. There are many ways to control database access and even options for only serving a copy of the data externally for queries. There are reasonable expectations for limiting queries

[8] TOPS-20 ARPANET USER UTILITIES GUIDE, TOPS-20 (KL MODEL B), V6.0 1983 by Digital Equipment Corporation. http://bitsavers.informatik.uni-stuttgart.de/pdf/dec/pdp10/TOPS20/arpanet/5221bm.mem.txt
[9] http://tenex.opost.com/tenex72.txt
[10] http://www.ietf.org/rfc/rfc954.txt

including IP logging and CAPTCHA codes. As far as the public is concerned, *listening* on Port 43. Listening means the port is open to accept traffic from outside the machine. TCP/IP ports are designated for different functions such as web (HTTP) and email (SMTP) traffic.[11] Ports can, of course, be configured for any type of traffic, but the point of having common designated ports allows the traffic to be standardized throughout the Internet. A WHOIS port is configured to wait for a query for a domain record.

6.3 FINDING THE RIGHT SERVER

Locating the right server and database for a WHOIS query has been a problem since the Internet became distributed. The ideal situation would be a single WHOIS service that accepts any data point (domain, IP, name server, ISP, etc.) and returns the appropriate information without switches or knowledge of specific servers. Even though there are hundreds of databases and servers with different formats, a proper single-entry process is completely possible. In the previous chapter on WHOIS code, we saw client-side solutions as well as user-level solutions in the chapter on WHOIS use. Attempts are made on the server side through referrals, but proposals to use the DNS to find the proper WHOIS service have been submitted. The draft 2003 RFC *Using DNS SRV records to locate whois servers*[12] by Marcos Sanz proffers a scheme of using a DNS Server Resource Record[13] (DNS SRV) to create a central "master" or "meta" WHOIS server used to refer to the correct source. This is not a proposal to centralize the data, but rather centralize the route to a WHOIS server by imbedding in the DNS. This recommendation did not leave the draft stage.

Because the tracking of WHOIS servers is done on an ad hoc, volunteer basis, there are few complete and routinely updated lists. A clear example of this can be seen in what is often used as a "standard" list of WHOIS servers[14] collected by Matt Power of M.I.T.

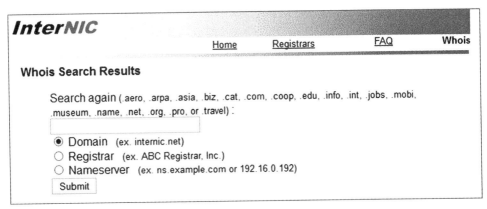

FIGURE 6.2   Domain WHOIS.

[11] http://www.iana.org/assignments/service-names-port-numbers/service-names-port-numbers.xhtml
[12] http://tools.ietf.org/html/draft-sanz-whois-srv-00
[13] http://tools.ietf.org/html/rfc2782
[14] http://www.mit.edu/afs.new/sipb/project/gopher-links/whois-servers.list

```
Domain Name: OPENWORLDSHOP.COM
Registrar: DYNADOT, LLC
Whois Server: whois.dynadot.com
Referral URL: http://www.dynadot.com
Name Server: NS1.DYNADOT.COM
Name Server: NS2.DYNADOT.COM
Status: clientTransferProhibited
Updated Date: 05-sep-2012
Creation Date: 08-sep-2011
Expiration Date: 08-sep-2013
```

FIGURE 6.3 WHOIS server in WHOIS record.

The list is frequently found in the source code of WHOIS clients and referenced generally, but it has not been updated since March 2000.

Determining the right server to get a record from first can save frustration. Since there is no single central database and registrars are only required to have records for the domains they sponsor, some upfront helps find the right record sooner. Follow these steps: If the domain is a gTLD *other than* .COM and .NET, use this form: reports.internic.net/cgi/whois or this form: http://www.internic.org/whois.html.

This query will get the record automatically from the registry. By doing this, you can skip the step of going to the specific registry WHOIS and will ensure all the formats are the same. By using the registry WHOIS, you can bypass all the format variations used by different registrars.

If the domain is .COM or .NET, use the internic.org/whois.html to find the specific registrar WHOIS server from the *thin* record and then query that server for the whole WHOIS record. Example:

If for some reason the InterNIC WHOIS query does not work, use the registry specific WHOIS server:

.INFO: whois.afilias.net

.BIZ: whois.neulevel.biz

.ORG: whois.pir.org

.AERO: whois.information.aero

.ARPA: whois.internic.net

.ASIA: whois.nic.asia

.COOP: whois.nic.coop

.EDU: whois.internic.net

.INT: whois.iana.org

.JOBS: jobswhois.verisign-grs.com

.MOBI: whois.dotmobiregistry.net

.MUSEUM: whois.museum

.PRO: whois.registrypro.pro

.TRAVEL: whois.nic.travel

A full list of WHOIS servers is provided in the Appendix. The JWhois Manual[15] provides some insights into internal WHOIS coding and options for proper server selection as well as using different options for each[16]:

```
whois-servers {
        type = regex;
        ".*-[A-Z]+$" = "struct handles";
        ".*" = "whois.internic.net";
};
handles {
        type = regex;
        ".*-RIPE$" = "whois.ripe.net";
        default = "whois.arin.net";
};
```

6.4   INSTALLING AND CONFIGURING WHOIS SERVERS

Deploying a WHOIS server even as an exercise can be an important tool for understanding WHOIS. If you are creating a WHOIS server as a domain provider, I would strongly recommend consulting with someone who has successfully done this task before. Maintaining the server is a completely different ongoing adventure that requires additional training. If this is for experimentation, you can create and destroy the server over and over until you are happy with the results. This section focuses on one server package as an example, but there are other free WHOIS server versions available such as the RIPE WHOIS server.[17]

6.4.1   JWhoisServer by Klaus Zerwes

JWhoisServer is a Java-based WHOIS server with a small load that runs on various Linux versions as well as Windows and can be configured for different database platforms.[18] The developer, Klaus Zerwes, maintains detailed documentation[19] and regularly issues updates. The current versions support IPv6 and IDNs and anticipate the deployment of new gTLDs. The free version (under a GNU license[20]) is a great package to use when learning and testing WHOIS server development. The commercial version is used by registrars and has been recommended by industry professionals.[21] The Indonesian registrar JogjaCamp instructs their resellers to download and install JWhoisServer.[22]

In speaking to Zerwes, I heard the passion for technology and problem solving that drives many the people of his caliber in this field. He started in the early IBM the Windows-based personal computer days eventually taking the leap to Linux at which point he gained

[15] http://www.gnu.org/software/jwhois/manual/jwhois.html#Whois-servers

[16] http://www.gnu.org/software/jwhois/manual/jwhois.html#Server-options

[17] http://www.ripe.net/data-tools/support/documentation/ripe-database-user-manual-getting-started

[18] http://jwhoisserver.net/

[19] http://jwhoisserver.sourceforge.net/

[20] http://www.gnu.org/licenses/agpl-3.0.html

[21] http://jwhoisserver.net/index.html

[22] http://resellercamp.wordpress.com/2010/03/21/installing-jwhoisserver/

a true appreciation of networking. By 2000, he was freelancing services for computing and networking. In 2006, his work for a ccTLD provider plunged him into the world of WHOIS and its server development. Being tasked with deploying the service, he realized there were no open-source, configurable packages on the market. The RIPE WHOIS server seemed oversized and impractical. In discussing the issue with a colleague, the two bet a round of drinks to see who could code a custom first. Zerwes used Java and his coworker tried in Perl. Zerwes won. He chose Java for its platform independence and the ability to use Java Database Connectivity (JDBC) as an abstract layer to support different relational database management systems (RDBMS).

6.4.1.1   Linux Installation of JWhoisServer   This is a detailed commentary of the author's own experience. It is not intended as a criticism of the existing documentation but rather as additional detail that may assist other users. The following example was performed on Fedora release 10, KDE 4.3.3. To start, open your Linux shell command window.

6.4.1.2   Dependencies   In order to install and run the package, there are a number of dependencies to install or verify before setting up the actual server. As this is Java based, you will need to have Java on your Linux system. Java is probably there but may not be the most current version, which is required for JWhoisServer. You will also need to use the root account or use the super user **sudo** prefix for the commands because you are making modifications to the core functions of the machine. Using **sudo** ("super user do") will prompt you for the administrator password.[23] The command for verifying, updating, and installing dependencies is **yum**. Yellowdog Updater Modified[24] (yum) is a common command for updating systems using **rpm**, the Linux package manger.[25] The dependencies we need are called java (the Java complier and libraries), log4j (Apache logging services), ant (Apache Java library[26]), and velocity (Linux performance management[27]). These must be done in proper order as the next installation in a sequence can fail if the previous dependency is not present. All of these are case sensitive; Linux upper- and lowercase switches have very different meanings. Run these commands:

```
sudo yum install java
sudo yum install log4j
sudo yum install ant
sudo yum install velocity
```

It is possible errors may be returned if some download locations are not available. The installation utility should check several mirrors until it finds a good installation.

6.4.1.3   Downloading the Server Packages   For security reasons, it is a good idea to import the GnuPG key to verify the integrity of downloads:

```
gpg --keyserver subkeys.pgp.net --recv-key ED7D414C
```

[23] http://www.linux.com/learn/tutorials/306766:linux-101-introduction-to-sudo
[24] http://www.linuxcommand.org/man_pages/yum8.html
[25] http://www.linuxfoundation.org/collaborate/workgroups/networking/rpm-commands
[26] http://ant.apache.org/bindownload.cgi
[27] http://www.velocity-software.com/

Here, we make a special directory (**mkdir**), navigate to it (**cd**), and then **wget** the installation file. If wget is not present, simply use **sudo yum install wget**. Check with the JWhoisServer website for the most current package:

```
sudo mkdir jwhoisserver
cd /root/jwhoisserver
wget <JWhoisServer-VERSION-src.tar.gz>
```

You will have to verify the location and name of the most current download and replace "JWhoisServer-VERSION-src.tar.gz" with that. As of this writing, this was jwhoisserver_0.4.1.1.orig.tar.gz.[28] There is an unfortunate space character in the directory name, which may cause some grief in downloading. After successfully getting the file, unpack it with **tar**, the "tape archives" compression utility[29]:

```
tar -xzf jwhoisserver-0.4.1.1.org.tar.gz
```

The –**xzf** switch tells tar to extract the file, filter it through gzip, and archive; the variation **tar xvz –f** should also work. You will then need the mysql-java-connector, also verify the current version. If you download different versions of any of these files, you will also have to modify the name in the tar commands. The first things to check whenever errors occur are the letter case, spacing, and exact spelling of file names:

- `wget http://downloads.mysql.com/archives/mysql-connector-java-5.1/mysql-connector-java-5.1.25.tar.gz`

```
tar -xzf mysql-connector-java-5.1.25.tar.gz
```

Then download the Apache Velocity package (this is optional):

```
wget http://archive.apache.org/dist/velocity/engine/ 1.7 /
velocity-1.7-dep.jar
```

Copy (**cp**) these downloads into the usr/share directory being sure to change version numbers as needed:

- `cp mysql-connector-java-5.1.25-bin.jar /usr/share/java/mysql-connector.jar`

```
cp velocity-1.7-dep.jar /usr/share/java/velocity-1.7-dep.jar
```

Navigate to the JWhoisServer build directory, the name of which will depend on the version you downloaded. In our case:

---

[28] http://sourceforge.net/projects/jwhoisserver/
[29] http://www.computerhope.com/unix/utar.htm
• The bullet point represents the code breaks

```
cd /root/jwhoisserver/JWhoisServer-0.4.1.1/build
```

At this point, you may need to configure a **classpath**. This command may help:

```
ant help-classpath
```

Or to set manually, use this:

- ```
  export CLASSPATH=/path/mysql-connector-java-5.1.25-bin.
  jar:$CLASSPATH
  ```

6.4.1.4   *Installing and Configuring the Server Package*   Now, we get to see if all of our previous steps were done correctly. Use these commands to install the server:

```
ant -Dpackage.log4j.jar=/usr/share/java/log4j.jar
ant -Dpackage.jdbc.jar=/usr/share/java/mysql-connector.jar
```
- ```
  ant -Dpackage.velocity.jar=/usr/share/java/velocitylibs/
  velocity-1.6.2/velocity-1.6.2.jar
  ```

- ```
  ant -Dpackage.velocity.deps=/usr/share/java/velocitylibs/
  velocity-1.6.2/velocity-1.6.2-dep.jar
  ```

```
ant -Dpackage.installdir.etc=/etc/jwhoisserver
ant -Dpackage.installdir.init=/etc/init.d
```

```
jar install
```

It is possible to bundle these seven lines into one, but for the sake of troubleshooting and learning the process, it is best to run them one at a time. If errors are returned, it is easier to see which line caused the problem. The Java complier (**javac**) will confirm the successful build, which means we can actually start our server! But first, we have to turn on the database with:

```
service mysqld start
```

In a production environment, these services would have to be set to self-start on boot. The server start is:

```
jwhoisserver
```

If everything is in place, the response should be "*JWhoisServer: up and running.*" This window is now your monitoring space; you will have to open a new shell window to run additional commands. It is also possible to install JWhoisServer with Red Hat Package Manager[30] (RPM), which can avoid some of the pitfalls of not having the previously installed dependencies.

---

[30] http://jwhoisserver.sourceforge.net/#install_rpm
• The bullet point represents the code breaks
```

6.4.1.5 Loading and Testing the Database   Zerwes has included a test database structure with sample data that can be installed with these commands from a new window:

```
mysql -u root -p < db.sql
mysql -u root -p < user.sql
mysql -u root -p jwhoisserver < struct.sql
mysql -u root -p jwhoisserver < data.sql
mysql -u root -p jwhoisserver < test.sql
```

A fuller discussion of what these commands do is in the database section of this chapter. If the commands ran successfully, we should now be able to test our WHOIS database with this:

```
whois -h localhost test.tld
```

or

```
jwhois -h localhost -- test.tld
```

Because we are not going out to the Internet to look for a WHOIS server, we use "localhost" to ensure we check our local database. If you toggle back to the monitoring shell we started JWhoisServer in, you should see the request for database data being displayed along with what was requested and where the request came from. In our case, the source is "127.0.0.1," which is the address of our local machine. If the query came from the Internet, it would show the IP address that submitted the WHOIS query. This is how IP addresses can be logged and blocked for excessive queries on the server side. The WHOIS record returned should look in part like this:

```
domain:     test.tld
mntnr:      MNTNR1
changed:    2006-10-14 16:21:09.0
nameserver: ns1.tld
nameserver: ns2.tld

[holder]
mntnr:      MNTNR1
type:       PERSON
name:       persona non grata
address:    two dead ends
pcode:      NWR
country:    AZ
phone:      +77 31 123454321
fax:        +77 31 123454321
email:      mail@domain.tld
changed:    2006-10-14 16:20:00.0
```

Switch to the monitoring shell and there should be an output similar to this:

```
1110073577 [Thread-13] WARN JWhoisServer  - ServerClientThread-
13::127.0.0.1 request: 'test.tld'
```

Compare that display to the one produced when a domain not present in the database is queried:

```
55785872 [Thread-11] WARN JWhoisServer  - ServerClient-
Thread-11::127.0.0.1 invalid syntax for domain: 'yahoo.com'
```

The IP address where the query came from is recorded along with the failed look up. At this point, it is fairly trivial for the server administrator to filter out or block repeated bad requests from someone who might be abusing the service. If someone excessively uses a WHOIS server, it is reasonable to set limits or request they sign up for some registered access with terms and conditions.

6.4.1.6 Windows Installation   Installing the Windows version is easier but not nearly as rewarding as the real Linux experience:

Download the setup EXE from sourceforge.net/projects/jwhoisserver/.

Run JWhoisServer-Setup-0.4.x.x.exe.

Agree to the GNU Affero General Public License.

Make sure all options are checked.

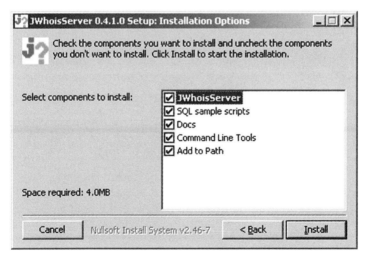

FIGURE 6.4   Whois Server configuration.

Navigate to the JWhoisServer folder in the Start menu and go to Doc.

Open jwhoisserver.html for instructions.

6.4.2 WHOIS Daemon

The word "Daemon" looks like "demon" but has a slightly different meaning. In classical Greek mythology, daemons were benign nature spirits that have specific function and held special wisdom. In computing, a Daemon is a process that runs silently in the background persistently but does not reveal itself unless specifically called, as opposed to a command that is called and terminates after running or when the user exists. Within different systems, Daemons are often named for the process or protocol they serve with a "d" on the end like **fingerd** for finger. A mailer daemon waits to process email, which may have been seen by many users in rejected emails as MAILER-DAEMON, which simply means the process could not deliver the message for some reason. In our context, a WHOIS daemon waits for a WHOIS query on Port 43. The SWhoisd[31] by Dan Anderson is a free BSD license package that can be installed independent of a WHOIS server or database. With this, it is possible to run and test a WHOIS service independent of the other components. Instructions and download: http://dan.drydog.com/swhoisd/

6.5 WHOIS DATABASE

A database stores collections information in an ordered and useful way. We think of databases as complex modern digital records but they are in fact and ancient tool used by humans for time immemorial. In 2013, researchers found what they believe are ancient clay balls in Iran that functioned like databases.[32] Being a database administrator is a distinct discipline just like network administration or program development. For our purposes, a WHOIS database is fairly straightforward in comparison to all the types of complex systems in existence today. A WHOIS database usually uses the *relational* model that employs unordered tables containing fields or attributes where specific data points are stored. We define relationships between the tables and fields with a set of transactional logic called Standard Query Language (SQL). SQL is used to read, write, and compare data as well as manage the architecture of our database. SQL can also be used to generate very detailed reports on the data we store. In terms of WHOIS for the outside world, there is one simple function: executing a **SELECT** statement for a record behind a domain name or IP address. However, as a manger of a WHOIS database, inserting new data, performing maintenance, and running reports are part of the job behind the scenes.

There are many database packages available including MSSQL Server, Sybase, and Oracle. Continuing with the example provided in this chapter with Klaus Zerwes' JWhoisServer, we will test with the free MySQL platform that is used for databases big and small around the world. However, RIPE NCC offers an online test version of its WHOIS

---

[31] http://freecode.com/projects/swhoisd

[32] http://www.foxnews.com/science/2013/10/11/clues-to-lost-prehistoric-code-discovered-in-mesopotamia/

database,[33] which allows object creation and modification. This is a good way to learn without installing your own server.

Within the JWhoisServer installation directory, there is a folder called "sql." Within this folder, there are a number of sample scripts; some were used when setting up the server:

- db.sql creates the empty database.
- user.sql creates a user for the database.
- struct.sql creates the structure of the WHOIS database.
- data.sql populates some default data.
- test.sql populates our sample domain and IP records.

In order to explore the database, open a command line and start the MySql program:

mysql -u root -p

The prompt will change to **mysql>**; type exit to quit at any time. All SQL commands must be terminated with a semicolon. This allows multiline queries to be entered before execution. The most basic operation is to get a list of tables in the database:

mysql> show tables;

This query should produce:

```
+------------------------+
| Tables_in_jwhoisserver |
+------------------------+
| country                |
| domain                 |
| inetnum                |
| mntnr                  |
| nameserver             |
| person                 |
| type                   |
+------------------------+
7 rows in set (0.00 sec)
```

With a list of table names, we can get additional information about a specific table, for example, "domain" with **describe**:

```
mysql> describe domain;
```

---

[33] http://www.ripe.net/data-tools/db/ripe-test-database

This will return the structure of the table with all field names, types, and other attributes:

```
+---------------------+----------------------+------+-----+-------------------+----------------+
| Field               | Type                 | Null | Key | Default           | Extra          |
+---------------------+----------------------+------+-----+-------------------+----------------+
| domain_key          | bigint(20) unsigned  | NO   | PRI | NULL              | auto_increment |
| domain              | varchar(255)         | NO   | UNI | NULL              |                |
| registered_date     | datetime             | NO   |     | NULL              |                |
| registerexpire_date | datetime             | NO   |     | NULL              |                |
| changed             | timestamp            | NO   |     | CURRENT_TIMESTAMP |                |
| remarks             | varchar(255)         | YES  |     | NULL              |                |
| holder              | bigint(20) unsigned  | NO   | MUL | NULL              |                |
| admin_c             | bigint(20) unsigned  | NO   | MUL | NULL              |                |
| tech_c              | bigint(20) unsigned  | NO   | MUL | NULL              |                |
| zone_c              | bigint(20) unsigned  | NO   | MUL | NULL              |                |
| mntnr_fkey          | bigint(20) unsigned  | NO   | MUL | NULL              |                |
| publicviewabledata  | tinyint(1) unsigned  | NO   | MUL | 1                 |                |
| disabled            | tinyint(1) unsigned  | NO   | MUL | 0                 |                |
+---------------------+----------------------+------+-----+-------------------+----------------+
```

To get a specific record from a table, we use the select query:

*mysql> select * from domain;*

This returns, in part:

```
+------------+----------+---------------------+---------------------+---------------------+
| domain_key | domain   | registered_date     | registerexpire_date | changed             |
+------------+----------+---------------------+---------------------+---------------------+
|          1 | test.tld | 2006-10-14 16:21:09 | 2016-10-14 16:21:09 | 2006-10-14 16:21:09 |
+------------+----------+---------------------+---------------------+---------------------+
1 row in set (0.00 sec)
```

We see this is just a domain record with no owner data. That information is kept in a different table. The owner data in "person" is connected to the domain by codes in the "domain" table.

*mysql> select * from person;*

This query will return, in part:

```
+------------+----------+------------------+----------------+---------+-------------
| person_key | type_fkey | name            | address        | pcode   | city
+------------+----------+------------------+----------------+---------+-------------
|          1 |        1 | persona non grata | two dead ends  | NWR     | and you still have to
|          2 |        3 | no name company   | last resort    | D-12345 | Berlin
+------------+----------+------------------+----------------+---------+-------------
2 rows in set (0.01 sec)
```

7

WHOIS POLICY ISSUES

With a firm technical and historical background in WHOIS, we will leap into the fiery pit of controversies. Specifically, how has the Internet Corporation for Assigned Names and Numbers (ICANN) succeed or failed in its mission? ICANN is the true nexus of WHOIS policy and related issues. How can we address concerns over privacy and mass surveillance? What can we do about falsification by criminals or obfuscation by service providers? What are the legal implications of WHOIS proxies, malicious use of WHOIS by spammers and marketers, and denial of WHOIS access by registrars? What of the international disputes over WHOIS? Thin and thick WHOIS records; lawsuits from the intellectual property (IP) sector; how the police use WHOIS in various societies; issues of technical access; bulk WHOIS record access; government investigations in mass WHOIS inaccuracy; failures of registrars to comply with WHOIS policy; systems for handling WHOIS complaints; and various studies over the years on the impact of WHOIS—these are just a few of the myriad of controversial topics. This chapter will provide a very real-world perspective, and the reader will clearly see where their interests fit in the grand scheme. The chapter attempts to offer a balanced presentation through arguments drawn from various perspectives along with meaningful suggestions for solutions.

7.1 THE WHOIS POLICY DEBATE

The Internet is not just wires, signals, and "tubes" but also a political structure. There is an alphabet soup of international organizations with their hand on the policy. In addition to IANA and ICANN, we also have at the table:

- World Wide Web Consortium (W3C)—http://www.w3.org/
- Internet Engineering Task Force (IETF)—http://www.ietf.org/

WHOIS Running the Internet: Protocol, Policy, and Privacy, First Edition. Garth O. Bruen.
© 2016 John Wiley & Sons, Inc. Published 2016 by John Wiley & Sons, Inc.

- Internet Engineering Steering Group (IESG)—http://www.ietf.org/iesg/
- Institute of Electrical and Electronics Engineers (IEEE)—http://www.ieee.org
- Internet Architecture Board (IAB)—http://www.iab.org/
- Internet Society (ISOC)—http://www.internetsociety.org/
- Governmental Advisory Committee (GAC)—gacweb.icann.org
- Internet Governance Forum (IGF)—http://www.intgovforum.org/
- ICANN's At-Large Advisory Committee (ALAC)—http://atlarge.icann.org/en/
- Generic Names Supporting Organization (GNSO)—http://gnso.icann.org/en/
- Non-Commercial Stakeholder Group (NCSG)
- Non-Commercial Users (NCUC)
- Not-for-Profit Operational Concerns Constituency (NPOC)
- Registrar and Registry Stakeholder Groups (RrSG/RySG)
- Country Code Names Supporting Organization (CCNSO)—http://ccnso.icann.org/
- Electronic Frontier Foundation (IEF)—https://www.eff.org/
- Internet Service Providers and Connectivity Providers (ISPCP) Constituency
- Security and Stability Advisory Committee (SSAC)—http://www.icann.org/en/groups/ssac
- Intellectual Property Constituency (IPC)—http://www.ipconstituency.org/
- Commercial and Business Users Constituency (CBUC)—http://www.bizconst.org/
- Address Supporting Organization (ASO)—http://aso.icann.org/
- International Telecommunication Union (ITU)—http://www.itu.int

All of these groups have their hands on WHOIS somewhere and try to change or interpret the policy. This is by no means a complete list, either. Within these groups, there are differing opinions on WHOIS policy.

In 2000, A. Michael Froomkin, a professor at the University of Miami School of Law, writing in the *Duke Law Journal* raised the concern that even the creation is dubious. In reference to WHOIS, Froomkin expressed this concern:

> *"The power to create is also the power to destroy, and the power to destroy carries in its train the power to attach conditions to the use of a domain name. Currently, this power is used to require domain name registrants to publish their addresses and telephone numbers on a worldwide readable list and to agree that any trademark holder in the world aggrieved by their registration can demand arbitration regarding ownership of the name under an eccentric set of rules and standards."* [1]

The concern is that ICANN's powers could drift perilously into content monitoring and control. Perhaps the presence of WHOIS itself is problematic.

Froomkin's concerns are directly related to the way ICANN conducts its business. *"ICANN's cumbersome process shuts out the true community,"*[1] he related in a phone interview. *"If you don't show up for the ICANN meetings three times a year across the globe in person you don't count."* This flies in the face of ICANN's public commitment, and there is no true user representation. *"Remote participation at ICANN meetings is*

---

[1] Froomkin interview.

seriously inadequate; comments from remote participants are heavily edited by ICANN staff and shelved." Froomkin insists that privacy should be implemented *by design* in any system and this failure to implement it within the Domain Name System (DNS) at the beginning kept it from taking hold. ICANN inherited WHOIS from previous entities and never updated it for the real world. According to Froomkin, ICANN listens to whoever has the most money and points a finger at the IP constituencies for holding WHOIS privacy back. As to what might fix ICANN and make it more accountable, Froomkin has two suggestions. One is that IANA IP function should be completely separate; there is too much control under one organization. The second is to not allow the ICANN board to have face-to-face meetings; all board business should be done remotely with the very technology proffered; making the board see things the way Internet users do would go a long way to truly democratizing ICANN.

Froomkin's remote board meeting suggestion immediately put me in mind of Doug Engelbart's 1968 *Mother of All Demos* during which he used the experimental oN-Line System (NLS) remotely to share a vision of communication technology. How have we fallen so far that Engelbart's "decedents" must meet in windowless rooms without community participation to decide the global network policy?

7.1.1 Basic Policy

While WHOIS policy is wide and varied subject depending on the Internet resource in question, there is a baseline standard laid out in 2004 by Leslie Daigle in RFC 3912.[2] In the standard, which continues to be current, WHOIS is defined as a service that:

- Exists for a number of informational reasons in addition to domain names
- Delivers "human-readable" data (that is text and not machine code)
- Is TCP based, through Port 43
- Has no language support
- Lacks security
- Is for nonsensitive information
- Is intended to be accessible to everyone

The fact that WHOIS lacks security and language support is really a question of technical implementation, which can be added on to the protocol at any time. The other definitions are matters of policy that can only be changed with a rewrite of the policy. Services that block Port 43, do not dispense information, or are closed to the general public are not WHOIS but rather subversions of the standard.

7.1.2 ICANN Registrar Accreditation Agreement WHOIS Standards

Under the Registrar Accreditation Agreement (RAA) extends the requirement of WHOIS specifically by dividing the responsibilities between registry, registrar, and registration. RFC 3912 defines what WHOIS is; the RAA defines who has to do what. The RAA applies

[2] http://tools.ietf.org/html/rfc3912

to ICANN gTLDs and establishes expectations of various parties of the contract as well as guaranteeing a service level to the public. Among other things, the RAA requires:

- Registrars to collect registration data at the time of registration
- Registrars to submit this data to the registry
- Registrars to allow persistent access to the data though Port 43 and a web-based interface
- Registrants to enter into an agreement to provide accurate data
- Registrars to accept complaints from any person about inaccurate data
- Registrars to investigate and correct inaccurate data
- Registrants to respond to complaints within a certain time frame

The contract is problematic in that it does not truly require registrars to validate the data due to the vagueness of the contract language. The RAA also fails to define what constitutes inaccurate data in the various categories of email address, phone number, postal addresses, etc.

The RAA also has a curious section on bulk WHOIS:

> 3.3.6 In addition, Registrar shall provide third-party bulk access to the data subject to public access under Subsection 3.3.1.[3]

This allows access to a registrar's entire WHOIS record for up to $10,000 per year. Attempts to actually purchase this access has been met with mixed results.[4] Registrars have been trying to delete this section from the contract and may be successful in the 2013 revision.[5]

The importance of WHOIS in ICANN business is made even more critical in the *Affirmation of Commitments* (AoC), the official document acknowledging ICANN's move to the private sector in 2009 and away from the direct oversight of the US Department of Commerce. Section 9.3.1 is completely devoted to WHOIS:

> ICANN additionally commits to enforcing its existing policy relating to WHOIS, subject to applicable laws. Such existing policy requires that ICANN implement measures to maintain timely, unrestricted and public access to accurate and complete WHOIS information, including registrant, technical, billing, and administrative contact information.[6]

This could not be clearer; WHOIS policy remains as it is. The section also demands ICANN to continue to study and improve WHOIS while involving a cross section of the community:

> One year from the effective date of this document and then no less frequently than every three years thereafter, ICANN will organize a review of WHOIS policy and its implementation to assess the extent to which WHOIS policy is effective and its implementation meets the legitimate needs of law enforcement and promotes consumer trust. The review will be performed by volunteer community members and the review team will be constituted and published for public comment.[7]

---

[3] http://www.icann.org/en/resources/registrars/raa/ra-agreement-21may09-en.htm#3.3.6
[4] http://www.circleid.com/posts/who_is_blocking_whois_part_2/
[5] https://community.icann.org/download/attachments/30344497/RAA+Summary+Notes.pdf?version=1&modific ationDate=1340437979000
[6] http://www.icann.org/en/about/agreements/aoc/affirmation-of-commitments-30sep09-en.htm#9
[7] See note 6.

Most importantly, the work has to result in action:

The Board will take action within six months of receipt of the recommendations.[8]

The concern at hand is consumer trust as the Internet as a global network works on mutual trust. However, the relationship between the US government and ICANN continued to shift through 2014 when the Department of Commerce announced it would release ICANN from its contractual oversight in September 2015.[9] This was seen by many as the next logical step in true Internet global governance, but also one causing concern especially as to how WHOIS issues would be dealt with in the future.

7.1.3 Lack of Language Support in WHOIS

The official standard for WHOIS, RFC 3912, lists two major problems with the protocol.[10] One is the lack of security considerations and the second is missing internationalization. The issue of security, in terms of both privacy and falsification of WHOIS, takes up the bulk of the debates and resources within ICANN space. This leaves very little space and air for internationalization. Considering that the WHOIS standard RFC is from 2004 and ICANN has a mandate to improve language access,[11] there has not been much improvement in this area. In the chapter on WHOIS use, we covered work by Ram Mohan in the area of Internationalized Domain Names (IDNs). Mohan cites a missing interest in language on technical issues. There are many people requesting interpretation services at ICANN meetings and more translation of ICANN documents, but the technical inclusion of language in the DNS is an extremely low priority. "*Language is an afterthought which is strange because most of the world does not use English,*"[12] related Mohan in a phone interview. There are also no domain industry entities wading into language expansion in the DNS, not even from registrars in non-English-speaking countries. This has real impacts according to Mohan. He related a case of rural non-English-speaking domain registrant who had their domains stolen.[13] This community-based organization did not understand the English documentation and could not read the WHOIS record, the two key elements needed to protect their domains. The idea that non-English-speaking registrants have fewer rights in a de facto sense is chilling. Mohan also noted that in order to get real movement on internationalization, there need to be clarity of purpose and a push from the Internet community to bring language down to the DNS. He continued to say that even among the new gTLDs, there is little discussion of language outside of specific IDN new gTLDs.

7.1.4 Abuses

What is "WHOIS abuse?" It means different things to different people. One of the biggest complaints about the open WHOIS system is that it permits mass harvesting of email addresses used in spam campaigns. That requiring the domain owner to leave their email

---

[8] See note 6.
[9] http://www.washingtonpost.com/business/technology/us-to-relinquish-remaining-control-over-the-internet/2014/03/14/0c7472d0-abb5-11e3-adbc-888c8010c799_story.html
[10] See note 2.
[11] http://www.icann.org/en/about/agreements/aoc/affirmation-of-commitments-30sep09-en.htm#5
[12] Mohan interview.
[13] See note 12.

addresses out in the open unfairly exposes them to unsolicited email, phishing attempts, and viruses. Let us be clear, email-based threats are very serious but actually provide much more argument for ensuring accuracy and availability of WHOIS to prevent spam. The argument that email addresses should not be listed in public WHOIS records because the owner might get spam is a fallacious argument. The ICANN SSAC examined this concern and determined that email addresses in WHOIS are clearly more vulnerable to spam harvesting, but they are no more prevalent in spam than any other email address.[14] It is not fallacious that WHOIS email addresses get spam, but the specificity of a threat against WHOIS email addresses versus other email addresses is not valid. The first thing to understand about creating registration record for a domain is not to use a *personal* email, especially as the WHOIS RFC standard states only "*nonsensitive information*" should be supplied in the public registration. Keep in mind that domain owners have the ability to create new email addresses along with their domain. Anyone who operates a domain needs to create a special administrator or contact email account to be used in the WHOIS record, not only to avoid spam but also for simple management reasons. In monitoring but keeping the WHOIS email address separate from personal email addresses, no one realistically needs to be a victim of WHOIS spam. The domain administrator should set up an automatic reply reminding the sender that the email address is for domain-related issues and not for unsolicited commercial email. The administrator should store all unsolicited email for reasons explained in the following text.

The problem of WHOIS spam can also be addressed through proper enforcement from registrars and ICANN. Using WHOIS contacts for unsolicited commercial contact is already prohibited by the RAA.[15] Domain owners need to proactively report these messages to their registrar and to ICANN. Registrars have sued organized WHOIS spammers before,[16] and such efforts can be made more effective if ICANN were to take a responsible lead. The Registration Abuse Policies Working Group issued a massive report in 2010 on domain registration abuses.[17] The cross-constituency collaboration identified a broad range of threats in the DNS such as cybersquatting, consumer deception, traffic diversion, and illicit *fast flux*.[18]

Fast flux is part of a category of threats that include domain generation algorithms (DGAs), systems, and semiautonomous malware registering many domains[19] for a variety of malicious uses. A subfunction of any of the DGAs is to populate WHOIS with bogus data. These are cases of the DNS being turned into a high-volume weapon against Internet users with WHOIS easily subverted. A well-known example is the so-called Confiker worm,[20] which was presented to the public as an infectious botnet operation, but lost in the discussion was its function of creating malicious domains en mass. The point was to create 50,000 new domains daily to be used for spamming or distributing malware, making traditional blacklisting techniques useless. Arguments over WHOIS abuse are often cast in terms of innocent users trying to protect their identities by using fake registrations.

[14] http://www.icann.org/en/groups/ssac/documents/sac-023-en.htm
[15] http://www.icann.org/en/resources/registrars/raa/ra-agreement-21may09-en.htm#3.3.5
[16] http://archive.wired.com/politics/law/news/2000/08/38014
[17] gnso.icann.org/issues/rap/rap-wg-final-report-29may10-en.pdf
[18] http://www.theregister.co.uk/2009/01/28/icann_fast_flux_report/
[19] https://media.blackhat.com/us-13/US-13-Geffner-End-To-End-Analysis-of-a-Domain-Generating-Algorithm-Malware-Family-WP.pdf
[20] http://www.gpo.gov/fdsys/pkg/CHRG-111hhrg72884/html/CHRG-111hhrg72884.htm

However, the DGA cases show that not only are the bulk of fake registrations used maliciously, but there is ultimately no real user whose rights need protecting. The user or registrant of the domain is malware program, a phantom, not someone part of the global stakeholder community.

The report frequently circles back to WHOIS-related problems underlying or accompanying the threats, specifically citing general WHOIS access problems and poor enforcement of existing rules. The team found registrars who were not providing WHOIS services as contracted or provided bad data in response to WHOIS queries.

7.1.5 Privacy

In 1999, Sun Microsystems CEO Scott McNealy famously said, *"Privacy is dead – get over it."*[21] Whether or not this should be true and whether or not citizens should accept it lying down are different issues. McNealy is right in the de facto sense. There is too much information in too many locations about too many people without their consent. The courts are becoming more and more preoccupied with this issue.[22] Beyond the general concern that various entities are collecting and using the data, there are two additional concerns. One is that unauthorized third parties are accessing the data through leaks and intrusions; some may consider government access to private data "unauthorized" as well. The second is that the data collected is often wrong; anyone trying to resolve issues on their credit report understands. The bottom line is that anyone desiring privacy needs to take direct responsibility for their data and be ever vigilant. The privacy fight should not be surrendered.

As technology marches on, there is no question that more and more of our personal data is being gathered, stored, shared, and misused by persons unknown. This is an undeniable fact. While government and business have been gathering our information for generations with few real expectations of security, the game is now about any individual being able to locate and invade the privacy of other citizens. However, there is a question about whether WHOIS records are a legitimate part of the overall privacy argument. The problem with applying the privacy standard to WHOIS is that domain holders are a tiny, voluntary population in comparison to the larger and nonvoluntary population. Existing in a modern society means we have to pay taxes, drive cars, use telephones, and now have email. While many still resist, existing without a credit card is becoming nearly impossible. Employment increasingly requires a bank account for direct deposit of salary. Consider that information storage combined with data collected by nationalized healthcare models and the compulsory collection in our society becomes enormous. Owning a domain name is not compulsory.

Beyond the fact that domain registration is completely voluntary, the number of people exposed by WHOIS is extremely small. The general privacy debate has been energized by mass government "sweeps" of telephone records and Internet logs. These collections affect nearly everyone. When US Social Security records are leaked or stolen or private data breaches expose our credit card information, our righteous indignation is justified. Unlike WHOIS records, these datasets are intended to be private and not accessed outside of the intended entities. WHOIS databases do not contain data on large swaths of the population

[21] http://www.wired.com/politics/law/news/1999/01/17538

[22] http://www.politico.com/story/2013/11/digital-era-technology-supreme-court-cases-100410.html

the way that government or utility databases do. Medical, banking, driving, travel, and other such common record sets should get the kind of privacy protections being demanded by critics of WHOIS.

However, none of this precludes that protections be offered to domain registrants, and we should not assume that threats against domain owners are not serious. One of the serious concerns with public WHOIS records is that the specific record set can be used to engage identity (ID) theft. The combination of name, address, email, and phone number is more than an ID thief needs to build a profile and launch an attack to get more information and compromise secure accounts.

The issue is about up-front disclosure, advice about privacy options, and personal responsibility. There is absolutely a serious open question as to whether ICANN, registries, and registrars are properly informing registrants that their domain registration record is intended to be *public*. Certainly, some registrars are going above and beyond the call of duty and communicating the issues to their customers, but voluntary goodwill is not a standard. The responsibility of ensuring the registrant is aware of WHOIS policy needs to start at the top and flow down.

Privacy is a concept that is largely misunderstood in a legal context and incorrectly conflated with *secrecy* and *anonymity*. In the United States, for example, the citizenry frequently speaks of a *right* to privacy, but in the legal sense, it does not exist. What citizens have is an *expectation* of privacy that can be a subtle difference but an important one to acknowledge. This expectation of privacy all but vanishes when one steps into the *Public Square*. All behavior, even in a free society, has limits. The law is about establishing those limits. An invasion of privacy occurs when a person's private affairs are the subject of unwarranted exploitation and humiliation initiated usually, but not exclusively, by the government. The requirement to have public WHOIS does not constitute an invasion of privacy. The right to be "left alone," as it is often called, is not extended in cases where public interest is genuine. Clearly, the public has interest in domain records engaged in commerce. Subjects raising concerns of privacy invasions include wiretapping or surveillance through the use of "unusual devices" to capture communication without court approval. Since WHOIS is a standard protocol, it does not constitute an unusual device. Furthermore, WHOIS records are not conversation or correspondence.

In the United States, persons are covered by the protection of the Fourth Amendment, part of the Bill of Rights of the Constitution, which states:

> *"The right of the people to be secure in their persons, houses, papers, and effects, against unreasonable searches and seizures, shall not be violated, and no Warrants shall issue, but upon probable cause, supported by Oath or affirmation, and particularly describing the place to be searched, and the persons or things to be seized."*[23]

The Bill of Rights is an agreement between citizens and the government, not between domain owners and private parties. The government is not requiring or collecting WHOIS data. Public WHOIS records also do not fall into the definitions of what is protected by the amendment. There are various statutes and legal decisions that update law for the modern world, like the Privacy Act of 1974,[24] but again, this act only applies to data held in US government databases and does not extend to WHOIS held by private companies.

---

[23] US Constitution, Bill of Rights, Fourth Amendment, http://www.law.cornell.edu/constitution/fourth_amendment
[24] http://www.law.cornell.edu/jureeka/index.php?doc=USPubLaws&cong=93&no=579

With that said, people do have a reason to be concerned in this day and age about too much disclosure. There are reasonable solutions, all of which exist today. Eliminating WHOIS altogether is not a serious proposal. Once a person or entity connects a commercial domain to the global network, its ownership becomes an issue of public interest. The privacy expectations of persons involved with the domain do not vanish, but they do change as a matter of fact.

7.1.6 Source of Concerns

Avri Doria,[25] vice president of policy at dotgay LLC and former ICANN board candidate, has been active in WHOIS policy debates since 2005 when she realized there was a security threat within WHOIS due to its lack of privacy. Doria notes that various individuals who champion social causes have been stalked and threatened through WHOIS.[26] Having a domain that represents controversial ideas can make one a target of those who hold more extreme opposing views or even repressive governments. The information superhighway works in several directions, and one enables parties of different types to get information about private individuals. For populations already under threat, minority political activists, or victimized population, having a public record connected to a public voice is extremely dangerous. Doria and many others feel there is a lack of awareness or concern over this, not to mention the basic privacy everyone should experience. A new 2014 program of WHOIS email verification immediately received criticism as being ineffective and too far reaching.[27] Instead of focusing on domains that were the subject of consumer complaints, ICANN issued a broad check of all domains that may have resulted in completely legitimate domains being disabled.

7.1.7 Creating Balance

Bernard "Bernie" Turcotte is a ubiquitous yet humble presence within the domain name world. The first time I spoke to him after an ICANN meeting, he never mentioned he had been the first CEO of the Canadian Internet Registration Authority (CIRA),[28] or Autorité Canadienne pour les Enregistrements Internet (ACEI) in French.[29] Turcotte stepped down in 2007[30] but only after implementing one of the most rational and balanced WHOIS policies for a ccTLD. Turcotte's early start developing communication emulators in the 1980s at McGill University and then connecting all the branches of a Canadian bank gave him an understanding of the issues of identifying parties on the network long before WHOIS became controversial. *"Telcos (telephone companies) were suspicious when asked for data circuits; they wanted to know why someone wanted a modem,"*[31] he related in our interview. Even in the early days of the national or global network, when there were few players as compared to now, knowing who was on the network and what they planned on doing was serious. Turcotte's work then moved to the Computer Research

---

[25] http://avri.doria.org/
[26] Doria interview.
[27] http://domainincite.com/16375-are-whois-email-checks-doing-more-harm-than-good#comment-68777
[28] http://www.cira.ca/about-cira/history/
[29] http://www.acei.ca/home-fr/
[30] http://blog.webnames.ca/cira-president-bernard-turcott/
[31] Turcotte interview.

Institute of Montreal[32] (CRIM) with hooking up their network, which was a system of BITNET mainframes. McGill wanted to use IP packets instead of DEC packets in order to connect to the fledgling New York State Education and Research Network[33] (NYSERNet) in the United States. This resulted in the first IP network in Quebec, which of course lead to the creation of the Canadian Internet, which is one of Turcotte's two proudest accomplishments.

His second was founding CIRA as the sponsor of .ca, the Canadian ccTLD. In order to preserve the integrity of these institutions, Turcotte recognized the importance of sound policy. From his perspective, WHOIS started to become controversial around 2001 as "crazy things" started happening in the gTLD world preceded by the dot-com boom,[34] which caused technical as well as financial problems. *"When mail relays failed, there was no way to recover what was lost."*[35] This was not an issue before the dot-com explosion. Without reliable WHOIS contacts, the technical problems became unresolvable. *"WHOIS is a dance between all the actors,"*[36] with two major partners being Internet abusers and government. Turcotte realized that criminals were setting up shop in Canada but also that demands from police could be at times unreasonable. Most of CIRA's customers are completely law-abiding responsible citizens, and the minority of miscreants, taking advantage of the network, do not justify unfettered access to customer information by government. At the same time, the rest of Canada's consumers deserve protection from domain owners targeting them for various illicit activities. Turcotte developed the first true domain registration privacy policy in 2004.[37] The first, and most important piece, was to create a clear delineation between commercial and personal domain names. Domains engaged in business, especially businesses requiring normal public disclosure, cannot have private WHOIS, while individual domain holders can have their information held privately.[38] Beyond keeping specific individuals information private, this is also intended to block mass harvesting of WHOIS data with .ca.[39] This is balanced on the other end with extensive dispute, contact, and disclosure procedures to deal with problems arising from the improper use of private domain names[40] as well as a clear protocol[41] for the Royal Canadian Mounted Police (RCMP). What is more, this development was done to comply with Canadian national laws[42] and with aggressive public consultation.[43] CIRA also has a robust trademark dispute system.[44] Believe it or not, CIRA also reviews every new .ca application for accuracy. The result, according to Turcotte, is 95% WHOIS accuracy within .ca, which is unheard of in the rest of the WHOIS world.

So where is the problem in the gTLDs, if this model can be demonstrated as successful? According to Turcotte, the gTLD policy for WHOIS is basically missing, and the few policies that do exist are being implemented. Accuracy can be implemented in the gTLD

---

[32] http://www.crim.ca/en/
[33] https://www.nysernet.org/about-nysernet/history/
[34] http://www.nethistory.info/History%20of%20the%20Internet/dotcom.html
[35] See note 32.
[36] See note 32.
[37] http://www.circleid.com/posts/cira_proposes_new_standard_for_domain_name_whois_privacy/
[38] http://www.cira.ca/utility-pages/WHOIS-Backgrounder/
[39] http://whoissecurity.com/category/whois/
[40] http://www.cira.ca/whois/
[41] http://www.cira.ca/assets/Documents/Legal/Registrants/disclosurelaw.pdf
[42] http://www.itbusiness.ca/news/cira-revamps-privacy-policy-for-pipeda-compliance/8785
[43] http://www.icann.org/en/news/correspondence/turcotte-to-twomey-25jul06-en.pdf
[44] http://www.cira.ca/legal/cdrp/dispute-resolution-decisions/

space as a technical matter, but the various players must acknowledge that domain ownership is a responsibility and not just a business, in the opinion of Turcotte. In the opinion of this author, the only thing blocking this commonsense policy in the gTLD world is the politics of ICANN. It is important to step outside the ICANN bubble to get more thoughts about the debate because the environment can become dulled and repetitive in its debate. The following perspectives are from people involved in WHOIS but not regular attendees of ICANN meetings.

Klaus Zerwes, creator of JWhoisServer, notes the WHOIS privacy issue and actually cites it in his motivation for creating WHOIS server software with a desire to have maximum configurability, including the possibility to associate recursive queries on special configurable fields ("recursecondition"). Zerwes knows WHOIS is not scalable by design and wants to see implementation of RWhois to close that gap. He believes that the privacy issue must be handled somehow but acknowledges the difficult balance of preserving privacy and offering the information required for domain handling and ownership. He cites a hypothetical comprehensive solution, which involves IP-based access control lists (ACL), improved UTF8 character encoding, as well as standardization of WHOIS output, commands, and source records.

Mary Stahl, one of the coauthors of the early WHOIS RFC, noted that one of the DDN ARPANET directories, the hard copy version, was somehow removed or leaked outside of the network. A person who got their hands on the directory started sending unsolicited commercial emails to people listed in the directory. SRI responded to this incident by placing a disclaimer in the printed version of the directory warning people about the misuse of the data contained within the directory and limiting the type of use of the data.[45] This disclaimer in basic policy restriction about data use is virtually the same as the one applied today for domain WHOIS. The ICANN RAA clearly lays out the conditions for making WHOIS data public but also places severe restrictions on how that data can be used.

Brian Harvey, coauthor of the original NAME/FINGER RFC,[46] acknowledges that early users of the network were oblivious to privacy concerns. This changed quickly as various users noted that natural data tracking and logging within the system could be used by their bosses to determine how hard they were working. In particular, the "last login" data could be used to see how long somebody was actually working on the network. Additionally, the *where am I now* feature was often used to physically locate people who might be working on the network. Dr. Harvey actually teaches a course on the social invocations of computers at Berkeley.[47] He acknowledges that there is definitely virtue in having public records in terms of accountability. However, he is somewhat critical of the public attitude toward privacy. *"People say they want privacy but they don't act like it. They dump their whole lives on Facebook and allow Google to scan their e-mails."*[48] He notes that if people really knew how WHOIS was used, they would opt for more privacy.

Simone Carletti, creator of Ruby WHOIS, stated that privacy is important in Italy. Privacy is a concern and something people talk about. However, he said, *"fake information is not a solution. The registry should collect real information and apply different layers of*

---

[45] Stahl interview.
[46] http://tools.ietf.org/html/rfc742
[47] http://www.eecs.berkeley.edu/Courses/Data/22.html
[48] Harvey interview.

access. There needs to be a clear specification of who is and each registry should be communicating to customers about the responsibilities and the registrar should be removed from that part of the policy cycle."[49] As somebody who deals with DNS issues, Carletti knows the importance of being able to contact a responsible party.

7.1.8 European Privacy Laws and WHOIS

A topic that comes up frequently in WHOIS policy discussions is the difference between European and US privacy laws. Since the early development and deployment of the Internet started in the United States and branched out to the rest of the world, it dragged most of the US viewpoint with it, especially through direct sponsorship of the DNS by the US government for over a decade. Critics point out that the US model does not work globally and the WHOIS policy as is does not meet the legal privacy criteria required in the European Union and other countries. The question before us is whether or not the privacy code in Europe applies to domain WHOIS records. "European privacy law" is often cited but not explained or understood in terms of WHOIS. The actual code in play is Article 8 of the European Convention on Human Rights, which states:

Right to respect for private and family life

1. *Everyone has the right to respect for his private and family life, his home and his correspondence.*

2. *There shall be no interference by a public authority with the exercise of this right except such as is in accordance with the law and is necessary in a democratic society in the interests of national security, public safety or the economic well-being of the country, for the prevention of disorder or crime, for the protection of health or morals, or for the protection of the rights and freedoms of others.*[50]

The most important part of the wording, in terms of applicable authority, is "*There shall be no interference by a public authority*"—meaning this is intended to apply to the government treatment of private citizens. The relationship between a domain registrant, registrar, and ICANN does not fall under this article. However, among other things, the privacy protection applies to "*correspondence,*" but placing a domain name on the global network is not correspondence, and correspondence is not contained in a WHOIS record. Using a domain to send email could be considered correspondence, but this is a separate issue. There is of course the reference of "*his home,*" which could be relevant in terms of displaying a residential address in a public WHOIS record, but this may also not be applicable in the context for reasons explained in the following text.

There are European laws like the Data Protection Directive[51] (Directive 95/46/EC) that provide protections for individuals and rules for the collection of data but do not prohibit the collection. Quite the opposite in fact of stopping collection, the directive spells out the conditions for transmitting personal data to assist international commerce. This is the sticking point: international commerce is virtually impossible without some transfer of

---

[49] Carletti interview.
[50] http://www.echr.coe.int/Documents/Convention_ENG.pdf
[51] http://eur-lex.europa.eu/LexUriServ/LexUriServ.do?uri=CELEX:31995L0046:en:HTML

personal information. What the directive does demand in terms of personal data is that its collection must be disclosed to and consented by the person. The data has to be for a clear purpose, and the collection must be *"relevant and not excessive."* In fact, some of the more discrete concerns are about how long data is to be held after a domain expires and not so much about the collection itself.[52]

Robin Gross, founder and executive director of IP Justice,[53] explained in a very detailed and eloquent letter to the ICANN WHOIS Review Team the various legal issues with WHOIS.[54] While all the cases and statutes covered in the letter are important for understanding the international spectrum of privacy law, it fails to make a real case that the existence of WHOIS violates any of these laws. The letter also seems to come from a single perspective of the battles waged by copyright and trademark attorneys against domain owners. Gross misses the enormous need of consumers to combat Internet fraud.

ICANN has actually addressed these issues fairly consistently by developing a Procedure for Handling WHOIS Conflicts with Privacy Law.[55] A registrar or registry must receive a specific order from a government with proper citations and forward this information to ICANN staff. A consultation will occur to determine how the local privacy law and the RAA obligations can be met. The ICANN general council will review, come to a conclusion, and issue a public notice. So, to be clear, there is a formal process for determining if WHOIS violates any privacy law; one cannot simply claim "European privacy law" as a reason to not supply WHOIS information—it is much more complicated.

7.1.9 Drawing the Line

When asked why some want WHOIS eliminated completely, Steve DelBianco, executive director of NetChoice,[56] says that *"at ICANN the ends define the middle"*—referring to somewhat extreme privacy advocates who want complete anonymity throughout the DNS.[57] Privacy should be important to Internet users and woven into policy, but we need to be realistic about the specific role of domain names. The question before us is not whether the *user* of Google deserves privacy but whether the *owner* of google.com deserves privacy. Certainly, the WHOIS records for google.com, amazon.com, twitter.com, and facebook.com should not be anonymous. These are entities that are first and foremost online businesses. To grant them WHOIS anonymity is to permit corporate secrecy; this is far distant from preserving the privacy of ordinary citizens. Should girlscouttrooplocal209.com have a public WHOIS record? Probably not, but the top-level Girl Scout organization should.

Vinton Cerf, early Internet architect and former ICANN board member, said in an interview where he supported the privacy of Google users in terms of browsing privacy: *"There*

---

[52] http://domainincite.com/10606-european-privacy-watchdog-says-icanns-whois-demands-are-unlawful
[53] http://www.imaginelaw.com/
[54] http://ipjustice.org/WSIS/ICANNthreat.shtml
[55] ICANN Procedure for Handling WHOIS Conflicts with Privacy Law
[56] http://netchoice.org/about/netchoice-staff/
[57] DelBianco interview.

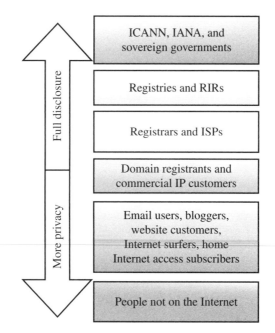

FIGURE 7.1   Privacy versus disclosure chart.

are cases where in the transactions both parties really need to know who we are talking to."[58] The privacy line should be drawn along the reasonable existing lines of commerce and transactions reflecting the disclosure policy of the specific industry represented. For example, if brick-and-mortar drug stores need to disclose ownership and license, so should a pharmacy website. If radio and television advertising for pharmaceuticals needs to follow certain regulations, so should Internet advertising for pharmaceuticals—including domains used to support drug sales. The balance of protection flips when the consumer is on the other end—a domain owner is no longer the "consumer" of public concern when regulated commercial activity is in play. The following chart shows the rough relationships from the top-level Internet authorities down to individual people.

This chart begins to ask the question as to where the privacy line should be drawn in Internet use. At opposite ends of the spectrum, we have the managers of the global network and the lowly users. Starting from the bottom, parties gain more access and control as they move up the ladder so to speak. The scope of control becomes larger as we move up; therefore, the burden of public responsibility becomes greater. Clearly, the root managers should not be anonymous, and neither should their contracted parties on various levels, but the disclosure requirement should stop at some layer. The fierce privacy battles mostly exist at the lowest levels of this chart with individual Internet user and consumers having the greatest expectation of privacy. People not yet engaging on the Internet clearly have the greatest expectation—noting that this refers to Internet *use* and not public records relating to offline individuals. Obviously, the problem is that domain ownership has an ambiguous placement between the private and public space. The most reasonable way to address this discrepancy is with a distinction between commercial domains and other types of domains.

---

[58] http://www.pcmag.com/article2/0,2817,2416242,00.asp

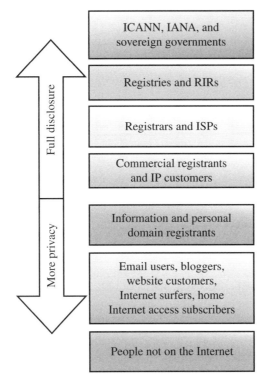

FIGURE 7.2   Suggested privacy versus disclosure model.

A commercial IP customer and a residential IP customer use the same resource but are treated differently. The same can be done for domain owners. The division of commercial and other types of domains is difficult, but not impossible to establish. The question is whether the domain engages in financial transactions, accepts funds for political campaigns, is used to advertise a product, or is monetized in some significant way. Of course, many websites support their operations through micropayments, donations, or banner advertising, and this may be a gray area requiring further definition.

7.1.10   Uniform Domain-Name Dispute-Resolution Policy

As described in the chapter on WHOIS use, cybersquatting has become a massive legal game and income generator for various parties. Brand owners have been continuously befuddled by the fact that any person can "buy" their trademarked ID in the form of a domain. The conundrum is captured by Tim Berners-Lee in *Weaving the Web: "The trademark-law criterion of separation in location and market does not work for domain names."* [2] WHOIS plays a major part in trademark illicit activity. The ICANN process for dealing with disputed names is called the Uniform Domain-Name Dispute-Resolution Policy[59] (UDRP). Cybersquatted domains are referred to registrations made in *bad faith*. Registrants must affirm that their domain *"will not infringe upon or otherwise violate the rights of any*

---

[59] http://www.icann.org/en/help/dndr/udrp/policy

third party."[60] Designated dispute providers serve as courts for this process, conduct investigations, and issue decisions.[61] As part of the process, domain registrars are required to comply with UDRP decisions[62] as part of their contract and transfer disputed domains to complaining brand owners per decision. Steve DelBianco, who represents the interests of several major companies in the ICANN space, thinks that UDRP is largely successful with the bulk of complaints rewarding the legitimate brand owner. He acknowledges that it has been used in some cases unscrupulously to gain control over a domain,[63] so-called *reverse domain name hijacking.*

Steven Metalitz, president of the IPC at ICANN, was part of the original drafting committee for the UDRP[64] who also believes the policy is a success, but there are many areas for improvement especially within WHOIS. Metalitz provides frequent advice on WHOIS policy including what became known as the "Metalitz comment," a recommendation to collect data on UDRP cases brought against registrants who used proxy or private registration services to determine if the use reduced the registrant's ability to contest a UDRP proceeding.[65] The issue is serious since many registrars' WHOIS privacy/proxy services do not relay notices to the registrant. The way some WHOIS services are configured, it would be impossible for the registrant to receive notices of a UDRP. Metalitz points out a major flaw in the system—that some of these services more or less remove WHOIS, thus breaking the trust foundation of the DNS. Trademark violators are of course playing a game; they are taking a risk of purchasing a domain with a trademark due to losing it to a UDRP, but they also risk being sued in the real world for IP theft. Completely illicit parties will attempt to conceal their ID as much as possible with the UDRP either by using a privacy shield or by completely falsifying the WHOIS.[66]

In terms of WHOIS, the UDRP requires that the registrar verify sponsorship of the domain name and supply the registrant contact data from WHOIS. The registrant is notified and has an opportunity to respond to the complaint and present their evidence. More often than not, infringing registrants with private WHOIS end up in default in UDRP cases by failing to reply to the complaint. In all these cases, the domain is transferred to the complainant. So, in essence, UDRP works as designed by awarding the trademark owner with control over the domain. However, there is more going on in the background. A registrant who is knowingly trying to exploit a trademark suffers no damages and remains anonymous in the UDRP procedure. While a complainant brand owner technically wins the case, the domain is often itself worthless to the complainant. *"Privacy and anonymity are not the same things,"* related DelBianco. *"There are people in this space who not only want to block their domain contact details, but also want to be un-contactable."*[67] This situation is frequently found at ICANN meetings with different registrant groups claiming that because this or that country does not have postal codes or street addresses, there should not be any WHOIS requirements.

---

[60] See note 59.

[61] http://www.icann.org/en/help/dndr/udrp/providers

[62] http://www.icann.org/en/resources/registrars/raa/ra-agreement-21may09-en.htm#3.8

[63] See note 58.

[64] http://archive.icann.org/en/udrp/staff-report-29sept99.htm

[65] http://www.icann.org/en/news/public-comment/whois-study-suggestion-summary-15feb08-en.pdf

[66] http://www.buchalter.com/wp-content/uploads/2013/06/summer-2006-patents.pdf

[67] See note 58.

Another problem with UDRP is that it is completely after-the-fact. Efforts to create a better process have resulted in the Trademark ClearingHouse (TCH), which notifies registrant that they might be using a protected name. Some critics claim this has a chilling effect on free speech by scaring legitimate registrants. DelBianco responds this by stating that *"The trademark notices are a favor to the registrant alerting them to a potential violation, it does not stop anything."* This is an important distinction—no one is blocked from registering a domain name with a trademark, and UDRP ultimately comes down to issues of use. For example, if a consumer believes that a particular product is dangerous and creates a domain called "aspirinisunhealthy.com," this could be a completely legitimate use of a trademark. While the battles over WHOIS are often framed as fights between privacy advocates and powerful copyright attorneys, Metalitz reminds us that *"WHOIS exists for the protection of every consumer, it has nothing to do with intellectual property ultimately, it is the trust foundation of our public network."*[68] This is, of course, one of the main arguments of this text, that every user should have access to accurate WHOIS for the protection of us all. If a brand is being infringed on the Internet with knockoff products, it does more harm to the consumer than the brand owner.

The problems presented by anonymous registrations in IP cases are made even more difficult by registrars who do not comply with the process and go unpunished by ICANN. In June 2012, one of the UDRP providers, the National Arbitration Forum (NAF), attempted to process a complaint about a domain sponsored by the ICANN-accredited registrar ABSystems.[69] The registrar never responded to any of the procedural requests of the UDRP. According to the UDRP decision, the *"Registrar's non-compliance has been reported to ICANN."*[70] The respondent (registrant) also never responded to the UDRP, so the default judgment was to award the complainant with the domain. According to historical WHOIS records, the domain was never transferred as ordered.[71] This means ABSystems violated their contract twice within this UDRP, yet there are no enforcement notices issued by ICANN over these issues.

Adding insult to injury, ICANN would eventually deaccredit ABSystems over an unrelated issue[72] but—even with sufficient published evidence concerning the illicit nature of the ABSystems operation—transferred all their domains to a different registrar. This became a massive headache for the accepting registrar, EnCirca, who had to deal with the mess, but to their credit handled it well[73]:

> *"Although not required for registrar transfers,* [EnCirca President Thomas Barrett] *decided to put all of the customers through email verification. 75% of the customer emails bounced and no customer verified their account."*[74]

Specifically, the WHOIS records for the bulk of ABSystems domains were invalid. ICANN had advance warning that there were issues with ABSystems yet still allowed an unsuspecting registrar to spend time and resources dealing with the problem.

---

[68] Metalitz interview.

[69] http://domains.adrforum.com/domains/decisions/1448633.htm

[70] See note 69.

[71] http://research.domaintools.com/research/whois-history/search/?q=nabpvipps.com

[72] http://www.icann.org/en/news/announcements/announcement-10mar14-en.htm

[73] http://domainnamewire.com/tag/encirca/

[74] http://domainnamewire.com/tag/encirca/#sthash.9mxxr6df.dpuf

This was not an anomaly; there are unenforced UDRPs for the registrars Interdominios,[75] UKRNAMES,[76] WEBAGENTUR.AT,[77] Bargin Register,[78] Web Werks India,[79] Todaynic. com,[80] URL SOLUTIONS,[81] and several others that beg explanation. This seems to indicate that some registrars and ultimately ICANN are part of this problem, which appears to reward the obscuring of WHOIS. When asked explicitly what happened in these cases during a recorded 2014 ICANN meeting in Singapore, Compliance representatives blamed *"global compliance communication problems"* for the UDRP issues without explaining further.[82]

The issue is further exemplified in the case of Bargin Register, Inc. who appears to be a serial violator of UDRP noncompliance not only with the NAF but also with the World Intellectual Property Organization (WIPO). As with ABSystems, their noncompliance was reported more than once in previous years, but ICANN only recently began to enforce against them. In what seems a rare example, ICANN would eventually breach and terminate Bargin Register for failing to comply with a UDRP but also for owing $5,873.03 in accreditation fees.[83] While this registrar was deaccredited eventually, the question still remains what happened in the cases of onduclair.com (D2011-1129[84]), regionsbabk.com (FA1204001439913[85]), thomsonreuters.com (FA1208001460785[86]), and copapetrobras. com (D2011-1250[87]). The last case on the list is interesting because WIPO felt the need to admonish the registrar in a dedicated section of the ruling, which states in part:

> *"D. The Registrar's Inaction: As noted the Registrar failed to respond to four requests from the Center, each seeking verification of the registrant's contact information and standard assurances regarding its registration agreement. Prior to commencing this proceeding Complainant made four inquiries of the Registrar to ascertain the language of the registration agreement, in order to file its Complaint in that language. See Rules, paragraph 11(a). No reply was forthcoming."*[88]

If this paragraph does not make the issue clear, it goes on to state:

> *"The Registrar's continued silence, which until an explanation be provided the Panel will presume to be intentional, is unhelpful and irresponsible."*[89]

WIPO does not stop with the registrar, but continues with a message to ICANN itself:

> *"The Panel also urges ICANN (as the registrar-accrediting agency) to take appropriate steps to encourage or require as a matter of standard contracting practice timely registrar replies to*

---

[75] http://domains.adrforum.com/domains/decisions/1479740.htm

[76] http://domains.adrforum.com/domains/decisions/1515636.htm

[77] http://domains.adrforum.com/domains/decisions/1514438.htm

[78] http://domains.adrforum.com/domains/decisions/1460785.htm

[79] http://domains.adrforum.com/domains/decisions/1475512.htm

[80] http://domains.adrforum.com/domains/decisions/1457832.htm

[81] http://domains.adrforum.com/domains/decisions/1450159.htm

[82] http://audio.icann.org/meetings/singapore2014/alac-regional-2-23mar14-en.mp3

[83] http://www.icann.org/en/news/correspondence/serad-to-wall-20feb13-en.pdf

[84] http://www.wipo.int/amc/en/domains/search/text.jsp?case=D2011-1129

[85] http://www.adrforum.com/domaindecisions/1439913.htm

[86] See note 78.

[87] http://www.wipo.int/amc/en/domains/search/text.jsp?case=D2011-1250

[88] See note 87.

[89] See note 87.

UDRP provider verification requests. A failure on ICANN's part to take appropriate steps to address registrar conduct such as has occurred in this and the Onduline case can only come at a cost to the credibility of its processes in the eyes of interested parties—mark owners properly invoking the Policy to enforce their rights and domain name owners who might fail to receive timely notice of UDRP proceedings brought against them."[90]

While this decision was rendered in September 2011, there is no accompanying enforcement from ICANN. It would take another 2 years and additional UDRPs without response before ICANN would act.

Some brand owners have completely sidestepped the UDRP and sued registrars directly with varying results. Verizon has sued the registrar DirectNIC twice for cybersquatting.[91] In these cases, Verizon charged that hundreds of infringing domains were registered not by customers of the registrar but by the registrar itself. Filed documents show a maze of shell companies behind the allegedly false WHOIS record leading back to officers of the registrar.[92]

7.1.10.1 *Proxy and Privacy in the ICANN gTLDs*

ICANN has conducted studies of privacy/proxy abuse,[93] which show criminal use of these services.[94] More studies in this area are pending.[95] While rarely fully disclosed, most private WHOIS services are run by registrars. In fact, the contract seems to dictate that privacy services must be run by the registrar or another contracted party[96]:

" [3.4.1] registrar shall either (1) include in the database the name and postal address, e-mail address, and voice telephone number provided by the customer of any privacy service or licensee of any proxy registration service offered or made available by Registrar or its affiliate companies."

The format and quality of privacy services vary wildly, but they generally fall into three format categories: (i) single-contact services, (ii) by-registrant services, and (iii) by-registration services. Single-contact services, like contactprivacy.org, have the same contact information for all registrations.

```
Registrant:
PrivacyProtect.org
Domain Admin (contact@privacyprotect.org)
ID#10760, PO Box 16
Note - All Postal Mails Rejected, visit Privacyprotect.org
Nobby Beach
null,QLD 4218
AU
Tel. +45.36946676
```

FIGURE 7.3 Privacy protection WHOIS record.

[90] See note 87.

[91] http://www.thedomains.com/2012/01/30/verizon-sues-parked-com-directnic-for-cybersquatting-on-over-600-domain-names/

[92] http://www.domainnamenews.com/legal-issues/verizon-suits-directnic-sigmund-solares-al-cybersquatting-288-million-dollars-damage-sought/7360

[93] http://botnetlegalnotice.com/citadel/files/Cox_Decl_EX01.pdf

[94] http://securityskeptic.typepad.com/the-security-skeptic/INET2010-PiscitelloSheng.pdf

[95] http://www.icann.org/en/news/announcements/announcement-24sep13-en.htm

[96] http://www.icann.org/en/resources/registrars/raa/ra-agreement-21may09-en.htm#3.4.1

These services are technically invalid since there is no way to contact the specific owner of a domain, which is the point of the WHOIS record. Paradoxically, the registrars behind single-contact services have been more cooperative, frequently suspending the privacy shields for illicit domains upon complaint. GoDaddy's single-contact proxy service has started revealing the name of the registrant without any other specific contact details. By-registrant privacy services are the most useful to investigators because even though the ID of the registrant is unknown, it is possible to link the domains owned by a single person or entity. For example, genericmedications.com and candrugstore.net both used the RebelPrivacy address AI0M7CWKK0COJL8G@rebelprivacy.com. Both of these domains redirect to CanadaDrugs, which supports the connection. By-registration privacy services like WhoisGuard are the most difficult to track because each registration has a different email address regardless of the owner behind them.

The following table shows which registrar is affiliated with which service; this is not always transparent to the consumer:

contactprivacy.com	Tucows
domainsbyproxy.com	GoDaddy
dynadot.com	Dynadot
dynamicdolphin.com	Dynamic Dolphin
emailaddressprotection.com	DomainDiscover
monikerprivacy.net	Moniker
myprivateregistration.com	Melbourne IT
networksolutionsprivateregistration.com	Network Solutions
privacy.com.ua	Ukrainian Names
privacypost.com	Dotster
privacyprotect.org	Directi
protecteddomainservices.com	Name.com
proxy.dreamhost.com	New Dream Network
rebelprivacy.com	Namescout
whoisguard.com	Namecheap
whoisprivacyprotect.com	eNom
whoisprivacyprotection.info	GMO Internet

There are many more out there, but these are the most commonly used. Some privacy services are completely ad hoc and not affiliated with a contracted party, which makes them invalid. The issue of transparency to the Internet user is extremely problematic. For example, the service whoisprivacyservices.com cannot be clearly linked to any registrar, and its home page is a pornographic site. For years, the registrar Internet.BS provided a service called privatewhois.net, which did not include a street address in the WHOIS record rather the lines:

```
******PLEASE DO NOT SEND LETTERS******
****Contact the owner by email only****
```

Following a series of revelations about Internet.BS,[97] the registrar changed its privacy record format.[98] The customers of the registrar BizCn use a service called privacy-protect.cn,

---

[97] http://krebsonsecurity.com/2012/03/half-of-all-rogue-pharmacies-at-two-registrars/
[98] http://www.webhostingtalk.com/showthread.php?t=1143482

which has been shown to be completely invalid; that case is detailed in Section 7.3.1, "Tracking ICANN's Response to WHOIS Inaccuracy."

The various privacy shields used for WHOIS have had their share of legal challenges when used illicitly. In 2010, a US 9th Circuit court concluded that WHOIS privacy is considered "material falsification" when used in conjunction with an online crime.[99] The crime in question is the violation of the US CAN-SPAM law, which prohibits unsolicited email unless it follows very strict guidelines. Part of the law dictates that a spam victim must show continued and excessive email from the same source. In order to avoid being caught, spammers will use multiple "identities" to avoid the violation. In using shielded registration, they are in effect misleading consumers.[100] The mass deception on the Internet through WHOIS leads us to our next section.

7.1.11 WHOIS Inaccuracy, Falsification, Obfuscation, and Access Denial

The deliberate falsification of WHOIS is a pervasive problem that has been widely studied and documented. The prevalence of false data and its direct link to cybercrime demonstrates an issue much larger and more specific than individual registrants trying to protect their privacy. Various registrants deliberately falsify their WHOIS records for obvious reasons. Doing something illegal or abusive on the Internet with a domain name is likely to attract the attention of police, private companies, and consumers. As with any illicit activity, Internet *malusers* want to cover their tracks and be anonymous. The desire of criminals to be anonymous is not related to an Internet user's need to be anonymous. One can exist without the other, regardless of what some more extreme privacy advocates would have us believe. While cybercriminals falsify records as a matter of course, they often get additional help with registrars blocking WHOIS access and further obscuring the records. Many ICANN-contracted and independent researchers have been drawing these conclusions year after year with little visible improvement. The problem is captured in public statements from Interpol representative Michael Moran at the ICANN San Francisco meeting in 2011:

> "Accurate Whois is a joke. It just doesn't happen…We don't see it, we never get it. Even if we do see something within it that might give us indications, it's always a dead end and it's a waste of time even trying. What's the point in having a Whois database if it can't be accurate? Somebody has to be responsible for having that accurate, and whoever that somebody is, can you please step up to the plate and do your work?"[101]

7.2 STUDIES, REPORTS, AND ACTIVITIES ON WHOIS

There have been a number of attempts to recognize and address the problems with WHOIS over the years, some with moderate success, but overall it is a tale of inaction. The data and recommendations from working groups and independent research have been sound; it is the failure of execution that has left WHOIS floundering.

---

[99] http://sedo.com/us/news/2575/WHOIS-Privacy-Considered-%9CMaterial-Falsification%9D/?tracked=&partnerid=&language=us

[100] http://blog.wordtothewise.com/2013/06/can-spam-ruling-against-whois-privacy-protection/

[101] http://www.theregister.co.uk/2011/03/17/child_abuse_cop_slams_icann/

7.2.1 SSAC (2002)

For over 10 years, the SSAC has issued advice to ICANN on risk and improvements.[102] The SSAC has made regular comments about WHOIS. In 2002, the committee declared that *"Whois data is thus important for the security and stability of the Internet as the administration and control of Internet resources is widely distributed."*[103] Because of the grave importance, SSAC plainly stated that WHOIS accuracy *"must be improved."* The improvements listed include a standard format for WHOIS, a date of the last verification in each WHOIS record, a published list of WHOIS servers, and enhanced privacy protections for registrants.[104] The recommendations of the committee are yet to be realized. This is made clear in the SSAC report from 2008, which stated: *"To date, little progress has been made towards the development of a formal directory service for the Internet."*[105] The report also notes the "poor" condition of WHOIS and makes many of the same recommendations to ICANN it did in 2002.

7.2.2 Benjamin Edelman Congressional Testimony on WHOIS (2003)

The US House of Representatives Committee on the Judiciary (Subcommittee on Courts, the Internet, and Intellectual Property) convened a hearing in 2003 about the to review the problems associated with WHOIS inaccuracy.[106] In 2003, Benjamin Edelman—a fellow at Harvard Law School Berkman Center for Internet and Society— testified before this congressional subcommittee about the accuracy database and serious flaws within the WHOIS system in general. Edelman's testimony from 2003 reads like a biblical prophecy of the state of WHOIS 10 years later. The Berkman Center engages in ongoing research into how the Internet affects society. Edelman stated the way the DNS currently works as an *honor system*. There is no economic incentive for registrars to enforce WHOIS accuracy. While registrars have a contractual obligation to address issues of accuracy, there is nothing concrete to make them take it seriously. As a result, *"whois database is substantially fiction."* Edelman was not just giving his opinion; he actually conducted intense research on the subject and even consulted ICANN on potential problems with an expanding DNS. He noted that various independent researchers and working groups had come to the same conclusion, yet nothing serious had been done to address it. This was not only criticism. Edelman offered comprehensive plans or policies and procedures that would incentivize registrants and registrars to create a more accurate record. ICANN had only been in operation for 5 years and the situation had already become dire. Within a week of Edelman's testimony, the *Memorandum of Understanding* between ICANN and the US government would be amended[107] to ensure proper WHOIS policy was in place within 1 year.

---

[102] http://www.icann.org/en/groups/ssac
[103] http://www.icann.org/en/groups/ssac/documents/sac-003-en.htm
[104] See note 103.
[105] http://www.icann.org/en/groups/ssac/documents/sac-027-en.pdf
[106] http://commdocs.house.gov/committees/judiciary/hju89199.000/hju89199_0f.htm
[107] http://www.icann.org/en/about/agreements/mou-jpa/amend6-jpamou-17sep03-en.htm

7.2.3 US Government Accountability Office Report on Prevalence of False Contact Information in WHOIS (2005)

The Government Accountability Office (GAO) is an independent US congressional agency often called the "congressional watchdog." It reviews how the federal government spends the people's money[108] and issues comprehensive reports to the US Congress. In 2005, GAO conducted research noting not only problems of accuracy within the database but also general problems of following documented procedure.[109] The GAO, for example, actually submitted inaccuracy reports to ICANN for patently false WHOIS records and found that 33% were not corrected by the closure of the complaint cycle. While this report tends to suggest that larger percentage of WHOIS records are not inaccurate, the handling of inaccuracies in the obviousness of those inaccuracies presents a serious threat to the validity of the system. While concerns about the data had been emerging for some time, it was also becoming apparent that the processes put in place to address the issue were not entirely effective.

7.2.4 WHOIS Study Hypotheses Group Report to the GNSO Council (2008)

The GNSO Council voted to convene a WHOIS study hypothesis group tasked with reviewing recommendations submitted in public comment periods as well as an official request from the GAC. The report issued by the group constitutes a summary and aggregation of various findings on WHOIS. The number of topics shows the complexity and seriousness of WHOIS in terms of real impact on Internet users whether they be consumers, registrants, or contracted parties:

> *"Whois databases are being used and mined regularly by direct mail."*

> *"Some Registrars knowingly tolerate inaccurate or falsified Whois data so as to attract and retain registrations by spammers."*

> *"Some registrars operating proxy/privacy services are not revealing registrant data when requested in a UDRP proceeding."*

> *"Registrants would be less likely to falsify their Whois data if the sensitive information of private persons can be secured."*

> *"A significant number of Registrars do not apply effective methods to detect fraudulent domain name registrations."*

There is a common thread running through all the comments that may not be apparent to those on different sides of the debate. The culprits in all problems are rogue commercial players victimizing consumers. In one scenario, the victim is a domain consumer fending off unsolicited advertising from bad actors. On the opposite side, email users are the victims of domain-owning spammers. In some, but clearly not all cases, the rogue commercial player is a contracted party. Unfortunately, instead of recognizing the general source of the problem, a false battle line has been drawn between domain owners and nondomain owners with WHOIS as the focus of the struggle. The contracted parties will naturally side with the domainers who are their paying customers. In analyzing statements by various registrars,

---

[108] http://www.gao.gov/about/index.html
[109] http://www.gao.gov/products/GAO-06-165

they are generally tired of taking the blame for rogue registrars but at the same time failing to take a stand against the abusers in the industry. This situation has created an "us against them" mentality in addressing WHOIS issues. The only people who benefit from this in the end are the rogue players.

7.2.5 National Opinion Research Center at the University of Chicago (2009)

The National Opinion Research Center (NORC) at the University of Chicago collaborated with ICANN in 2009 to sample WHOIS records and test them for validity.[110] Rigorous checks of records behind a sample set of domains showed that only 23% of the WHOIS records were accurate.[111] This leaves 77% of the sampled WHOIS records in some state of inaccuracy. Not all of these domains were malicious, and not all were deliberately falsified, but the overall poor standard makes criminal falsification all the more trivial.

7.2.6 WHOIS Policy Review Team Final Report (2012)

One of the most damning assessments of ICANN's performance in terms of WHOIS came from the WHOIS Policy Review Team (WIRT) cross-constituency working group tasked with reviewing WHOIS policy and drafting recommendations for ICANN's new path.[112] While the WIRT came to some very troubling conclusions about the state of WHOIS, ICANN's reaction to the report and follow-up handling of the recommendations may be worse. The report found not only multiple problems with the WHOIS system but specifically with ICANN's response to those problems. In a letter to ICANN's Compliance director, Maguy Serad, the WIRT chair Emily Taylor wrote about the difficulties of working with Compliance while conducting their research. Taylor states that Compliance was *"laboring under an attitude of inordinate defensiveness and distrust of the review team and the review process."*[113] For some reason, ICANN felt the need to have their lawyers present whenever the WIRT met with Compliance, limiting the open interaction. As for the report itself, it notes poor compliance performance on achieving an acceptable level of WHOIS accuracy,[114] a lack of transparency, and generally confusing data on staffing levels. The most shocking finding is that the WIRT was unable to locate an actual ICANN WHOIS policy document, which should have been developed following the *AoC*. The SSAC comment[115] on the WIRT report goes right this issue; the fact that the policy was never defined by ICANN makes solving any related problems extremely difficult. Much to Taylor's dismay, instead of going right to work on the WIRT recommendations, ICANN created a *new* working group to look at WHOIS issues.[116] Additional critics felt that the ICANN response to WIRT was akin to asking someone else the question because it did not like the answer it got the first time.[117] However, one needs to wonder if Taylor and the others should

---

[110] http://www.icann.org/en/resources/compliance/norc-whois-accuracy-study-design-04jun09-en.pdf

[111] https://www.icann.org/en/resources/compliance/reports/whois-accuracy-study-17jan10-en.pdf

[112] http://www.icann.org/en/about/aoc-review/whois/final-report-11may12-en.pdf

[113] http://www.icann.org/en/about/aoc-review/whois/draft-final-report-appendix-whois-compliance-10jan12-en.pdf

[114] See note 112.

[115] http://www.icann.org/en/groups/ssac/documents/sac-055-en.pdf

[116] http://www.emilytaylor.eu/articles/2013/January/ICANN-WHOIS-and-George-Orwell

[117] http://krebsonsecurity.com/2013/09/whois-privacy-plan-draws-fire/

have been surprised since ICANN did not implement the improvements from the other cited studies going back a decade.

However, the various studies and recommendations have had an impact. ICANN has issued a series of advisories to registrars concerning WHOIS data accuracy,[118] steps to improve WHOIS data accuracy,[119] and clarification of contract language.[120] ICANN also instituted a WHOIS Data Reminder Policy[121] in 2003, which requires registrars to send out regular notices to registrants asking them to verify their WHOIS data.[122] However, these policies have been criticized for the lack of measurable results.[123] ICANN also created a WHOIS Data Problem Report System (WDPRS) for the public:

> *This form allows Internet users to submit a complaint to ICANN regarding incomplete or incorrect Whois data, including privacy or proxy contact information. The complaint is then forwarded to the sponsoring registrar, who must take reasonable steps to investigate and correct inaccurate data.*[124]

However, the process has been criticized for ICANN's inability to process complaints on the back end effectively, as we will see in the following. Some Internet users also note the system has been offline at various times for extended periods.[125]

7.3 WHOIS ENFORCEMENT AND NONENFORCEMENT AT ICANN

So far, we have highlighted situations where specific WHOIS records are not available or WHOIS services are not available. VeriSign/Network Solutions received one of the earliest breaches for WHOIS issues in 2002.[126] However, there have been situations where an entire WHOIS database vanished. Let us remember that the main point of WHOIS is to show who registered a domain name; if the record is deleted, it creates significant issues. Following an avalanche of allegations of fraud against the registrar RegisterFly[127] in 2007, their website went offline and along with it access to their WHOIS database. This concerned some two million domain names. Following extensive legal action, ICANN terminated its contract with RegisterFly.[128] But the amount of control a rogue registrar has in such situations became obvious. Even if a registrar loses its accreditation with ICANN, the registrar still has to cooperate by transferring domains to a new registrar while maintaining the accurate ownership of each domain. Control over the WHOIS record is vital to the stability of the DNS, and critics charged that ICANN ignored complaints about RegisterFly for too long and allowed the situation to get out of control.[129] To keep this from happening again,

[118] http://www.icann.org/announcements/advisory-10may02.htm

[119] http://www.icann.org/announcements/announcement-03sep02.htm

[120] http://www.icann.org/announcements/advisory-03apr03.htm

[121] http://www.icann.org/announcements/advisory-16jun03.htm

[122] http://www.icann.org/en/resources/registrars/consensus-policies/wdrp

[123] http://www.mcit.gov.eg/Upcont/Documents/Reports%20and%20Documents_182012000_final-report-11may12-en.pdf

[124] http://www.icann.org/en/resources/compliance/complaints/whois/inaccuracy-form

[125] https://groups.google.com/forum/#!topic/news.admin.net-abuse.email/JuyqIVx5ToM

[126] http://www.icann.org/en/news/correspondence/touton-letter-to-beckwith-03sep02-en.htm

[127] http://www.theregister.co.uk/2007/03/03/icann_registerfly_domain/

[128] http://www.icann.org/en/news/litigation/icann-v-registerfly

[129] https://omblog.icann.org/?p=6

ICANN instituted a required Data Escrow Program with Iron Mountain,[130] demanding registrars to regularly deposit copies of their WHOIS with the remote storage provider. It sounds like an excellent plan, but data escrow had actually always been required but never formalized by ICANN until the RegisterFly incident, even with these policies in place:

- In October 2008, the registrars Joker.com and Beijing Innovative Linkage Technology Ltd. were breached by ICANN for failing to investigate WHOIS inaccuracies.[131]
- The next year, the registrar Parava Networks, Inc. was breached, and eventually terminated, for not complying with the data escrow.[132]
- The registrar Alantron was the first company to be *suspended* in 2010 from registering new domains after repeatedly not having functional WHOIS.[133]
- Escrow issues continued to be a problem in 2011 with Samjung Data Service breached[134] and Best Bulk Register terminated.[135]
- In 2012 and 2013, more registrars continued to be cited for WHOIS issues including Mat Bao[136] and USA Webhost.[137]

In one of the most unusual WHOIS-related enforcement cases, the third largest ICANN registrar, Tucows, was breached in 2012 over a single WHOIS record.[138] The public paper trail shows a long back-and-forth between ICANN and Tucows over this one WHOIS record, but what sparked the issue or why Tucows could not turn over the record is a mystery to the public. The issue was eventually resolved, but how is not disclosed.

The number of public issues concerning WHOIS, issues that reach the level of enforcement, is continuous and problematic, but this is a fraction of the activity. Most of the WHOIS violations never reach the level of public record. Most of the enforcement activity from ICANN remains financial, that is, failure to pay accreditation fees.[139] One might think WHOIS enforcement actions would be the most prevalent type of enforcement since it is the most common complaint type at ICANN.[140] The second most common complaint for ICANN has been the issue of domain transfers. Part of this problem is tied to WHOIS, especially as registrars deal with other registrars. Incoming transfers from other registrars with incompatible WHOIS formats will often fail. If the WHOIS is unreadable, is missing, or has invalid characters, the process of reading, parsing, and inserting WHOIS data into another database will cause significant delays in a domain transfer. Since online entities depend on constant availability, the issue of WHOIS becomes a business problem as well. The gaining registrar can be made to look incompetent in this situation when it is in fact the prior registrar's fault.

---

[130] http://www.ironmountain.com/Knowledge-Center/Reference-Library/View-by-Document-Type/Data-Sheets-Brochures/R/Registrar-Data-Escrow.aspx
[131] http://www.icann.org/en/news/announcements/announcement-01oct08-en.htm
[132] http://www.icann.org/en/news/correspondence/burnette-to-valdes-27feb09-en.pdf
[133] www.icann.org/en/news/correspondence/burnette-to-acir-16apr10-en.pdf
[134] http://www.icann.org/en/news/correspondence/burnette-to-kim-02sep11-en.pdf
[135] http://www.icann.org/en/news/correspondence/burnette-to-gurung-09feb11-en.pdf
[136] http://www.icann.org/en/news/correspondence/serad-to-binh-21dec12-en.pdf
[137] 2013 www.icann.org/en/news/correspondence/serad-to-hill-10may13-en.pdf
[138] http://www.icann.org/en/news/correspondence/burnette-to-eisner-22jun12-en.pdf
[139] http://www.circleid.com/posts/20130924_icann_and_your_internet_abuse/
[140] http://www.icann.org/en/resources/compliance/update/update-may13-en.htm

It behooves ICANN and the industry to adopt single standards and acceptable service levels of WHOIS to ensure continuity beyond just settling issues of consumer complaints. But the consumer complaints are legion. ICANN's absence in speaking for the consumer, especially as it applies to WHOIS, makes the problems of cybercrime and Internet abuse much worse. Rather than covering the litany of malicious domain uses, the volume of WHOIS inaccuracies, and ICANN's lack of meaningful enforcement in the area, we will follow one real-world example of false WHOIS and its impact and ICANN's response.

7.3.1 Tracking ICANN's Response to WHOIS Inaccuracy

This analysis is wholly based on research conducted by the author. The story begins in June 2011 with a spam-advertised rogue pharmacy domain called approvedonlinepharmacy.net sponsored by the ICANN-accredited registrar BizCn.com, Inc.[141] Domains of this type cross several lines of concern for the community with abuse of email users being the first issue. Beyond spam, rogue pharmacy sites violate trademarks by selling potentially counterfeit or mislabeled products. Many of these domains themselves contain trademarked strings, which is an additional problem. These sites are also blatantly criminal and pose a health risk to the public. The criminal nature of these operations is undisputable, and they have been linked to organized crime; this is the suspected situation with approvedonlinepharmacy.net specifically.[142] Finally, there is the WHOIS problem that is what makes it ICANN's problem. The WHOIS for this domain was behind a privacy shield called privacy-protect.cn, which uses a mix of contact information in China and France. Attempts to contact the owners of this domain through email resulted in a rejection.

There are various reasons why email rejections occur; in this case, it is because the domain name, privacy-protect.cn, is not deployed in the DNS. A check of that record indicates it is on HOLD.

This is a clear WHOIS inaccuracy, so a complaint was filed with ICANN's WDRPS on June 10, 2011, and given the WDPRS ticket number c6e6d0835bdb4112636fceb7d8c5c1a-27744cabe. The full life cycle of a WDPRS complaint is 45 days, meaning this issue should have been resolved one way or another by July 11, 2011. However, as the deadline passed, the WHOIS record was not corrected, and the domain had not been deleted. To clarify what should have happened, we note that BizCN has a contract, the RAA,[143] with ICANN that has a number of specific conditions. Among other things, the contract requires the registrar to collect, maintain, and make available to the public:

> *3.3.1.8 The name, postal address, **e-mail address**, voice telephone number, and (where available) fax number of the administrative contact for the Registered Name.*[144]

This is, of course, a requirement of the registrant to supply accurate contact information, but the contractual obligation is ultimately on the registrar to keep it accurate and public. However, the specific condition for the registrant is:

> *3.7.7.2 A Registered Name Holder's willful provision of inaccurate or unreliable information, its willful failure promptly to update information provided to Registrar, or its failure to respond*

[141] http://www.internic.net/registrars/registrar-471.html
[142] http://www.legitscript.com/pharmacy/approvedonlinepharmacy.net
[143] http://www.icann.org/en/resources/registrars/raa/ra-agreement-21may09-en.htm
[144] http://www.icann.org/en/resources/registrars/raa/ra-agreement-21may09-en.htm#3.3

```
I'm afraid I wasn't able to deliver your message to the following addresses.
This is a permanent error; I've given up. Sorry it didn't work out.

<contact@privacy-protect.cn>:
Sorry, I couldn't find any host named privacy-protect.cn. (#5.1.2)
```

FIGURE 7.4 Mail rejection.

```
Checking server [whois.cnnic.net.cn]
Results:
Domain Name: privacy-protect.cn
ROID: 20091005s10001s18845131-cn
Domain Status: clientTransferProhibited
Domain Status: clientHold
Registrant ID: hh1254757178772
Registrant: Privacy-Protect cn
Registrant Contact Email: contact@privacy-protect.cn
Sponsoring Registrar: åŽ¦é—¨äˌœå—èžé€šåœ¨ç°¿ç§'æŠ€ä
—¨åŽå•ᵀç›»äˌ-ç½'ç»œæœ‰é™å…¬åˌ)
Name Server: ns3.cnmsn.com
Name Server: ns4.cnmsn.com
Registration Date: 2009-10-05 23:39:43
Expiration Date: 2013-10-05 23:39:43
DNSSEC: unsigned
```

FIGURE 7.5 Hold record status.

for over fifteen (15) calendar days to inquiries by Registrar concerning the accuracy of contact details associated with the Registered Name Holder's registration shall constitute a material breach of the Registered Name Holder-registrar contract and be a basis for cancellation of the Registered Name registration.[145]

In terms of addressing WHOIS inaccuracies, the registrar is required, among other things:

3.7.8 … Registrar shall, upon notification by any person of an inaccuracy in the contact information associated with a Registered Name sponsored by Registrar, take reasonable steps to investigate that claimed inaccuracy. In the event Registrar learns of inaccurate contact information associated with a Registered Name it sponsors, it shall take reasonable steps to correct that inaccuracy.

As the 3.7.7.2 clause states that willful provision of false data is terms for breach of the agreement, the registrar is required to act under these conditions:

3.7.5.3 … a domain name must be deleted within 45 days of either the registrar or the registrant terminating a registration agreement.[146]

Because of this obvious problem, ICANN Compliance was contacted directly about the situation, as the domain remained online continuously in violation of these agreements.

[145] http://www.icann.org/en/resources/registrars/raa/ra-agreement-21may09-en.htm#3.7.7.2
[146] http://www.icann.org/en/resources/registrars/raa/ra-agreement-21may09-en.htm#3.7.5.3

After nearly a year of regular requests for updates on this case, ICANN Compliance declared on March 25, 2012, in reference to the complaint:

> *"Registrar provided steps taken to investigate alleged inaccuracies. NO ACTION required. RESOLVED."*

The response was not verified by the facts; nevertheless, the contact details of approvedonlinepharmacy.net were tested again and found to be still invalid. It would impossible for BizCn to *"verify that the data was correct,"* suggesting that the registrar supplied false information to ICANN Compliance. Further checks of privacy-protect.cn with DiG showed it had no IP address (no "A" record, let alone MX records) or name servers, meaning it simply did not exist as far as the DNS was concerned—hence, it would be impossible to receive email. Given these facts, ICANN Compliance was queried again but inexplicably reaffirmed that:

> *"Registrar verified that the data was correct in response to initial W-Ticket notice. Ticket Closed."*

While this was going on, further research was conducted on privacy-protect.cn and its related domains. Because the domain privacy-protect.cn was not active, there was no other method for contacting the supposed privacy service except through the WHOIS record, but the phone number was disconnected as well, so the record was proved to be further invalid. Additional research revealed around 2000 domain names using this same invalid WHOIS information, meaning the registrants used the privacy-protect.cn. Many of the related domains were collected and examined. A pattern quickly emerged; all of the domains using this service appeared to be of an illicit nature including more rogue pharmacies, malware distributions, media piracy, and so-called reshipping scam sites. One of the most disturbing domains using this invalid privacy service was called rapetube.org. The site offered exactly what the name says: access to brutal and explicit rape-themed video material. Given the seriousness of the issue, Compliance was asked again to reexamine the case of privacy-protect.cn and the domains using its WHOIS protection. At this point, Compliance refused to discuss the issue further and declined to supply any additional documentation.

ICANN has a Documentary Information Disclosure Policy (DIDP[147]) for requesting information not disclosed to the public, which should be in the interests of transparency. However, ICANN rejected the request in the case citing that it would interfere with their contractual relationship with BizCn.[148] A letter was also sent directly to the ICANN CEO, Fadi Chehade, alerting him to the situation and the "rape tube" site with false WHOIS, but no public response or visible action occurred.[149] ICANN also has an ombudsman who is supposed to advocate on behalf of the Internet user, but he also declined to investigate the matter.[150] The ombudsman even included in his report the following statement:

> *"I also mention one registrar in particular which has been openly criticised, being Bizcn.com. As part of the monitoring by Compliance, scorecards of requests are kept. Compliance informed me that Bizcn.com is a registrar that is prompt & cooperative with Compliance inquiries, including Whois inaccuracy complaints. I was shown the scorecard, of all complaints since January 2013, which shows that all were resolved before a 3rd notice was needed."[151]*

---

[147] http://www.icann.org/en/about/transparency

[148] http://www.icann.org/en/about/transparency/bruen-response-07mar13-en.pdf

[149] http://www.icann.org/en/news/correspondence/bruen-to-chehade-22apr13-en.pdf

[150] https://omblog.icann.org/?p=1023

[151] See note 150.

This endorsement of BizCn by ICANN does not match the facts presented in the BizCn complaints, and the ombudsman made no effort to refute the factual inaccuracy of BizCn's WHOIS records. All of the ICANN processes have been exhausted in this inaccurate WHOIS case with general failure.

The result is that after more than 2 years, approvedonlinepharmacy.net, rapetube.org, and the other illicit domains are still sponsored by BizCn, BizCn is still accredited, the WHOIS records are still invalid, and ICANN staff will not discuss the issue. The ALAC leadership filed an additional complaint concerning rapetube.org in February 2014.[152] Following the complaint, the domain was placed on "CLIENTHOLD" by the registrar, meaning it was removed from the DNS. However, shortly before the March 2014 ICANN Singapore meeting, the CLIENTHOLD status was removed for rapetube.org, making the domain viable again after only appearing to comply with the process. The WHOIS record remained invalid and the domain was not deleted. When asked in a recorded session,[153] ICANN Compliance could not explain the situation.

It appears, from this case, which ICANN's WHOIS process and ancillary procedures do not work as claimed by ICANN. The Internet community deserves to know what happened in this case, as Polybius wrote: "*If history is deprived of the Truth, we are left with nothing but an idle, unprofitable tale.*" We will attempt to explain at least one reason why ICANN would not enforce the contract in the next section.

7.3.2 ICANN Compliance Designed for Failure

In understanding why ICANN Compliance does not produce results, one only needs to look at their own documentation. For years, ICANN relied on a Compliance flowchart[154] to explain their process, but a review seemed to show something curious: there was no enforcement end to the loop of the flowchart. The only terminating points in the ICANN Compliance Program for Registries and Registrars are *dismissal* or *closure* of the complaint. The issuing of breach notices is not part of the process, and contracted parties are only mentioned in passing. The process, as stated, only provides a potentially endless cycle of a complainant submitting additional information. If this flowchart is a true representation of the duties of Compliance, it exists only to shuffle paper. Analysis of the Compliance flowchart leads to a problem with the third leg of Compliance: enforcement.[155] Entry into the compliance cycle yields two choices: (i) The complaint is dismissed and not investigated (ii) The complaint is investigated.

After the investigation, there are two possible choices: (i) The case is closed. (ii) The complainant submits more information. If a case is not closed, it is simply resubmitted to the beginning of the process for further investigation. This precludes the third tool of Compliance.

There was no path for ICANN Compliance in this process to enforce the contract with registrars. If this is in fact a true representation of the ICANN Compliance function, it is not actually designed to enforce the contract but only drop complaints or endlessly

[152] http://atlarge-lists.icann.org/pipermail/alac-excom/2014-February/005551.html
[153] See note 82.
[154] http://www.knujon.com/compliance-flowchart.gif
[155] http://www.icann.org/en/resources/compliance

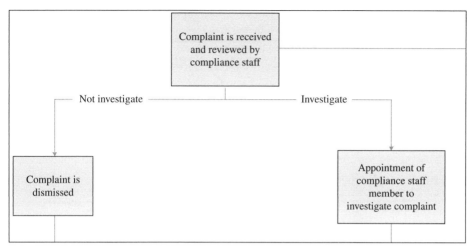

FIGURE 7.6   ICANN Compliance investigation chart.

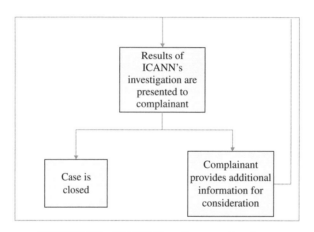

FIGURE 7.7   ICANN Compliance endless loop.

investigate them. The result is that ICANN Compliance is failing in its professed mission and seemingly on basic functional levels as well.

7.3.3   ICANN's Contract with Registrars Not Enforceable on WHOIS Accuracy

While there have been multiple studies concerning the accuracy of the gTLD WHOIS record set and problems presented by this issue, there are no known studies of the effectiveness of ICANN's process for dealing with WHOIS inaccuracy. Given what we understand about the problem, our question is: can ICANN actually handle complaints as expected?

The ICANN coordinates the DNS[156]; it does this in particular by accrediting domain name registrars who sponsor domain names.[157] The AoC is a document in which ICANN

---

[56] http://www.icann.org/en/about/welcome

[57] http://www.icann.org/en/resources/registrars

pledges that coordination of the DNS is made in the public interest and is accountable and transparent.[158] In short, ICANN administers agreements with the companies who sell domain names, and their procedures in this core function must be open for public viewing and documented in such a way that responsibility is clearly defined.

All domain owners and operators must supply accurate contact information for each domain they register.[159] Failure to supply truthful and accurate data in domain WHOIS records is a material breach of the registrar–registrant agreement.[160] A WHOIS record is a publicly available domain name database entry that can be accessed through a registrar or registry supplied service.[161] For its part, the sponsoring registrar is obligated to take reasonable steps to investigate and correct WHOIS inaccuracies.[162] These obligations are stipulated in the standard ICANN–registrar contract called the RAA[163]. False WHOIS is considered to be a widespread and serious problem. A recent cross-constituency review of the issue found that ICANN had failed to meet its expectations for managing this portion of the DNS and specifically to regulate or be effective in dealing with registrars on this issue.[164]

The WDPRS is ICANN's system for accepting and tracking complaints of WHOIS inaccuracies.[165] The reports are forwarded to the sponsoring registrar, who is responsible for investigating and correcting the data.[166] The full cycle for the complaint is 45 days inclusive of a 15-day response period for registrants.[167]

It is the function of ICANN's Compliance department to process WDPRS complaints and enforce contractual breaches against registrars. In theory, ICANN Compliance is supposed to accept complaints, investigate them thoroughly, and if needed enforce the RAA contract. Since ICANN's core function is in accrediting registrars, the oversight of these entities is critical for preserving the security, stability, and resiliency of the DNS. By adhering to this practice, ICANN Compliance can promote consumer trust. In short, what we want to know is: does this ICANN Compliance process work as documented, and is it effective? Our analysis has revealed a major stumbling block to true effectiveness.

This may or may not come as a shock to some readers, but the ICANN contract with the domain name registrars, in terms of WHOIS inaccuracy, is not enforceable. The ability of ICANN to enforce against a registrar who fails to correct or delete a domain with false WHOIS does not exist. There are two clauses to RAA 3.7.8: the first can be completely ignored because it is conditional on nonexistent "established policies":

> *Registrar shall abide by any specifications or policies established according to Section 4 requiring reasonable and commercially practicable (a) verification, at the time of registration, of contact information associated with a Registered Name sponsored by Registrar or (b) periodic re-verification of such information.[168]*

---

[158] http://www.icann.org/en/about/agreements/aoc/affirmation-of-commitments-30sep09-en.htm

[159] http://www.icann.org/en/resources/registrars/raa/ra-agreement-21may09-en.htm#3.7.7.1

[160] See note 145.

[161] See note 2.

[162] http://www.icann.org/en/resources/registrars/raa/ra-agreement-21may09-en.htm#3.7.8

[163] See note 143.

[164] See note 112.

[165] http://wdprs.internic.net/

[166] http://www.icann.org/en/news/announcements/advisory-10may02-en.htm

[167] http://www.icann.org/en/news/announcements/advisory-03apr03-en.htm

[168] See note 162.

At first blush, this clause reads like tough policy until the referenced "Section 4"[169] is reviewed and we find that Section 4 merely outlines the procedure for adopting specifications rather than detailing any actual specifications. This means there is in fact no established policy requiring verification of WHOIS. Because there is no policy, there is no way to actually enforce the contract since the registrar does not have guidance or specifications. "Shall" in a legal context will usually refer to a requirement, whereas the use of "may" suggests possible actions. However, in this context, the registrar is required to verify the WHOIS record (i) when created or (ii) periodically. The word "or" in this clause ultimately removes obligation because it allows the registrar to select one option or the other with no firm mandate or ability for ICANN to ensure either is being performed. Hence, the use of "shall" here is a complete red herring as it is conditional on the ephemeral.

The second clause is the one that is truly problematic:

Registrar shall, upon notification by any person of an inaccuracy in the contact information associated with a registered Name sponsored by Registrar, take reasonable steps to investigate that claimed inaccuracy. In the event Registrar learns of inaccurate contact information associated with a Registered Name it sponsors, it shall take reasonable steps to correct that inaccuracy.[170]

We have been operating under the false assumption that the registrar has to correct the record and has to delete the domain if the record is not corrected. However, the only obligation here is for the registrar to "take reasonable steps." There is no obligation to actually correct and there is no obligation to delete the domain if the WHOIS record is not corrected. This is clarified in a 2003 advisory issued by ICANN,[171] which states in part that the RAA contract "does not require a registrar to cancel a registration" and that registrars are "are not bound to a fixed timetable." This policy only gives the registrar the authority to delete the domain at their *discretion*. The registrar cannot be compelled to delete the domain and therefore cannot be held in breach of their contract for failing to do so. The registrar could hypothetically say, "we checked the WHOIS record, it's fine. Mickey Mouse lives at 1600 Pennsylvania Ave, we called him at 800-HEEHAHA and he told us so." So, walking backwards, because a registrar cannot be held in breach for failing to correct or delete, a registrant cannot be obligated to correct inaccurate WHOIS data. Because there is no direct obligation on the registrant, any affirmation in the registrant agreement to provide truthful and accurate statements is ultimately wishful thinking. WHOIS inaccuracy studies and enforcement efforts are ineffective if the registrar chooses to ignore them.

The implications are profound. A registrar in a noncooperative, lawless country can sponsor the most heinously illegal domains with fake WHOIS as long they "take reasonable steps" to investigate. This also renders the implied compact between ICANN, registrar, registrant, and Internet consumer virtually meaningless. This is not conjecture, but a situation that has played out in fact on multiple occasions.

Now, we must view the apparent WHOIS unenforceability in the contract alongside the problems discussed previously concerning UDRPs, which also appear unenforceable. WHOIS inaccuracy complaints are an entry point for ordinary Internet users to participate

---

[169] http://www.icann.org/en/resources/registrars/raa/ra-agreement-21may09-en.htm#4

[170] See note 162.

[171] See note 167.

in the policy. UDRP is an entry point for businesses to access the policy. Both, upon analysis, appear ineffective. While complex procedures have been put in place to ensure trust, they simply do not work when tested. These are perfect examples of the "tussles" predicted in 2002.[172] The political mismanagement of these tussles by ICANN leads to an erosion of trust by allowing the subversion of ID.

Unfortunately, ICANN has never addressed this concern and had two conflicting answers on record concerning the enforceability of the RAA contract on WHOIS inaccuracy. In response to the WIRT, ICANN Compliance stated: *"there is no requirement in the RAA for registrars to ensure that WHOIS data is accurate,"*[173] which is in line with the Review Team's own findings that *"If data is found to be intentionally false registrars are not obligated to cancel the registration."*[174] Because of this serious issue ICANN Compliance staff was asked specifically[175] to clarify the contract language at a public meeting in Prague on June 24, 2012.[176] The confusing Compliance response was that *"ICANN is authorized to breach a registrar for failure to delete or failure to correct inaccurate WHOIS."*[177] This Compliance statement seems to be in direct conflict with Compliance's advisory on the subject, which states in part that "[the RAA] *does not require a registrar to cancel a registration."*[178] Compliance was asked in another session to cite the specific authority that allows them to breach a registrar for failure to delete, but the compliance staff merely answered by restating that ICANN had the authority to enforce against a registrar who did not delete a domain with false WHOIS[179] and not by clarifying the actual contractual authority. The following chart compares the three documented statements on the enforceability of the contract on WHOIS inaccuracy.

2003 Compliance Advisory	Compliance Quoted in WIRT, May 2012	Compliance in Prague Session
"Registrar Accreditation Agreement does not require a registrar to cancel a registration ... the registrar has the ability to cancel after 15 days of no response in very serious cases ... registrars also have flexibility to decide when to use that right ... "	*"there is no requirement in the RAA for registrars to ensure that WHOIS data is accurate"*	*"ICANN is authorized to breach a registrar for failure to delete or failure to correct inaccurate whois"*

http://www.icann.org/en/about/aoc-review/whois/final-report-11may12-en.pdf

[172] http://groups.csail.mit.edu/ana/Publications/PubPDFs/Tussle2002.pdf
[173] See note 112.
[174] See note 112.
[175] https://community.icann.org/display/atlarge/At-Large+Compliance+Questions+for+Prague+Workspace?focusedCommentId=34605706#comment-34605706
[176] http://prague44.icann.org/node/31569
[177] https://community.icann.org/download/attachments/34606099/ICANN+44+-+Contractual+Compliace+-+ALAC.pptx
[178] See note 167.
[179] http://audio.icann.org/meetings/prague2012/alac-regional-4-24jun12-en.mp3

At this same Prague meeting, Compliance presented a number of WHOIS complaint process enhancements and improvements in automation. However, the issue on the table was actual enforcement of the contract, which seems to be lacking. Setting the tone for this missing enforcement was the apparent removal from ICANN's website of a flowchart entitled "ICANN Compliance Program for Registries and Registrars,"[180] which had no enforcement phase documented in the flow, only compliant dismissal, closure, and circular shuffling. However, this was replaced with three new charts,[181] which show significant improvement in the stated process. Unfortunately, the question is still open as to if these processes will actually be used as presented as there is not a good track record of real follow-through. The three legs of ICANN Compliance are (i) prevention through collaboration, (ii) transparency through communication, and (iii) enforcement.

ICANN, governments, and private researchers have poured resources into addressing the WHOIS inaccuracy problem, but the issue is ultimately unfixable under the existing contract. This issue cannot be understated; RAA 3.7.8 is the crossroads of public participation. RAA 3.7.8 is in fact the only way ordinary Internet users may file a grievance through ICANN about a domain name. At the moment, enforceability is completely at the discretion of the sponsoring registrar, even outside of ICANN. The failure of RAA 3.7.8 precludes the goal of ensuring accountability, transparency, and the interests of global Internet users as stated in the ICANN AoC[182] document as it robs the community of meaningful grievance process.

While ICANN never formally acknowledged the loophole in the contract, they fixed it in the 2013 version of the RAA. The new 3.7.8 language now reads:

> *Registrar shall comply with the obligations specified in the Whois Accuracy Program Specification.*[183]

The WHOIS Accuracy Program[184] is a very detailed addition to the contact, which explains what accuracy and validity really mean for each data element and what the registrar is obligated to do. Included in this specification is the requirement that the registrar shall either terminate or suspend the domain name for the "*willful provision of inaccurate or unreliable WHOIS information.*"[185]

REFERENCES

1 Froomkin, M. 2000. Wrong turn in cyberspace, Duke Law Journal 50:17.

2 Berners-Lee, T. 1999. Weaving the Web. San Francisco, CA: HarperSanFrancisco.

---

[180] See note 154.

[181] http://www.icann.org/en/resources/compliance/approach-processes

[182] http://www.icann.org/en/about/aoc-review

[183] http://www.icann.org/en/resources/registrars/raa/approved-with-specs-27jun13-en.htm#3.7.8

[184] http://www.icann.org/en/resources/registrars/raa/approved-with-specs-27jun13-en.htm#whois-accuracy

[185] See note 184.

8

THE FUTURE OF WHOIS

There are several major WHOIS issues on the table for coming years: the release of new Generic Top-Level Domains (i.e. "dotANYTHING"), the growing deployment of Internet Protocol Version 6, the new proposed model for WHOIS, further internalization, and the emergence of Alternate DNS. All are fraught with controversy and complexity. These issues impact and are impacted by WHOIS policy. Web Extensible Internet Registration Data Service (WEIRDS) is an attempt to standardize the data framework in simple ways, which will support internationalized registration data and be based on client authorization. But WEIRDS is just one of the emerging projects. The Aggregated Registration Directory Service (ARDS) project, called the next-generation WHOIS, is a massive push to reform WHOIS. There is also a new version of the Registrar Accreditation Agreement (RAA), which contains very specific enforcement enhancements and WHOIS requirements[1] including a specific *WHOIS Accuracy Program Specification.*[2] In summary, we have WEIRDS that is supposed to improve access, ARDS that is supposed to improve management, and RAA 2013 that is supposed to be an enforcement. If history is any guide, we may end up with something else in implementation. All efforts will fail if ICANN operates as it has in previous attempts. In terms of information, ICANN finally created a comprehensive portal for WHOIS: whois.icann.org as ICANN had been criticized for not providing such a top-level presentation for WHOIS. Time will be the test of any effectiveness of this site.

There is plentiful and convincing proof that a number of ICANN-accredited registrars support, benefit from, or actually engage in illicit online activity. There are also bountiful

[1] http://www.icann.org/en/news/announcements/announcement-31jul13-en.htm
[2] http://www.icann.org/en/resources/registrars/raa/approved-with-specs-27jun13-en.htm#whois-accuracy

WHOIS Running the Internet: Protocol, Policy, and Privacy, First Edition. Garth O. Bruen.
© 2016 John Wiley & Sons, Inc. Published 2016 by John Wiley & Sons, Inc.

examples showing that ICANN is not effectively managing the registrars and carrying out enforcement. The WHOIS Review Team (WIRT) has plainly stated that *"ICANN the corporation has failed to meet expectations."*[3] WHOIS data collection and storage is entrusted to the registrars; they control WHOIS. ICANN exists to accredit and manage registrar contracts. The failure to manage WHOIS is the failure of ICANN to manage the registrars. If the registrars ostensibly exist to provide technical access to domains and collect fees, they are the wrong party to manage WHOIS policy in an ad hoc fashion. Starting in 2002, ICANN has failed to implement WHOIS recommendations from a number of bodies, year after year. ICANN is supposed to have a bottom-up policy process, but rather than the community managing ICANN and ICANN managing the registrars, it actually appears the registrars are attempting to manage ICANN and the community. WHOIS has been criticized for not having a policy, but the sad fact is that it does have a policy. The ICANN SSAC *Report on WHOIS Terminology and Structure* from September 2011 reiterates that RFC 3912 is standard and cites several related existing policies.[4] The 2013 Congressional Research Service report *Internet Domain Names: Background and Policy Issues* continues to clarify that the policy is determined by the contractual relationships between ICANN and the registrars.[5] While there continues to be confusion over what the policy is, this is a manufactured confusion. Rather than improving the policy or develop true standards of implementation, attempts are being made to obscure the policy and discard it.

8.1 NEW gTLDs

There have been about 1900 applications for 1400 unique new gTLDs. How many will actually make it the Internet is unknown. ICANN delegated 100 new gTLDs in January 2014[6] and routinely releases more.[7] However, there are a few issues to be aware of. First, all new gTLDs are mandated to have Thick WHOIS only. Also, the highly scrutinized application process shows applicants putting forth rigorous WHOIS requirements to ensure the public of better security and compliance. All the new gTLD applications and their status are published for review at http://gtldresult.icann.org/application-result/applicationstatus. Clicking on a particular new gTLD string allows review of the application details. Within each application under section 26, there are details about the WHOIS record scheme proposed by the applicant. The major flaw from the beginning is that the applicant chooses the format. The format for each registry should be the same and dictated by ICANN. Here, there is not only failure to address the problem of clashing WHOIS formats but a situation that actually makes it worse by expanding it drastically. Even if the applicants propose a standard, this is only as good as ICANN's enforcement, which has a poor track record for registrars and is almost nonexistent for registries.

---

[3] http://www.thedomains.com/2012/05/11/whois-review-team-issues-scathing-report-on-icann-icann-the-corporation-has-failed-to-meet-expectations/
[4] http://www.icann.org/en/groups/ssac/documents/sac-051-en.pdf
[5] http://www.fas.org/sgp/crs/misc/97-868.pdf
[6] http://www.thewhir.com/web-hosting-news/icann-delegates-100-new-gtlds-root-zone
[7] http://newgtlds.icann.org//en/program-status/delegated-strings

8.2   WHOIS-BASED EXTENSIBLE INTERNET REGISTRATION DATA SERVICE (WEIRDS)

The application of RESTful services by ARIN and RIPE NCC to IP WHOIS has been largely successful. The IETF[8] has been developing a similar scheme for domain WHOIS as WEIRDS through a chartered[9] working group. The working group acknowledges many of the inherent shortcomings of the current WHOIS architecture discussed in this the text. Not only is the goal to address the general problems but also to make the service better overall. Improvements beyond corrective actions include *differential* services depending on what a particular client or query needs. A differential service would eliminate the need to retrieve an entire WHOIS record for certain needs, thus streamlining the output and improving privacy on an incremental level. WEIRDS would be able to deliver specific portions of the WHOIS record for technical tools or abuse notifications. Some earlier attempts have been made to address the WHOIS formatting problem by providing a central interface as a gateway. The Internet Registry Information Service (IRIS) Core Protocol is a 2005 proposal[10] to use Extensible Markup Language (XML) for the query–response structure and a custom schema.[11] WEIRDS is being developed and released in stages with various IETF drafts, which preceded official RFC designation, presented at public sessions:

- HTTP usage in the Registration Data Access Protocol (RDAP): RDAP is, of course, the varying model for accessing information in general,[12] not just for WHOIS, and the document *draft-ietf-weirds-using-http-07*[13] marks a specific attempt to depart from WHOIS as the dominant paradigm by introducing a different way to refer to the concepts, specifically *Registration Data Directory Services*. This is not simply a marketing tactic, but covers a concept that is truly different from WHOIS. If WHOIS as we know it uses Port 43 to connect to a database to retrieve a record, then directory services are definitely not WHOIS. As we see from the title, data is intended to be accessed through Hypertext Transfer Protocol (HTTP), which is the common way we access web content. WHOIS uses TCP to establish a specific connection where HTTP uses **Get** and **Post** requests to retrieve files or submit data.[14] One of the quick benefits offered by HTTP is the dynamic tool set built-in to it; the TCP-based WHOIS protocol is fundamentally limiting. HTTP uses status codes to indicate to the client (browsers or other software) how the remote server responded, the codes are up to the client software to interpret.[15] In TCP WHOIS, when something goes wrong within a query, it is nearly impossible to find out what happened or where the problem exists without a review of network logs on either end. HTTP status codes offer a series of explanations, which a client can use for troubleshooting. For example, codes 400 and 500 mean HTTP content were not returned but for different reasons, not possible in a WHOIS

---

[8] http://datatracker.ietf.org/wg/weirds/

[9] http://datatracker.ietf.org/wg/weirds/charter/

[10] http://tools.ietf.org/html/rfc3981

[11] http://tools.ietf.org/html/rfc3982

[12] http://www.icann.org/en/news/announcements/announcement-18feb12-en.htm

[13] http://tools.ietf.org/html/draft-ietf-weirds-using-http-07

[14] http://tools.ietf.org/html/draft-ietf-weirds-using-http-07#section-5

[15] http://www.w3.org/Protocols/rfc2616/rfc2616-sec10.html

response. In addition to HTTP, this draft introduces the use of JavaScript Object Notation[16] (JSON) for message exchange within this model. JSON is crucial part of the model, and its use is described in a separate WEIRDS draft briefed later. Also, an extremely important space is provided for internationalization.[17] Overall, the document begins to address many of the shortcomings acknowledged in the WHOIS protocol.

- Security services for RDAP in the draft *draft-ietf-weirds-rdap-sec-05*[18] addresses one of the key concerns in WHOIS along with the language and technical limitations covered in *draft-ietf-weirds-using-http-07*. Because WHOIS was originally deployed with no security or expectations of security, the proposed replacement seeks to provide authentication, authorization, and data confidentiality. Authentication is part of the HTTP framework,[19] which allows for different level of access depending on the type of user with a password-based challenge; the specification requires Transport Layer Security[20] (TLS) be used to secure the connection, although anonymous access must also be supported. Authorization allows for different levels of access for the authenticated clients, who may be able to get more or less registration record data depending on their *relationship* to the record[21]—relationships are not defined here. Data confidentiality covers the privacy of the transaction by requiring encryption of messages between the client and server, meaning the request and the registration data returned must be a *private* communication.[22] There is a fourth category of *availability*, which allows for rate limiting of queries as a defense against denial-of-service attacks.[23] A fifth consideration for data integrity is detailed to ensure record data is not modified in transit.[24] These proposals constitute a fairly comprehensive address of the security shortcomings of WHOIS. The only concern is in the implementation of the authentication regime as to whether it will maintain effective public access to registration data.

- Redirection Service for RDAP puts query referrals on the server end as opposes to client-side solutions as described in the draft draft-ietf-weirds-redirects-02.[25] As we have seen throughout this text, finding the right WHOIS server, or the authoritative server, is a major task largely left to the user or client software. There are redirects and referrals available from some services, but it is so inconsistent and lacking in sufficient server updates when present. The most robust referrals are handled by dynamic WHOIS client programming as seen in the chapters on use and code. This problem only becomes bigger as more registries and registrars enter the field. RDAP seeks to move this responsibility up the chain by returning specific HTTP codes to clients.[26] The draft shows some pseudo code as a guide:

---

[16] http://tools.ietf.org/html/rfc4627
[17] http://tools.ietf.org/html/draft-ietf-weirds-using-http-07#section-9
[18] http://tools.ietf.org/html/draft-ietf-weirds-rdap-sec-05
[19] http://tools.ietf.org/html/rfc2617
[20] http://tools.ietf.org/html/rfc2246
[21] http://tools.ietf.org/html/draft-ietf-weirds-rdap-sec-05#section-3.2
[22] http://tools.ietf.org/html/draft-ietf-weirds-rdap-sec-05#section-3.4
[23] http://tools.ietf.org/html/draft-ietf-weirds-rdap-sec-05#section-3.3
[24] http://tools.ietf.org/html/draft-ietf-weirds-rdap-sec-05#section-3.5
[25] http://tools.ietf.org/html/draft-ietf-weirds-redirects-02
[26] http://tools.ietf.org/html/draft-ietf-weirds-using-http-01#section-5.2

```
while(true) {
    query = read_query_from_network()
    auth_rdap_svr = redirect_table_lookup (query.resource)
    if (auth_rdap_svr != null) {
        write_http_301(auth_rdap_svr)
    } else {
        write_http_404("resource not in redirect table")
    }
}
```

In essence, this routine checks the server table list for the correct resource until either it finds it or runs out of choices, only then returning the failure to the client. However, there is an acknowledged *bootstrapping problem* inherent here, which is still being considered, specifically where the list of resources will be kept: on the server or the client? The second part of the problem is how the list will be maintained. Unfortunately, some of the proposals include using record sets we already know to be problematic, for example, the IANA registry table. The draft also points to an innate security flaw in recursion or looping, which is that a malicious user could create and endless loop as a kind of denial-of-service attack. There are methods for preventing this kind of attack; it is not hopeless, but it is an important consideration;

- RDAP query format is discussed in draft *draft-ietf-weirds-rdap-query-08*.[27] It presents the use of Uniform Resource Identifiers (URIs) to access registration data, a URI being the HTTP strings we are all familiar with. This is one of the major departures in the scheme, which distinguishes WEIRDS from WHOIS. A WHOIS query, as we have seen, is generally constituted by

whois –h whois.somesever.com example.com.

A WEIRDS query might appear like this:

http://somesever.com/whois/rdap/domains?name=example.com

This uses the web's inherent directory structure to access discrete records. As part of the plan, substituting "domains" with "nameservers" or "ip" would search those records. Because the data is stored and presented atomically, rather than a whole WHOIS record, specific data is easier to obtain, and cross-referencing becomes possible in ways limited by the current WHOIS protocol:

- JSON responses for RDAP as described in the draft *draft-ietf-weirds-json-response-06*[28] refers to the proposed use of this lightweight data interchange format for WEIRDS. As indicated by the name, this is a use of a specific potion of the JavaScript library, which is commonly available in standard Internet browsers. JSON is an object-oriented code, which employs a structure similar to other standard languages like C and Perl.[29] Data structures created within JSON allow for the record data to be dynamically represented for RDAP. Various elements within registration records can be formatted according to their data type and presented to requesters as

---

[27] http://tools.ietf.org/html/draft-ietf-weirds-rdap-query-08
[28] http://tools.ietf.org/html/draft-ietf-weirds-json-response-06
[29] http://www.json.org/

vCards, or in this case *jCards,*[30] which are common structure for contact information transmitted over email and elsewhere. The use of JSON opens additional paths for internationalization and parsing on the fly. There are some criticisms of JSON functionality, but it is miles ahead of static WHOIS formats.

- Registration Data Access Protocol Object Inventory Analysis described in draft draft-ietf-weirds-object-inventory-01[31] is a collection and overview of existing record elements that exist across the broad spectrum of inconsistent WHOIS records. While formats from different registries and registrars conflict, they share basic requirements albeit with varying field names and orders. This comprehensive study takes inventory WHOIS field variations and determines which tags are the most popular in use, a commendable effort.
- The Bootstrapping Protocol has not yet been drafted. How the source records will be reached is still a matter of debate.[32] Some options being considered are a DNS model, an IANA model, or even a mixed solution. It comes down to how the relevant RDAP server is identified, either from the TLD zone file (DNS) or the IANA registry database. Each method has benefits and potential drawbacks.

WEIRDS is a bold attempt to reform WHOIS as a technical matter, a project long overdue in many minds. Andrew Newton, chief engineer of ARIN, is one of the project champions and main developers and has summed up the work succinctly:

"The WEIRDS approach to this problem is based not on a new protocol but on the reuse of existing application strata …WEIRDS is unlike the RWhois, WHOIS++, and IRIS work. Many more constituencies are participating….the technology model is simple and well within the mainstream of most programmers. And, as with all IETF activities, everyone is welcome and voices can be heard."[33]

Because the work is ongoing as of this publishing, there is still time to get involved (see http://tools.ietf.org/wg/weirds/charters).

8.3 AGGREGATED REGISTRY DATA SERVICES (ARDS)

Developed by the Expert Working Group (EWG) and commissioned by ICANN, ARDS is an outgrowth of the WIRT but a controversial one. While the plans of EWG may seem like an obvious direction for WHOIS, there is a discrepancy between its impetus and foundation. The WIRT gave ICANN a mandate to *fix* WHOIS, but the stated goal of ARDS is to *replace* WHOIS. In this context, ARDS may appear to be an attempt to change WHOIS without changing the policy. Regardless, the EWG is made up of cross section of experts who are prepared to answer questions and accept suggestions, all expressing the seriousness and complexity of the issue. The main specific goals of ARDS are to:

- Centralize the data and access to it
- Provide validation of the data
- Handle accuracy complaints

[30] http://tools.ietf.org/html/draft-ietf-jcardcal-jcard-06
[31] http://tools.ietf.org/html/draft-ietf-weirds-object-inventory-01
[32] http://www.ietf.org/proceedings/88/slides/slides-88-weirds-1.pdf
[33] http://www.internetsociety.org/articles/something-weirds-way-comes

ARDS will collect domain registration data from all the gTLD registries, which originally come from the registrars, and serve it from a central repository. The managers of ARDS will also manage access, granting different levels of access to different users. Steve Delbianco, of the Business Constituency, likes portions of ARDS idea especially the centralization and single standards, but he is concerned about the management of access, which has not been finalized.[34] The centralization of ARDS could doom its development since few will be able to agree on its national location in the current climate of international surveillance suspicion. Ram Mohan of Afilias also wants to see more attention to language and internationalization in the system.[35] There are a variety of public comments on ARDS filling the debate space[36] as it will likely take some time to create a final model. ARDS may not even be a new idea.

One concern with ARDS is completely technical and has yet to be fully explored. If ARDS is intended to replace current WHOIS access streams, it is presumed that existing registrar and registrar WHOIS services will be turned off. So far, few people are asking the EWG what will happen when this change occurs. The loss of Port 43 could turn out to be catastrophic for the Internet. We have seen throughout this text WHOIS being hardcoded into low-level processes everywhere. In interviewing many of the WHOIS developers for this book, it was discovered that few knew about the implications of ARDS or about the project at all. Many of the WHOIS-related functions that underlie the DNS were written 5 or 10 years ago by people who have moved on to other projects. WHOIS "just works" right now, but so apparently, it will not. It is unknown at this point if ARDS will break the DNS. The EWG needs to partner directly with developers who support various open and free portions of the Internet and conduct a proper survey to determine how shutting off WHOIS will impact the basic functionality of the network.

In general, ARDS is flawed in the sense that it is designed to sit on top of an existing system, which is accused of being broken to begin with. A solution should start at the record level and work its way up. It would be better to institute corrective policy to the records at their creation and renewal points rather than an after-the-fact cosmetic application. Otherwise, we have garbage in, garbage out. The primary issue is whether or not ICANN even has the authority to limit WHOIS access. All policies so far acknowledge the need of all users to be able to access WHOIS, including the Affirmation of Commitments (AoC), which requires *unrestricted* access to WHOIS for the public.[37] The authority of ARDS is traced from the AoC. If the main function of ARDS is to in fact restrict WHOIS, then it violates the integrity of the AoC.

8.4   TRULY SOLVING THE PROBLEM

The problem with WHOIS is not technical; it is purely political and specifically in the politics of money. Fixes are ultimately blocked by a minority of players benefiting financially from the status quo. The various problems cited by different sectors of the

---

[34] Delbianco interview.

[35] Mohan interview.

[36] http://krebsonsecurity.com/2013/09/whois-privacy-plan-draws-fire/

[37] http://www.icann.org/en/about/agreements/aoc/affirmation-of-commitments-30sep09-en.htm

community can be addressed. The registrars will not police themselves, and ICANN has demonstrated it cannot either. Some of the suggestions below are already being developed and considered, but these should be starting point of fixing WHOIS. Placing data access behind arbitrary barriers without fixing the records and process first will prove futile:

- Recognize that a minority of bad players as domain owners, WHOIS harvesters, stalkers, spammers, and rogue registrars are the true source of the problem. Confront these problems directly with effective existing tools.
- Move the responsibility of informing domain registrants about their privacy and obligations up to the registry level. Pushing this down to the registrars creates too many different standards and complete gaps in coverage with the registrars who will not implement the solutions.
- Ensure all registrants are duly notified of the purpose of WHOIS and that their entries are displayed publicly.
- Move .COM and .NET to a thick registry WHOIS model. Relive registrar obligations to distribute the data through Port 43 and unify the WHOIS record format within VeriSign.
- Create a single standard within the gTLDs for WHOIS records.
- Drop billing contact data from public display; there is no need for this portion to be public.
- Certify the privacy protection services and make them truly accountable.
- Create clear distinctions between private and public WHOIS based on commercial use.
- Employ a registration system, which limits fraud. This is not hard; algorithms already exist. Data must be verified as it is collected, not after the fact. Systems that would allow for on-the-fly validation can be employed without impacting registration speed or domain cost. Existing registrations can be reprocessed at the annual expiration date.
- Permanently remove the IANA function from under ICANN. This is too much authority focused in one organization. Making the domain and IP oversight truly separate will remove some politics from the WHOIS issue and allow more innovation on either side.
- Remove the WHOIS-related compliance function from ICANN and put it to a third party with community oversight. Internet users and domain registrants are the people directly impacted by WHOIS so they should have review of enforcement.
- Dramatically increase the development of language accessibility of WHOIS and truly extend the Internet globally on the technical level.

8.5 CONCLUSION: THE DOMAIN MONEY WALL—OR WHY ICANN WILL NEVER FIX WHOIS

We might believe that civilization has come a long way from signaling with torches on towers, but Polybius would think otherwise. ICANN professes to be democratic in its multistakeholder model of bottom-up policy development, but more than a decade of nonaction on WHOIS proves that this democracy is a myth. Artful ICANN players will cite a "lack of consensus" on WHOIS policy, but this is not the truth. Cross-constituency groups have presented ICANN time and time again with specific plans for WHOIS that are not implemented. Apologist for ICANN inaction will point to the need to balance between privacy rights and the needs of law enforcement, but this is a red herring. Privacy advocates, personal domain owner, trademark holders, consumer advocates, and governments could all be satisfied with a common sense WHOIS policy, which for the most part already exists. Holding back solutions is the fact that loose WHOIS standards fuel the financial pace of ICANN and its contracted parties. We have discussed previously the specifics of augmenting and/or transitioning WHOIS in its technical aspects. The greater problem that requires separate addressing is the overall barrier to a functioning WHOIS and the existential threat to the entire Internet that exists due to the needs of an extreme commercial minority.

What the general public does not see is a massive, coordinated effort to deceptively drive Internet money in to a small pool. This *innovation* is for a tiny segment of the electronic economy and does not benefit telecommunications or consumer value. ICANN manages the contracts with registrars, and the registrars fund ICANN. This is an extremely rare situation, which would be considered an obvious and outright corruptible relationship in any other industry, but here it is the norm.

Anything that represents even the most minute delay or restrictions on domain purchasing is seen as threat to ICANN and the contracted parties and is met with extreme resistance. Efforts by the Internet community and consumers to negotiate better conditions are given lip service than ignored by the body politic or manipulated by unseen hands. Critics of this situation are frequently cast as fringe freaks or false community representatives while simultaneously being paraded by ICANN as evidence of the their commitment to the multistakeholder model. From the beginning, contracted parties of ICANN have been manipulating the process for their own benefit, ensuring that money flows up to ICANN and then back down to the industry. The Domain Name System has been converted into a weapon aimed at consumers, and an extremely small number of people benefit.

There is no greater example the upward money flow than the curious practice of superfluous accreditation purchases by registrars through shell companies. A registrar only realistically needs one accreditation to sell domains, but some registrars have more than one hundred. ICANN has never adequately explained this practice.

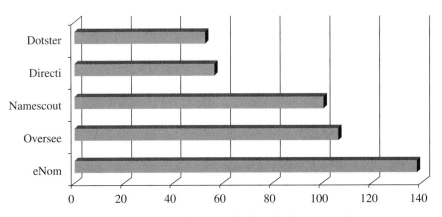

FIGURE 8.1   Excessive accreditations by five companies.

Who controls ICANN's extra annual $2,336,000?

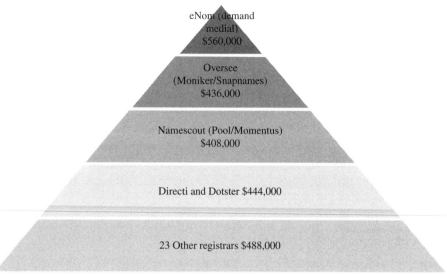

FIGURE 8.2   Who controls ICANN's extra money?

FIGURE 8.3   Rejected mail sent to a spam-advertized domain owner.

At US$4000.00 each year, the purchase of extra accreditations would seem a frivolous waste of money, yet the phenomena appear only to increase. A handful of companies pass millions of dollars each year to ICANN.

This also leads to a second realization, which is one of perceived market competition. Instead of 1000 independent registrars, we actually have five or six mega-registrars and a dozen or more mid-sized pools of shell companies, which leave less than 50% truly independent.

The two practices that drive bulk domain purchases are speculative domains as a commodity and junk product marketing. The massive purchase, parking, and auctioning of domains creates profits for domain insiders closely linked to registrars. Spam, click fraud, botnetting, illicit traffic, multilevel marketing, and other deceptive online operations need lots of domains. The following is an image of a rejected demand letter from a registrant with dozens of spammed domains:

This would seem an open-and-shut case of the willful provision of false WHOIS, yet ICANN did not respond to complaint about these registrations and did not explain why. Unfortunately, this was one of 5344 WHOIS inaccuracy complaints ICANN never responded to in 2012.[38]

These two industries drive domain sales but does little to benefit the Internet user, improve telecommunications, or drive other online business while at the same time rely on loose WHOIS rules. More domain sales mean more funds for registrars and ICANN.

There is nothing inherently wrong with monetizing domains, but power brokers at ICANN would have us believe this is the *only* way to fund the Internet and needs the most care and attention. This is not the mindset of the entire domain industry but is for the sectors with the most influence. ICANN has an inherent conflict of interest culture with board members also working for registrars and critical ICANN committee chairs populated by domain industry representatives.[39] There is also a persistent flow back and forth between ICANN and the domain name industry, with the last board chair moving directly to a new gTLD company after developing the policies that made new gTLDs possible.[40] This leads critics to claim ICANN has been captured by the domain industry.[41] With this system in place, there is no incentive to fix WHOIS.

WHOIS will likely be replaced or severely modified in the coming years, but its need is only going to grow. The purpose of WHOIS must remembered and retained in any Internet, which claims a democratic policy development structure, as that of a foundation of consumer trust on a massive network where consumers need to be able to clearly identify certain remote parties they are dealing with. Unfortunately, ICANN is playing a passive and sometimes active role in obfuscating those sources of information while accepting payment for permitting unidentified commercial players on the network. We need to get back to the ARPANET-type sense of camaraderie where everyone working on the network has a stake in mutual success. ICANN needs to live up to its pledge of putting the Internet community above commercial interests. Because the alternative to a responsible Internet industry (one accountable to the community) is a segmented global network heavily regulated by governments. WHOIS exits to make domains accountable to other Internet users, but the continued insistence that domain owner data only be made available to law enforcement is begging for a bad situation. The address of cybercrime and abuse should involve a direct dialog between registrars and consumers. For ICANN and registrars to shove all abuse issues to the police is either a complete admission of failure or an irresponsible dodge. If the police are brought in to solve a problem, everything else in society has failed.

---

[38] http://www.knujon.com/icann_compliance_2012.pdf
[39] http://www.techdirt.com/articles/20120323/03201418221/massive-conflict-interests-icann-called-out-ceo-start-to-get-some-attention.shtml
[40] http://domainnamewire.com/2011/08/22/icanns-peter-dengate-thrush-problem/
[41] http://www.internetsociety.ca/a-call-for-icann-to-embrace-its-inner-regulator/

Over 2000 years ago, Polybius wrote of *anacyclosis*, which is a common cycle of political decline in that even the most seemingly benign forms of government devolve into the worst forms through self-corruption[42] because the inheritors of power lack virtue:

> *"Those who know how to win are much more numerous than those who know how to make proper use of their victories."*[43]

Yes, specific entrepreneurs have taken the power of the Internet granted by the original developers and enriched themselves, but the newfound wealth and power is not being applied wisely. Polybius addressed the inevitable decline of good governance with well-balanced power sharing, but in the ICANN space, different stakeholders are completely unequal. True equal knowledge of all sources of information through WHOIS is a built-in check on the system. Do not allow the torches on the tower to go out.

---

[42] http://penelope.uchicago.edu/Thayer/E/Roman/Texts/Polybius/4*.html
[43] Polybius, The Histories Book X, chapter 31.

APPENDIX A: WHOIS CODE

A.1   C CODE EXAMPLE 1: BERKELEY WHOIS.c 8.1

```
/*
 * Copyright (c) 1980, 1993
 *     The Regents of the University of California.  All
 *     rights reserved.
 *
 * Redistribution and use in source and binary forms, with
 *   or without modification, are permitted provided that the
 *   following conditions are met:
 * 1. Redistributions of source code must retain the above
 *     copyright notice, this list of conditions and the fol-
 *     lowing disclaimer.
 * 2. Redistributions in binary form must reproduce the
 *     above copyright notice, this list of conditions and
 *     the following disclaimer in the documentation and/or
 *     other materials provided with the distribution.
 * 3. All advertising materials mentioning features or use
 *     of this software must display the following acknowl-
 *     edgement:
```

WHOIS Running the Internet: Protocol, Policy, and Privacy, First Edition. Garth O. Bruen.
© 2016 John Wiley & Sons, Inc. Published 2016 by John Wiley & Sons, Inc.

```
*      This product includes software developed by
       the University of California, Berkeley and its
       contributors.
* 4. Neither the name of the University nor the
     names of its contributors may be used to
     endorse or promote products derived from
     this software without specific prior written
     permission.
*
* THIS SOFTWARE IS PROVIDED BY THE REGENTS AND
  CONTRIBUTORS ''AS IS'' AND ANY EXPRESS OR IMPLIED
  WARRANTIES, INCLUDING, BUT NOT LIMITED TO, THE
  IMPLIED WARRANTIES OF MERCHANTABILITY AND FITNESS FOR
  A PARTICULAR PURPOSE
* ARE DISCLAIMED.  IN NO EVENT SHALL THE REGENTS OR
  CONTRIBUTORS BE LIABLE
* FOR ANY DIRECT, INDIRECT, INCIDENTAL, SPECIAL, EXEMPLARY,
  OR CONSEQUENTIAL
* DAMAGES (INCLUDING, BUT NOT LIMITED TO, PROCUREMENT OF
  SUBSTITUTE GOODS
* OR SERVICES; LOSS OF USE, DATA, OR PROFITS; OR BUSINESS
  INTERRUPTION)
* HOWEVER CAUSED AND ON ANY THEORY OF LIABILITY, WHETHER IN
  CONTRACT, STRICT
* LIABILITY, OR TORT (INCLUDING NEGLIGENCE OR OTHERWISE)
  ARISING IN ANY WAY
* OUT OF THE USE OF THIS SOFTWARE, EVEN IF ADVISED OF THE
  POSSIBILITY OF
* SUCH DAMAGE.
*/


#ifndef lint
static const char copyright[] =
"@(#) Copyright (c) 1980, 1993\n\
     The Regents of the University of California.
     All rights reserved.\n";
#endif /* not lint */


#if 0
#ifndef lint
static char sccsid[] = "@(#)whois.c   8.1 (Berkeley)
6/6/93";
#endif /* not lint */
#endif
```

```
#include <sys/cdefs.h>
#ifndef __APPLE__
__FBSDID("$FreeBSD: src/usr.bin/whois/whois.c,v 1.41
2004/08/25 15:34:44 mbr Exp $");
#endif

#include <sys/types.h>
#include <sys/socket.h>
#include <netinet/in.h>
#include <arpa/inet.h>
#include <ctype.h>
#include <err.h>
#include <netdb.h>
#include <stdarg.h>
#include <stdio.h>
#include <stdlib.h>
#include <string.h>
#include <sysexits.h>
#include <unistd.h>

#define    ABUSEHOST              "whois.abuse.net"
#define    NICHOST                "whois.crsnic.net"
#define    INICHOST               "whois.networksolutions.com"
#define    DNICHOST               "whois.nic.mil"
#define    GNICHOST               "whois.nic.gov"
#define    ANICHOST               "whois.arin.net"
#define    LNICHOST               "whois.lacnic.net"
#define    RNICHOST               "whois.ripe.net"
#define    PNICHOST               "whois.apnic.net"
#define    MNICHOST               "whois.ra.net"
#define    QNICHOST_TAIL          ".whois-servers.net"
#define    SNICHOST               "whois.6bone.net"
#define    BNICHOST               "whois.registro.br"
#define    NORIDHOST              "whois.norid.no"
#define    IANAHOST               "whois.iana.org"
#define    GERMNICHOST            "de.whois-servers.net"
#define    DEFAULT_PORT           "nicname"
#define    WHOIS_SERVER_ID        "Whois Server: "
#define    WHOIS_ORG_SERVER_ID    "Registrant Street1:Whois
                                  Server:"

#define WHOIS_RECURSE      0x01
#define WHOIS_QUICK        0x02

#define ishost(h) (isalnum((unsigned char)h) || h == '.' ||
h == '-')
```

```
const char *ip_whois[] = { LNICHOST, RNICHOST, PNICHOST,
BNICHOST, NULL };
const char *port = DEFAULT_PORT;

static char *choose_server(char *);
static struct addrinfo *gethostinfo(char const *host, int
exit_on_error);
#ifdef __APPLE__
static void s_asprintf(char **ret, const char *format, …)
__attribute__((__format__(printf, 2, 3)));
#else
static void s_asprintf(char **ret, const char *format, …)
__printflike(2, 3);
#endif
static void usage(void);
static void whois(const char *, const char *, int);

int
main(int argc, char *argv[])
{
        const char *country, *host;
        char *qnichost;
        int ch, flags, use_qnichost;

#ifdef  SOCKS
        SOCKSinit(argv[0]);
#endif

        country = host = qnichost = NULL;
        flags = use_qnichost = 0;
        while ((ch = getopt(argc, argv, "aAbc:dgh:iIlmp:
        QrR6")) != -1) {
                switch (ch) {
                case 'a':
                        host = ANICHOST;
                        break;
                case 'A':
                        host = PNICHOST;
                        break;
                case 'b':
                        host = ABUSEHOST;
                        break;
                case 'c':
                        country = optarg;
                        break;
```

```
                case 'd':
                        host = DNICHOST;
                        break;
                case 'g':
                        host = GNICHOST;
                        break;
                case 'h':
                        host = optarg;
                        break;
                case 'i':
                        host = INICHOST;
                        break;
                case 'I':
                        host = IANAHOST;
                        break;
                case 'l':
                        host = LNICHOST;
                        break;
                case 'm':
                        host = MNICHOST;
                        break;
                case 'p':
                        port = optarg;
                        break;
                case 'Q':
                        flags |= WHOIS_QUICK;
                        break;
                case 'r':
                        host = RNICHOST;
                        break;
                case 'R':
                        warnx("-R is deprecated; use '-c ru'
                        instead");
                        country = "ru";
                        break;
                case '6':
                        host = SNICHOST;
                        break;
                case '?':
                default:
                        usage();
                        /* NOTREACHED */
                }
        }
        argc -= optind;
        argv += optind;
```

```
        if (!argc || (country != NULL && host != NULL))
                usage();


        /*
         * If no host or country is specified determine the
           top level domain
         * from the query.  If the TLD is a number, query
           ARIN.  Otherwise, use
         * TLD.whois-server.net.  If the domain does not
           contain '.', fall
         * back to NICHOST.
         */
        if (host == NULL && country == NULL) {
                use_qnichost = 1;
                host = NICHOST;
                if (!(flags & WHOIS_QUICK))
                        flags |= WHOIS_RECURSE;
        }
        while (argc-- > 0) {
                if (country != NULL) {
                        s_asprintf(& qnichost, "%s%s",
                        country, QNICHOST_TAIL);
                        whois(*argv, qnichost, flags);
                } else if (use_qnichost)
                        if ((qnichost = choose_server(*argv))
                        != NULL)
                                whois(*argv, qnichost,
                                flags);
                if (qnichost == NULL)
                        whois(*argv, host, flags);
                free(qnichost);
                qnichost = NULL;
                argv++;
        }
        exit(0);
}


/*
 * This function will remove any trailing periods from
   domain, after which it returns a pointer to newly
   allocated memory containing the whois server to be
   queried, or a NULL if the correct server couldn't be
   determined.  The caller must remember to free(3) the
   allocated
   memory.
 */
```

```c
static char *
choose_server(char *domain)
{
        char *pos, *retval;

        for (pos = strchr(domain, '\0'); pos > domain && *--
        pos      == '.';)
                *pos = '\0';
        if (*domain == '\0')
                errx(EX_USAGE, "can't search for a null string");
        if (strlen(domain) > sizeof("-NORID")-1 &&
            strcasecmp(domain + strlen(domain) - sizeof
            ("-NORID") + 1,
                "-NORID") == 0) {
                s_asprintf(&retval, "%s", NORIDHOST);
                return (retval);
        }
        while (pos > domain && *pos != '.')
                --pos;
        if (pos <= domain)
                return (NULL);
        if (isdigit((unsigned char)*++pos))
                s_asprintf(&retval, "%s", ANICHOST);
        else
                s_asprintf(&retval, "%s%s", pos, QNICHOST_TAIL);
        return (retval);
}

static struct addrinfo *
gethostinfo(char const *host, int exit_on_error)
{
        struct addrinfo hints, *res;
        int error;

        memset(&hints, 0, sizeof(hints));
        hints.ai_flags = 0;
        hints.ai_family = AF_UNSPEC;
        hints.ai_socktype = SOCK_STREAM;
        error = getaddrinfo(host, port, &hints, &res);
        if (error) {
                warnx("%s: %s", host, gai_strerror(error));
                if (exit_on_error)
                        exit(EX_NOHOST);
                return (NULL);
        }
        return (res);
}
```

```c
/*
 * Wrapper for asprintf(3) that exits on error.
 */
static void
s_asprintf(char **ret, const char *format, …)
{
        va_list ap;

        va_start(ap, format);
        if (vasprintf(ret, format, ap) == -1) {
                va_end(ap);
                err(EX_OSERR, "vasprintf()");
        }
        va_end(ap);
}

static void
whois(const char *query, const char *hostname, int flags)
{
        FILE *sfi, *sfo;
        struct addrinfo *hostres, *res;
        char *buf, *host, *nhost, *p;
        int i, s;
        size_t c, len;

        hostres = gethostinfo(hostname, 1);
        for (res = hostres; res; res = res->ai_next) {
                s = socket(res->ai_family, res->ai_socktype,
                res->ai_protocol);
                if (s < 0)
                        continue;
                if (connect(s, res->ai_addr, res->ai_addrlen)
                == 0)
                        break;
                close(s);
        }
        freeaddrinfo(hostres);
        if (res == NULL)
                err(EX_OSERR, "connect()");
        sfi = fdopen(s, "r");
        sfo = fdopen(s, "w");
        if (sfi == NULL || sfo == NULL)
                err(EX_OSERR, "fdopen()");
        if (strcmp(hostname, GERMNICHOST) == 0) {
                fprintf(sfo, "-T dn,ace -C US-ASCII %s\r\n",
                query);
        } else {
                fprintf(sfo, "%s\r\n", query);
```

```
        }
        fflush(sfo);
        nhost = NULL;
        while ((buf = fgetln(sfi, &len)) != NULL) {
                while (len > 0 && isspace((unsigned char)buf
                [len - 1]))
                        buf[--len] = '\0';
                printf("%.*s\n", (int)len, buf);


                if ((flags & WHOIS_RECURSE) && nhost == NULL) {
                        host = strnstr(buf, WHOIS_SERVER_ID,
                        len);
                        if (host != NULL) {
                                host += sizeof(WHOIS_SERVER_ID)
                                - 1;
                                for (p = host; p < buf + len;
                                p++) {
                                        if (!ishost(*p)) {
                                                *p = '\0';
                                                break;
                                        }
                                }
                                s_asprintf(&nhost, "%.*s",
                                        (int)(buf + len - host),
                                        host);
                        } else if ((host =
                           strnstr(buf, WHOIS_ORG_SERVER_ID,
                           len)) != NULL) {
                                host += sizeof(WHOIS_ORG_SERVER_
                                ID) - 1;
                                for (p = host; p < buf + len;
                                p++) {
                                        if (!ishost(*p)) {
                                                *p = '\0';
                                                break;
                                        }
                                }
                                s_asprintf(&nhost, "%.*s",
                                        (int)(buf + len - host),
                                host);
                        } else if (strcmp(hostname, ANICHOST)
                        == 0) {
                                for (c = 0; c <= len; c++)
                                        buf[c] = tolower((int)
                                        buf[c]);
                                for (i = 0; ip_whois[i] !=
                                NULL; i++) {
```

```
                                    if (strnstr(buf, ip_
                                    whois[i], len) !=
                                        NULL) {
                                            s_asprintf
                                            (&nhost, "%s",
                                                ip_whois[i]);
                                            break;
                                    }
                                }
                            }
                        }
                    }
                }
                if (nhost != NULL) {
                        whois(query, nhost, 0);
                        free(nhost);
                }
        }
}

static void
usage(void)
{
        fprintf(stderr,
            "usage: whois [-aAbdgiIlmQrR6] [-c country-code
            | -h hostname] "
            "[-p port] name -\n");
        exit(EX_USAGE);
}
```

A.2   C CODE EXAMPLE 2: RIPE WHOIS3.c BY SHANE KERR AND CAN BICAN

```
/*
 * This file is part of
 * ===========================================================
 *
 * whois3
 *
 * Copyright 2003 RIPE NCC
 * See the file "COPYING" for licensing information
 *
 *
 * =========================================================== */

/* $Id: whois3.c,v 1.5 2005/01/17 11:15:15 bican Exp $ */

#include <string.h>
#include <stdlib.h>
```

```c
#include <stdio.h>
#include <limits.h>
#include <netdb.h>
#include <errno.h>
#include <netdb.h>
#include <sys/types.h>
#include <sys/socket.h>
#include <netinet/in.h>
#include <unistd.h>

#include <unistd.h>
#include <stdarg.h>

#ifdef HAVE_STDINT_H
#include <stdint.h>
#endif                          /*  */

#ifdef HAVE_STRTOL
#include <errno.h>
#include <limits.h>
#endif                          /*  */

#include <assert.h>

/* default name to query - can be set at runtime via the
   "-h" option */
#define DEFAULT_WHOIS_HOST "whois.ripe.net"

/* default port - only used if there is no entry for "whois"
   in the
   /etc/services file and no "-p" option is specified */
#define DEFAULT_WHOIS_PORT "43"

/* maximum length of the string representing an IP address */
#define MAX_IP_ADDRLEN
sizeof("0000:0000:0000:0000:0000:0000: 255.255.255.255")
#define MAX_PORTLEN     sizeof("65535")
typedef struct address_t {
    char *address;
    char *port;
} address;


#if !defined(HAVE_SS_FAMILY_IN_SS) && defined(HAVE___SS_
FAMILY_IN_SS)
# define ss_family __ss_family
#endif /* !defined(HAVE_SS_FAMILY_IN_SS) && defined(HAVE_SA_
FAMILY_IN_SS) */
```

```c
int   ipv4_flag = 0;                          /*  -4  */
int   ipv6_flag = 0;                          /*  -6  */

/* program name */
static char *program_name = NULL;

/*
 * FUNCTIONS
 */
const char *get_program_name()
{

    return program_name;
}

/* exit the program with an error message */
void fatal(const char *template, ...)
{
    va_list ap;
    fprintf(stderr, "%s: ", get_program_name());
    va_start(ap, template);
    vfprintf(stderr, template, ap);
    va_end(ap);
    fprintf(stderr, "\n");
    exit(EXIT_FAILURE);
}

/* this function opens a socket, connects the socket to
   the address specified by "remote" and returns the file
   descriptor of the socket. */
static int tcp_connect(sa_family_t family, address *
remote)
{
    int err, fd;
    socklen_t destlen;
    struct addrinfo hints, *res = NULL, *ptr;
    struct sockaddr_storage dest;

    /* make sure that the preconditions on the addresses and
       on the flags
     * are respected */
    assert(remote != NULL);
    assert(remote->address != NULL && strlen(remote-
>address) > 0);
    assert(remote->port != NULL && strlen(remote->port)
    > 0);
```

```
    /* setup hints structure to be passed to getaddrinfo */
    memset(&hints, 0, sizeof(hints));
    hints.ai_family = family;
    hints.ai_socktype = SOCK_STREAM;

    /* get the IP address of the remote end of the
       connection */
    err = getaddrinfo(remote->address, remote->port, &hints,
    &res);
    if (err != 0)
       fatal("getaddrinfo error: %s", gai_strerror(err));

    /* check the results of getaddrinfo */
    assert(res != NULL);
    assert(res->ai_addrlen <= sizeof(dest));

    /* if the connect to the first address returned by
       getaddrinfo fails,
     * then we keep trying with the other addresses */
    err = -1;
    for (ptr = res; ptr != NULL; ptr = ptr->ai_next) {

        /* get the first sockaddr structure returned by
           getaddrinfo */
        memcpy(&dest, ptr->ai_addr, ptr->ai_addrlen);
        destlen = ptr->ai_addrlen;

#ifdef  AF_INET
        if ((dest.ss_family == AF_INET)  && ipv6_flag)
            continue;
#endif  /* AF_INET */
#ifdef  AF_INET6
        if ((dest.ss_family == AF_INET6)  && ipv4_flag)
            continue;
#endif  /* AF_INET6 */
        /* create the socket */
        fd = socket(dest.ss_family, SOCK_STREAM, 0);
        if (fd < 0)
        {
            fprintf(stderr, "Warning cannot create the socket
            (family %d): %s\n", dest.ss_family, strerror(errno));
        }
        else
        {
            /* perform the connection */
            err = connect(fd, (struct sockaddr *) &dest,
            destlen);
```

```
            if (err == 0)
                break;
        }
    }

    /* cleanup to avoid memory leaks */
    freeaddrinfo(res);

    /* if we have reached the end of the loop without
       having err == 0 then * we have failed to establish
       the connection */
    if (err < 0)
        fatal("cannot establish connection: %s",
        strerror(errno));
    return fd;
}


/*
  whois_query

  Writes the query string in "query" to the "out" descriptor,
  and reads the result in the "in" descriptor.  The "out"
  buffer may have either no buffering or line buffering, but
  must NOT have full buffering.

  The routine then outputs each line the server returns,
  until the server ends the connection.  If the "check_for_
  blank" variable is set to non-zero, then the routine will
  also return when two consecutive blank

  lines appear in the server response.

  If an error occurs sending or reading the query, -1 is
  returned.
 */
int whois_query(FILE * in, FILE * out, char *query, int
check_for_blank)
{
    char buf[1024];
    int last_line_blank;
    char *p, *query_copy;

    /* manipulate a copy of the query */
    query_copy = (char *) malloc(strlen(query) + 4);
    strcpy(query_copy, query);
```

```c
/* remove any newline or carriage return */
p = strchr(query_copy, '\r');
if (p != NULL) {
    *p = '\0';
}
p = strchr(query_copy, '\n');
if (p != NULL) {
    *p = '\0';
}

/* add CR+LF */
strcat(query_copy, "\r\n");

/* send query */
if (fputs(query_copy, out) == EOF) {
    return (-1);
}

/* wait for reply to finish, printing until then */
last_line_blank = 0;
for (;;) {

    /* read next line */
    if (fgets(buf, sizeof(buf), in) == NULL) {
        return (-1);
    }

    /* output the line */
    fputs(buf, stdout);

    /* if entire line fit in buffer */
    if (strchr(buf, '\n')) {

        /* if line is empty */
        if (!strcmp(buf, "\n")) {

            /* if the last line was also blank, we're done */
            if (check_for_blank && last_line_blank) {
                return 1;
            }
            last_line_blank = 1;
        }

        /* non-empty line */
        else {
            last_line_blank = 0;
        }
    }
```

```
        /* otherwise read until end of line */
        else {

            do {
                if (fgets(buf, sizeof(buf), in) == NULL) {
                    return 0;
                }
                fputs(buf, stdout);
            } while (!strchr(buf, '\n'));
            last_line_blank = 0;
        }
    }
}

/* usage_error - output proper syntax and exit */
void usage_error(const char *exename)
{
    fprintf(stderr,
            "%s: [-4|-6] [-h host | --host=host] [-p port |
            --port=port] -k | query\n",
            exename);
    exit(1);
}

/* main - program entry point */
int main(int argc, char *argv[])
{

    /* name of executable */
    char *exename;

    /* variables used to parse arguments */
    int p;

    /* arguments to forward to whois server */
    char **whois_argv;
    int whois_argc;

    /* server name and port to query */
    char *host;
    char *port;
    char src_addr[MAX_IP_ADDRLEN + 1];
    char src_port[MAX_PORTLEN + 1];
    sa_family_t family;
    address remote;
```

```c
/* persistent mode flag */
int persistent_mode;
char linebuf[BUFSIZ];

/* connection information */
int whois_fd;
FILE *whois_in, *whois_out;
char whois_in_linebuf[BUFSIZ];

/* query string */
char *query;
int query_len;

/* the all-seeing i */
int i;

/* */
/* parse command line */
/* */

/* get the name of this executable */
if (argc > 0) {
    program_name = exename = "whois3";
} else {
    program_name = exename = argv[0];
}

/* set defaults for parameters */
host = NULL;
port = NULL;
persistent_mode = 0;
family = AF_UNSPEC;

/* allocate enough space for our argument list */
whois_argv = (char **) malloc(sizeof(char *) *
(argc + 1));
if (whois_argv == NULL) {
    fprintf(stderr, "%s: out of memory\n", exename);
    exit(1);
}
whois_argc = 0;

/* parse command-line arguments */
p = 1;
while (p < argc) {
```

```c
    /* check for short host name */
    if (!strncmp(argv[p], "-h", 2)) {

        /* only specify host once */
        if (host != NULL) {
            usage_error(exename);
        }

        /* see if the host was specified after the 'h' */
        host = argv[p] + 2;

        /* if not, then it must be the next argument */
        if (*host == '\0') {
            p++;
            if (p >= argc) {
                usage_error(exename);
            }
            host = argv[p];
        }
        p++;
    }

    /* check for long host name */
    else if (!strncmp(argv[p], "--host=", 7)) {

        /* only specify host once */
        if (host != NULL) {
            usage_error(exename);
        }

        /* grab host name */
        host = argv[p] + 7;
        if (*host == '\0') {
            usage_error(exename);
        }
        p++;
    }

    /* check for short port name */
    else if (!strncmp(argv[p], "-p", 2)) {

        /* only specify port once */
        if (port != NULL) {
            usage_error(exename);
        }
```

```
        /* see if the port was specified after the
            'p' */
        port = argv[p] + 2;
        if (*port == '\0') {
            p++;
            if (p >= argc) {
                usage_error(exename);
            }
            port = argv[p];
        }
        p++;
    }

    /* check for ipv4 flag, -4 */
    else if (!strncmp(argv[p], "-4", 2)) {
        ipv4_flag = 1;
        p++;
    }

    /* check for ipv6 flag, -6 */
    else if (!strncmp(argv[p], "-6", 2)) {
        ipv6_flag = 1;
        p++;
    }

    /* check for long port name */
    else if (!strncmp(argv[p], "--port=", 7)) {

        /* only specify port once */
        if (port != NULL) {
            usage_error(exename);
        }
        port = argv[p] + 7;
        p++;
    }

    /* check for stand-alone persistent flag */
    else if (!strcmp(argv[p], "-k")) {

        /* note we explicitly allow multiple -k options,
            as this doesn't
            add any ambiguity, even if it is pointless */
        persistent_mode = 1;
        p++;
    }
```

```c
        /* other flags or arguments */
        else {

            /* check to see if -k was used - this will
               cause an error below,
               as you can only use -k by itself */
            if ((argv[p][0] == '-') && strchr(argv[p],
            'k')) {
                persistent_mode = 1;
            }

            /* add our argument in any case */
            whois_argv[whois_argc++] = argv[p];
            p++;
        }
    }
}

/* don't allow any arguments with a persistent mode */
if (persistent_mode) {
    if (whois_argc > 0) {
        fprintf(stderr, "%s: do not specify arguments
        with -k\n",
                exename);
        exit(1);
    }
    /* set to line buffering if we are in persistent
    mode,
     * to allow programs to pipe the result without
    block buffering */
    setvbuf(stdout, linebuf, _IOLBF, BUFSIZ);
}


/* require options otherwise */
else {
    if (whois_argc <= 0) {
        usage_error(exename);
    }
}

/* */
/* arguments look good - connect to server */
/* */

/* set port address if not specified */
if (port == NULL) {
    remote.port = DEFAULT_WHOIS_PORT;
```

```
} else {
    strncpy(src_port, port, sizeof(src_port) - 1);
    src_port[sizeof(src_port) - 1] = '\0';
    remote.port = src_port;
}

/* set host address if not specified */
if (host == NULL) {
    remote.address = DEFAULT_WHOIS_HOST;
} else {
    strncpy(src_addr, host, sizeof(src_addr) - 1);
    src_addr[sizeof(src_addr) - 1] = '\0';
    remote.address = src_addr;
}

/* create a socket, exit if no connection possible */
whois_fd = tcp_connect(family, &remote);

/* bind FILE structures to our file descriptor for easy
handling */
whois_in = fdopen(whois_fd, "r");
if (whois_in == NULL) {
    fprintf(stderr, "%s: error %d creating input stream;
    %s\n",
            exename, errno, strerror(errno));
}
setvbuf(whois_in, whois_in_linebuf, _IOLBF,
sizeof(whois_in_linebuf));
whois_out = fdopen(whois_fd, "w");
if (whois_out == NULL) {
    fprintf(stderr, "%s: error %d creating input stream;
    %s\n",
            exename, errno, strerror(errno));
}
setbuf(whois_out, NULL);

/* */
/* Query away */
/* */

/* if we had flags, we're running in "interactive"
mode */
if (whois_argc > 0) {

    /* combine our arguments into a single string */
    query_len = 0;
    for (i = 0; i < whois_argc; i++) {
```

```
            query_len += (1 + strlen(whois_argv[i]));
    }
    query = (char *) malloc(query_len + 1);
    if (query == NULL) {
        fprintf(stderr, "%s: out of memory\n", exename);
        exit(1);
    }
    strcpy(query, whois_argv[0]);
    for (i = 1; i < whois_argc; i++) {
        strcat(query, " ");
        strcat(query, whois_argv[i]);
    }

    /* now send our query to the server */
    whois_query(whois_in, whois_out, query, 0);
}

    /* otherwise we're in "batch" mode - read each query a
    line at a time */
    else {
        /* make a buffer to read into */
        query_len = 8192;
        query = (char *) malloc(query_len);
        if (query == NULL) {
            fprintf(stderr, "%s: out of memory\n", exename);
            exit(1);
        }

    /* enter persistent mode */
    if (whois_query(whois_in, whois_out, "-k", 1) == -1) {
        fprintf(stderr, "%s: unable to send query\n", exename);
        exit(1);
    }

    /* loop and query */
    while (fgets(query, query_len, stdin) != NULL) {
        if (strchr(query, '\n') == NULL) {
            fprintf(stderr, "%s: query line too long\n",
            exename);
            exit(1);
        }
        if (whois_query(whois_in, whois_out, query, 1) == -1) {
            fprintf(stderr, "%s: unable to send query\n",
            exename);
            exit(1);
        }
    }
}
```

```
        /* exit persistent mode */
        fputs("-k\n", whois_out);
    }

    /* everything exited fine */
    return 0;
}
```

A.3 C CODE EXAMPLE 3: RIPE WHOIS.c BY MARCO D'ITRI

```
/* Copyright 1999-2007 by Marco d'Itri <md@linux.it>.
 *
 * This program is free software; you can redistribute
it and/or modify * it under the terms of the GNU General
Public License version 2 as * published by the Free
Software Foundation.
 */

/* for AI_IDN */
#define _GNU_SOURCE

/* System library */
#include <stdio.h>
#include <stdlib.h>
#include <stdarg.h>
//#include <unistd.h>
#include "config.h"
#include <string.h>
#include <ctype.h>
//#include <sys/types.h>
//#include <sys/socket.h>
//#include <netinet/in.h>
//#include <netdb.h>
#include <errno.h>
//#include <signal.h>
//#ifdef HAVE_GETOPT_LONG
//#include <getopt.h>
//#endif
//#ifdef HAVE_REGEXEC
//#include <regex.h>
//#endif
//#ifdef HAVE_LIBIDN
//#include <idna.h>
//#endif
```

```
//#ifndef AI_IDN
//#define AI_IDN 0
//#endif

/* Application-specific */

#include <winsock.h>
#include "data.h"
#include "whois.h"
#include "win_funcs.h"

#define streq(a, b) (strcmp(a, b) == 0)
#define strneq(a, b, n) (strncmp(a, b, n) == 0)

/* Global variables */
int sockfd, verb = 0;

#ifdef ALWAYS_HIDE_DISCL
int hide_discl = HIDE_UNSTARTED;
#else
int hide_discl = HIDE_DISABLED;
#endif

char *client_tag = (char *)IDSTRING;

//#ifdef HAVE_GETOPT_LONG
//static struct option longopts[] = {
//    {"help",     no_argument,       NULL, 0  },
//    {"version",  no_argument,       NULL, 1  },
//    {"verbose",  no_argument,       NULL, 2  },
//    {"server",   required_argument, NULL, 'h'},
//    {"host",     required_argument, NULL, 'h'},
//    {"port",     required_argument, NULL, 'p'},
//    {NULL,       0,                 NULL, 0  }
//};
//#else
//extern char *optarg;
//extern int optind;
//#endif

int main(int argc, char *argv[])
{
    int ch, nopar = 0;
    const char *server = NULL, *port = NULL;
    char *p, *qstring, fstring[64] = "\0";

        WSADATA wsad;
```

```c
#ifdef ENABLE_NLS
    setlocale(LC_ALL, "");
    bindtextdomain(NLS_CAT_NAME, LOCALEDIR);
    textdomain(NLS_CAT_NAME);
#endif

    while ((ch = GETOPT_LONGISH(argc, argv,
                "abBcdFg:Gh:Hi:KlLmMp:q:rRs:St:T:v:V:x", lon-
                gopts, 0)) > 0) {
        /* RIPE flags */
        if (strchr(ripeflags, ch)) {
            for (p = fstring; *p; p++);
            sprintf(p--, "-%c ", ch);
            continue;
        }
        if (strchr(ripeflagsp, ch)) {
            for (p = fstring; *p; p++);
//          snprintf(p--, sizeof(fstring), "-%c %s ", ch,
            optarg);
                _snprintf(p--, sizeof(fstring), "-%c %s ",
                ch, optarg);
            if (ch == 't' || ch == 'v' || ch == 'q')
                nopar = 1;
            continue;
        }
        /* program flags */
        switch (ch) {
        case 'h':
            server = strdup(optarg);
            break;
        case 'V':
            client_tag = optarg;
        case 'H':
            hide_discl = HIDE_UNSTARTED;   /* enable dis-
            claimers hiding */
            break;
        case 'p':
            port = strdup(optarg);
            break;
        case 2:
            verb = 1;
            break;
        case 1:
#ifdef VERSION
            fprintf(stderr, _("Version %s.\n\nReport bugs to %s.\n"),
                    VERSION, "<md+whois@linux.it>");
```

```
#else
            fprintf(stderr, "%s %s\n", inetutils_package, in-
            etutils_version);
#endif
            exit(0);
        default:
            usage();
        }
    }
    argc -= optind;
    argv += optind;

    if (argc == 0 && !nopar)   /* there is no parameter */
        usage();

    /* On some systems realloc only works on non-NULL buffers */
    qstring = malloc(64);
    *qstring = '\0';

    /* parse other parameters, if any */
    if (!nopar) {
        int qslen = 0;

        while (1) {
            qslen += strlen(*argv) + 1 + 1;
            qstring = realloc(qstring, qslen);
            strcat(qstring, *argv++);
            if (argc == 1)
                break;
            strcat(qstring, " ");
            argc--;
        }
    }

//    signal(SIGTERM, sighandler);
//    signal(SIGINT, sighandler);
//    signal(SIGALRM, alarm_handler);

    if (getenv("WHOIS_HIDE"))
        hide_discl = HIDE_UNSTARTED;

    /* -v or -t has been used */
    if (!server && !*qstring)
        server = strdup("whois.ripe.net");

#ifdef CONFIG_FILE
    if (!server) {
```

```
            server = match_config_file(qstring);
            if (verb && server)
                printf(_("Using server %s.\n"), server);
        }
#endif

    if (!server) {
        char *tmp;

        tmp = normalize_domain(qstring);
        free(qstring);
        qstring = tmp;
        server = whichwhois(qstring);
    }


        WSAStartup(MAKEWORD(1,1), &wsad);

    handle_query(server, port, qstring, fstring);

        WSACleanup();

    exit(0);
}


/* server may be a server name from the command line, a
server name got * from whichwhois or an encoded command/
message from whichwhois. * server and port are allocated
with malloc.
 */
const char *handle_query(const char *hserver, const char
*hport,
        const char *qstring, const char *fstring)
{
    const char *server = NULL, *port = NULL;
    char *p;

    if (hport) {
        server = strdup(hserver);
        port = strdup(hport);
    } else if (hserver[0] < ' ')
        server = strdup(hserver);
    else
        split_server_port(hserver, &server, &port);

    switch (server[0]) {
        case 0:
```

```
          if (!(server = getenv("WHOIS_SERVER")))
              server = DEFAULTSERVER;
          break;
      case 1:
          puts(_("This TLD has no whois server, but you
          can access the "
                      "whois database at"));
          puts(server + 1);
          return NULL;
      case 2:
          puts(server + 1);
          return NULL;
      case 3:
          puts(_("This TLD has no whois server."));
          return NULL;
      case 5:
          puts(_("No whois server is known for this kind
          of object."));
          return NULL;
      case 6:
          puts(_("Unknown AS number or IP network. Please
          upgrade this program."));
          return NULL;
      case 4:
          if (verb)
              puts(_("Connecting to whois.crsnic.net."));
          sockfd = openconn("whois.crsnic.net", NULL);
          server = query_crsnic(sockfd, qstring);
          break;
      case 7:
          if (verb)
              puts(_("Connecting to whois.publicinter-
              estregistry.net."));
          sockfd = openconn("whois.publicinterestregistry.
          net", NULL);
          server = query_pir(sockfd, qstring);
          break;
      case 9:
          if (verb)
              puts(_("Connecting to whois.nic.cc."));
          sockfd = openconn("whois.nic.cc", NULL);
          server = query_crsnic(sockfd, qstring);
          break;
      case 0x0A:
          p = convert_6to4(qstring);
          /* XXX should fail if p = 0.0.0.0 */
```

```c
            printf(_("\nQuerying for the IPv4 endpoint %s of
            a 6to4 IPv6 address.\n\n"), p);
            server = whichwhois(p);
            /* XXX should fail if server[0] < ' ' */
            qstring = p;        /* XXX leak */
            break;
        case 0x0B:
            p = convert_teredo(qstring);
            printf(_("\nQuerying for the IPv4 endpoint %s of
            a Teredo IPv6 address.\n\n"), p);
            server = whichwhois(p);
            qstring = p ;
            break;
        default:
            break;
    }

    if (!server)
        return NULL;

    p = queryformat(server, fstring, qstring);
    if (verb) {
        printf(_("Using server %s.\n"), server);
        printf(_("Query string: \"%s\"\n\n"), p);
    }

    sockfd = openconn(server, port);

    strcat(p, "\r\n");
    server = do_query(sockfd, p);

    /* recursion is fun */
    if (server) {
        printf(_("\n\nFound a referral to %s.\n\n"), server);
        handle_query(server, NULL, qstring, fstring);
    }

    return NULL;
}

#ifdef CONFIG_FILE
const char *match_config_file(const char *s)
{
    FILE *fp;
    char buf[512];
    static const char delim[] = " \t";
```

```
    if ((fp = fopen(CONFIG_FILE, "r")) == NULL) {
        if (errno != ENOENT)
            err_sys("Cannot open " CONFIG_FILE);
        return NULL;
    }

    while (fgets(buf, sizeof(buf), fp) != NULL) {
        char *p;
        const char *pattern, *server;
#ifdef HAVE_REGEXEC
        int i;
        regex_t re;
#endif

        for (p = buf; *p; p++)
            if (*p == '\n')
                *p = '\0';

        p = buf;
        while (*p == ' ' || *p == '\t')  /* eat leading blanks */
            p++;
        if (!*p)
            continue;     /* skip empty lines */
        if (*p == '#')
            continue;     /* skip comments */

        pattern = strtok(p, delim);
        server = strtok(NULL, delim);
        if (!pattern || !server)
            err_quit(_("Cannot parse this line: %s"), p);
        p = strtok(NULL, delim);
        if (p)
            err_quit(_("Cannot parse this line: %s"), p);

#ifdef HAVE_REGEXEC
        i = regcomp(&re, pattern, REG_EXTENDED|REG_
        ICASE|REG_NOSUB);
        if (i != 0) {
            char m[1024];
            regerror(i, &re, m, sizeof(m));
            err_quit("Invalid regular expression '%s': %s",
            pattern, m);
        }

        i = regexec(&re, s, 0, NULL, 0);
        if (i == 0) {
            regfree(&re);
```

```
                return strdup(server);
            }
            if (i != REG_NOMATCH) {
                char m[1024];
                regerror(i, &re, m, sizeof(m));
                err_quit("regexec: %s",  m);
            }
            regfree(&re);
#else
            if (domcmp(s, pattern))
                return strdup(server);
#endif
        }
    return NULL;
}
#endif

/* Parses an user-supplied string and tries to guess the
right whois server.
 * Returns a statically allocated buffer.
 */
const char *whichwhois(const char *s)
{
    unsigned long ip, as32;
    unsigned int i;
    char *colon;

    /* IPv6 address */
    if ((colon = strchr(s, ':'))) {
        unsigned long v6prefix, v6net;

        /* RPSL hierarchical objects */
//          if (strncasecmp(s, "as", 2) == 0) {
        if (strnicmp(s, "as", 2) == 0) {
            if (isasciidigit(s[2]))
                return whereas(atoi(s + 2));
            else
                return "";
        }

        v6prefix = strtol(s, NULL, 16);

        if (v6prefix == 0)
            return "\x05";                    /* unknown */

        v6net = (v6prefix << 16) + strtol(colon + 1, NULL,
        16);/* second u16 */
```

```
        for (i = 0; ip6_assign[i].serv; i++) {
            if ((v6net & (~0UL << (32 - ip6_assign[i].
            masklen)))
                    == ip6_assign[i].net)
                return ip6_assign[i].serv;
        }

        return "\x06";        /* unknown allocation */
    }

    /* email address */
    if (strchr(s, '@'))
        return "\x05";

    /* no dot and no hyphen means it's a NSI NIC handle or
    ASN (?) */
    if (!strpbrk(s, ".-")) {
//      if (strncasecmp(s, "as", 2) == 0 &&   /* it's an AS */
        if (strnicmp(s, "as", 2) == 0 &&   /* it's an AS */
                (isasciidigit(s[2]) || s[2] == ' '))
            return whereas(atoi(s + 2));
        if (*s == '!')   /* NSI NIC handle */
            return "whois.networksolutions.com";
        else
            return "\x05";   /* probably a unknown kind of
            nic handle */
    }

    /* ASN32? */
//      if (strncasecmp(s, "as", 2) == 0 && s[2] &&
        if (strnicmp(s, "as", 2) == 0 && s[2] &&
            (as32 = asn32_to_long(s + 2)) != 0)
        return whereas32(as32);

    /* smells like an IP? */
    if ((ip = myinet_aton(s))) {
        for (i = 0; ip_assign[i].serv; i++)
            if ((ip & ip_assign[i].mask) == ip_assign[i].net)
                return ip_assign[i].serv;
        return "\x05";        /* not in the unicast IPv4
        space */
    }

    /* check the TLDs list */
    for (i = 0; tld_serv[i]; i += 2)
        if (domcmp(s, tld_serv[i]))
            return tld_serv[i + 1];
```

```
        /* no dot but hyphen */
        if (!strchr(s, '.')) {
            /* search for strings at the start of the word */
            for (i = 0; nic_handles[i]; i += 2)
//                if (strncasecmp(s, nic_handles[i], strlen(nic_
                handles[i])) == 0)
                    if (strnicmp(s, nic_handles[i], strlen(nic_
                    handles[i])) == 0)
                    return nic_handles[i + 1];
            /* it's probably a network name */
            return "";
        }

        /* has dot and maybe a hyphen and it's not in tld_
        serv[], WTF is it? */
        /* either a TLD or a NIC handle we don't know about
        yet */
        return "\x05";
}

const char *whereas32(const unsigned long asn)
{
    int i;

    for (i = 0; as32_assign[i].serv; i++)
        if (asn >= as32_assign[i].first && asn <= as32_
        assign[i].last)
            return as32_assign[i].serv;
    return "\x06";
}

const char *whereas(const unsigned short asn)
{
    int i;

    for (i = 0; as_assign[i].serv; i++)
        if (asn >= as_assign[i].first && asn <= as_
        assign[i].last)
                return as_assign[i].serv;
    return "\x06";
}

char *queryformat(const char *server, const char *flags,
const char *query)
{
    char *buf, *p;
    int i, isripe = 0;
```

```c
    /* 64 bytes reserved for server-specific flags added
    later */
    buf = malloc(strlen(flags) + strlen(query) + strlen
    (client_tag) + 64);
    *buf = '\0';
    for (i = 0; ripe_servers[i]; i++)
        if (streq(server, ripe_servers[i])) {
            strcat(buf, "-V ");
            strcat(buf, client_tag);
            strcat(buf, " ");
            isripe = 1;
            break;
        }
    if (*flags) {
        if (!isripe && !streq(server, "whois.corenic.net"))
            puts(_("Warning: RIPE flags used with a tradi-
            tional server."));
        strcat(buf, flags);
    }

#ifdef HAVE_LIBIDN
    /* why, oh why DENIC had to make whois "user
    friendly"?
     * Do this only if the user did not use any flag.
     */
    if (streq(server, "whois.denic.de") && domcmp(query,
    ".de")
            && !strchr(query, ' ') && !*flags)
        sprintf(buf, "-T dn,ace -C US-ASCII %s", query);
    else
    /* here we have another registrar who could not make
    things simple
     * -C sets the language for both input and output
     */
    if (!isripe && streq(server, "whois.cat")
    && domcmp(query, ".cat")
            && !strchr(query, ' '))
        sprintf(buf, "-C US-ASCII ace %s", query);
    else
#endif
    if (!isripe && (streq(server, "whois.nic.mil") ||
            streq(server, "whois.nic.ad.jp")) &&
//          strncasecmp(query, "AS", 2) == 0 && isasciidigit
            (query[2]))
                strnicmp(query, "AS", 2) == 0
                && isasciidigit(query[2]))
        /* FIXME: /e is not applied to .JP ASN */
```

```c
        sprintf(buf, "AS %s", query + 2);   /* fix query for
        DDN */
    else if (!isripe && (streq(server, "whois.nic.ad.jp") ||
            streq(server, "whois.jprs.jp"))) {
        char *lang = getenv("LANG");   /* not a perfect
        check, but… */
        if (!lang || !strneq(lang, "ja", 2))
            sprintf(buf, "%s/e", query);   /* ask for english
            text */
        else
            strcat(buf, query);
    } else if (!isripe && streq(server, "whois.arin.net") &&
            (p = strrchr(query, '/'))) {
        strncat(buf, query, p - query);     /* strip CIDR */
    } else
        strcat(buf, query);
    return buf;
}

/* the first parameter contains the state of this simple
state machine:
 * HIDE_DISABLED: hidden text finished
 * HIDE_UNSTARTED: hidden text not seen yet
 * >= 0: currently hiding message hide_strings[*hiding]
 */
int hide_line(int *hiding, const char *const line)
{
    int i;

    if (*hiding == HIDE_DISABLED) {
        return 0;
    } else if (*hiding == HIDE_UNSTARTED) {  /* looking for
    smtng to hide */
        for (i = 0; hide_strings[i] != NULL; i += 2) {
            if (strneq(line, hide_strings[i], strlen(hide_
            strings[i]))) {
                *hiding = i;          /* start hiding */
                return 1;                /* and hide this line */
            }
        }
        return 0;                 /* don't hide this line */
    } else if (*hiding > HIDE_UNSTARTED) {   /* hiding
    something */
        if (*hide_strings[*hiding + 1] == '\0') { /*look for
        a blank line?*/
            if (*line == '\n' || *line == '\r' || *line ==
            '\0') {
```

```
                *hiding = HIDE_DISABLED;     /* stop hiding */
                return 0;                     /* but do not hide the
                                                 blank line */

          }
      } else {            /*look for a matching string*/
          if (strneq(line, hide_strings[*hiding + 1],
                   strlen(hide_strings[*hiding + 1]))) {
              *hiding = HIDE_DISABLED;         /* stop hiding */
              return 1;                        /* but hide the
                                                  last line */

          }

  }
  return 1;            /* we are hiding, so do it */
    } else
  return 0;
}
/* returns a string which should be freed by the caller, or NULL */
const char *do_query(const int sock, const char *query)
{
    char buf[2000], *p;
//    FILE *fi;
    int hide = hide_discl;
    char *referral_server = NULL;

//    fi = fdopen(sock, "r");
//    if (write(sock, query, strlen(query)) < 0)
        if (sock_write(sock, query, strlen(query)) < 0)
        err_sys("write");
/* Using shutdown used to break the buggy RIPE server. Would
   this work now?
    if (shutdown(sock, 1) < 0)
        err_sys("shutdown");
*/

//    while (fgets(buf, sizeof(buf), fi)) {
        while (sock_gets(buf, sizeof(buf), sock)) {
        /* 6bone-style referral:
         * % referto: whois -h whois.arin.net -p 43 as 1
         */
        if (!referral_server && strneq(buf, "% referto:", 10)) {
            char nh[256], np[16], nq[1024];

            if (sscanf(buf, REFERTO_FORMAT, nh, np, nq) == 3) {
                /* XXX we are ignoring the new query string */
                referral_server = malloc(300);
                sprintf(referral_server, "%s:%s", nh, np);
            }
        }
```

```c
        /* ARIN referrals:
         * ReferralServer: rwhois://rwhois.fuse.net:4321/
         * ReferralServer: whois://whois.ripe.net
         */
        if (!referral_server && strneq(buf, "ReferralServer:", 15)) {
            char *q;

            q = strstr(buf, "rwhois://");
            if ((q = strstr(buf, "rwhois://")))
                referral_server = strdup(q + 9);
            else if ((q = strstr(buf, "whois://")))
                referral_server = strdup(q + 8);
            if (referral_server) {
                if ((q = strchr(referral_server, '/'))
                        || (q = strchr(referral_server, '\n')))
                    *q = '\0';
            }
        }

        if (hide_line(&hide, buf))
            continue;

        for (p = buf; *p && *p != '\r' && *p != '\n'; p++);
        *p = '\0';
        fprintf(stdout, "%s\n", buf);
        }
//      if (ferror(fi))
//      err_sys("fgets");
//      fclose(fi);

    if (hide > HIDE_UNSTARTED)
        err_quit(_("Catastrophic error: disclaimer text has
                    been changed.\n"
                "Please upgrade this program.\n"));

    return referral_server;
}

const char *query_crsnic(const int sock, const char *query)
{
    char *temp, buf[2000], *ret = NULL;
//    FILE *fi;
    int hide = hide_discl;
    int state = 0;

    temp = malloc(strlen(query) + 1 + 2 + 1);
    *temp = '=';
```

```
      strcpy(temp + 1, query);
      strcat(temp, "\r\n");

//    fi = fdopen(sock, "r");
//    if (write(sock, temp, strlen(temp)) < 0)
       if (sock_write(sock, temp, strlen(temp)) < 0)
       err_sys("write");
//    while (fgets(buf, sizeof(buf), fi)) {
      while (sock_gets(buf, sizeof(buf), sock)) {
      /* If there are multiple matches only the server of
         the first record
         is queried */
      if (state == 0 && strneq(buf, "   Domain Name:", 15))
          state = 1;
      if (state == 1 && strneq(buf, "   Whois Server:", 16)) {
          char *p, *q;

          for (p = buf; *p != ':'; p++);  /* skip until colon */
          for (p++; *p == ' '; p++);           /* skip colon and
                                                  spaces */
          ret = malloc(strlen(p) + 1);
          for (q = ret; *p != '\n' && *p != '\r' && *p != '
              '; *q++ = *p++)
            ; /*copy data*/
          *q = '\0';
          state = 2;
      }
      /* the output must not be hidden or no data will
         be shown for host records and not-existing
         domains */
      if (!hide_line(&hide, buf))
          fputs(buf, stdout);
      }
//     if (ferror(fi))
//      err_sys("fgets");

      free(temp);
      return ret;
}

const char *query_pir(const int sock, const char *query)
{
      char *temp, buf[2000], *ret = NULL;
      FILE *fi;
      int hide = hide_discl;
      int state = 0;
```

```
        temp = malloc(strlen(query) + 5 + 2 + 1);
        strcpy(temp, "FULL ");
        strcat(temp, query);
        strcat(temp, "\r\n");

        fi = fdopen(sock, "r");
//      if (write(sock, temp, strlen(temp)) < 0)
        if (sock_write(sock, temp, strlen(temp))
            < 0)
        err_sys("write");

//      while (fgets(buf, sizeof(buf), fi)) {
        while (sock_gets(buf, sizeof(buf), sock)) {
        /* If there are multiple matches only the server of
           the first record
           is queried */
        if (state == 0 &&
                strneq(buf, "Registrant Name:SEE SPONSORING
                REGISTRAR", 40))
            state = 1;
        if (state == 1 &&
                strneq(buf, "Registrant Street1:Whois
                            Server:", 32)) {
            char *p, *q;

            for (p = buf; *p != ':'; p++);  /* skip until colon */
            for (p++; *p != ':'; p++);           /* skip until
                                                    2nd colon */
            for (p++; *p == ' '; p++);       /* skip colon
                                                and spaces */
            ret = malloc(strlen(p) + 1);
            for (q = ret; *p != '\n' && *p != '\r'; *q++ =
                                                *p++); /*copy
                                                data*/
            *q = '\0';
            state = 2;
        }
        if (!hide_line(&hide, buf))
            fputs(buf, stdout);
    }
//      if (ferror(fi))
//       err_sys("fgets");

    free(temp);
    return ret;
}
```

```c
int openconn(const char *server, const char *port)
{
        int fd = -1;
#ifdef HAVE_GETADDRINFO
        int err;
        struct addrinfo hints, *res, *ai;
#else
        struct hostent *hostinfo;
        struct servent *servinfo;
        struct sockaddr_in saddr;
#endif

//      alarm(60);
#ifdef HAVE_GETADDRINFO
        memset(&hints, 0, sizeof(struct addrinfo));
        hints.ai_family = AF_UNSPEC;
        hints.ai_socktype = SOCK_STREAM;
        hints.ai_flags = AI_IDN;

        if ((err = getaddrinfo(server, port ? port : "nic-
name", &hints, &res)) != 0)
            err_quit("getaddrinfo(%s): %s", server, gai_
            strerror(err));
        for (ai = res; ai; ai = ai->ai_next) {
            if ((fd = socket(ai->ai_family, ai->ai_socktype,
            ai->ai_protocol)) < 0)
            continue;          /* ignore */
            if (connect(fd, (struct sockaddr *)ai->ai_addr, ai-
                >ai_addrlen) == 0)
            break;                 /* success */
//          close(fd);
            closesocket(fd);
        }
        freeaddrinfo(res);

        if (!ai)
            err_sys("connect");
#else
        if ((hostinfo = gethostbyname(server)) == NULL)
            err_quit(_("Host %s not found."), server);
        if ((fd = socket(PF_INET, SOCK_STREAM, IPPROTO_IP)) < 0)
            err_sys("socket");
        memset(&saddr, 0, sizeof(saddr));
        saddr.sin_addr = *(struct in_addr *) hostinfo->h_addr;
        saddr.sin_family = AF_INET;
        if (!port) {
            saddr.sin_port = htons(43);
```

```
        } else if ((saddr.sin_port = htons(atoi(port))) == 0) {
            if ((servinfo = getservbyname(port, "tcp")) == NULL)
                err_quit(_("%s/tcp: unknown service"), port);
            saddr.sin_port = servinfo->s_port;
        }
        if (connect(fd, (struct sockaddr *)&saddr,
            sizeof(saddr)) < 0)
            err_sys("connect");
#endif
        /*
         * Now we are connected and the query is supposed to
           complete quickly.
         * This will help people who run whois … | less
         */
//      alarm(0);

        return fd;
}

void alarm_handler(int signum)
{
//      close(sockfd);
        err_quit(_("Timeout."));
}

void sighandler(int signum)
{
//      close(sockfd);
        err_quit(_("Interrupted by signal %d..."), signum);
}

/* check if dom ends with tld */
int domcmp(const char *dom, const char *tld)
{
        const char *p, *q;
        for (p = dom; *p; p++); p--;  /* move to the last char */
        for (q = tld; *q; q++); q--;
        while (p >= dom && q >= tld && tolower(*p) == *q) {
                /* compare backwards */
            if (q == tld)                 /* start of the second
                                             word? */
                return 1;
            p--; q--;
        }
        return 0;
}
```

```c
char *normalize_domain(const char *dom)
{
      char *p, *ret;
      char *domain_start = NULL;
      ret = strdup(dom);
      for (p = ret; *p; p++); p--;   /* move to the last char */
      /* eat trailing dots and blanks */
      for (; *p == '.' || *p == ' ' || *p == '\t' || p == ret; p--)
         *p = '\0';

#ifdef HAVE_LIBIDN
      /* find the start of the last word if there are spaces
         in the query */
      for (p = ret; *p; p++)
         if (*p == ' ')
            domain_start = p + 1;

      if (domain_start) {
         char *q, *r;
         int prefix_len;

         if (idna_to_ascii_lz(domain_start, &q, 0) != IDNA_
            SUCCESS)
            return ret;

         /* reassemble the original query in a new buffer */
         prefix_len = domain_start - ret;
         r = malloc(prefix_len + strlen(q) + 1);
         strncpy(r, ret, prefix_len);
         r[prefix_len] = '\0';
         strcat(r, q);

         free(q);
         free(ret);
         return r;
      } else {
         char *q;

         if (idna_to_ascii_lz(ret, &q, 0) != IDNA_SUCCESS)
            return ret;

         free(ret);
         return q;
      }
#else
      return ret;
#endif
}
```

```c
/* server and port have to be freed by the caller */
void split_server_port(const char *const input,
        const char **server, const char **port) {
    char *p;
    if (*input == '[' && (p = strchr(input, ']'))) {   /* IPv6 */
        char *s;
        int len = p - input - 1;

        *server = s = malloc(len + 1);
        memcpy(s, input + 1, len);
        *(s + len) = '\0';

        p = strchr(p, ':');
        if (p && *(p + 1) != '\0')
            *port = strdup(p + 1);        /* IPv6 + port */
    } else if ((p = strchr(input, ':')) && /* IPv6, no port */
            strchr(p + 1, ':')) {          /*    and no brackets */
        *server = strdup(input);
    } else if ((p = strchr(input, ':'))) {   /* IPv4 + port */
        char *s;
        int len = p - input;

        *server = s = malloc(len + 1);
        memcpy(s, input, len);
        *(s + len) = '\0';

        p++;
        if (*p != '\0')
            *port = strdup(p);
    } else {                                 /* IPv4, no port */
        *server = strdup(input);
    }

    /* change the server name to lower case */
    for (p = (char *) *server; *p && *p != '\0'; p++)
        *p = tolower(*p);
}

char *convert_6to4(const char *s)
{
    char *new = malloc(sizeof("255.255.255.255"));
    unsigned int a, b;

    if (sscanf(s, "2002:%x:%x:", &a, &b) != 2)
        return (char *) "0.0.0.0";

    sprintf(new, "%d.%d.%d.%d", a >> 8, a & 0xff, b >> 8, b & 0xff);
    return new;
}
```

```c
char *convert_teredo(const char *s)
{
    char *new = malloc(sizeof("255.255.255.255"));
    unsigned int a, b;

    if (sscanf(s, "2001:%*[^:]:%*[^:]:%*[^:]:%*[^:]:%*[^:]:%
        x:%x", &a, &b) != 2)
        return (char *) "0.0.0.0";
    a ^= 0xffff;
    b ^= 0xffff;
    sprintf(new, "%d.%d.%d.%d", a >> 8, a & 0xff, b >> 8, b & 0xff);
    return new;
}

unsigned long myinet_aton(const char *s)
{
    unsigned long a, b, c, d;
    int elements;
    char junk;

    if (!s)
        return 0;
    elements = sscanf(s, "%lu.%lu.%lu.%lu%c", &a, &b, &c, &d, &junk);
    if (!(elements == 4 || (elements == 5 && junk == '/')))
        return 0;
    if (a > 255 || b > 255 || c > 255 || d > 255)
        return 0;
    return (a << 24) + (b << 16) + (c << 8) + d;
}

unsigned long asn32_to_long(const char *s)
{
    unsigned long a, b;
    char junk;

    if (!s)
        return 0;
    if (sscanf(s, "%lu.%lu%c", &a, &b, &junk) != 2)
        return 0;
    if (a > 65535 || b > 65535)
        return 0;
    return (a << 16) + b;
}

int isasciidigit(const char c) {
    return (c >= '0' && c <= '9') ? 1 : 0;
}
```

```c
/* http://www.ripe.net/ripe/docs/databaseref-manual.html */

void usage(void)
{
    fprintf(stderr, _(
"Usage: whois [OPTION]... OBJECT...\n\n"
"...l                      one level less specific lookup
                          [RPSL only]\n"
"...L                      find all Less specific matches\n"
"...m                      find first level more specific
                          matches\n"
"...M                      find all More specific matches\n"
"...c                      find the smallest match containing
                          a mnt-irt attribute\n"
"...x                      exact match [RPSL only]\n"
"...d                      return DNS reverse delegation
                          objects too [RPSL only]\n"
"...i ATTR[,ATTR]...       do an inverse lookup for specified
                          ATTRibutes\n"
"...T TYPE[,TYPE]...       only look for objects of TYPE\n"
"...K                      only primary keys are returned
                          [RPSL only]\n"
"...r                      turn off recursive lookups for
                          contact information\n"
"...R                      force to show local copy of the
                          domain object even\n"
"                         if it contains referral\n"
"...a                      search all databases\n"
"...s SOURCE[,SOURCE]...   search the database from SOURCE\n"
"...g SOURCE:FIRST...LAST  find updates from SOURCE from
                          serial FIRST to LAST\n"
"...t TYPE                 request template for object of
                          TYPE ('all' for a list)\n"
"...v TYPE                 request verbose template for
                          object of TYPE\n"
"...q [version|sources|types]  query specified server info
[RPSL only]\n"
"...F                      fast raw output (implies ...r)\n"
"...h HOST                 connect to server HOST\n"
"...p PORT                 connect to PORT\n"
"...H                      hide legal disclaimers\n"
"      ......verbose       explain what is being done\n"
"      ......help          display this help and exit\n"
"      ......version       output version information and exit\n"
));
    exit(0);
}
```

```c
/* Error routines */
void err_sys(const char *fmt, ...)
{
    va_list ap;
    va_start(ap, fmt);
    vfprintf(stderr, fmt, ap);
    fprintf(stderr, ": %s\n", strerror(errno));
    va_end(ap);
    exit(2);
}
void err_quit(const char *fmt, ...)
{

    va_list ap;
    va_start(ap, fmt);
    vfprintf(stderr, fmt, ap);
    fputs("\n", stderr);
    va_end(ap);
    exit(2);
}
```

A.4   JAVA WHOIS BY ERIK THAUVIN

```java
/*
 * Package: GeekTools Whois Java Client 1.0.2
 * File: Whois.java (Java source file)
 * Author: Erik C. Thauvin <erik@skytouch.com>
 * Comments: Part of the GeekTools Whois Java Client package.
 *
 * See the README.TXT file for more information.
 *
 * Copyright (C) 2000-2001 SkyTouch Communications. All
   Rights Reserved.
 * This program is distributed under the terms of the GNU General
 * Public License as published by the Free Software Foundation.
 * See the COPYING.TXT file for more information.
 *
 * $Id$
 */
import java.io.*;
import java.net.Socket;
import java.util.Properties;

/**
 * Class Whois
 *
```

```java
* @author Erik C. Thauvin (erik@skytouch.com)
* @version 1.0.2
*/
public class Whois
{
        /**
         * Method main
         *
         * The Truth is Out There!
         *
         * @param args Command line arguments
         */
        public static void main(String[] args)
        {
                // Display usage if there are no command line
                   arguments
                if (args.length < 1)
                {
                        System.out.println("Usage: java Whois
                        query[@&lt;whois.server&gt;]");

                         return;
                }
                // Default server is whois.geektools.com
                String server = "whois.geektools.com";

                // Default server port is 43
                int port = 43;

                // Load the properties file.
                try
                {
                        final FileInputStream in = new
                        FileInputStream("Whois.properties");
                        final Properties app = new Properties();

                        app.load(in);

                        // Get the server property
                        server = (app.getProperty("server",
                                server));

                        // Get the port property
                        try
                        {
                                port = Integer.parseInt(app.
                                        getProperty("port"));
```

```
            }
            catch (NumberFormatException e)
            {
                    // Do nothing!
            }
            in.close();
    }
    catch (FileNotFoundException e)
    {
            // Do nothing!
    }
    catch (IOException e)
    {
            System.err.println("Whois: an error
            occurred while loading the prop-
            erties file: " + e);
    }

    // Build the whois query using command line
       arguments
    final StringBuffer buff = new
    StringBuffer(args[0]);

    for (int i = 1; i < args.length; i++)
    {
            buff.append(" " + args[i]);
    }

    // Convert string buffer to string
    String query = buff.toString();
    // The whois server can be specified after
       "@"
    // e.g.: query@whois.networksolutions.com
    final int at = query.lastIndexOf("@");
    final int len = query.length();

    if ((at != -1))
    {
            // Remove the @ if last character in
               query
            // e.g.: john@doe.com@
            if (at == (len - 1))
            {
                query = query.substring(0, len - 1);
            }
            else
            {
```

```
                    // The whois server is specified
                       after "@"
                 server = query.substring(at + 1, len);
                 // The whois query is specified
                    before "@"
                 query = query.substring(0, at);
             }
         }

         try
         {
                 // Establish connection to whois
                    server & port
                 final Socket connection = new
                 Socket(server, port);
                 final PrintStream out =
                   new PrintStream(connection.getOut-
                   putStream());
                 final BufferedReader in = new
                 BufferedReader(
                   new InputStreamReader(connection.
                   getInputStream()));
                 String line = "";
                 // Send the whois query
                 out.println(query);
                 // Display the whois server's
                    address & port
                 System.out.println("[" + server + ":"
                 + port + "]");

                 // Read/display the query's result
                 while ((line = in.readLine()) != null)
                 {
                   System.out.println(line);
                 }
         }
         catch (java.net.UnknownHostException e)
         {
                 // Unknown whois server
                 System.err.println("Whois: unknown
                 host: " + server);

                 return;
         }
         catch (IOException e)
         {
                 // Could not connect to whois server
```

```
                              System.err.println("Whois: " + e);
                              return;
                          }
              }
```

A.5   LISP WHOIS BY METIN EVRIM ULU

```
;; Core Server: Web Application Server

;; Copyright (C) 2006-2008 Metin Evrim Ulu, Aycan iRiCAN

;; This program is free software: you can redistribute it
   and/or modify it under the terms of the GNU General Public
   License as published by the Free Software Foundation,
   either version 3 of the License, or (at your option) any
   later version.

;; This program is distributed in the hope that it will be
   useful, but WITHOUT ANY WARRANTY; without even the implied
   warranty of MERCHANTABILITY or FITNESS FOR A PARTICULAR
   PURPOSE. See the GNU General Public License for more details.

;; You should have received a copy of the GNU General Public
   License along with this program. If not, see <http://www.
   gnu.org/licenses/>.

(in-package :core-server)

;;+---------------------------------------------------------
;;| Whois Service
;;+---------------------------------------------------------
;;
;; This file implements whois service
;;
;;---------------------------------------------------------
;; Whois Service Specific Variables
;;---------------------------------------------------------
(defparameter *default-whois-port* 43
  "Remote whois server port")

(defparameter *whois-servers*
  '(("com" . "whois.internic.net")
    ("net" . "whois.internic.net")
    ("org" . "whois.internic.net")
    ("edu" . "whois.internic.net")
    ("uk.com" . "whois.uk.com")
```

```
    ("eu.org" . "whois.eu.org")
    ("ac" . "whois.nic.ac")
    ("al" . "whois.ripe.net")
    ("am" . "whois.amnic.net")
    ("am" . "whois.amnic.net")
    ("as" . "whois.nic.as")
    ("at" . "whois.nic.at")
    ("au" . "whois.aunic.net")
    ("az" . "whois.ripe.net")
    ("ba" . "whois.ripe.net")
    ("be" . "whois.dns.be")
    ("bg" . "whois.ripe.net")
;; ("bm" . "rwhois.ibl.bm:4321")
    ("biz" . "whois.biz")
    ("br" . "whois.nic.br")
    ("by" . "whois.ripe.net")
    ("ca" . "whois.cira.ca")
    ("cc" . "whois.nic.cc")
    ("ch" . "whois.nic.ch")
    ("cl" . "whois.nic.cl")
    ("edu.cn" . "whois.edu.cn")
    ("cn" . "whois.cnnic.cn")
    ("cx" . "whois.nic.cx")
    ("cy" . "whois.ripe.net")
    ("cz" . "whois.ripe.net")
    ("de" . "whois.ripe.net")
    ("dk" . "whois.ripe.net")
    ("dz" . "whois.ripe.net")
    ("ee" . "whois.ripe.net")
    ("eg" . "whois.ripe.net")
    ("es" . "whois.ripe.net")
    ("fi" . "whois.ripe.net")
    ("fo" . "whois.ripe.net")
    ("fr" . "whois.nic.fr")
    ("gov" . "whois.nic.gov")
    ("gr" . "whois.ripe.net")
    ("gs" . "whois.adamsnames.tc")
    ("hk" . "whois.hknic.net.hk")
    ("hm" . "webhost1.capital.hm")
    ("hr" . "whois.ripe.net")
    ("hu" . "whois.ripe.net")
    ("ie" . "whois.domainregistry.ie")
    ("il" . "whois.ripe.net")
    ("in" . "whois.ncst.ernet.in")
    ("info" . "whois.afilias.net")
    ("int" . "whois.isi.edu")
    ("is" . "whois.isnet.is")
```

```
("it"  .  "whois.nic.it")
("jp"  .  "whois.nic.ad.jp")
("kr"  .  "whois.krnic.net")
("kz"  .  "whois.domain.kz")
("li"  .  "whois.nic.li")
("lk"  .  "whois.nic.lk")
("lt"  .  "whois.ripe.net")
("lu"  .  "whois.ripe.net")
("lv"  .  "whois.ripe.net")
("ma"  .  "whois.ripe.net")
("md"  .  "whois.ripe.net")
("mil" .  "whois.nic.mil")
("mk"  .  "whois.ripe.net")
("mm"  .  "whois.nic.mm")
("mobi" . "whois.dotmobiregistry.net")
("ms"  .  "whois.adamsnames.tc")
("mt"  .  "whois.ripe.net")
("mx"  .  "whois.nic.mx")
("my"  .  "whois.mynic.net")
("nl"  .  "whois.domain-registry.nl")
("no"  .  "whois.norid.no")
("nu"  .  "whois.nic.nu")
("pe"  .  "whois.rcp.net.pe")
("pk"  .  "whois.pknic.net.pk")
("pl"  .  "whois.ripe.net")
("pt"  .  "whois.dns.pt")
("ro"  .  "whois.ripe.net")
("ru"  .  "whois.ripn.net")
("se"  .  "whois.nic-se.se")
("sg"  .  "whois.nic.net.sg")
("sh"  .  "whois.nic.sh")
("si"  .  "whois.ripe.net")
("sk"  .  "whois.ripe.net")
("sm"  .  "whois.ripe.net")
("st"  .  "whois.nic.st")
("su"  .  "whois.ripe.net")
("tc"  .  "whois.adamsnames.tc")
("tf"  .  "whois.adamsnames.tc")
("th"  .  "whois.thnic.net")
("tj"  .  "whois.nic.tj")
("tm"  .  "whois.nic.tm")
("tn"  .  "whois.ripe.net")
("to"  .  "whois.tonic.to")
("tr"  .  "whois.metu.edu.tr")
("tw"  .  "whois.twnic.net")
("tv"  .  "tvwhois.verisign-grs.com")
("ua"  .  "whois.ripe.net")
```

```
      ("ac.uk" . "whois.ja.net")
      ("gov.uk" . "whois.ja.net")
      ("uk" . "whois.nic.uk")
      ("us" . "whois.isi.edu")
      ("va" . "whois.ripe.net")
      ("vg" . "whois.adamsnames.tc")
      ("yu" . "whois.ripe.net")
      ("gb.com" . "whois.nomination.net")
      ("gb.net" . "whois.nomination.net")
      ("za" . "whois.co.za"))
   "Addresses of whois servers around around the world")

;; com, net, org, edu -> type1
;; info -> type2
;; tv -> type1
;; mobi -> type2
;; biz -> type3
(defun render-type1 (fqdn)
  (format nil "=~a~c~c" fqdn #\return #\linefeed))

(defun render-type2 (fqdn)
  (format nil "~a~c~c" fqdn #\return #\linefeed))

(defun render-type3 (fqdn)
  (format nil "~a~c~c" fqdn #\return #\linefeed))

(defun parser-type1 (text)
  (search "No match for" text))

(defun parser-type2 (text)
  (search "NOT FOUND" text))

(defun parser-type3 (text)
  (search "Not found:" text))

(defparameter +whois-map+
  (list (cons '("com" "net" "org" "edu" "tv")
          '(render-type1 . parser-type1))
        (cons '("info" "mobi")
          '(render-type2 . parser-type2))
        (cons '("biz")
          '(render-type3 . parser-type3))))

(defun whois-map-lookup (dpart)
  (reduce (lambda (i a) (if (null i) a i))
    (mapcar (lambda (l)
        (if (member dpart (car l) :test #'string=) (cdr l)))
        +whois-map+)))
```

```lisp
(defun root-domain-part (fqdn)
  (awhen (position #\. fqdn :from-end t)
    (subseq fqdn (1+ it))))

(defun whois-server (fqdn &optional (server-list *whois-
servers*))
  "Returns whois server associated to 'fqdn'"
  (flet ((resolve (addr)
           (sb-bsd-sockets:host-ent-address (sb-bsd-
             sockets:get-host-by-name addr))))
    (awhen (root-domain-part fqdn)
      (let ((s (assoc it server-list :test #'equal)))
        (aif (and s (cdr s) (position #\: (cdr s)))
          (values (resolve (subseq (cdr s) 0 it))
                  (or (parse-integer (subseq (cdr s) (1+ it))
                        :junk-allowed t)
                      *default-whois-port*)
                  (subseq (cdr s) 0 it))
          (values (resolve (cdr s))
                  *default-whois-port*
                  (cdr s)))))))

;; look for this top level domains: com info net org tv mobi biz
;; domain-availablep :: string -> bool
(defun domain-availablep (fqdn)
  "Returns t if domain is available"
  (let ((res (whois fqdn)))
    (if (funcall (car res) (cdr res)) t nil)))

(defun whois (fqdn)
  "Executes whois query on 'fqdn'"
  (handler-bind ((error (lambda (condition)
                          (restart-case (swank::swank-debug-
ger-hook condition nil)
                          (ignore-error ()
                          :report "ignore error"
                          (return-from whois nil))))))
    (multiple-value-bind (server port) (whois-server fqdn)
      (let ((s (make-instance 'sb-bsd-sockets:inet-socket
          :type :stream :protocol 6))
            (out "")
            (whois-map (whois-map-lookup (root-domain-part
            fqdn))))
        (sb-bsd-sockets:socket-connect s server port)
        (with-open-stream (s (sb-bsd-sockets:socket-make-
          stream s :input t :output t :buffering :none
                                   :external-format :iso-8859-9
```

```
                                  :element-type 'character))
(format s (funcall (car whois-map) fqdn))
(force-output s)
;; no need to read all output, just search every line
(do ((line (read-line s nil :eof)
         (read-line s nil :eof)))
((eq line :eof))
(setf out (concatenate 'string out (format nil
 "~A~%" line))))
(format t "~A" out)
(cons (cdr whois-map) out))))))
```

APPENDIX B: WHOIS SERVERS

B.1 TOP-LEVEL INTERNET ORGANIZATIONAL WHOIS SERVERS

whois.internic.net   ICANN gTLD WHOIS (run by Verisign)
whois.iana.net   IANA
whois.crsnic.net   Network Solutions, Inc. for Shared Registration System

B.2 RIR WHOIS SERVERS

ARIN, North America: whois.arin.net
APNIC, Asia-Pacific: whois.apnic.net
AfriNIC, Africa: whois.afrinic.net
RIPE NCC, Europe: whois.ripe.net
LACNIC, Latin America-Caribbean: whois.lacnic.net

B.3 ADDITIONAL REGIONAL REGISTRAR WHOIS SERVERS

China Telecom Corporation Limited (CHINANET)
Indian Registry for Internet Names and Numbers (IRINN) 192.168.1.88
Japan Network Information Center (JPNIC) whois.nic.ad.jp, whois.jprs.jp, whois.jp
Korea Network Information Center (KRNIC) whois.kisa.or.kr, whois.krnic.net
Taiwan Network Information Center (TWNIC) whois.twnic.net.tw
Nippon Telegraph and Telephone (NTTCOM) rr.ntt.net

WHOIS Running the Internet: Protocol, Policy, and Privacy, First Edition. Garth O. Bruen.
© 2016 John Wiley & Sons, Inc. Published 2016 by John Wiley & Sons, Inc.

B.4 INTERNET ROUTING REGISTRIES (IRR) WHOIS SERVERS

Current lists of mirrored databases can be obtained from irr.net.[1]

ALTDB: whois.altdb.net	ALTDB free registry, mirrors: RADB, CW, RIPE, ANS, CANET (whois.canet.ca)
AOLTW: whois.aoltw.net	AOLTW General Internet Community, mirrors: RADB
BCNET: whois.bc.net	BCNET
BELL whois.in.bell.ca	Bell and Customer's objects, mirrors: AOLTW, ARIN, GT, LEVEL3, RADB, NTTCOM, RISQ, SAVVIS
BBOI: irr.bboi.net	BBOI Customer's objects, mirrors: ALTDB, ARIN, HOST, LEVEL3, NTTCOM, RADB, SAVVIS, WVGDB, WVFIBER
CANARIE: whois.canarie.ca	CANARIE Network, mirrors: BCNET, OTTIX, RISQ
D: whois.depository.net	Depository, customers
DERU: whois.deru.net	Deru communications and customers, mirrors: ANS, RADB, VERIO, DODNIC
DIGITALREALM: rr.digitalrealm.net	DIGITALREALM, mirrors: RADB, RIPE, ARIN, LEVEL3, CW, BELL, ANS
EASYNET: whois.noc. easynet.net	Easynet and customers, mirrors: RIPE, RADB
EBIT: whois.ebit.ca	eBit networks customer data
EPOCH: whois.epoch.net	EPOCH general Internet community
GT: rr.gt.ca	GT group telecom owned objects and objects of routed customers, mirrors: RADB, ANS, CW, VERIO, BELL, LEVEL3, SPRINT
GW: whois.gw.net	GW peers, mirrors: PANIX, RADB, RIPE
HOST: rr.host.net	Host.net customers and general Internet community, mirrors: ALTDB, AOLTW, APNIC, ARIN, DoDNIC, EPOCH, LEVEL3, PANIX, RADB, REACH, RIPE, SAVVIS, SPRINT, VERIO, WCGDB
InternetMCI whois.mci.net	
JPIRR: jpirr.nic.ad.jp	JPIRR IRR data, mirrors: APNIC, RADB, RIPE
LEVEL3: rr.Level3.net	LEVEL3, mirrors: ALLTEL, ALTDB, ANS, AOLTW APIRR APNIC, ARRBOR, ARCSTAR, AREA151, ARIN, AUNIC, BCONNEX, BELL, CANET, CARYNET, CRC, CSAS, CW, DAKNET, DERU, DoDNIC, DROW, EASYNET, EPOCH, FASTVIBE, FGC, GT, GTS, GW, HS, I2, IIJ, JPNI,C KOREN, KRNIC, NESTEGG, OPENFACE, OTTIX, PANIX, RADB, REACH, RGNET, RIPE, RISQ, SAKURA, SINET, SOUNDINTERNET, SPRINT, TELSTRA, TWNIC, VERIO, WL2K
MTO: rr.mtotelecom.com	MTO customers, mirrors: ARIN, RADB, OPENFACE, RISQ
NESTEGG: whois.nestegg. net	Nestegg specific, mirrors: ALTDB, APNIC, ARIN, BELL, GT, BBOI, JPIRR, LEVEL3, RADB, RGNET, RIPE, SAVVIS
NTTCOM: rr.ntt.net	NTTCOM
OPENFACE: whois. openface.ca	Openface customers
OttIX: whois.ottix.net	OttIX and member routing policies, mirrors: ALTDB, LEVEL3, RADB, DODNIC, ARCSTAR, SINET CW, TELSTRA

---

[1] http://www.irr.net/docs/list.html

PANIX: rrdb.access.net	PANIX community
PEGASUS: whois.abranet. org.br	ABRANET members and general Internet community, mirrors: ALTDB, ARIN, HOST, LEVEL3, NTTCOM, OTTIX, RADB, SAVVIS, RIPE, WVFIBER
RADB: whois.radb.net	RADB general Internet community, mirrors: RIPE, SAVVIS, BELL, APNIC, NTTCOM, ARCSTAR, ALTDB, PANIX, EPOCH, DERU, RISQ, NESTEGG, GW, LEVEL3, REACH, AOLTW, OPENF, ARIN, GT, OTTIX, EASYNET, JPIRR, DIGITALREALM, MTO, BCNET, HOST, D, EICAT, EBIT, RGNET, ROGERS, PEGASUS, BBOI
REACH: rr.net.reach.com	REACH route objects
RG: whois.rg.net	RGnet routing plus DevCon domain whois
RISQ: rr.risq.net	RISQ customers, mirrors: RADB, BELL, CW
ROGERS: whois. rogerstelecom.net	Rogers IP network
SAVVIS: rr.savvis.net	SAVVIS customer/commercial, mirrors: RIPE, ARIN, APNIC, RADB, BELL, EPOCH, ALTDB, ARCSTAR, GT, LEVEL3, VERIO
SCW: whois.scw.net.br	SCW telecom customers and general, mirrors: ALTDB, AOLTW, APNIC, ARIN, BBOI, BCNET, BELL, D, DERU, DIGITALREALM, EASYNET, EBIT, EPOCH, GT, GW, HOST, JPIRR, LEVEL3, MTO, NESTEGG, NTTCOM, OPENFACE, OTTIX, PANIX, PEGASUS, RADB, REACH, RETINA, RGNET, RIPE, RISQ, ROGERS, SAVVIS

B.5 gTLD REGISTRY WHOIS SERVERS

.arpa	whois.iana.org
.aero	whois.information.aero, whois.aero
.asia	whois.nic.asia
.biz	whois.nic.biz, whois.neulevel.biz
.cat	whois.cat
.com	whois.verisign-grs.com, whois.crsnic.net (use specific registrar)
.coop	whois.nic.coop
.edu	whois.educause.net
.gov	whois.nic.gov
.int	whois.iana.org, whois.isi.edu
.info	whois.afilias.info, whois.afilias.net
.jobs	jobswhois.verisign-grs.com
.mobi	whois.dotmobiregistry.net
.museum	whois.museum
.name	whois.nic.name
.net	whois.verisign-grs.com, whois.crsnic.net (use specific registrar)
.org	whois.publicinterestregistry.net, whois.pir.org (subdomain: eu.org at whois.eu.org)
.post	whois.dotpostregistry.net
.pro	whois.registrypro.pro, whois.registry.pro
.tel	whois.nic.tel
.travel	whois.nic.travel
.xxx	whois.nic.xxx

B.6 .PRO SUBDOMAINS

All use whois.registry.pro

aaa.pro, aca.pro, acct.pro, arc.pro, avocat.pro, bar.pro, bus.pro, cfp.pro, chi.pro, chiro.pro, cpa.pro, dds.pro, den.pro, dent.pro, ed.pro, eng.pro, jur.pro, law.pro, med.pro, min.pro, ntr.pro, nur.pro, nurse.pro, opt.pro, pa.pro, pha.pro, pharma.pro, pod.pro, pr.pro, prof.pro, prx.pro, psy.pro, pt.pro, recht.pro, rel.pro, teach.pro, and vet.pro

B.7 NEW gTLD WHOIS SERVERS LISTED IN 2013

The following use whois.donuts.co

.bike, .camera, .clothing, .construction, .contractors, .diamonds, .directory, .enterprise, .equipment, .estate, .gallery, .graphics, .holdings, .kitchen, .land, .lighting, .photography, .plumbing, .singles, .technology, .tips, .today, .ventures

The following use whois.uniregistry.net

.sexy, .tattoo

```
.menu     whois.nic.menu
.ruhr     whois.nic.ruhr
```

B.8 ccTLD WHOIS SERVERS

The two-letter country-code TLDs are derived from the ISO 3166 table[2] and are completely inconsistent in their format and even existence. Many ccTLDs have no WHOIS server or only allow lookups through a web page. Servers marked with a "!" have had problems reported or have been offline for extended periods. Several ccTLDs have subdomain registrations, listed beside with additional servers noted as appropriate.

.ac	whois.nic.ac		
.ad	whois.nic.ad	!	
.ae	whois.nic.ae, whois.uaenic.ae	!	
.af	whois.nic.af	!	
.ag	whois.nic.ag		
.ai	whois.ainic.ai, whois.offshore.ai	!	
.al	http://www.inima.al/Domains.html		
.am	whois.amnic.net, whois.nic.am		
.an	http://www.una.net/an_domreg/	!	
.ao	http://www.dns.ao		
.aq	None		
.ar	http://www.nic.ar/consultas/consdom.html		
.as	whois.nic.as		
.at	whois.nic.at	(Subdomains: co.at, or.at)	
.au	whois.aunic.net, whois.ausregistry.net.au	(Subdomains: asn.au, com.au, id.au, net.au, org.au)	
.aw	www.setarnet.aw		

[2] http://www.iso.org/iso/iso-3166-1_decoding_table

.az	www.whois.az, www.nic.az	
.ba	http://www.nic.ba/stream/whois/	
.bb	http://domains.org.bb/regsearch/	
.bd	http://www.bttb.net/	
.be	whois.dns.be	
.bf	http://www.onatel.bf/	
.bg	whois.register.bg	
.bh	http://www.inet.com.bh/	
.bi	whois.nic.bi	
.bj	whois.nic.bj	
.bm	rwhois.ibl.bm:4321, rwhois.bermudanic. bm:4321	
.bn	http://www.brunet.bn	
.bo	http://www.nic.bo/	
.br	whois.nic.br	(Subdomains: adm.br, adv.br, am.br, arq.br, art.br, bio.br, cng.br, cnt.br, com.br, ecn. br, eng.br, esp.br, etc.br, eti.br, fm.br, fot. br, fst.br, g12.br, gov.br, ind.br, inf.br, jor. br, lel.br, med.br, mil.br, net.br, nom.br, ntr.br, odo.br, org.br, ppg.br, pro.br, psc. br, psi.br, rec.br, slg.br, tmp.br, tur.br, tv. br, vet.br, zlg.br)
.bs	http://www.nic.bs/cgi-bin/search.pl	
.bt	whois.netnames.net	
.bv	whois.ripe.net	
.bw	http://www.botsnet.bw btc.bw/	
.by	http://www.tld.by/indexeng.html	
.bz	whois.belizenic.bz	
.ca	whois.cira.ca	(Subdomains: mb.ca, nb.ca, nf.ca, nl.ca, ns. ca, nt.ca, nu.ca, on.ca, pe.ca, qc.ca, sk.ca, yk.ca, ab.ca, bc.ca)
.cc	whois.nic.cc	
.cd	whois.nic.cd	
.cf	http://www.nic.cf/whois.php3	
.cg	http://www.nic.cg/cgi-bin/whoiscg.pl	
.ch	whois.nic.ch	
.ci	whois.nic.ci	!
.ck	whois.nic.ck	
.cl	whois.nic.cl	
.cm	http://info.intelcam.cm/	
.cn	whois.cnnic.cn, whois.cnnic.net.cn	(Subdomains: ah.cn, bj.cn, com.cn, cq.cn, fj.cn, gd.cn, gs.cn, gx.cn, gz.cn, ha.cn, hb.cn, he.cn, hi.cn, hk.cn, hl.cn, hn.cn, jl.cn, js.cn, jx.cn, ln.cn, mo.cn, net.cn, nm.cn, nx.cn, org.cn, qh.cn, sc.cn, sd.cn, sh.cn, sn.cn, sx.cn, tj.cn, tw.cn, xj.cn)
.co	https://www.nic.co/	
.cr	http://www.nic.cr/consulta-dns.html	
.cu	http://www.nic.cu/consult.html	
.cv	dns.cv	!
.cx	whois.nic.cx	!

.cy	whois.ripe.net	
.cz	whois.nic.cz	
.de	whois.denic.de	
.dj	http://www.nic.dj/	!
.dk	whois.dk-hostmaster.dk, whois.nic.dk	
.dm	whois.nic.cx, whois.nic.dm	
.do	whois.nic.do	!
.dz	whois.ripe.net	
.ec	www.nic.ec	(Subdomains at whois.lac.net: com.ec, org.ec, net.ec, mil.ec, fin.ec, med.ec, gov.ec)
.ee	whois.eenet.ee	
.eg	whois.ripe.net	
.eh	Not in zone	
.er	http://www.afridns.org/er/tld_er.txt	
.es	whois.nic.es	
.et	http://www.telecom.net.et/	
.eu	whois.eu	
.fi	whois.ficora.fi	
.fj	whois.usp.ac.fj	
.fk	http://www.fidc.org.fk/domain-registration/home.htm	
.fm	http://www.dot.fm/whois.html	
.fo	whois.ripe.net	
.fr	whois.nic.fr	(Subdomains: asso.fr, com.fr, gouv.fr, nom.fr, tm.fr)
.ga	http://www.inet.ga/	
.gb	whois.ripe.net	
.gd	whois.nic.gd	
.ge	whois.sanet.ge	!
.gf	whois.nplus.gf	!
.gg	whois.channelisles.net, whois.isles.net	
.gh	http://www.ghana.com.gh/domain.htm	
.gi	whois2.afilias-grs.net	
.gl	whois.nic.gl	
.gm	http://www.nic.gm/htmlpages/whois/nic.htm	
.gn	http://www.psg.com/dns/gn/	
.gp	whois.nic.gp	
.gq	http://www.intnet.gq/	
.gr	whois.grnet.gr	
.gs	whois.gs, 203.119.12.22, whois.adamsnames.tc	
.gt	http://www.gt	
.gu	http://gadao.gov.gu/Scripts/wwsquery/wwsquery.dll?hois=guamquery	
.gw	http://www.register.gw	
.gy	whois.registry.gy	
.hk	whois.hkdnr.net.hk, whois.hknic.net.hk	(Subdomains: com.hk, org.hk, net.hk, edu.hk)
.hm	whois.registry.hm	
.hn	whois2.afilias-grs.net	

.hr	www.dns.hr	
.ht	whois.nic.ht	!
.hu	whois.nic.hu	
.id	whois.idnic.net.id, whois.net.id	
.ie	whois.iedr.ie, whois.domainregistry.ie	
.il	whois.isoc.org.il	(Subdomains: co.il, org.il, net.il, ac.il, k12.il, gov.il, muni.il)
.im	whois.nic.im	
.in	whois.registry.in, whois.inregistry.net	(Subdomains: firm.in, gen.in, ind.in, net.in, org.in)
.io	whois.nic.io	
.iq	whois.cmc.iq	
.ir	whois.nic.ir	
.is	whois.isnet.is, whois.isnic.is	
.it	whois.nic.it	
.je	whois.je, whois.channelisles.net, whois. isles.net	
.jm	uwimona.edu.jm/ http://nic.jm/	
.jo	http://www.nis.jo/dns/	
.jp	whois.jprs.jp	(Subdomains at whois.nic.ad.jp: ac.jp, co.jp, go.jp, or.jp, ne.jp)
.ke	whois.kenic.or.ke	
.kg	whois.domain.kg	!
.kh	http://www.mptc.gov.kh/Reculation/DNS. htm	
.ki	whois.nic.ki	
.km	http://www.domaine.km/	
.kn	None	
.kp	http://www.star.co.kp	
.kr	whois.krnic.net	(Subdomains at whois.nic.or.kr: ac.kr, co.kr, go.kr, ne.kr, nm.kr, or.kr, re.kr)
.kw	http://www.domainname.net.kw/	
.ky	http://146.115.157.215/whoisfrontend.asp	
.kz	whois.nic.kz	
.la	whois.nic.la, whois2.afilias-grs.net	
.lb	cgi.aub.edu.lb	
.lc	http://www.isisworld.lc/domains/	
.li	whois.nic.li	
.lk	whois.nic.lk	!
.lr	http://www.psg.com/dns/lr/	
.ls	None	
.lt	whois.domreg.lt	
.lu	whois.dns.lu, whois.restena.lu	
.lv	whois.nic.lv	
.ly	whois.lydomains.com, whois.nic.ly	
.ma	whois.iam.net.ma	
.mc	whois.ripe.net	
.md	whois.nic.md	
.me	whois.nic.me, whois.meregistry.net	
.mg	http://www.nic.mg/	
.mh	http://www.nic.net.mh/	

.mk	whois.ripe.net	
.ml	http://www.sotelma.ml/	
.mm	whois.nic.mm	! (Subdomains: com.mm, org.mm, net.mm, edu.mm, gov.mm)
.mn	whois.nic.mn	!
.mo	whois.umac.mo	
.mp	whois.nic.mp	
.mq	http://www.nic.mq	!
.mr	http://www.univ-nkc.mr/nic_mr.html	
.ms	whois.adamsnames.tc, whois.ms, whois.nic.ms	
.mt	www.um.edu.mt	
.mu	whois.nic.mu	
.mv	dhiraagu.com.mv	
.mw	http://www.registrar.mw/	
.mx	whois.nic.mx	(Subdomains: com.mx, edu.mx, gob.mx, net.mx, org.mx)
.my	whois.mynic.net.my	
.mz	http://www.uem.mz/	
.na	whois.na-nic.com.na	
.nc	whois.cctld.nc	
.ne	http://www.intnet.ne/	
.nf	whois.nic.nf	
.ng	whois.rg.net	
.nl	whois.sidn.nl, whois.domain-registry.nl	
.no	whois.norid.no	
.np	http://www.mos.com.np/domsearch.html	
.nr	http://www.cenpac.net.nr/dns/whois.html	
.nu	whois.nic.nu	
.nz	whois.domainz.net.nz	(Subdomains through whois.srs.net.nz : ac.nz, co.nz, cri.nz, geek.nz, gen.nz, govt.nz, iwi.nz, maori.nz, mil.nz, net.nz, org.nz, parliament.nz, school.nz)
.om	http://www.gto.net.om/	
.pa	http://www.nic.pa/	
.pe	whois.nic.pe	
.pf	whois.registry.pf	
.pg	http://www.unitech.ac.pg/Unitech_General/ITS/ITS_Dns.htm	
.ph	http://www.domains.ph/DomainSearch.asp	
.pk	pknic.net.pk	
.pl	whois.dns.pl	(Subdomains: com.pl, net.pl, org.pl, aid.pl, agro.pl, atm.pl, auto.pl, biz.pl, edu.pl, gmina.pl, gsm.pl, info.pl, mail.pl, miasta.pl, media.pl, mil.pl, nom.pl, pc.pl, priv.pl, realestate.pl, rel.pl, shop.pl, sklep.pl, sos.pl, targi.pl, tm.pl, tourism.pl, travel.pl, turystyka.pl)
.pm	whois.nic.pm	
.pn	http://www.pitcairn.pn/PnRegistry/CheckAvailability.html	

.pr	whois.nic.pr, whois.uprr.pr	
.ps	http://www.nic.ps/whois/	
.pt	whois.dns.pt, whois.nic.pt	
.pw	whois.nic.pw	
.py	http://www.nic.py/consultas/	
.qa	http://www.qatar.net.qa/services/virtual. htm	
.re	whois.nic.re, whois.nic.fr	
.ro	whois.rotld.ro	(Subdomains: arts.ro, co.ro, com.ro, firm.ro, info.ro, nom.ro, nt.ro, org.ro, rec.ro, ro.ro, store.ro, tm.ro, www.ro)
.ru	whois.ripn.ru, whois.ripn.net	(Subdomains: com.ru, int.ru, net.ru, org.ru, pp.ru)
.rw	http://www.nic.rw/cgi-bin/whoisrw.pl	
.sa	saudinic.net.sa	
.sb	whois.nic.net.sb	
.sc	whois2.afilias-grs.net	
.sd	http://www.sudatel.sd/	
.se	whois.nic-se.se, whois.nic.se, whois.iis.se	(Subdomains: org.se, pp.se, tm.se)
.sg	whois.nic.net.sg	(Subdomains: com.sg, org.sg, net.sg, gov.sg)
.sh	whois.nic.sh	
.si	whois.arnes.si	
.sj	whois.ripe.net	
.sk	whois.sk-nic.sk	
.sl	http://www.sierratel.sl/	
.sm	whois.ripe.net	
.sn	http://www.nic.sn/	
.so	http://www.nic.so/	!
.sr	whois.register.sr	
.st	whois.nic.st	
.su	whois.ripn.net	
.sv	http://www.uca.edu.sv/dns/	
.sy	whois.tld.sy	
.sz	http://www.sispa.org.sz/	
.tc	whois.tc, whois.adamsnames.tc	
.td	http://www.tit.td/	
.tf	whois.nic.tf, whois.afnic.fr	
.tg	http://www.nic.tg/	
.th	whois.thnic.net	(Subdomains: ac.th, co.th, go.th, mi.th, net. th, or.th)
.tj	whois.nic.tj	
.tk	whois.dot.tk, whois.nic.tk	
.tl	whois.domains.tl, whois.nic.tl	
.tm	whois.nic.tm	!
.tn	whois.ati.tn	!
.to	whois.tonic.to	
.tp	whois.domains.tl	
.tr	whois.nic.tr	(Subdomains at whois.metu.edu.tr : bbs.tr, com.tr, edu.tr, gov.tr, k12.tr, mil.tr, net.tr, org.tr)
.tt	http://www.nic.tt/cgi-bin/search.pl	

.tv	whois.tv, whois.nic.tv, tvwhois.verisign-grs.com	
.tw	whois.apnic.net, whois.twnic.net.tw	(Subdomains com.tw, org.tw, net.tw)
.tz	http://www.psg.com/dns/tz/	
.ua	whois.com.ua, whois.net.ua	
.ug	whois.co.ug	
.uk	whois.nic.uk	(Subdomains: co.uk, ltd.uk, org.uk)
.um	whois.nic.us	
.us	whois.nic.us	(Subdomain: fed.us through whois.nic.gov)
.uy	nic.uy, www.rau.edu.uy	
.uz	whois.cctld.uz, www.noc.uz	!
.va	whois.ripe.net	
.vc	whois.opensrs.net, whois2.afilias-grs.net	
.ve	whois.nic.ve, rwhois.reacciun.ve:4321	
.vg	whois.adamsnames.tc, whois.vg	
.vi	http://www.nic.vi/whoisform.htm	
.vn	http://www.vnnic.net.vn/english/reg_domain/	
.vu	http://www.vunic.vu/whois.htm	
.wf	whois.nic.wf	
.ws	whois.worldsite.ws, whois.nic.ws, www.nic.ws	
.ye	http://www.y.net.ye/	
.yt	whois.nic.yt	
.yu	whois.ripe.net	
.za	http://www2.frd.ac.za/uninet/zadomains.html	
.zm	http://www.zamnet.zm/domain.shtml	
.zr	Not in zone	
.zw	zptc.co.zw	

B.9   AUTHORITATIVE gTLD REGISTRAR WHOIS SERVERS

This is a list of ICANN-accredited registrar WHOIS servers listed by server. All entries are based on either queries of the InterNIC registrar database or found in an actual WHOIS record of a domain sponsored by the registrar. Some registrars have more than one server, and some servers are used by multiple registrar accreditations owned by the same parent company. Company names in this list followed by "Et Al." indicate the server is used by more than one registrar. Some of the listed registrars are definitely defunct or terminated but were still listed in the InterNIC database with an active WHOIS server. There are, of course, many registrar entries in the InterNIC database without a WHOIS server listed as discussed in the chapter on WHOIS and DNS, but those are not listed here. Server locations can change without warning, and not all on this list have been tested.

comnet-whois.humeia.com	Humeia Corporation
domains.experianinteractive.com	Experian Services Corp.
grs.hichina.com	Hichina Web Solutions (Hong Kong) Limited (2)
grs-whois.hichina.com	Hichina Zhicheng Technology Ltd.

its.yourwhois.com	Shaver Communications, Inc.
ken.mailclub.fr	Mailclub Sas
nic.entorno.es	Entorno Digital S.A.
ns.pam.net	American Domain Name Registry
nswhois.domainregistry.com	Domainregistry.com, Inc.
pds.verisigninc.com	Pds
rcube.ipmirror.com/rblWhois.do	Brights Consulting Inc.
registrar.amazon.com	Amazon Registrar Inc.
rs.internic.net	Registry Installation
secure.communigal.net	Sitename.com Llc
whois.007names.com	007names, Inc.
whois.0101domain.com	0101 Internet, Inc.
whois.101domain.com	101domain, Inc.
whois.123domainregistry.com	Hi-Tech Information and Marketing Pvt. Ltd.
whois.123-reg.co.uk	Webfusion Ltd.
whois.123registration.com	123 Registration, Inc.
whois.1accredited.com	1 Accredited Registrar
whois.1api.net	Atak Tercume Teknoloji Yayincilik Bilgisayar Ins.
whois.1dni.com	#1 Domain Names International, Inc. Dba 1dni.com
whois.1hostbrazil.com	1 Host Brazil, Inc.
whois.1hostcanada.com	! #1 Host Canada Inc.
whois.1hostchina.com	! #1 Host China, Inc.
whois.1hostgermany.com	! #1 Host Germany, Inc.
whois.1hostjapan.com	! #1 Host Japan, Inc.
whois.1hostkorea.com	! #1 Host Korea, Inc.
whois.1hostkuwait.com	! #1 Host Kuwait, Inc.
whois.1hostmalaysia.com	! #1 Host Malaysia, Inc.
whois.1hostunitedkingdom.com	! #1 Host United Kingdom, Inc.
whois.1isi.com	#1 Internet Services International Inc. Dba 1isi
whois.1morename.com	Drophub.com Inc., Et Al.
whois.1stdomain.net	1stdomain Llc
whois.22.cn	Beijing Tong Guan Xin Tian Technology Ltd. (Novaltel)
whois.2day.com	2day Internet Limited D/B/A 2day.com
whois.2imagen.net	Tecnologia Desarrollo Y Mercado
whois.35.com	35 Technology Co., Ltd.
whois.3721.com	Inter China Network Software (Beijing) Co., Ltd.
whois.4domains.com	4domains, Inc.
whois.51hkidc.com	Hkidc International Limited
whois.55hl.com	Jiangsu Bangning Science & Technology Co. Ltd.
whois.625domains.com	Enom625, Inc.
whois.72dns.com	Foshan Yidong Network Co., Ltd.
whois.7dc.com	7dc, Inc.
whois.8hy.cn	Hu Yi Global Information Resources (Holding) Company Hong Kong Limited
whois.aaaq.com	Aaaq.com, Inc.
whois.abansysandhostytec.com	Abansys & Hostytec, Sl
whois.abdomainations.ca	Abdomainations.ca Inc.
whois.aboutdomainsolutions.com	About Domain Dot Com Solutions Pvt. Ltd.
whois.above.com	Above.com Pty. Ltd.
whois.accentdomains.com	Accentdomains Llc
whois.aceofdomains.com	Ace of Domains, Inc.

whois.acquirednames.com	Acquirednames Llc
whois.active24.com	Active 24 Asa
whois.activeregistrar.com	Active Registrar, Inc.
whois.addresscreation.com	Address Creation Llc
whois.adknowledge.com	Adknowledge Inc.
whois.adomainofyourown.com	Adomainofyourown.com Llc
whois.adoptadomain.net	Adoptadomain.net Inc.
whois.advancedregistrar.com	Netearth One Inc. D/B/A Netearth
whois.advantage-interactive.com	Lcn.com Ltd.
whois.aerotek.com.tr	Aerotek Bilisim Taahut Sanayi Ve Ticaret Ltd. Sti.
whois.affinity.com	Affinity Internet, Inc.
whois.afforda.com	Affordable Computer Solutions, Inc.
whois.afriregister.com	Afriregister S.A.
whois.afterdarkdomainsincorporated.com	Afterdark Domains, Incorporated
whois.afternic.com	Domainadministration.com Llc
whois.airnames.com	Airnames.com, Inc.
whois.aitdomains.com	Advanced Internet Technologies Inc. (Ait)
whois.akky.mx	Network Information Center Mexico, S. C.
whois.alantron.com	Alantron Bilisim Ltd. Sti.
whois.alfena.com	Alfena, Llc
whois.alibaba.com	Alibaba (China) Technology Co. Ltd.
whois.alices-registry.com	Alice's Registry, Inc.
whois.allearthdomains.com	Allearthdomains.com Llc
whois.allglobalnames.com	Allglobalnames, S.A. Dba Cyberegistro.com
whois.allindomains.com	Allindomains, Llc
whois.allworldnames.com	Allworldnames.com Llc
whois.alohanic.com	! Alohanic Llc/Name105, Inc.
whois.alpinedomains.com	Alpine Domains Inc.
whois.anchovy.com	Hogan Lovells International Llp
whois.anessia.com	Anessia Inc.
whois.annulet.com	Annulet, Inc.
whois.answerable.com	Answerable.com (I) Pvt. Ltd.
whois.antagus.de	1st Antagus Internet Gmbh
whois.apexregistry.com	Apex Registry, Inc.
whois.apisrs.com	Tuonome.it Srl
whois.arabinternetnames.com	Arab Internet Names, Incorporated
whois.arcticnames.com	Arctic Names, Inc.
whois.argotech.us	Argo Technologies, Llc/Name104, Inc.
whois.aruba.it	Aruba Spa
whois.asadal.com	Asadal, Inc.
whois.ascio.com	Ascio Technologies Inc.
whois.asiadomains.biz	Asiadomains, Incorporated
whois.asiaregister.com	Asiaregister, Inc.
whois.assorted.com	Assorted, Ltd.
whois.astutium.com	Astutium Limited
whois.asusa.net	Asusa Corporation
whois.atcomtechnology.com	Atcom Technology Llc
whois.atlanticfriendnames.com	Atlanticfriendnames.com Llc
whois.atozdomainsmarket.com	Atozdomainsmarket, Llc
whois.ausregistry.com	Ausregistry Group Pty. Ltd.

whois.ausregistryinternational.com	Ausregistry Group Pty. Ltd.
whois.autica.com	Autica Domain Services, Inc.
whois.availabledomains.ca	Availabledomains.ca Inc.
whois.aviddomain.com	Aviddomain Llc
whois.aviddomains.com	Aviddomains.com, Inc.
whois.awregistry.net	All West Communications, Inc.
whois.az.pl	Az.pl Inc.
whois.azprivatez.com	Annulet Incorporated/Azdomainz Llc
whois.backslapdomains.com	Backslap Domains Inc.
whois.backup.ca	Backup.ca Corporation
whois.badger.com	Badger Inc.
whois.barginregister.com	Bargin Register Inc.
whois.baronofdomains.com	Baronofdomains.com Llc
whois.basicfusion.com	Basic Fusion, Inc.
whois.batdomains.com	Batdomains.com Ltd.
whois.beartrapdomains.com	Beartrapdomains.com Llc
whois.belgiumdomains.com	Belgiumdomains, Llc
whois.belizenic.bz	University Management Ltd.
whois.belmontdomains.com	Belmontdomains.com Llc
whois.bemydomain.net	Bemydomain.net, Inc.
whois.bestpriceregister.com	Best Bulk Register Inc.
whois.bestregistrar.com	Best Registration Services, Inc.
whois.bestsitenames.com	Best Site Names, Inc.
whois.betterthanaveragedomains.com	Betterthanaveragedomains.com Llc
whois.bigdomainshop.com	Big Domain Shop, Inc.
whois.bighouseservices.com	Big House Services, Inc.
whois.biglizarddomains.com	Biglizarddomains.com Llc
Whois.bigrock.com	Bigrock Solutions Private Limited
whois.binero.se	Binero Ab
whois.bizcn.com	Bizcn.com, Inc.
whois.blacknight.com	Blacknight Internet Solutions Ltd.
whois.blastdomains.com	Blastdomains Llc
whois.blisternet.net	Blisternet, Incorporated
whois.blockhost.com	Blockhost Llc
whois.bluefractal.com	Blue Fractal, Inc.
whois.bluerazor.com	Blue Razor Domains, Llc
whois.bookmyname.com	Online Sas
whois.boterosolutions.net	Boterosolutions.com S.A.
whois.bottledomains.com	Bottle Domains, Inc.
whois.bravename.com	Bravenames Inc.
whois.briarwoodtechnologies.com	Briarwood Technologies Inc.
whois.broadspire.com	Broadspire Inc.
whois.bt.com	British Telecommunications, Plc
whois.budgetnames.com	Compana Llc
whois.bulkregister.com	Bulkregister, Llc.
whois.bullrundomains.com	Bullrundomains.com Llc
whois.burnsidedomains.com	Burnsidedomains.com Llc
whois.canyongate.biz	Name111, Inc.
whois.capdom.com	Capitoldomains, Llc
whois.casdns.net	Casdns, Inc.
whois.catalog.com	Catalog.com, Inc.

whois.ccdomain.co.kr	Korea Electronic Certification Authority, Inc. (Crosscert, Inc.)
whois.ccireg.com	Central Comercializadora
whois.cdmon.com	10dencehispahard, S.L.
whois.centergate.com	Centergate Research Group, Llc
whois.centralregistrar.com	Central Registrar, Inc. D/B/A Domainmonger.com
whois.centrohost.ru	Cjsc Registrar R01
whois.cheapies.com	Cheapies.com Inc.
whois.chinaegov.cn	Service Development Center of the Service Bureau State Commission Office for Public Sector Reform
whois.chinagov.cn	China Organizational Name Administration Center (Conac)
whois.ChinaNet.cc	Chinanet Technology (Suzhou) Co., Ltd.
whois.cihost.com	C I Host Inc.
whois.cirs.us	Name112, Inc.
whois.claimeddomains.com	Claimeddomains Llc
whois.clertech.com	Clertech.com, Inc.
whois.clouddomainregistry.com	Siliconhouse.net Pvt. Ltd.
whois.cn.hooyoo.com	Hooyoo Information Technology Co. Ltd.
whois.cndns.com	Shanghai Meicheng Technology Information Development Co., Ltd.
whois.cnolnic.com	Xiamen Chinasource Internet Service Co., Ltd.
whois.codycorp.com	Codycorp.com, Inc.
whois.columbianames.com	Columbianames.com Llc
whois.comfydomains.com	Comfydomains Llc
whois.comlaude.com	Nom-Iq Ltd. Dba Com Laude
whois.commerceisland.com	Commerce Island, Inc.
whois.communigal.net	Gal Communication (Communigal) Ltd.
whois.compuglobalhypermega.com	Compuglobalhypermega.com Llc
whois.condomainium.com	Condomainium.com Inc.
whois.coolhosting.ca	Coolhosting.ca Inc.
whois.coolocean.com	Cool Ocean, Inc.
whois.corenic.net	Core Internet Council/Nameshield
whois.corporatedomains.com	Csc Corporate Domains, Inc., Et Al.
whois.cps-datensysteme.de	Cps-Datensysteme Gmbh
whois.crispnames.com	Crisp Names, Inc.
whois.cronon.net	Cronon Ag Berlin Niederla
whois.crystalcoal.com	Crystal Coal, Inc.
whois.csiregistry.com	Csiregistry.com, Inc.
whois.curiousnet.com	Curious Net, Inc.
whois.cvo.ca	Cvo.ca, Inc.
whois.cypack.com	Cydentity, Inc. D/B/A Cypack.com
whois.dagnabit.biz	Dagnabit, Incorporated
whois.dancue.com	Dancue Inc.
whois.dandomain.dk	Dandomain A/S
whois.data-hotel.net	Datahotel Co., Ltd.
whois.datasource.com.au	Datasource Network Australia Limited
whois.dattatec.com	Dattatec.com Srl
whois.dbms.com	Dbms (Internal)
whois.dbmsdomains.com	Dbms, Incorporated
whois.deerwood.name	Deerwood Investments Llc/Name113, Inc.

whois.demand.com	Vayala Corporation D/B/A Demand.com
whois.demys.com	Demys Limited
whois.deschutesdomains.com	Deschutesdomains.com Llc
whois.desertdevil.com	Desert Devil, Inc.
whois.desktopdomainer.com	Vocalspace, Llc
whois.desto.com	Desto! Inc.
whois.df.eu	Domainfactory Gmbh
whois.dfordomains.com	Web Werks India Pvt. Ltd.
whois.dharanadomains.com	Dharana Domains Inc./Name114, Inc.
whois.dinahosting.com	Dinahosting Sl
whois.directnic.com	Assorted, Ltd./Dnc Holdings, Inc.
whois.discount-domain.com	Gmo Internet, Inc. D/B/A Onamae.com
whois.discountdomainsuk.com	Discount Domains Ltd.
whois.distributeit.com.au	Tpp Wholesale Pty. Ltd.
whois.division120.com	Pacific Online Inc.
whois.dm3networks.com	Gulf Computer Society Fz-Llc
whois.dnglobe.com	Dnglobe Llc
whois.dns.com.cn	Beijing Innovative Linkage Technology Ltd. Dba Dns. com.cn
whois.dns-net.de	Dns Net Internet Service Gmbh
whois.dnsvillage.com	Dnsvillage.com
whois.documentdata.li	Documentdata Anstalt
whois.domain.com	Dotster Inc., Et Al.
whois.domain1source.com	1 Domain Source, Ltd. Dba Domain 1 Source, Inc.
whois.domainagent.co.nz	Web Drive Ltd.
whois.domainahead.com	Domainahead Llc
whois.domainallies.com	Domainallies.com, Inc.
whois.domainarmada.com	Domainarmada.com Llc
whois.domainauthority.ca	Domainauthority.ca Inc.
whois.domainband.com	Domain Band, Inc.
whois.domainbonus.com	Mobiline Usa, Inc. Dba Domainbonus.com
whois.domainbuzz.ca	Domainbuzz.ca Inc.
whois.domainca.com	Korea Information Certificate Authority Inc.
whois.domaincannon.com	Domaincannon.com Llc
whois.domaincapitan.com	Domaincapitan.com Llc
whois.domaincentral.ca	Domaincentral.ca Inc.
whois.domaincentral.com.au	Australian Style Pty. Ltd.
whois.domaincentral.com.au	Domain Central Australia Pty. Ltd.
whois.domaincentre.ca	Super Registry Inc.
whois.domaincity.com	Venture.com, Inc. Dba Domaincity
whois.domainclip.com	Domainclip Domains, Inc.
whois.domainclub.com	Domainclub.com Llc
whois.domainclub.net	!!!$0 Cost Domain And Hosting Services, Inc.
whois.domaincomesaround.com	Domaincomesaround.com Llc
whois.domaincontext.com	Imperial Registrations Inc.
whois.domaincraze.com	Domaincraze Llc
whois.domaincreek.com	Domaincreek Llc
whois.domaincritics.com	Domaincritics Llc
whois.domaindelights.com	Domaindelights Llc
whois.domaindiscover.com	Tierranet Inc. D/B/A Domaindiscover
whois.domaindomain.com	Interactive Telecom Network, Inc.

whois.domaindoorman.com	Domaindoorman, Llc
whois.domainestic.com	Domainestic.com Inc.
whois.domainevent.ca	Domainevent.ca Inc.
whois.domainextreme.com	Domainextreme Llc
whois.domainfalcon.com	Domainfalcon Llc
whois.domainfighter.ca	Domainfighter.ca Inc.
whois.domaingazelle.com	Domaingazelle.com Llc
whois.domaingetter.com	Domaingetter Llc
whois.domainguardians.com	Domain Guardians, Inc.
whois.domainhawks.net	Domainhawks.net Llc
whois.domainheadz.ca	Domainheadz.ca Inc.
whois.domainhip.com	Domainhip.com, Inc.
whois.domainhood.com	Domainhood Llc
whois.domainhysteria.com	Domainhysteria.com Llc
whois.domainiac.ca	Domainiac.ca Inc.
whois.domainideas.ca	Domainideas.ca Inc.
whois.domaininfo.com	Domaininfo Ab
whois.domaininthebasket.com	Domaininthebasket.com Llc
whois.domaininthehole.com	Domaininthehole.com Llc
whois.domainit.com	Domain-It!, Inc.
whois.domainjingles.com	Domain Jingles, Inc.
whois.domainjungle.net	Domainjungle.net Llc
whois.domainladder.com	Domainladder Llc
whois.domainlink.ca	Domainlink.ca Inc.
whois.domainlocal.com	Domainlocal Llc
whois.domainluminary.ca	Domainluminary.ca Inc.
whois.domainmall.ca	Domainmall.ca Inc.
whois.domainmantra.com	Domain Mantra, Inc.
whois.domainmap.com	Premierename.ca Inc.
whois.domainmarketplace.ca	Domainmarketplace.ca Inc.
whois.domainmonarch.com	Western United Domains Inc.
whois.domainmonkeys.com	Domain Monkeys, Llc
whois.domainmonster.com	Domainmonster.com, Inc.
whois.domainname.com	Domainname, Inc.
whois.domainnameshop.com	Domeneshop As
whois.domainnetwork.ca	Domainnetwork.ca Inc.
whois.domainnote.com	Dext Co., Ltd.
whois.domainnovations.com	Domainnovations, Incorporated
whois.domainparadise.ca	Domainparadise.ca Inc.
whois.domainparkblock.com	Domainparkblock.com Llc
whois.domainpeople.com	Domainpeople, Inc.
whois.domainpicking.com	Domainpicking Llc
whois.domainplaza.ca	Domainplaza.ca Inc.
whois.domainprime.com	Domainprime.com Llc
whois.domainprocessor.com	Funpeas Media Ventures, Llc
whois.domainraker.net	Domainraker.net Llc
whois.domainreg.com	Blue Gravity Communications, Inc.
whois.domainregi.com	Domainregi Llc
whois.domainregservices.com	Name115, Inc.
whois.domainreign.ca	Domainreign.ca Inc.
whois.domainrg.com	Echo, Inc.

whois.domainrouge.com	Domain Rouge Inc.
whois.domainroyale.com	Domainroyale.com Llc
whois.domains.co.za	Diamatrix C.C.
whois.domains.domreg.lt	Kaunas University Of Technology
whois.domains2be.ca	Domains2be.com Inc.
whois.domains4u.ca	Domains4u.ca Inc.
whois.domainsails.net	Domainsails.net Llc
whois.domainsalsa.com	Domainsalsa.com Llc
whois.domainsareforever.net	Domainsareforever.net Llc
whois.domainsatcost.ca	Namescout, Et Al.
whois.domainscape.ca	Domainscape.ca Inc.
whois.domainscostless.ca	Domainscostless.ca Inc.
whois.domainscout.com	Domainscout.com Inc.
whois.domainservicesrotterdam.nl	Domain Services Rotterdam Bv
whois.domainsfirst.ca	Domainsfirst.ca Inc.
whois.domainsforme.ca	Domainsforme.ca Inc.
whois.domainshype.com	Domainshype.com, Inc.
whois.domainsinthebag.com	Domainsinthebag.com Llc
whois.domainsite.com	Spot Domain Llc Dba Domainsite.com
whois.domainsofcourse.com	Domainsofcourse.com Llc
whois.domainsoftheday.net	Domainsoftheday.net Llc
whois.domainsoftheworld.net	Domainsoftheworld.net Llc
whois.domainsofvalue.com	Domainsofvalue.com Llc
whois.domainsonly.com	Domains Only Inc.
whois.domainsouffle.com	Domainsouffle.com Llc
whois.domainsoverboard.com	Domainsoverboard.com Llc
whois.domainsovereigns.com	Domainsovereigns.com Llc
whois.domainspa.com	Domainspa Llc
whois.domainsprouts.com	Domainsprouts.com Llc
whois.domainsrs.com	Indialinks Web Hosting Pvt. Ltd.
whois.domainsrs.com	Indialinks Web Hosting Pvt. Ltd.
whois.domainstream.ca	Domainstream.ca Inc.
whois.domainstreet.ca	Domainstreet.ca Inc.
whois.domainstreetdirect.com	Domainstreetdirect.com Llc
whois.domainsurgeon.com	Domainsurgeon.com Llc
whois.domainsystems.com	Domain Systems, Inc.
whois.domaintact.com	Domaintact Llc
whois.domainthenet.com	Domain The Net Technologies Ltd.
whois.domaintimemachine.com	Domaintimemachine.com Llc
whois.domainventures.ca	Domainventures.ca Internet Services Corporation
whois.domainwards.com	Domainwards.com Llc
whois.domainyeti.com	Domainyeti.com Llc
whois.domainz.com	Domainz Limited
whois.domainzoo.com	Domainzoo.com, Inc.
whois.domerati.com	Domerati, Inc.
whois.domoden.com	Deviation, Llc D/B/A/ Domoden
whois.domrobot.com	Internetworx Ltd. & Co. Kg
whois.domus-llc.com	Domus Enterprises Llc Dba
whois.dontaskwhy.ca	Dontaskwhy.com Inc.
whois.do-reg.jp	Firstserver Inc.
whois.doregi.com	Hangang Systems, Inc.

whois.dot.es	Sync Intertainment S.L.
whois.dotalliance.com	Dotalliance Inc.
whois.dotarai.com	Dotarai Co., Ltd.
whois.dotearth.com	Domain Registration Services Inc. Dba Dotearth.com
whois.dotname.co.kr	Dotname Korea Corp.
whois.dotroll.com	Dotroll Kft.
whois.dotster.com	Dotster Inc., Et Al.
whois.dottedventures.com	Dotted Ventures, Inc.
whois.dreamhost.com	New Dream Network Llc
whois.droplimited.com	Droplimited.com Inc.
whois.dropnation.com	Domain Guardians, Inc.
whois.dropoutlet.com	Dropoutlet, Incorporated
whois.duckbilleddomains.com	Duckbilleddomains.com Llc
whois.dynadot.com	Dynadot Llc, Et Al.
whois.dynadot0.com	Dynadot0 Llc
whois.dynadot1.com	Dynadot1 Llc
whois.dynadot2.com	Dynadot2 Llc
whois.dynadot3.com	Dynadot3 Llc
whois.dynadot4.com	Dynadot4 Llc
whois.dynadot5.com	Dynadot5 Llc
whois.dynadot6.com	Dynadot6 Llc
whois.dynadot7.com	Dynadot7 Llc
whois.dynadot8.com	Dynadot8 Llc
whois.dynamicdolphin.com	Dynamic Dolphin, Inc.
whois.dynanames.com	Dynanames.com, Inc.
whois.dyndns.com	Dynamic Network Services, Inc.
whois.eachnic.com	Ejee Group Holdings Limited
whois.eaiti.com	Eai Technologies
whois.eastcom.com	Eastern Communications Co., Ltd.
whois.eastnames.com	Eastnames Inc.
whois.easydns.com	Dummy Easydns Technologies, Inc.
whois.easyspace.com	Internetters Ltd.
whois.eb.com.cn	Hangzhou E-Business Services Co., Ltd.
whois.ebrandsecure.com	Ebrandsecure, Llc
whois.echodomain.com	Echodomain Llc
whois.edong.com	Shanghai Oweb Network Co., Ltd.
whois.educause.net	Educause
whois.ekados.com	Ekados Inc. D/B/A Groundregistry.com
whois.elserver.com	Elserver Srl
whois.empirestatedomains.com	Empirestatedomains Inc.
whois.ename.com	Xiamen Ename Network Technology, Et Al.
whois.enameco.com	Enameco Llc
whois.encirca.com	Encirca Inc.
whois.enetica.com.au	Enetica Pty. Ltd.
whois.enetregistry.net	Enetregistry.com Corporation
whois.enic.cc	Enic Corporation2
whois.enom1.com	Enom1 Inc.
whois.enom2.com	Enom2 Inc.
whois.enom3.com	Enom3 Inc.
whois.enom371.com	Enom371 Incorporated
whois.enom373.com	Enom373 Incorporated

whois.enom375.com	Enom375 Incorporated
whois.enom377.com	Enom377 Incorporated
whois.enom379.com	Enom379 Incorporated
whois.enom381.com	Enom381 Incorporated
whois.eNom383.com	Enom383 Incorporated
whois.eNom385.com	Enom385 Incorporated
whois.enom387.com	Enom387 Incorporated
whois.enom389.com	Enom389 Incorporated
whois.enom391.com	Enom391 Incorporated
whois.eNom393.com	Enom393 Incorporated
whois.enom395.com	Enom395 Incorporated
whois.enom397.com	Enom397 Incorporated
whois.enom399.com	Enom399 Incorporated
whois.enom4.com	Enom4 Inc.
whois.enom403.com	Enom403 Incorporated
whois.enom405.com	Enom405 Incorporated
whois.enom407.com	Enom407 Incorporated
whois.enom409.com	Enom409 Incorporated
whois.enom411.com	Enom411 Incorporated
whois.enom413.com	Enom413 Incorporated
whois.eNom415.com	Enom415 Incorporated
whois.enom417.com	Enom417 Incorporated
whois.enom419.com	Enom419 Incorporated
whois.enom421.com	Enom421 Incorporated
whois.enom423.com	Enom423 Incorporated
whois.enom425.com	Enom425 Incorporated
whois.enom427.com	Enom427 Incorporated
whois.enom429.com	Enom429 Incorporated
whois.enom431.com	Enom431 Incorporated
whois.enom433.com	Enom433 Incorporated
whois.enom435.com	Enom435 Incorporated
whois.enom437.com	Enom437 Incorporated
whois.enom439.com	Enom439 Incorporated
whois.enom441.com	Enom441 Incorporated
whois.enom443.com	Enom443 Incorporated
whois.enom445.com	Enom445 Incorporated
whois.enom447.com	Enom447 Incorporated
whois.enom449.com	Enom449 Incorporated
whois.enom451.com	Enom451 Incorporated
whois.enom453.com	Enom453 Incorporated
whois.enom455.com	Enom455 Incorporated
whois.enom457.com	Enom457 Incorporated
whois.enom459.com	Enom459 Incorporated
whois.eNom461.com	Enom461 Incorporated
whois.enom463.com	Enom463 Incorporated
whois.enom465.com	Enom465 Incorporated
whois.enom467.com	Enom467 Incorporated
whois.enom469.com	Enom469 Incorporated
whois.enom5.com	Enom5, Inc.
whois.enoma1.com	Enoma1 Inc.
whois.enomate.com	Enomate Inc.

whois.enomau.com	Enomau Inc.
whois.enombre.com	Enombre Corporation
whois.enomcorporate.com	Enom Corporate Inc.
whois.enomeu.com	Enomeu Inc. 1
whois.enomfor.com	Enomfor Inc.
whois.enomgmpservices.com	Enom Gmp Services Inc.
whois.enommx.com	Enommx Inc.
whois.enomnz.com	Enomnz Inc.
whois.enomsky.com	Enomsky Inc.
whois.enomten.com	Enomten Inc.
whois.enomtoo.com	Enomtoo Inc.
whois.enomv.com	Enomv Inc.
whois.enomworld.com	Enom World Inc.
whois.enomx.com	Enomx Inc.
whois.enterprice.net	Epag Domainservices Gmbh
whois.enterthedomain.com	Enterthedomain.com
whois.entorno.es	Entorno Digital, S.A.
whois.epik.com	Epik, Inc.
whois.esoftwiz.com	Esoftwiz, Inc.
whois.estdomains.com	Estdomains, Inc.
whois.eunameflood.com	Eunameflood.com Llc
whois.eunamesoregon.com	Eunamesoregon Llc
whois.eurodns.com	Eurodns S.A./Above Inc.
whois.europeanconnectiononline.com	Europeanconnectiononline.com Llc
whois.europeannic.eu	European Nic, Inc.
whois.europedomainsllc.com	Europe Domains Llc
whois.eurotrashnames.com	Eurotrashnames.com Llc
whois.euturbo.com	Euturbo.com Llc
whois.everreadynames.com	Ever Ready Names, Inc.
whois.evonames.com	Evoplus Ltd.
whois.exai.com	Black Ice Domains, Inc.
whois.experianinteractive.com	Experian Services Corp.
whois.experinom.com	Experinom Inc.
whois.expertsrs.com	Nj Tech Solutions, Inc.
whois.extendnames.com	Extend Names, Inc.
whois.extranetdeclientes.com	Estrategias Website S.L.
whois.extrathreads.com	Extra Threads Corporation
whois.extremedomains.ca	Extremedomains.ca, Inc.
whois.extremelywild.com	Extremely Wild, Inc.
whois.ezhosting.ca	Ezhosting.ca Internet Services Corporation
whois.fabulous.com	Fabulous.com Pty. Ltd.
whois.fastdomain.com	Fastdomain, Inc.
whois.fenominal.com	Fenominal Inc.
whois.fiducia.lv	Fiducia Llc, Latvijas Parstavnieciba
whois.findgooddomains.com	Find Good Domains, Inc.
whois.finduaname.com	Finduaname.com Llc
whois.findyouadomain.com	Findyouadomain.com Llc
whois.findyouaname.com	Findyouaname.com Llc
whois.flancrestdomains.com	Flancrestdomains.com Llc
whois.freeparking.co.uk	Freeparking Domain Registrars, Inc.
whois.freestyleholdings.com	Freestyle Name Holdings Inc./Name116, Inc.

whois.freeyellow.com	Free Yellow.com, Inc.
whois.french-connexion.com	French Connexion Dba Domaine.fr
whois.freshbreweddomains.com	Freshbreweddomains.com Llc
whois.frontstreetdomains.com	Frontstreetdomains.com Llc
whois.fullnic.com	Fullnic
whois.fushitarazu.com	Fushi Tarazu, Incorporated
whois.gabia.com	Gabia Inc., Et Al.
whois.gamefornames.com	Game For Names, Inc.
whois.gandi.net	Gandi Sas
whois.gatekeeperdomains.net	Gatekeeperdomains.net Llc
whois.geewhizdomains.com	Gee Whiz Domains, Inc.
whois.generalnames.com	General Names, Inc.
whois.genious.net	Genious Communications Sarl/Au
whois.genuinenames.com	Genuine Names, Inc.
whois.gesloten.an	Gesloten Domain N.V.
whois.getdomainsiwant.ca	2003300 Ontario Inc.
whois.getrealnames.com	Get Real Names, Inc.
whois.getyername.com	Aim High!, Inc.
whois.getyourdotinfo.com	3349608 Canada Inc.
whois.ghana.com	Ghana Dot Com Ltd.
whois.gi.net	Netracorp 1
whois.gkg.net	Gkg.net, Inc.
whois.glamdomains.com	Glamdomains Llc
whois.glis.in	Good Luck Internet Services Pvt., Ltd.
whois.globalnamesonline.com	Global Names Online, Inc.
whois.globedom.com	Globedom Datenkommunikations Gmbh
whois.globehosting.net	Globe Hosting, Inc.
whois.goaustraliadomains.com	Go Australia Domains, Llc
whois.gocanadadomains.com	Go Canada Domains, Llc
whois.gochinadomains.com	Go China Domains, Llc
whois.godaddy.com	Godaddy.com Inc., Et Al.
whois.godomaingo.com	Godomaingo.com Llc
whois.gofrancedomains.com	Go France Domains, Llc
whois.gofullhouse.com	Go Full House, Inc.
whois.gomontenegrodomains.com	Go Montenegro Domains, Llc
whois.gonames.ca	Gonames.ca Inc.
whois.gonbei.jp	Interlink Co. Ltd.
whois.gooddomainregistry.com	Good Domain Registry Pvt. Ltd.
whois.google.com	Google Inc.
whois.goserveyourdomain.com	Goserveyourdomain.com Llc
whois.gotnames.ca	Gotnames.ca Inc.
whois.gozerdomains.com	Gozerdomains.com Llc
whois.gpdomains.com	Gp Domains Inc.
whois.grabton.ca	Grabton.ca Inc.
whois.gradeadomainnames.com	Gradeadomainnames.com Llc
whois.greenzonedomains.com	Greenzonedomains Inc.
whois.groundinternet.com	Ground Internet, Inc.
whois.gungagalunga.biz	Gunga Galunga, Incorporated
whois.guoxuwang.cn	Beijing Guoxu Network Technology Co. Ltd.
whois.gzidc.com	Guangdong Jinwanbang Technology Investment Co. Ltd.
whois.haveaname.com	Haveaname Llc

whois.hawthornedomains.com	Hawthornedomains.com Llc
whois.heavydomains.net	Heavydomains.net Llc
whois.hebeidomains.com	Hebei Guoji Maoyi (Shanghai) Ltd.
whois.hectamedia.com	Minds + Machines Registrar Limited
whois.hichina.com	Hichina Zhicheng Tech
whois.hipsearch.com	Hipsearch.com Inc.
whois.hkidc.com	Hkidc International Limited
whois.hoapdi-inc.com	Hoapdi Inc.
whois.home.pl	Home.pl Sp. J. Jurczyk, Stypula, Kapcio T/A Home.pl
whois.hooyoo.com	Hooyoo (Us) Inc.
whois.host.uol.com.br	Universo Online S/A (Uol)
whois.hostaliadomains.com	Acens Technologies Inc.
whois.hosteur.com	Ab Connect
whois.hosting.kr	Megazone Corp.
whois.hostinger.com	Hostinger Uab
whois.hostingservicesinc.net	Cloud Group Limited/Uk2 Group Ltd.
whois.hostlane.com	Hostlane Inc. 2
whois.hostmaster.ca	Hostmaster.ca Inc.
whois.hostnameservices.net	Host Name Services Inc./Name117, Inc.
whois.hostway.com	Hostway Services, Inc.
whois.hotdomaintrade.com	Hotdomaintrade.com, Inc.
whois.http.net	Http.net Internet Gmbh
whois.hughes.net	Hughes Electronic Commerce Inc.
whois.hupo.com	Guangzhou Ming Yang Information Technology Co., Ltd.
whois.hyperstreet.com	Hyperstreet.com Inc.
whois.iana.org	Iana And Many Defunct Registrars
whois.iaregistry.com	The Registry at Info Avenue, Llc D/B/A Spirit Communications
whois.ibi.net	Netpia.com, Inc.
whois.icann.org	Terminated Registrar
whois.idgenesis.com	Id Genesis, Llc
whois.idindi.com	Indirection Identity Corporation
whois.idirections.com	Namezero.com, Inc.
whois.igempresas.com	Internet Group Do Brasil S/A
whois.ihs.com.tr	Ihs Telekom, Inc.
whois.iisp.com	Zhuhai Naisinike Information Technology Co. Ltd.
whois.ikano.com	Ikano Communications
whois.ilait.com	Ilait Ab
whois.imena.ua	Internet Invest, Ltd. Dba Imena.ua
whois.imminentdomains.net	Imminentdomains.net Llc
whois.in2net.com	In2net Network Inc.
whois.inames.co.kr	Inames Co., Ltd.
whois.indiatimes.com	Times Internet Limited
whois.indom.com	Indom Sas
whois.inic.ch	Cadiware Ag
whois.ininaf.com	Internet Internal Affairs Corporation
whois.initialesonline.net	Acropolis Telecom Sarl
whois.inname.net	Webagentur.at Internet Services Gmbh Dba Domainname.at
whois.inplaza.net	Internetplaza City Co., Ltd.
whois.instantnames.com	Instantnames Llc

whois.instinctsolutions.com	Instinct Solutions, Inc.
whois.instra.net	Instra Corporation Pty. Ltd.
whois.interaccess.com	Hosting.com Inc.
whois.interdomain.com	Acens Technologies, S.L.U.
whois.interdomain.net	Acens Technologies, S.L.U.
whois.interdominios.com	Interdominios, Inc.
whois.interlakenames.com	Interlakenames.com Llc
whois.interlink.hu	Globix Kft.
whois.intermedia.net	Intermedia.net, Inc.
whois.internet.bs	Internet.bs Corp.
whois.internetcap.us	Internet Capital Inc/Name118, Inc.
whois.internetdomainnameregistrar. org	Campoint Ag
whois.internetters.co.uk	Internetters Ltd.
whois.internetwire.de	Registrygate Gmbh
whois.internetworks.com	Internet Networks S.A. De C.V.
whois.internext.fr	Internext
whois.intlregistrationservices.com	International Registration Services Inc./Name119, Inc.
whois.intrustdomains.com	Intrust Domains Inc., Et Al.
whois.ipmirror.com	Ip Mirror Pte. Ltd. Dba Ip Mirror
whois.ipxcess.com	Ipxcess.com Sdn Bhd
whois.ireg.net	Imperial Registrations, Inc.
whois.iregisterdomainnameshere.com	Iregisterdomainshere.com, Inc.
whois.iregistry.com	Iregistry Corp./Uniregistrar Corp.
whois.ironmountain-ipm.com	Iron Mountain Intellectual Property Management, Inc.
whois.is.co.za	Internet Solutions (Pty.) Ltd.
whois.is.com	Bp Holdings Group, Inc. Dba Is.com
whois.iserveyourdomain.com	Iserveyourdomain.com Llc
whois.isimtescil.net	Fbs Inc.
whois.ispreg.com	Ispreg Ltd.
whois.isregistrar.com	Internet Service Registrar Inc.
whois.itpan.com	Itpan.com, Limited
whois.itpan.com	Itpan.com, Limited
whois.itsyourdomain.com	Innerwise, Inc. D/B/A Itsyourdomain.com
whois.iwelt.de	Iwelt Ag
whois.jazdomainnames.com	Jaz Domain Names Ltd.
whois.jetpackdomains.com	Jetpack Domains, Inc.
whois.joinup.jp	Wixi Incorporated
whois.joker.com	Csl Computer Service Langenbach Gmbh
whois.jprs.jp	Japan Registry Services Co., Ltd.
whois.jumboname.com	Jumbo Names, Inc.
whois.jumpingdot.com	Aftergen, Inc. Dba Jumpingdot
whois.jungbo.net	Jungbonet Co., Ltd.
whois.k8.com.br	Digirati Informatica Servicos E Telecomunicacoes Ltda
whois.kagoya.jp	Kagoya Japan Inc.
whois.keyregistrar.com	Key Registrar, Inc.
whois.kheweul.com	Kheweul.com Sa
whois.kheweul.org	Kheweul.com Sa
whois.king-domains.com	Kingdomains, Incorporated
whois.klaatudomains.com	Klaatudomains.com Llc
whois.knipp.de	Knipp Medien Und Kommunikation Gmbh

whois.komplex.net	Komplex.net Gmbh
whois.ksdom.kr	Korea Server Hosting Inc.
whois.kudo.com	Crazy8domains.com Inc.
whois.kuwaitnet.net	Kuwaitnet General Trading Co.
whois.ladasdomains.com	Ladas Domains Llc
whois.lakeodomains.com	Lakeodomains.com Llc
whois.launchpad.com	Launchpad.com, Inc.
whois.lcn.com	Lcn.com Ltd.
whois.leadnetworks.com	Lead Networks Domains Pvt. Ltd.
whois.ledl.net	Ledl.net Gmbh
whois.lemonregistry.com	Znet Technologies Pvt. Ltd.
whois.lexsynergy.com	Lexsynergy Limited
whois.libris.com	Domreg Ltd.
whois.limedomains.com	Lime Labs, Llc
whois.liquidnetlimited.com	Liquidnet Ltd.
whois.litedomains.com	Litedomains Llc
whois.locaweb.com.br	Locaweb Servicos De Internet S/A Dba Locaweb
whois.LTNIC.com	Fujian Litian Network Technology Co., Ltd.
whois.luckydomains.ca	Luckydomains.ca, Inc.
whois.lunarpages.com	Add2net Inc.
whois.lws.fr	Ligne Web Services Sarl
whois.maff.com	Maff Inc.
whois.magicfriday.com	Magic Friday, Inc.
whois.mailclub.net	Mailclub Sas
whois.maindomain.ca	Maindomain.ca Inc.
whois.maprilis.com.vn	April Sea Information Technology Corporation
whois.marcaria.com	Mango Moods Inc.
whois.markbark.com	Mark Barker, Incorporated
whois.markmonitor.com	Markmonitor Inc.
whois.marksonline.com	Marksonline, Inc.
whois.masterofmydomains.net	Masterofmydomains.net Llc
whois.matbao.net	Mat Bao Trading & Service Company Limited D/B/A Mat Bao
whois.matchnames.ca	Matchnames.ca Inc.
whois.maximinternet.com	Maxim Internet, Inc.
whois.megabyte.ca	6230644 Canada Inc. Dba Megabyte.ca Internet Services
whois.melbourneit.com	Melbourne It Ltd., Et Al.
whois.meshdigital.com	Mesh Digital Limited, Et Al.
whois.metaregistrar.nl	Mijndomein.nl
whois.microbreweddomains.com	Microbreweddomains.com Llc
whois.mijninternetoplossing.nl	Mijn Internetoplossing B.V.
whois.misk.com	Misk.com Inc.
whois.mistername.com	Mister Name
whois.misternic.com	Misternic Llc
whois.mobile.pro	Mobile.pro Corporation
whois.mobilenameservices.com	Mobile Name Services, Inc.
whois.mojonic.com	Mojonic, L.L.C. Dba Mojonic.com
whois.moniker.com	Moniker Online Services Llc, Et Al.
whois.mountaindomains.net	Mountain Domains Inc./Name120, Inc.
whois.mouzz.com	Mouzz Interactive Inc.
whois.msintergate.com	Ms Intergate, Inc.

whois.mvpdomainnames.com	Mvpdomainnames.com Llc
whois.mynameonline.ca	Mynameonline.ca Inc.
whois.myobnet.com	Myob Australia E1 Pty. Ltd.
whois.myorderbox.com	Ipnic Inc., Et Al.
whois.mypreciousdomain.com	Mypreciousdomain.com Llc
whois.n1n.com	Nom D'un Net! Sarl
whois.name.com	Name.com Llc, Et Al.
whois.name.net	Name.net, Inc.
whois.name2host.com	Name 2 Host Inc. Dba Name2host.com
whois.nameaction.com	Nameaction, Inc.
whois.namearsenal.com	Namearsenal.com Llc
whois.namebake.com	Namebake Llc
whois.namebay.com	Namebay
whois.namebrew.com	Namebrew Llc
whois.namebright.com	Turncommerce Inc., Et Al.
whois.namecheap.com	Namecheap Inc.
whois.namecheap.getwhois.net	Namecheap Inc.
whois.namechild.com	Namechild Llc
whois.namecroc.com	Namecroc.com Llc
whois.nameemperor.com	Nameemperor.com Llc
whois.nameengine.com	Nameengine, Inc.
whois.nameescape.com	Nameescape.com Llc
whois.namefinger.com	Namefinger.com Llc
whois.nameforname.com	Name For Name, Inc.
whois.nameforward.com	Nameforward Llc
whois.namefrog.com	South America Domains Ltd.
whois.namefull.com	Datahotel Co., Ltd.
whois.namegame.ca	Namegame.ca Internet Services Corporation
whois.namehouse.net	Namehouse, Inc.
whois.nameintel.com	Cheap-Registrar.com
whois.nameisp.com	Ab Name Isp
whois.namejolt.com	Namejolt.com Llc
whois.namejuice.com	Brandon Gray Internet Services, Inc.
whois.nameking.com	Nameking.com, Inc.
whois.namemax.cn	Beijing Wangzun Technology Co. Ltd.
whois.namenelly.com	Name Nelly Corporation
whois.namepanther.com	Namepanther.com Llc
whois.nameperfections.com	Name Perfections, Inc.
whois.namerepublic.com	Namerepublic.com
whois.namerich.cn	China Springboard Inc.
whois.names4ever.com	Hostopia.com Inc. D/B/A Aplus.net
whois.namesalacarte.com	Namesalacarte.com Llc
whois.namesay.com	Namesay Llc
whois.namesbeyond.com	2030138 Ontario Inc.
whois.namesbond.net	Names Bond, Inc.
whois.namescout.com	Namescout Corp., Et Al.
whois.namesector.com	Namesector Llc
whois.namesecure.com	Namesecure.com
whois.nameshere.com	Nameshere Llc
whois.namesilo.com	Namesilo Llc
whois.namesinmotion.com	Names In Motion, Inc.

whois.namesreal.com	Names Real, Inc.
whois.namestrategies.com	Namestrategies Llc
whois.namestream.com	Namestream.com, Inc.
whois.namesystem.com	A Technology Company, Inc.
whois.nametell.com	Nametell.com Llc
whois.namethread.com	Name Thread Corporation
whois.nametofame.com	Name To Fame, Inc.
whois.nametree.com	Nametree, Inc.
whois.nameturn.com	Nameturn Llc
whois.namevault.com	Homestead Limited Dba Namevault.com
whois.nameview.com	Nameview, Inc.
whois.namevolcano.com	Namevolcano.com Llc
whois.NameWeb.biz	Nameweb Bvba
whois.namezero.com	Cat Inc. D/B/A Namezero.com
whois.naugus.com	Naugus Limited Llc.
whois.nawang.cn	Xiamen Nawang Technology Co., Ltd.
whois.nayana.com	Internet Nayana Inc.
whois.needservers.com	Need Servers, Inc.
whois.neen.it	Neen Srl
whois.neonic.com	Neonic Oy
whois.nerdnames.com	Nerd Names Corporation
whois.net.cn	Hichina Zhicheng Technology Limited
whois.net4domains.com	Net 4 India Limited
whois.netart-registrar.com	Netart Registrar Sp. Z O.O.
whois.netbulk.com	Netbulk Nv
whois.net-chinese.com.tw	Net-Chinese Co., Ltd.
whois.netclient.no	Netclient As
whois.netcn.net	Beijing Midwest Taian Technology Services Ltd.
whois.netcore.co.in	Netcore Solutions Pvt. Ltd.
whois.netdorm.com	Netdorm, Inc. Dba Dnsexit.com
whois.netestate.com	Netestate Llc
whois.netfirms.com	Netfirms, Inc.
whois.netim.com	Netim Sarl
whois.netjuggler.com	Net Juggler, Inc.
whois.netlogistics.com.au	Net Logistics Pty. Ltd.
whois.netlynx.com	Netlynx, Inc.
whois.netmediasystems.de	Netmedia Systems E.K.
whois.netnames.com	Group Nbt Plc Aka Netnames
whois.netregistry.net	Netregistry Pty. Ltd.
whois.netsavers.com	Small World Communications, Inc. D/B/A Netsavers
whois.nettica.com	Nettica Domains, Inc.
whois.networking4all.com	Networking4all B.V.
whois.networksavior.com	Network Savior, Inc.
whois.networksolutions.com	Network Solutions Llc, Et Al.
whois.neubox.com	Neubox Internet S.A. De C.V.
whois.neudomain.com	Neudomain Llc, Et Al.
whois.newgreatdomains.com	New Great Domains, Inc.
whois.nic.br	A. Telecom S.A.
whois.nic.cx	Indian Ocean Territories Telecom, Pty. Ltd.
whois.nic.ru	Regional Network Information Center, Jsc Dba Ru-Center
whois.nicco.com	Nicco Ltd.

whois.nicline.com	Arsys Internet S.L.
whois.nic-name.ca	3597245 Canada Inc. Dba Nic-Name Internet Service Corp.
whois.nicproxy.com	Nics Telekomünikasyon Hizmetleri Ltd. Sti
whois.nicreg.com	Nicreg Llc
whois.nictrade.se	Nictrade Internet Identity Provider Ab
whois.no-ip.com	Vitalwerks Internet Solutions Llc Dba No-Ip
whois.nomer.com	Nomer Registro De Dominio E Hospedagem De Sites Ltda.
whois.nomer.com.br	Nomer Registro De Dominio E Hospedagem De Sites Ltda.
whois.nominalia.com	Nominalia Internet S.L.
whois.nominate.net	Bb Online Uk Ltd.
whois.nominfinitum.com	Nom Infinitum, Incorporated
whois.nondotcom.com	Nondotcom, Inc.
whois.nordnet.net	Nordnet
whois.nordreg.com	Nordreg Ab
whois.northnames.com	Northnames Inc.
whois.notablenames.ca	Notablenames.ca Inc.
whois.noticeddomains.com	Noticeddomains Llc
whois.notsofamousnames.com	Notsofamousnames.com Llc
whois.novutec.com	Novutec Inc.
whois.octopusdomains.net	Octopusdomains.net Llc
whois.oiinternet.com.br	Internet Group Do Brasil S.A.
whois.oldtowndomains.com	Oldtowndomains.com Llc
whois.oldworldaliases.com	Oldworldaliases.com Llc
whois.oleane.net	France Telecom
whois.omnis.com	Omnis Network, Llc
whois.onlinenameservices.com	Online Name Services Inc./Name109, Inc.
whois.onlinenic.com	Onlinenic, Inc./Usa Intra Corp.
whois.openname.com	Openname Llc
whois.orangenames.com	Larsen Data
whois.oray.com	Shanghai Best Oray Information S&T Co., Ltd.
whois.oregoneu.com	Oregoneu.com Llc
whois.oregonurls.com	Oregonurls.com Llc
whois.othelloreg.net	Astutium Limited
whois.ourdomains.com	Ourdomains Limited
whois.ovh.com	Ovh
whois.ownidentity.com	Own Identity, Inc.
whois.ownregistrar.com	Trunkoz Technologies
whois.pacnames.com	Pacnames Ltd.
whois.pairnic.com	Pair Networks Inc. D/B/A Pairnic
whois.paknic.com	Paknic (Private) Limited
whois.pananames.com	Url Solutions Inc.
whois.parava.net	Parava Networks Inc.
whois.pasia.com	Pasia, Inc.
whois.pavietnam.vn	P.A. Vietnam Company Limited
whois.paycenter.com.cn	Xin Net Technology Corporation
whois.pdxprivatenames.com	Pdxprivatenames.com Llc
whois.pearlnamingservice.com	Pearlnamingservice.com Llc
whois.personalnames.com	Personal Names Limited

whois.pheenix.com	Pheenix, Inc., Et Al.
whois.philippineregistry.com	Philippine Registry.com, Inc.
whois.planetdomain.com	Planetdomain Pty. Ltd.
whois.planetonline.net	Planet Online Corp.
whois.platinumregistrar.com	Platinum Registrar, Inc.
whois.plisk.com	$$$ Private Label Internet Service Kiosk, Inc.
whois.pocketdomain.com	Alfena Llc
whois.populardomains.ca	Populardomains.ca Inc.
whois.portingxs.com	Porting Access B.V.
whois.portlandnames.com	Portlandnames.com, Llc
whois.postaldomains.com	Postaldomains, Incorporated
whois.powerbrandcenter.com	Power Brand Center Corp.
whois.powerbrandsolutions.com	Power Brand Solutions Llc
whois.powercarrier.com	Power Carrier, Inc.
whois.powernamers.com	Power Namers, Inc.
whois.ppcmarketingllc.com	$Ppc Marketing Llc
whois.premierwebsitesolutions.com	Premier Website Solutions
whois.premiumregistrations.com	Premium Registrations Sweden Ab
whois.PresidentialDomains.com	Presidentialdomains Llc
whois.pricedomain.ca	Pricedomain.ca Internet Services Corporation
whois.primedomain.ca	Primedomain.ca Inc.
whois.primeregistrar.ca	Primeregistrar.ca Inc.
whois.privatedomains.biz	Private Domains, Incorporated
whois.prodomaines.com	Bdl Systemes Sas Dba Prodomaines
whois.profilebuilder.com	Profile Builder, Llc
whois.pronamed.com	Pronamed Llc
whois.protondomains.com	Protondomains.com Llc
whois.psi.jp	Psi-Japan, Inc.
whois.psi-usa.info	Psi-Usa, Inc. Dba Domain Robot
whois.PublicDomainRegistry.com	Directi Internet Solutions, Et Al.
whois.puredomain.com	Variomedia Ag Dba Puredomain.com
whois.purenic.com	Purenic Japan Inc.
whois.puritynames.com	Purity Names Incorporated
whois.quark.ca	3684458 Canada, Inc. Dba Quark.ca Internet Service Corporation
whois.questfinancialco.com	Quest Financial
whois.r01.ru	Cjsc Registrar R01
whois.rainydaydomains.com	Rainydaydomains.com Llc
whois.rallydomains.com	Rallydomains.com, Inc.
whois.rankusa.com	Rank Usa, Inc.
whois.realtimeregister.com	Ranger Registration (Madeira) LLC
whois.rebel.com	Rebel.com Corp.
whois.reclaimdomains.com	Reclaimdomains Llc
whois.redomainder.com	Redomainder.com Inc.
whois.redregister.com	Red Register, Inc.
whois.reg.ru	Registrar Of Domain Names Reg.ru
whois.reg2c.com	Reg2c.com, Inc.
whois.register.ca	Register.ca Inc.
whois.register.com	Register.com, Inc.
whois.register.eu	Register Nv Dba Register.eu
whois.register.it	Register.it Spa

whois.register365.com	Register365, Inc.
whois.register4less.com	Register4less, Inc.
whois.registerfly.com	Registerfly.com, Inc.
whois.registermatrix.com	Media Elite Holdings Limited
whois.registermydomains.ca	Registermydomains.ca Inc.
whois.registerone.ca	Registerone.ca Inc.
Whois.Registrar.Amazon.com	Amazon Registrar, Inc.
whois.registrar.aol.com	Aol, Llc
whois.registrar.eu	Hosting Concepts B.V. D/B/A Openprovider
whois.registrar.telekom.de	Deutsche Telekom Ag
whois.registrardirect.com	Registrardirect Llc
whois.registrar-info.eu	Domainfactory Gmbh
whois.registrarmanager.com	Registrar Manager Inc.
whois.registrars.com	Internet Domain Registrars
whois.registrationtek.com	Registration Technologies, Inc., Et Al.
whois.registrator.com	Netplex
whois.registrygate.com	Registrygate Gmbh
whois.regnow.ca	Regnow.ca, Inc.
whois.regtons.com	Gransy S.R.O. D/B/A Subreg.cz
whois.relevad.com	Relevad Corporation
whois.resellercamp.com	Cv. Jogjacamp
whois.resellerid.com	Pt Ardh Global Indonesia
whois.ResellServ.com	Everyones Internet, Ltd. Dba Softlayer
whois.retaildomains.net	Retail Domains Inc.
whois.retailstudio.com	Elb Group, Inc.
whois.rethemhosting.net	Rethem Hosting Llc
whois.rgnames.com	Wooho T&C Co., Ltd. D/B/A Rgnames.com
whois.ride-domain.com	Ride Co., Ltd.
whois.riktad.se	Ab Riktad
whois.rockenstein.de	Rockenstein Ag
whois.rocketalk.com	Rocketalk India Pvt. Ltd.
whois.roka.net	Freenet Cityline Gmbh
whois.romel.ca	Romel Corporation
whois.rrpproxy.net	Key-Systems Gmbh
whois.rrproxy.net	Bdl Systemes Sas Dba Prodomaines
whois.rumahweb.com	Cv. Rumahweb Indonesia
whois.ruregistrar.com	Ooo Russian Registrar
whois.safenames.net	Safenames Ltd.
whois.sammamishdomains.com	Sammamishdomains.com Llc
whois.santiamdomains.com	Santiamdomains.com Llc
whois.savethename.com	Savethename.com Llc
whois.sbsnames.com	Sbsnames, Incorporated
whois.schlund.info	1&1 Internet Ag
whois.scip.es	Soluciones Corporativas Ip, Slu
whois.scoopdomain.ca	Scoopdomain.ca Inc.
whois.s-dns.de	Server-Service Gmbh
whois.sdsns.com	Samjung Data Service Co., Ltd.
whois.searchname.ca	Searchname.ca Internet Services Corporation
whois.searchnresq.com	Searchnresq Inc.
whois.securadomain.ca	Securadomain.ca Inc.
whois.secura-gmbh.de	Secura Gmbh

whois.secureadomain.ca	Securedomain.ca Internet Services Corporation
whois.serveisweb.com	Sw Hosting & Communications Technologies, S.L.
whois.serverplan.com	Server Plan Srl
whois.seymourdomains.com	Seymour Domains, Llc
whois.sfn.cn	Beijing Sanfront Information Tech
whois.shop4domain.com	Computerdatanetworks Dba Shop4domain/ Netonedomains
whois.sibername.com	Sibername Internet and Software Technologies Inc.
whois.sibername.com	Sibername Internet and Software Technologies Inc.
whois.sicherregister.com	Sicherregister, Incorporated
whois.signdomains.com	Visesh Infotecnics Ltd.
whois.silverbackdomains.com	Silverbackdomains.com Llc
whois.simplynamed.com	Simply Named, Inc. Dba Simplynames.com
whois.sipence.com	Sipence, Inc.
whois.sitefrenzy.com	Sitefrenzy.com Llc
whois.siteleader.com	Site Leader, Inc.
whois.siteregister.com	Globalhosting, Inc. Dba Siteregister
whois.skykomishdomains.com	Skykomishdomains.com Llc
whois.slimnames.com	Total Calories, Inc.
whois.smallbusinessnamescerts.com	Small Business Names and Certs, Incorporated
whois.snappyregistrar.com	Snappyregistrar.com Llc
whois.snoqulamiedomains.com	Snoqulamiedomains.com Llc
whois.softlayer.com	Everyones Internet, Ltd. Dba Softlayer
whois.southnames.com	Southnames Inc.
whois.soyouwantadomain.com	Soyouwantadomain.com Llc
whois.specificname.com	Specific Name, Inc.
whois.srsplus.com	Tlds/Enic Corporation
whois.ssandomain.com	Koreacenter.com Co., Ltd.
whois.sssasss.com	Sssasss, Incorporated
whois.standardnames.com	Standard Names, Llc
whois.star-domain.jp	Netowl Inc.
whois.submit.ca	Submit.ca Inc.
whois.subreg.cz	Gransy S.R.O. D/B/A Subreg.cz
whois.sudu.cn	Chengdu Fly-Digital Technology Co., Ltd.
whois.suempresa.com	Interplanet, S.A. De C.V.
whois.sundancegrp.com	Sundance Group, Inc.
whois.sunmounta.in	Name108, Inc.
whois.supernameworld.com	Super Name World, Inc.
whois.svenskadomaner.se	Ab Svenska Domäner
whois.sync.es	Sync Intertainment S.L.
whois.syra.com.au	Crazy Domains Fz-Llc/Dreamscape Networks Fz-Llc
whois.tagidomains.com	Abu-Ghazaleh Intellectual Property
whois.tahoedomains.com	Tahoe Domains, Inc.
whois.talk.com	Talk.com, Inc.
whois.tartondomainnames.com	Tarton Domain Names Ltd.
whois.techdogs.com	Tech Dogs, Inc.
whois.techtyrants.com	Tech Tyrants, Inc.
whois.theblackcow.ca	The Black Cow Corp.
whois.thedomainnamestore.ca	Thedomainnamestore.ca Inc.
whois.thedomainshop.ca	Thedomainshop.ca Inc.
whois.thenameco.com	Thenameco Llc
whois.thenamesregistration.com	The Names Registration, Inc.

whois.theplanet.com	Softlayer Technologies Inc.
whois.theregistrarservice.com	The Registrar Service, Inc.
whois.thirdfloordns.com	Thirdfloordns.com Llc
whois.threadagent.com	Threadagent.com, Inc.
whois.threadwalker.com	Threadwalker.com, Inc.
whois.threadwatch.com	Threadwatch.com, Inc.
whois.threadwise.com	Threadwise.com, Inc.
whois.tigertech.net	Tiger Technologies Llc
whois.tirupatidomains.in	Tirupati Domains and Hosting Private Limited
whois.titanichosting.com	Titanic Hosting, Inc.
whois.tldnames.com	7ways
whois.tldregistrarsolutions.com	Tld Registrar Solutions Ltd.
whois.todaynic.com	Todaynic.com, Inc.
whois.toglodo.com	Toglodo S.A.
whois.topsystem.com	Topsystem Llc
whois.topvhost.net	Guangzhou Ehost Tech. Co. Ltd.
whois.totallydomain.com	Totallydomain Llc
whois.totalregistrations.com	Total Web Solutions Ltd.
whois.towebs.com	Virtucom Networks Sa
whois.tppinternet.com	Tpp Domains Pty. Ltd. Dba Tpp Internet
whois.tradeindia.com	Infocom Network Ltd.
whois.tradenamed.com	Tradenamed Llc
whois.tradestarter.com	Trade Starter, Inc.
whois.trafficmedia.com	Black Ice Domains Inc, Et Al.
whois.trafficnames.net	Traffic Names, Incorporated
whois.transip.net	Transip B.V.
whois.traveldomainsincorporated.com	Traveldomains, Incorporated
whois.tregistrar.com	Tregistrar
whois.triara.com	Triara.com, S.A. De C.V.
whois.tropicregistry.com	Tropic Management Systems, Inc.
whois.trustnames.net	Research Institute For Computer Science, Inc.
whois.tsukaeru.net	Tsukaeru.net Kk
whois.ttpia.com	Hanilnetworks Co., Ltd.
whois.tucows.com	Tucows Domains Inc.
whois.turbosite.com.br	Open System Ltd.
whois.twt.it	Twt S.P.A.
whois.udag.net	United-Domains Ag
whois.udamain.com	Udamain.com Llc
whois.udomainname.com	Udomainname.com Llc
whois.ukrnames.com	Center Of Ukrainian Internet Names
whois.ultraregistrar.com	Ultra Registrar, Inc.
whois.ultrarpm.com	Ultrarpm Inc. Dba Metapredict.com
whois.unifiedservers.com	Unified Servers, Inc.
whois.uniregistrar.com	Uniregistrar Corp.
whois.uniteddomainregistry.com	United Domain Registry Inc.
whois.unpower.com	Unpower, Inc.
whois.usawebhost.com	Usa Webhost
whois.usefuldomains.net	Usefuldomains.net, Inc.
whois.vedacore.com	Vedacore.com, Inc.
whois.verelink.com	Verelink
whois.verisign-grs.com	Verisign Grs, Et Al.
whois.vertexnames.com	Vertex Names.com Inc.

whois.verzadomains.com	Verza Domain Depot Bv
whois.viaduc.fr	Sarl Viaduc
whois.viennaweb.at	Internet Viennaweb Service Gmbh
whois.vigson.com	Vigson, Inc.
whois.virtualis.com	Virtualis Systems Inc.
whois.virtualregistrar.com	Virtual Registrar, Inc. (Dootall)
whois.visualmonster.com	Visual Monster, Inc
whois.visualnames.com	Visualnames Llc
whois.vividdomains.com	Vivid Domains, Inc.
whois.volusion.com	Volusion, Inc.
whois.web.com	Web.com Holding Company, Inc.
whois.web4africa.net	Web4africa Inc.
whois.webair.com	Webair Internet Development
whois.webbusiness.biz	1 Domain Source Ltd.
whois.webcast-tv.com	Webcast-Tv Usa Llc
whois.webhosting24.com	Webhosting24 Inc.
whois.webinfinityinc.com	Name107, Inc.
whois.webmasters.com	Nettuner Corp.
whois.webnames.ca	Webnames.ca Inc.
whois.webnames.com	Infoback Corporation
whois.webnames.ru	Regtime Ltd.
whois.webnic.cc	Web Commerce Communications Limited
whois.website.ws	Global Domains International Inc.
whois.websitesource.com	Web Site Source, Inc.
whois.webtechnames.com	Name106, Inc.
whois.webtrends.net	Webtrends Corporation
whois.webyourcompany.com	New Era Information Systems Incorporation
whois.webzero.com	Webzero, Inc.
whois.welcomedomain.com	Welcomedomain.com Llc
whois.weregisterit.ca	Weregisterit.ca Inc.
whois.west263.com	Chengdu West Dimension Digital Tech
whois.whatisyourdomain.com	Whatisyourdomain Llc
whois.whatsyourname.ca	Whatsyourname.ca Inc.
whois.whitecowdomains.com	Whitecowdomains.com Inc.
whois.whiteglovedomains.com	Whiteglove Domains, Inc.
whois.whoistoolbar.com	Whoistoolbar.com Corp.
whois.wholesalesystem.com.au	Ventraip Group (Australia) Pty. Ltd.
whois.wildwestdomains.com	Wild West Domains, Llc
whois.willamettenames.com	Willamettenames.com Llc
whois.wiredwebsite.com	Wired Website, Inc.
whois.wisdomain.ca	Wisdomain.ca Inc.
whois.world4you.com	World4you Internet Services Gmbh
whois.worldbizdomains.com	World Biz Domains, Llc
whois.worldnames.ca	Worldnames.ca Inc.
whois.worthydomains.com	Worthydomains Llc
whois.www.tv	Tv Corporation
whois.xyz.com	Xyz.com Llc
whois.yahonic.com	Netblue Communications Co., Ltd.
whois.yellowname.com	Yellowiz Corp. D/B/A Yellowname.com
whois.yellowstart.com	Yellow Start, Inc.
whois.yesnic.com	Yesnic Co. Ltd.
whois.yexa.com	Yexa.com Pty. Ltd.

whois.youdamain.com	Youdamain.com Llc
whois.yourdomainco.com	Yourdomainco.com Inc.
whois.yourdomainking.com	Your Domain King, Inc.
whois.yourdomainnameregistrar.com	The Registrar Company B.V.
whois.yourjungle.com	Yourjungle, Inc., Et Al.
whois.yournamemonkey.com	Absystems Inc.
whois.your-server.de	Hetzner Online Ag
whois.yoursrs.com	Realtime Register Bv
whois.yovole.com	Shanghai Yovole Networks, Inc.
whois.z-core.com	One Putt Inc.
whois.zidodomain.ca	Zidodomain.ca Inc.
whois.zigzagnames.com	Zigzagnames.com Llc
whois.zipa.com	Zipa, Llc
whois.zippydomains.ca	Zippydomains.ca Inc.
whois.zognames.com	Zogmedia Inc. Dba Zognames
whois.zonecasting.com	Zone Casting, Inc.
whois.zoomregistrar.com	Zoomregistrar Llc
whois2.domain.com	Dotster Inc., Et Al.
whois2.softlayer.com	Softlayer Technologies, Inc.
whois2.virtualname.es	Estrategias Website S.L.
whois-farm.opensrs.net	The Planet Internet Service
whois-generic.marcaria.com	Marcaria.com, International, Inc.
ww.columbiadomains.net/whois	Columbiadomains, Llc (1)
www.101.com	Hangzhou Duomai E-Commerce Co. Ltd.
www.allwhois.com	Alldomains.com, Inc. D/B/A Alldomains.com
www.intra.com/domain/whois.php	Usa Intra Corp.
ynotdomains.myorderbox.com	Ynot Domains Corp.

B.10 CENTRALNIC SUBDOMAINS

All through whois.centralnic.net
.br.com, .cn.com, .de.com, .eu.com, .gb.com, .gb.net, .hu.com, .no.com, .qc.com, .ru.com, .sa.com, .se.com, .se.net, .uk.com, .uk.net, .us.com, .uy.com, .za.com, .jpn.com
.web.com, whois.centralnic.net

B.11 ZANET SUBDOMAINS

.za.net	whois.za.net
.za.orgs	whois.za.org

B.12 NONAUTHORITATIVE AND SPECIAL USE WHOIS SERVERS

Consolidated list of various servers from source code referenced in the appendix, the Matt Power List,[3] and general research. Not all servers may be active; some only serve local data and not Internet-wide information. Some, however, have unique properties or still allow Telnet connections for experimentation.

[3] http://stuff.mit.edu/afs/sipb/project/gopher-links/whois-servers.list

ac.nsac.ns.ca	Nova Scotia Agricultural College
archie.au	Australian Academic and Research Network
austin.onu.edu	Ohio Northern University
camis.stanford.edu	Stanford University
cc.fsu.edu	Florida State University
cgl.ucsf.edu	University of California at San Francisco, School of Pharmacy
chalmers.se	Chalmers University of Technology
companies.mci.net	RFC 2345 TLD-WHOIS demonstration server
condor.dgsca.unam.mx	Univ. Nacional Autonoma de Mexico
cs.hut.fi	Helsinki University of Technology
csufresno.edu	California State University—Fresno
csuhayward.edu	California State University—Hayward
csus.edu	California State University—Sacramento
directory.gatech.edu	Georgia Institute of Technology
directory.msstate.edu	Mississippi State University
directory.ucdavis.edu	University of California at Davis
directory.vuw.ac.nz	Victoria University, Wellington
dns411.com	Name.Space
domain-registry.nl	Stichting Internet Domeinregistratie Nederland
ds.internic.net	Network Solutions, Inc. (non-MILNET/non-POC)
dsa.fccn.pt	Fundacao para a Computacao Cientifica Nacional
dsa.nis.garr.it	GARR-NIS c/o CNR-CNUCE
dsa.shu.ac.uk	Sheffield Hallam University
dvinci.usask.ca	University of Saskatchewan, Engineering
earth.njit.edu	New Jersey Institute of Technology
finger.caltech.edu	California Institute of Technology
gettysburg.edu	Gettysburg College
gmu.edu	George Mason University
gopher.educ.cc.keio.ac.jp	Science and Technology Computing Center, Keio University
gopher.fme.vutbr.cz	Faculty of Mechanical Engineering, Technical University of Brno
hermes.informatik.htw-zittau.de HTW Zittau/Goerlitz Elektrotechnik	
hmc.edu	Harvey Mudd College
ibc.wustl.edu	Washington University
indiana.edu	Indiana University
info.cnri.reston.va.us	Corporation for National Research Initiatives, Knowbot interface
info.nau.edu	Northern Arizona University
info.psu.edu	Pennsylvania State University
isgate.is	Association of Research Networks in Iceland
isgate3.isnet.is	Internet a Islandi
kth.se	Royal Institute of Technology
larc.nasa.gov	NASA Langley Research Center
llnl.gov	Lawrence Livermore National Laboratory
lookup.umd.edu	University of Maryland
mit.edu	Massachusetts Institute of Technology
nd.edu	University of Notre Dame
netlia2.cs.utk.edu	The Innovative Computing Laboratory (ICL)

nii.isi.edu	US Domain Registry
nrtm.db.ripe.net	RIPE Mirror Database
ns.unl.edu	University of Nebraska at Lincoln
osu.edu	Ohio State University
oulu.fi	Oulu University
panda1.uottawa.ca	University of Ottawa
pcdc.net	Pacific Communications Development Corp.
pgebrehiwot.iat.cnr.it	Nigerian TLD Registration Service
ph.orst.edu	Oregon State University
phys.uvic.ca	University of Victoria, Physics & Astronomy
seda.sandia.gov	Sandia National Laboratories
sics.se	Swedish Institute of Computer Science
sorak.kaist.ac.kr	Korea Advanced Institute of Science & Technology
src.doc.ic.ac.uk	Imperial College
sserve.cc.adfa.oz.au	University College, Australian Defense Force Academy
stanford.edu	Stanford University
stjohns.edu	St. John's University
sunysb.edu	State University of New York, Stony Brook
uchicago.edu	University of Chicago
ucsd.edu	University of California at San Diego
umn.edu	University of Minnesota
uwa.edu.au	University of Western Australia
vax2.winona.msus.edu	Minnesota State University—Winona
vm1.hqadmin.doe.gov	US Department of Energy Headquarters
vm1.nodak.edu	North Dakota State University
vtt.fi	Technical Research Centre of Finland
waikato.ac.nz	Waikato University
weber.ucsd.edu	University of California at San Diego, Division of Social Sciences
whitepages.rutgers.edu	Rutgers University
whois-server.l.chiba-u.ac.jp	Chiba University
whois.6bone.net	6bone Registry
whois.abuse.net	Network Abuse Clearinghouse
whois.aco.net	Austrian Academic Computer Network
whois.adamsnames.tc	AdamsNames (.gs, .ms, .tc, .tf, and .vg)
whois.adelaide.edu.au	University of Adelaide
whois.aist-nara.ac.jp	Nara Institute of Science and Technology
whois.alabanza.com	Alabanza, Inc.
whois.aunic.net	The .AU Registry
whois.awregistry.net	All West Communications
whois.bcm.tmc.edu	Baylor College of Medicine
whois.belnet.be	Belgian National Research Network
whois.berkeley.edu	University of California at Berkeley
whois.camosun.bc.ca	Camosun College, Victoria, B.C.
whois.canet.ca	Bell Canada Internet Transit Service
whois.canterbury.ac.nz	University of Canterbury
whois.cary.net	CARYNET
whois.cc.keio.ac.jp	Keio University
whois.cc.rochester.edu	University of Rochester
whois.cc.uec.ac.jp	University of Electro-Communications
whois.cdnnet.ca	CDNnet

whois.ci.ucr.ac.cr	University of Costa Rica Computer Center
whois.cnnic.net.cn	Computer Network Center, Chinese Academy of Sciences
whois.compuserve.com	CompuServe Interactive Services, Inc.
whois.connect.com.au	Connect.com.au Pty. Ltd.
whois.cuni.cz	Charles University, Prague
whois.cw.net	Cable & Wireless USA
whois.cwru.edu	Case Western Reserve University
whois.dfci.harvard.edu	Dana–Farber Cancer Institute
whois.dhs.org	Domain Host Services
whois.discount-domain.com	interQ Inc.
whois.dit.upm.es	Tech. Univ. Madrid, Telecommunications Highschool
whois.dns.pt	Fundacao para a Computacao Cientifica Nacional
whois.elka.pw.edu.pl	Faculty of Electronic Engineering, Warsaw University
whois.eunet.es	EUnet, Goya, Spain
whois.fee.vutbr.cz	Faculty of Elec. Eng. and Computer Sci., Technical Univ. of Brno
whois.fh-koeln.de	Fachhochschule Koeln
whois.frd.ac.za	National Research Foundation
whois.fzi.de	Forschungszentrum Informatik
whois.geektools.com	CenterGate Research Group, Llc
whois.hinet.net	Chunghwa Telecom
whois.hiroshima-u.ac.jp	Hiroshima University
whois.hq.nasa.gov	NASA Headquarters
whois.ia.pw.edu.pl	Institute of Automatic Control, Warsaw University of Technology
whois.ibm.com	IBM
whois.icm.edu.pl	Interdyscyplinarne Centrum Modelowania Matematycznego i Komputero
whois.iii.org.tw	Institution for Information Industry
whois.iisc.ernet.in	Indian Institute of Science
whois.internetnamesww.com	Melbourne IT
whois.isi.edu	.INT Whois Service
whois.ja.net	JANET
whois.jpl.nasa.gov	NASA Jet Propulsion Laboratory
whois.krnic.net	Korea Network Information Center
whois.kuleuven.ac.be	Katholieke Universiteit Leuven
whois.lac.net	Latin America & Caribbean Whois Server
whois.larc.nasa.gov	NASA Langley Research Center
whois.lut.ac.uk	Loughborough University
whois.messiah.edu	Messiah College
whois.metu.edu.tr	Middle East Technical University
whois.mff.cuni.cz	Charles University, Faculty of Mathematics and Physics
whois.monash.edu.au	Monash University
whois.morris.org	Morris Automated Information Network
whois.ncst.ernet.in	National Centre for Software Technology
whois.ncsu.edu	North Carolina State University
whois.netnames.net	NetNames (.af, .bt, .pw, and .tm)
whois.nic-se.se	Network Information Centre Sweden
whois.nic.ad.jp	Japan Network Information Center
whois.nic.net.sg	Singapore Network Information Centre
whois.nic.or.kr	Korea Network Information Center

whois.nomination.net	NomiNation (.gb.com, .gb.net, .uk.com, and .uk.net)
whois.nordnet.fr	NordNet
whois.norid.no	UNINETT FAS (NORID)
whois.nrl.navy.mil	Naval Research Laboratory
whois.nsiregistry.net	Network Solutions, Inc.
whois.oleane.net	OLEANE SA
whois.opensrs.net	Open Shared Registration System
whois.oxy.edu	Occidental College
whois.pacbell.com	Pacific Bell
whois.patho.gen.nz	PATHOGEN
whois.queensu.ca	Queen's University, Kingston, Canada
whois.ra.net	The Routing Arbiter Project
whois.radb.net	Merit Routing Assets Database
whois.rcp.net.pe	Red Cientifica Peruana
whois.register.com	Forman Interactive Corp.
whois.registrars.com	Internet Domain Registrars
whois.registry.hm	HM Domain Registry
whois.risc.uni-linz.ac.at	Research Institute for Symbolic Computation, University of Linz
whois.rsmas.miami.edu	University of Miami, Rosentiel School
whois.sdsu.edu	San Diego State University
whois.seed.net.tw	Seednet
whois.sixxs.net	SixXS
whois.state.ct.us	Department of Administrative Services, State of Connecticut
whois.sunquest.com	Sunquest Information Systems
whois.th-darmstadt.de	Darmstadt University of Technology
whois.thnic.net	Thailand Network Information Center
whois.tonic.to	Tonic Domain Name Registry
whois.tu-chemnitz.de	Technische Universitaet Chemnitz
whois.twnic.net	Taiwan Network Information Center
whois.uakom.sk	SANET (WAN of Slovak academic institutions)
whois.ubalt.edu	University of Baltimore
whois.uh.edu	University of Houston
whois.umass.edu	University of Massachusetts at Amherst
whois.unb.ca	University of New Brunswick
whois.und.ac.za	University of Natal (Durban)
whois.uni-c.dk	Danish Computing Centre for Research and Education
whois.uni-regensburg.de	Universitaet Regensburg
whois.univ-lille1.fr	University of Sciences and Technologies of Lille—France
whois.upenn.edu	University of Pennsylvania
whois.usask.ca	University of Saskatchewan
whois.ut.ee	University of Tartu
whois.uwo.ca	University of Western Ontario
whois.virginia.edu	University of Virginia
whois.vutbr.cz	Technical University of Brno
whois.wfu.edu	Wake Forest University
whois.wu-wien.ac.at	Wirtschaftsuniversität Wien
whois.yamanashi.ac.jp	Yamanashi University
wisc.edu	University of Wisconsin
wp.doe.gov	US Department of Energy
wp.es.net	Energy Sciences Network

wp.nersc.gov	National Energy Research Supercomputer Center
wp.tuwien.ac.at	Technische Universität Wien
wpi.wpi.edu	Worcester Polytechnic Institute
www.binghamton.edu	State University of New York at Binghamton
www.fce.vutbr.cz	Faculty of Civil Engineering, Technical University of Brno
www.orions.ad.jp	Osaka Regional Information and Open Network Systems
www.restena.lu	RESTENA
x500.arc.nasa.gov	NASA Ames Research Center
x500.gsfc.nasa.gov	NASA Goddard Space Flight Center
x500.ivv.nasa.gov	NASA Software Independent Verification & Validation Facility
x500.jsc.nasa.gov	NASA Johnson Space Center
x500.msfc.nasa.gov	NASA Marshall Space Flight Center
x500.nasa.gov	National Aeronautics and Space Administration
x500.ssc.nasa.gov	NASA Stennis Space Center
x500.utexas.edu	University of Texas at Austin
x500.wstf.nasa.gov	NASA White Sands Test Facility

INDEX

WHOIS Running the Internet: Protocol, Policy, and Privacy, First Edition. Garth O. Bruen.
© 2016 John Wiley & Sons, Inc. Published 2016 by John Wiley & Sons, Inc.